THE ELLIS ISLAND SNOW GLOBE

A JOHN HOPE FRANKLIN CENTER BOOK

ERICA RAND

THE ELLIS ISLAND
SNOW GLOBE

DUKE UNIVERSITY PRESS   DURHAM AND LONDON 2005

THE DISTRIBUTION OF THIS BOOK
IS SUPPORTED BY A GENEROUS GRANT
FROM THE GILL FOUNDATION.

Designed by Rebecca Giménez.
Typeset in Scala by Tseng Information Systems.
Library of Congress Cataloging-in-Publication
Data appear on the last printed page
of this book.

An earlier version of chapter 2 appeared
as "Breeders on a Golf Ball: Normalizing
Sex at Ellis Island," in *Environment and
Planning D: Society and Space* 21, no. 3 (2003):
441–60. Reprinted by permission of
Pion Limited, London.

An earlier version of chapter 4 was published
in *Queer Migrations*, edited by Eithne
Luibhéid and Lionel Cantú, published by the
University of Minnesota Press. Copyright
by the Regents of the University of Minnesota,
reprinted with permission.

CONTENTS

PREFACE

RESPECT AND REVERENCE

"Don't forget to thank Mrs. Roosevelt, dear." That is what my grandmother's friend Marion told me when she learned I was writing a book about Ellis Island (as I had described the project in shorthand to my grandmother). Marion wanted me to thank Eleanor Roosevelt for getting her sister out of Siberia. In the 1920s, Marion told me, when her mother was a widow in Sanok, Poland, struggling to raise her five children, Marion's grandmother emigrated with two of the children to the United States, partly to help ease her daughter's burden. She brought the oldest and the middle child, having determined to take, of the second and third daughters, whichever one succeeded in getting up early enough to make the journey. Marion herself came over, after having been rejected three times for a visa, in 1933, by which time stringent U.S. quota laws put new obstacles before would-be migrants and she had to pretend to be her grandmother's daughter in order to get the papers. The second daughter, however, by then married, stayed in the area of Sanok. When the Nazi occupation began there in 1939, she was living on the side of the river that fell under Russian rule when the control of Poland was split between German and Russian forces. She and her family were sent to Siberia. After the war ended, Marion said, the Jews in Siberia were forgotten deportees, and might be there still had it not been for the efforts of Eleanor Roosevelt. According to Marion, Roosevelt, as "ambassador to the United Nations," worked with "a friend, a woman diplomat politician from England," and together they were responsible for having deportees returned to Poland. The sister left Siberia in 1949 and came to the United States soon thereafter.[1]

For several reasons, I thought of Marion's request often when writing this book. First, her description of family history nicely illustrates the intricate interrelations among big-picture forces, small-scale peculiarities, and perceptions about both that inform so many Ellis Island narratives. The early bird catches the train: the lack of fit between the consequence and the criterion, more suitable, perhaps, for making a choice such as who gets a pretty hair ribbon, seemed even more glaring with hindsight. Yet just as interesting to me was that Marion didn't seem to consider this part of the story remarkable at all. Maybe by then the course of events had the taken-for-grantedness of old news, or maybe it is just the fact that family weirdness sometimes comes to seem ordinary from within. In any case, not even my own expression of incredulity—"your sister overslept coming to America and wound up in Siberia?!"—induced her to do any more than affirm that I had heard correctly. Our interchange did, however, get the attention of my sister, Cynthia, who was in the room at the time. A veteran of winding up in my explanatory anecdotes, she frequently alerts others when she spots a conversational moment that she perceives to be drawing my writerly interests. "Marion, that's going into the book," she said. Fulfilling Cynthia's prediction several years later also heightens my awareness about the extent to which the listener's habits of perception (mine apparently habitual enough to be predictable) contribute, in turn, to how narratives generate other narratives.

Second, Marion's request came to epitomize for me the gap that I imagine to exist between the tone and content of my project and the expectations that many may have for a book about Ellis Island. With my grandmother, it is a gap to which I contributed by deliberately failing to elaborate. In talking to her, I addressed only the questions that she brought up herself, primary among which was the issue of genre: couldn't I write a novel this time? I didn't introduce other topics. Even mentioning sex, one major topic, would have named it more explicitly than ever before in our conversations. We hadn't gotten any closer than an oblique acknowledgment of arrangements presumed sexual, like her willingness, when I brought a lover to visit, to treat butch gallantries extended to her (helping her on with her coat, driving us around) as the appropriate solicitations of an aspiring grandson-in-law. At the same time, for both my grandmother and Marion, that gap was partly filled by their own histories, and the history of others like them, whose survival depended on migration out of Poland. Many of those who didn't leave, including people in both families, were killed in the Holocaust or barely survived the horrors they went through. What else would I be writing about regarding Ellis Island, and from what stance other than respect and reverence?

I have respect and reverence. But I am interested here especially in making respect and reverence an object of study rather than simply a position to enact. It is significant that Marion wanted me to tell the story of a sister who surely didn't pass through Ellis Island, since she arrived after it had ceased its storied function, begun in 1892, of processing new arrivals. Marion's notion that the story belongs nonetheless testifies to the way that the site, for many people, has come to stand more generally for immigrant journeys to the United States. Evidence appears also every time Ellis Island is used as a shorthand—when, for instance, a local newspaper quotes a comment that calls Omaha's Union Station, "sort of the Ellis Island of Nebraska," without providing any explanation of the historical reference.[2]

How did Ellis Island become the place, the experience, and the symbol that seems to need no explication? Since its recognizability rose dramatically after a big fund-raising campaign for its restoration in the 1980s, and since along with the federal government big corporations (like American Express) and big names (like Lee Iacocca) have contributed to the project of supplying resources and publicity, the question of Ellis Island's fame needs also to be a question about whose heritage does and doesn't get that kind of support. For numerous reasons, this question in turn involves matters of race. These reasons include the predominance, among migrants through Ellis Island, of people coming from Europe whose descendents today, sometimes unlike them, are largely considered white, as well as the use of mythic stories of their bootstrap individualism to dismiss how systemic inequalities, like disparate education funding, contribute to the struggles of people of color in the United States.

The question about whose heritage gets honored also involves matters concerning sexuality. Marion's story, like most Ellis Island narratives that I encountered, refers only, and only implicitly, to sexual relations understood to be involved in procreation and legitimized in heterosexual marriage. Marion has a mother, a grandmother, and sisters, who are married, unmarried, or widowed, implicitly in relation to men. Eleanor Roosevelt has a (deceased) husband, who made her "Mrs." Roosevelt, and a female friend. Do these relations gesture to all of those types that made meanings in the lives of the women mentioned? With Roosevelt, we know that they don't. I am not suggesting here that Roosevelt's friend was a lover as well as an activist colleague or that any information about Roosevelt's love for women belongs in this story. Nor do I presume that Marion knows nothing of this matter. Whatever she knows, however, "Mrs." is both Marion's only reference to Roosevelt's personal life and, importantly, the term she used to convey respect.

What might look different if habits of popular knowledge and the accordance of respect were such that Roosevelt's intimate affection for Lorena Hickok could reside as easily on the surface of Marion's picture of Roosevelt as does the relationship indicated by the designation "Mrs."?[3] How might gratitude toward "Mrs. Roosevelt" be reshaped, or what views might that gratitude toward a beloved "first lady" reshape? How might views toward sexuality and contemporary migrants be reshaped if the enshrined Ellis Island ancestors who came through Ellis Island were broadly understood to have desires and practices as varied and nuanced as they must have been? (This is not to suggest that we transpose contemporary identities to the past but rather to advocate against oversimplification; Freud's patients cannot have been the only complex early-twentieth-century Europeans.) How might laws and policies be reshaped, including those favoring heterosexual marriage bonds as a primary justification for migration—to the exclusion of many adults involved in differently linked relations and to the detriment of others forced by migration criteria to remain in harmful legal unions?

These are questions regarding justice, pleasure, knowledge, and the connections among them. Part of my argument in this book is that certain trappings of respect and reverence may function to obstruct all three, not only by disembodying the past and by failing to specify the beneficiaries of honor toward it, but also by missing or obfuscating seemingly crass or trivial dimensions of encounters with Ellis Island, past and present, that equally merit attention. One way that I attempt in this book to dislodge the naturalness of certain discretions and silences is by venturing sometimes into the realm of the unserious and the impolite; turning next, for instance, to my own far from reverent first encounter with Ellis Island. Revolving around a date, a snow globe, and a debate about requisite solemnity, my tale suggests the stakes, the gaps, and the contradictions in making reverence the primary pose. In pointing these out, however, regarding that narrative and throughout the book, I do not mean thereby to disrespect the histories of people who link themselves to Ellis Island. I hope, instead, by studying the production of respect, to contribute to the project of spreading it around.

ACKNOWLEDGMENTS

I have numerous people to thank here, beginning with Sallie McCorkle. In 1997, she suggested a trip to Ellis Island, a place I'd never considered visiting. This book began in the pleasure of that afternoon and I remain thankful as well for pleasures and support that followed.

In 1999, I presented my first paper related to Ellis Island for a conference organized by Inderpal Grewal and Caren Kaplan called the Transnational Politics of Gender and Consumption. I owe them much gratitude for the invitation. At and as a result of that conference I met people whose work on sexuality and migration inspired and influenced my own thinking. I thus also thank the other participants at that conference and the organizers and participants at three others: Sexuality and Space (2001); Sexuality and Migration (2002); and the Focus: Migration conference of the Sex, Race and Globalization Project of the Committee on Lesbian/Gay/Bisexual/Transgender Studies at the University of Arizona (2002). Particular thanks to Jasbir K. Puar, Dereka Rushbrook, Louisa Schein, Miranda Joseph, and Eithne Luibhéid, for including me in interdisciplinary conference and writing projects that turned out to stretch boundaries we hadn't always anticipated. I benefited as well from opportunities to present my work elsewhere including Bowdoin College; Penn State; San Francisco State; the University of California, Santa Cruz; the University of Maine, Orono; the University of Southern Maine; and the University of Wisconsin, Madison. Throughout my work on this project I have also had the amazing good fortune to know two people, Jed Bell and Wendy Chapkis, as great friends and wonderful allies; this project and my life have been greatly enriched by the joys and insights I have gleaned from our mutual engagements with sex and gender, culture and politics, rights and freedoms.

Because this book partly concerns what I would like to find at Ellis Island, it is essential to emphasize how much I did find: park rangers, tour guides, actors, and other employees who offer so much to visitors every day and who generously spoke to me in my role as researcher even when the very fact that I was taking notes must have made me look like one more hassle in what were often overloaded and undercompensated workdays. Jeff Dosik and Barry Moreno, at the Ellis Island library, are fabulous, enthusiastic guides to the collection who not only helped me find what I knew I was looking for, but also showed me what I didn't yet know to want. I hope they will want to direct future visitors to this book.

At Bates College, my research was supported by a Phillips Faculty Fellowship and by other faculty research development grants. I am also grateful for wonderful faculty and staff both within and outside my two institutional homes, the department of Art and Visual Culture and the program in Women and Gender Studies, for fantastic students in my courses, and for the activist work linked to the Women's Resource Center, the Multicultural Center, "justice," and OUTfront, the organization for people of all genders and sexualities. In addition, I thank Regan Richards, for charming help with my computer freak-outs, Lorelei Purrington, for helping me survive chairing, Sallie Hackett, for assistance in innumerable ways and through seemingly countless drafts ("was that sexspace8 or fantasybutch4?"), and six student research assistants who not only graciously handled tedious tasks but also contributed insightfully and creatively to research. They are, in order of appearance: Christine Quinn, Jason Goldman, Penelope Malakates, Julia Getzel, Alex Wenger, and Rory Stratton; Jason and Penni provided invaluable assistance after graduation as well.

Working with Duke University Press has, simply, been great for both me and the book. Thanks to Courtney Berger, Jean Brady, Justin Faerber, Rebecca Giménez, the manuscript readers, including the self-described six on the curmudgeon scale, the other people involved in editing, publicity, and production, and Ken Wissoker. If I hadn't gotten so wary during this project about mismatching analogies that work to obscure serious matters, I would say something with Ellis Island resonance about his help on the arduous journey of book writing from embarkation to landing and my gratitude for our by now long-term connection in migrations both personal and professional. Maybe it will be just as good to say, pulling from a lighter realm of travel reference, that he could sure teach Julie, your Cruise Director, a thing or two about how to facilitate making the good stuff happen. Thanks also to Laurie Prendergast from moonmarked for the great index.

Since this book questions rankings and concepts of affiliation that heritage sites (and, sometimes, the marriage craze) may encourage taking for granted, and since some people need to be acknowledged in oblique relation to the reason why, I forego some standard divisions here that put genetic links in a separate location and appear to designate more and less significant others. So I list together four people I miss whom I hoped would be able to see the book: Nadine McGann, Lionel Cantú, and my grandmothers Sophie Chananie and Adele Rand. Each, in different ways, enhanced my appreciation of close relations and their complexities. For various reasons, including hospitality, information, assistance, manuscript reading, collaborations, many pleasures, the moondance, and some other things they will know about, I want also to cite, besides the people already mentioned, Anne, Ahmad Azadi, Deborah Bright, Cynthia, Ron, Rebecca, Jacob, and Sophie Barabas, Johannah Burdin, Lorrayne Carroll, Rachel Cohen, David, Mathea Daunheimer, Gabriel Demaine, "Deep Throat (Two)," Robert Diamante, Dorn, Annette Dragon, Robert Feintuch, Debbie Gould, Marilyn, Waldo, and Iola Graton, Lynda Hathaway, Beth Helsinger, Paul Heroux, Rebecca Herzig, Leslie Hill, Sarah Holmes, John, Lise Kildegaard, Joanne Kalogeras, Anne Koenig, Kathryn Lattanzi, James Light, Limp Wrist, Francisca López, Louise, Roger Mayo, Heather McGrath, Joe Medley, Jim Neal, Jackie Parker, William Pope.L, Spencer, Liz, Ellie, and Isaac Rand, Lydia Savage, Susan Slohm, Annie Sprinkle, Beth Stephens, Norma Ware, Monday Night Dinner, Outright/Lewiston-Auburn, the adult figure skaters and staff at the Portland Ice Arena, JustUs/Come Out for Peace, and the editorial board of *Radical Teacher*.

Finally, writing acknowledgments in November 2004, when suppressing evidence of protest is only part of dominant media's dubious business as usual, it seems all the more imperative to take this and every opportunity to publicly recognize and honor the many, many people — in the streets, in coalitions, in varied, multiple, and glorious activist endeavors — working for gender and sexual freedom, for anti-racist visions of migration, borders, and belongings, and for peace.

INTRODUCTION

COMING TO ELLIS ISLAND

In August 1997 I made my first trip to Ellis Island, a strip of land off the tip of Manhattan, near the Statue of Liberty. It was here that the federal government in 1892 opened a processing, detention, and deportation center to deal with immigrants and other migrants arriving in the United States at New York Harbor. In 1907, the center's busiest year, as many as five thousand migrants came through each day, primarily from Europe. Most were admitted; only about 2 percent were refused entry. After 1924, with the passage of a new set of anti-immigration laws and the increasing role of embassies in handling immigration, deporting immigrants rather than admitting them began to become the site's dominant function. By the time the center closed in 1954 most of its functions had ceased, with the exception of the medical work and experimentation at its hospitals (notably with shock treatments).

In 1965, President Lyndon Johnson declared Ellis Island part of the Statue of Liberty National Monument, but the significant restoration of its buildings and grounds didn't occur until the 1980s, when the Statue of Liberty–Ellis Island Foundation, Inc. (SOLEIF) raised several hundred million dollars for both restoration projects in conjunction with the statue's centennial. In 1990, the Ellis Island Immigration Museum opened in the restored administration building. After an 1897 fire destroyed the original building, a second structure was erected in 1897–1904. This building, which stands today, is an imposing three-story French Renaissance structure intended to impress as well as accommodate those commanded to enter it; the grandeur of its huge central registry room was later enhanced by a tiled ceiling made by the same artisans famous for their work at Grand

Central Station. The present museum, operated by the National Park Service, now has about one and a half million visitors per year who arrive on the Circle Line Ferry from Battery Park in New York or from Liberty Park in New Jersey.[1]

Like many visitors, and like many Jews living in the United States, I have ancestors who, I have been told, came through Ellis Island, including a grandfather from Poland and great-grandparents from Russia. Further, my activism, teaching, and research activities all include issues regarding immigration. But on the occasion of my first trip to Ellis Island I was hardly on a long-planned pilgrimage to study either my own history or global migration. I was, instead, on a hot date, and in it for the ferry ride more than the destination. To me, the ferry ride is one of the sexiest summer activities: standing with a lover on the top deck—sun on skin, wind on sweat—as we watch the boat thrust forward while we weigh (perhaps enjoy) the pleasures and risks of violating public decorum. Frankly, I would have taken a tourist ferry just about anywhere.

Soon after our ride got underway I said to my date, Sallie, "Honey, when we get there, I want you to buy me an Ellis Island snow globe." I meant it as a joke, with the intended humor less in the souvenir than in the request for it. Through my tone, I vaguely parodied that (misogynist) stereotype of the woman who drains her man's finances either to satisfy a voracious hunger for luxury goods or as implicit payment for sex. Our actual sexual and gender identities added an extra twist of parody about dyke gender roles. There we were, just beginning to consider a more serious direction for our casual fling, and already I was commanding presents as if I knew I'd be lying around in lace someday, showered with baubles by my breadwinning butch. I thought I was pretty funny.

Sallie, however, wasn't laughing. "There won't be a snow globe at Ellis Island," she said. "That would be like having snow globes at a concentration camp. If there's a store, it will only have educational material, like books." She soon acknowledged that the concentration camp analogy was too extreme, but she was still certain about the snow globe. I disagreed. Sure, bad things happened at Ellis Island that would be grossly inappropriate to memorialize under shiny little flakes of falling snow. Yet several cheerful and gift-friendly spins seemed easily accessible. How about "the huddled masses yearning to breathe free," from the famous Emma Lazarus poem associated with our ferry's other destination, the Statue of Liberty? After all, many people conceived to have been part of the "huddled masses" did get admitted at Ellis Island to a country that is often promoted as the best place to "breathe free." Or how about "celebrate diversity"? The phrase, already on bumper stickers, encapsulates a popular model for understanding ethnic, national, and racial differences, often presented with a focus on products and productions to consume, such as jewelry, music, food, and festivals—more so, certainly, than on the inequities of power and resources that structure relations among "diverse" peoples. With Guatemalan purses available at shopping malls, "Asian chic" as a rising fashion trend, and increasing discussion in various arenas about the racial and ethnic specificities that contribute to the label "white,"[2] the many cultures of origin represented at Ellis Island seemed ripe for packaging both sober and carefree (or careless). Snow globes, I argued, could be the least of it. Sallie wasn't convinced, however. She remained horrified at the prospect of Ellis Island trinkets, adamant that we wouldn't find them.

We might have remained on this subject for the rest of the ferry ride if information hadn't emerged during our debate that wrenched my attention from imagined souvenirs. Sallie, it turned out, wasn't actually defending her own history from trivialization. In fact, she told me, both her father and mother had immigrant ancestors on the Mayflower. I was shocked, by both the news and my reaction to it. The whole notion of maintaining heritage criteria for friends or lovers seemed bigoted and preposterous. But my visceral response to the news, which I translated to myself as "oh, no, I let someone inside me who could join the DAR," exposed certain presumptions about my intimate relations, sexual and otherwise.[3] I don't date in Pilgrim territory. I hang out with people whose people had to struggle against everything enshrined in the myth of the first Thanksgiving, like colonialism, white supremacy, and Protestant domination; with people whose genetic material survived pogroms, the Middle Passage, the border police. Apparently, despite breezily tossing my ancestors into a snow globe for the sake of sexual banter, my own relation to the history of global migration was complicated, contradictory (I certainly know better than to segregate the gene pool), and deeply felt.

We arrived at Ellis Island, then, with some unsettled preconceptions, a bet in place, and an imperative first destination: the gift shop, if it existed. It did. Run by Aramark Corporation, which also runs the snack shop, it had the books that Sallie expected, and much more. One section displayed groups of products from various locations, many associated with emigration through Ellis Island. Varying in price, but most well under $50, the items seemed to have been chosen to represent craft or artisanal traditions that evoke the traditional and handmade, even if most are currently mass produced. Many products, like the Russian wooden nesting dolls, are widely marketed in other "world showcase" or "ethnic heritage" contexts. Besides these objects, which many might contend to honor, or to intend to honor, the gravity of the site, the store sold a vast array of items typically sold at tourist stops ranging from museums to minimarts: T-shirts, caps, shot glasses, key chains, and, of course, the very snow globes I'd teased Sallie about (figures 1 and 2).

Of these objects, some, like calculator keychains, lighters, and several of the T-shirts, were merely marked with the phrase "Ellis Island" to make them site specific. Others had designs geared to the site. The snow in the globes fell on six human figures, seen from behind, who are designated as immigrants by their luggage, big garments, the occasional kerchief, and, perhaps, by the scene's black-and-white rendering reminiscent of old photographs or woodcuts. Somewhat ambiguously grouped, although a father-mother-child seem loosely configured at the center, they look out from behind a ferry railing at the globe's flat backdrop. The backdrop's design, which also graced the shopping bags provided for customers, shows a monochrome abstraction of the Ellis Island administration building beneath a U.S. flag topped with the words "Destination America" and surrounded by a semicircular canopy of fourteen much smaller flags from other countries. Most of the flags, like those of Germany, Hungary, and Italy, refer to the primary countries of emigration through Ellis Island. But others, like that of Japan, most likely were included as the home countries of tourists. (As stated in a souvenir greeting card with an attached commemorative medallion, several hundred thousand Japanese immigrants did pass through Ellis Island. However, Japan's inclusion in this greeting card series—which must have the implicit theme "places you wouldn't associate with Ellis Island" since the other cards represent Mexico, France, and Africa—seems appro-

FIGURE 1. Ellis Island snow globe. Purchased at the gift shop in 1999.
(Photograph by Robert Diamante)

FIGURE 2. Ellis Island trinkets. Purchased at the gift shop in 1997 and 1999.
(Photograph by Robert Diamante)

priate, given that people from Asian countries more commonly migrated through the West Coast.⁴) Presumably, the big flag/little flags motif is supposed to signal "all the ethnicities that make up 'America,'" in the spirit of "e pluribus unum," not "the United States, imperialist bully."

The U.S. flag also appeared (twice) in a souvenir pen with floating parts (like the famous example where the pen is tipped to remove a woman's bikini). On the Ellis Island version, three pale-skinned children hold hands, girl-boy-girl in varied but vague European folk wear (puffed sleeves, wide skirts, bright colors), one waving a U.S. flag. By inverting the pen, one can make the figures travel from a position in front of a bigger flag on the left, portrayed as if wind blown, across the sea to the right, where they disappear behind the administration building. The flag and the building also make separate appearances on various T-shirts, hats, and golf balls; we are meant only, it seems, to swat them one at a time.

Confronted with actual products, my response changed drastically from the somewhat detached amusement with which I had contemplated the hypothetical items. My response had two strong components, which I first experienced as incompatible. One was a personalized version of Sallie's original horror, formulated tritely in the name of my grandfather who had been processed at Ellis Island after leaving Poland: "I'm glad Grandpa Irving didn't live to see this." I kept intoning this phrase to myself, although I knew that it was fundamentally false. I wasn't glad he didn't live this long, or even necessarily that he didn't see the refurbished building, gift shop and all. Thinking about his fondness for ordering Franklin Mint commemorative medals, long before "limited edition" offers appeared daily in magazine and TV ads, and the weirdly pagan Sabbath candlesticks, with putti that he had designated as my wedding present, I really had no idea how he would react. The phrase's truth value, I think, lay in its echo of the statements I used to hear from relatives hoping to generate behavior-changing guilt by invoking one or more grandparents as the fragile alleged possessor of the conservative values I was violating: "This [e.g., lesbian thing or, further back, a Puerto Rican boyfriend] will kill/would have killed your grandfather/grandparents." The resonance was in the illogic of portable shame —something public, bad for the family. Maybe heritage, like sex, risked descent into the realm of the tainted when certain money matters loomed too visibly. Immigrants in a snow globe, $3.99: my history for sale, and cheap.

The other component of my response I could state more directly: I wanted everything in sight. Well, not everything. I didn't want the international gifts. To be honest, I didn't even want to look at the books (although once in that section, the video about Ellis Island narrated by Telly Savalas, a.k.a. "Kojak," did tempt me).[5] It was the snow globes, the golf balls, the pens. I wanted to hold them, run my hands over them, stare at them from every angle. I wanted to dump snow on the immigrants and flip-flop the little white kids in the pen into an endless floating journey. I wanted to take them all home and keep them just for me. No gift buying here: before even owning them I knew that I couldn't ever part with them. Looking back later, I wonder if there's a connection between the "bad girl" haunting my articulation of disgust and how desperately I wanted those souvenirs. It was the kind of wanting that went way beyond the usual pull I feel toward glitter and fluids. My skin felt hot, my fingers tingled. Sallie wanted things, too, if not so urgently.

I can easily recreate those desires. My memory is vivid (not that vividness guarantees accuracy); my fingers still get prickly when I think about it. In contrast, all I remember about visiting the museum is that we decided to do it before buying anything. I must have learned some basics, at least, since I know I left with new information. But walking the halls, seeing exhibits, climbing stairs, reading wall texts—no activities stuck in my mind that would enable me to differentiate what I learned then from what I learned later. Afterward, we returned to the gift shop, where my dueling impulses battled it out in the manner of those cartoonish abstractions of angel and devil, Pleasure and Virtue—except that my impulses were so palpably inside me that separate externalized figures seemed ill-suited to represent them, as if I couldn't wrench them outside of me enough to look at them. What could I live with buying? What could I leave behind? Could I buy more stuff if I planned to write or teach about the objects? How much did I need to believe that I would? Finally, I bought for myself a pen, a lighter, maybe more. I bought Sallie a golf ball. It was her favorite outrageous item, and I wanted to give her a souvenir of our clearly memorable excursion. (Plus, the date was going well, so I figured I could visit the golf ball later.) Sallie bought me the snow globe, of course, and then chivalrously picked out for herself some objects, like the back scratcher, that she thought I might later regret leaving behind. Having fulfilled what had become the trip's mission, we left.

This book developed from my continuing interaction with Ellis Island and its products. From its first appearance as an object of unconfirmed existence invoked to spark sexual banter, the snow globe has remained central to my thinking. The subject to which I considered it central, however, has changed significantly several times.

ON THE ROAD

I put my souvenirs to work almost immediately. Maybe because I'd used the phrase "teaching tool" to bargain with myself for a bigger haul, or maybe because a weekend of play left me scrambling for a gimmick that might enhance a presentation I had to craft on the drive home, the souvenirs seemed perfect devices to illuminate the presentation, which was to be given on a panel about "social inequities." The panel was part of a program put together by the Affirmative Action Office and Multicultural Center at Bates College, where I teach, for the visiting adult chaperones at Seeds of Peace. As a camp in nearby Otisfield, Maine, Seeds of Peace, later chronicled in the 1999 documentary *Peace of Mind*,[6] brings together young people from sites of conflict, in this case, primarily Palestinians and Israelis.

The title of my talk, "The Ellis Island Gift Shop(!): Comments on the Diversity Rap," indicates the tenor of my first public presentation using the Ellis Island material. I went for shock value: Can you believe there even is a gift shop? Look how the snow globe says "Destination America" as if the United States were all of America. Look at those pale kids ("Two girls for every boy," as the Beach Boys might say, appropriately enough as the enshriners of blond); how come none of them look Jewish or Italian? In their casual national chauvinism and white centeredness, I argued, these products aptly symbolize the problems with multiculturalism in the United States today, where promoting diversity is so often a shallow and sentimental substitute for analyzing and fighting injustices based partly on those celebrated differences. It's easier, and more common, to buy a snow globe honoring immigrants of the past than to think or act critically about immigration. How about considering, instead, why a dubious category called "illegal alien" exists, or why those deemed its occupants can be denied health care and education due to the likes of California's Proposition 187, passed in 1994, and under review in California courts at the time. (It was about to be thrown out on the grounds that by enacting the 1996 Personal Responsibility and Work Opportunity Reconciliation Act, also known as "welfare reform," which curtailed basic benefits even to most legal immigrants, the federal government had claimed the sole right to pass such laws.[7])

My political critique was apt enough, but while my objects adequately assisted me in making my points, I could offer the items as emblems of lazy multiculturalism only by sidestepping the evidence of my own consumer response. Much of that I kept hidden, unless anyone noticed the way I kept fingering the plastic treasures or observed my reluctance to pass them around. This evidence, in turn, might rightly call into question the simple opposition I implied, but shouldn't have, between informed activists and snow globe fans, while presenting myself as only the activist. The opposition is a dubious one shored up by a number of common assumptions that I ordinarily work hard to challenge: that consumers lack critical skills or insight; that pop culture is necessarily shallow; that activists are dour by nature; that pleasures match, or should match, one's politics. When I returned to the material several years later, at my first real opportunity to undertake new research, I wanted to study both the products and how people engaged with them.

I still expected to consider the suggested politics of Ellis Island souvenirs in terms of their existence, their motifs, and their relation to the site. Especially since immigrants in the United States faced widespread hostility, violence, racism, and numerous policies that hurt them, such as the denial of benefits under "welfare reform" that I mentioned above, I wanted to study who and what was being promoted in this cheerleading for immigration. (This impetus for my project hasn't changed; the visibility and vociferousness of anti-immigrant sentiment and its effects have only increased in the aftermath of the events of September 11, 2001.)

A second visit to Ellis Island in summer 1999 confirmed that I had much to explore in this regard. This time, I devoted significant attention to areas beyond the gift shop. Part of what the museum offers is a chance to trace, loosely, the path of would-be entrants to the United States processed at Ellis Island, whose aims are often, inaccurately, subsumed under the term "immigrant." Although Ellis Island's reputation primarily concerns immigrants, which is also the museum's focus, the center processed others who are inadequately described by the term, including people arriving with the intention of leaving at a later point, as well as noncitizen residents who lived in the United States but had to be processed as newcomers every time they returned from a trip out of the country. Then as now, when noncitizens in the United States can be deported to countries they never lived in,[8] definitions of categories such as resident, citizen, and alien were not up to individuals to decide. (Given the diversity of circumstances that brought people through Ellis Island, I use the broader term "migrant" here unless I am referring to narratives or situations that specifically concern, or are imagined to concern, immigrants only. Besides a concern for accuracy, then, I want also to attend both to the politics and poetics of using terms like "immigrant."[9])

A visitor to Ellis Island today, who most likely enters, as did those in the past, through doors that led into what was once the baggage room, can walk up stairs as the early arrivals would then have done (although not precisely the same stairs), arriving in the registry room where the inspectors conducted interrogations. In addition, all three floors of the museum contain exhibits, most of which, appropriately enough, concern migration through Ellis Island. One series of rooms, "Through America's Gate," details the processing system at Ellis Island, from arrival to admission or exclusion. (People sometimes refer to refused entry as "deportation," but that term more properly belongs to people who have been admitted and then thrown out.) Although most rooms contain constructed exhibits with photographs, artifacts, and informational plaques, one, with period furnishings, re-creates one of the rooms in which the Board of Special Inquiry heard the cases of people deemed, on preliminary inspection, to have cause for being refused entry. Other exhibits on display include "Peak Immigration Years," which considers migrant life during the period from 1892 to 1924; "Treasures from Home," which offers a look at the kinds of items migrants brought with them; and an exhibit on the history of the site. Another permanent installation, called "The Peopling of America" (with "America" again misused, as it was on the snow globe, to designate the United States), seeks to situate Ellis Island in the context of migration to the United States in general, including forced migration and various forms of voluntary migration, ranging from indentured to unencumbered types.[10]

Besides the exhibits and the gift shop, areas of the building accessible to visitors include a library (for which making an appointment is preferred), a cafeteria, areas for groups such as those visiting from schools, and theaters for both plays and video showings. As of 2001, the building also houses the American Family Immigration History Center, where, for a fee, one can search a database of passenger lists, called ship manifests, for boats whose passengers might have passed through Ellis Island. This center is run by SOLEIF, which has been raising money for the two monuments since their restoration began in the early 1980s, when it was headed by Lee Iacocca, who was well known for securing a government loan to bail out Chrysler Corporation.[11] Visitors can also see one of SOLEIF's fund-raising projects behind the main building: called the American Immigrant Wall of Honor, it is a large circular structure composed of metal panels with the inscribed names of people whom donors have paid to honor. What visitors cannot approach are the many unrenovated buildings in the area, including hospitals, a contagious disease ward, and a laundry. These buildings are located in the sections called islands two and three, which were created by landfill that then enlarged the site from its original 3.3 acres to 27.5 acres.

Scanning the site as a whole suggested to me certain dominant representational trends present both inside and outside the gift shop. For instance, on souvenirs, like one of the erasers (figure 3), the huddled of the "huddled masses" were primarily female, while men more often looked heroically burdened. One such young man, head forward as if into the wind, appeared on key chains, miniature tea cups, tiles (figure 21, page 219), and the souvenir cups for the large sodas sold at the snack shops. This imagery was just one of the ways in which the clothing, poses, and dominant groupings of the figures on the souvenirs complemented the museum displays that seemed to presume heterosexual and gender normative immigrants.

On-site advertising for the Wall of Honor, which asked visitors especially to honor their parents or grandparents partly for the sake of their children, relatedly foregrounded procreative ties. Certain people, past and present, were missing from these representations. More than twelve million immigrants passed through Ellis Island. Surely, not all were married with chil-

FIGURE 3. Ellis Island eraser. Purchased at the gift shop in 1999. (Photograph by Kathryn Lattanzi)

dren (DOMA style) or aspiring to be so; surely not all fit easily, or at all, into the categories of "man" or "woman" offered as visual, statistical, and textual binary givens.[12] Could it really be possible, for instance, that each person wearing men's clothes in the exhibits' historical photos actually had a penis (of the fleshy sort)? What about today's visitors? Don't any of them want to buy an Ellis Island rainbow flag? In terms of gender, sex, and sexuality, I wanted to study Ellis Island representations in terms of both the migrants and the contemporary audience that they implied, validated, or worked to construct.

I had similar questions regarding race. Many figures on the souvenirs and other displays of imagery seemed to be raced in complex ways, with dark tones used to make them intelligible as immigrants according to prevailing representational codes but also with sufficient lightness to identify them as people whose descendents are now considered "white." I planned to consider these images in relation to racialized discourses and practices concerning immigration, looking especially at the two primary narratives about immigration presented at the Ellis Island museum. Interestingly, it is the broad contextualizing exhibit, "The Peopling of America," that most conspicuously addressed race. In a large central display, a wall with an accordionlike surface shows the U.S. flag when seen from one angle. When seen from the opposite angle, however, the wall displays a patchwork of smiling faces arranged to highlight an array of skin tones. If neither analytic nor realistic in its presentation of multiracial harmony, it at least signaled race as a major issue. With the more specific narrative about immigration through Ellis itself, racial matters appeared more subtextually and less visually identified as such. No clear iconic visual display, for instance, seemed to represent changing standards about who gets to be counted as white, which contributed to the 1924 restrictions that greatly curtailed immigration. In addition to closing loopholes in the already highly proscribed immigration of Asians, these restrictions also aimed to block the admission of southern and eastern Europeans—and intentionally, in the process, Jews—by imposing quotas based on country of origin that were correlated to census data not from 1920 but from 1890, before the huge influx of people from Russia, Italy, and Poland.

The need to use national quotas to restrict people by perceived race and/or religion raises another key issue: the straining required to sort people by nation. In 1999, I found this problem illustrated at the gift shop in a glittery fashion by a set of souvenir wall plaques. Each plaque, about the size of a postcard, had the words "Ellis Island" and a picture of the main building superimposed on varying images of a flag. Most of the flags represented primary countries of origin, such as Italy. One plaque, however, displayed the flag of Israel, with the white of the flag's background transformed into a more festive silver. It was probably offered to appeal to Jewish visitors, on the reasonable assumption, it seems logical to surmise, that many would not want to celebrate countries they fled from—and, probably, the less reasonable assumption that all Jews identify with Israel (figure 4). Here, the series' dominant logic of historical reference is abandoned in favor of an appeal to supposed contemporary affiliation. Israel became a state in 1948, long after Ellis Island's role as an immigration station had virtually ended.

While inconsistent signification in souvenirs may be more amusing than anything else, the recurrence of statistics, displays, and objects divided into

FIGURE 4. Ellis Island souvenir plaque. Purchased at the gift shop in 1999.
(Photograph by Robert Diamante)

categories named by country of origin plus "Jewish" or "Hebrew" is important. Besides gesturing in their particularities to a common sense that Jews do not really belong to the countries they inhabit, these lists point toward the cracks, past and present, in the use of nation and citizenship as organizing principles, which is quite noteworthy in showing up here since, among other functions, these categories determine the rules for designating certain types of relocation as immigrations; national borders would not exist without them. As Barbara Kirshenblatt-Gimblett writes in her important chapter on the museum in *Destination Culture*, the gift shop's "gallery of nations" approach reveals these cracks on many levels: in grouping products by countries that did not actually exist as independent states during the period of immigration or that may not "hold still long enough for the gift shop to clear its inventory," and in the lack of clear address, or sometimes any address, to many groups. "Which souvenirs," she asks, "are appropriate for Palestinians, Ukrainians, Armenians, Basques, Gypsies [Roma], Quebecois, and African Americans?"[13]

Which souvenirs, one might also ask, are appropriate for people whose identities cannot be described with singular or hyphenated compound terms. Ella Shohat, writing about her own identity as a Jewish-Arab and Iraqi-Israeli American, notes that "not all hyphenated identities are permitted entry into America's official lexicon of ethnicities and races." Jewish and Arab, for instance, are frequently considered not only mutually exclusive but also "antonyms," and, regarding immigrants to the United States, "only one geography is allowed prior to disembarking—the made-in-U.S.A. predicament of the single hyphen." In her case, this habit of labeling led to painful erasures: she explains that in being displaced from Iraq, "like most Jewish-Arab families after the colonial partition of Palestine," her family "became refugees from Iraq in the 1950s and ended up in Israel, due to what was styled a 'population exchange' that massively swapped Palestinians and Jewish-Arabs across borders." After migrating later to the United States, she notes, "I found that my scars of partition and traumatic memories of crossing the borders from Iraq to Israel/Palestine have no relevance or are rendered invisible."[14] What other erasures does the gallery of nations and cultures reinforce?

These were some of the issues that interested me concerning contemporary products at Ellis Island: products for sale, like snow globes, and products of interpretive work, like museum displays, that might function as producers of meanings. But what meanings? and for whom? Meanings do not reside in objects. No matter how directly objects might seem to express a message, no matter how transparent seem the intentions of the producer(s), people who derive meanings from the objects contribute to the production of those meanings. What they contribute, however, is often hard to determine. After all, even my consumer sample of one (me) indicated that the museum exhibits I describe above as important comparative material do not necessarily figure as significant components of consumer encounters with Ellis Island souvenirs. I brought to my own first encounter just about everything but that: some old and new information about matters personal and historical; some guiding ideas, beliefs, and echoes of which I was variously, if at all, conscious; and the dynamics of a particular hot date, with a particular person, at a particular stage of our relationship. While dissecting my experience is beside the point here (how much did the date's sexual buzz contribute to my giddy lust for the objects, for instance?), it is worth noting the discrepancy between what I noticed on my first visit and the early products of my research about what might be noticed.

So I could hardly expect to discern meanings for others from books, objects, and museum cues, especially if I presumed, as I do, that all visitors come to Ellis Island in the company of ideas, values, memories, histories, theories, and people (live and in mind) that form a mix at least as complicated as mine. To address questions of meaning, then, I needed to learn about what and whom other people brought to the Ellis Island gift shop and what they took away, in terms of both products and ideas. I hoped to interview a lot of visitors, as well as people connected to selling and to meaning making: the buyer and employees at the gift shop; the tour guides, most of whom are National Park Service rangers; and vendors at other sites, like the people at the Circle Line's New Jersey dock who sell $6 T-shirts, made in Bangladesh, that read "Ellis Island, New Jersey" in commemoration of the state's Supreme Court victory in a battle with New York over jurisdiction of the Island.[15]

TRIPS IN SHOPPING

After my initial research, I understood the Ellis Island snow globe as the anchor for a project about relations between production, consumption, and interpretation. The working title of this project, "The Ellis Island Snow Globe and Other Trips in Shopping," gestured toward the dominant overarching topic: the representation of political issues, positions, and affiliations through products for sale. Various objects have continued to lure me toward accompanying case studies. For example:

– The "great new sporty equality look in pigment-dyed fleece" advertised in the "Equal*idays*" catalog from the fall 1998 issue of the *Human Rights Campaign Quarterly*. The lavish detail of the ad copy stands in stark contrast to certain telling silences, beginning with the deliberate vagueness of the organization's name, which obscures the Human Rights Campaign's (HRC) singular focus on what it then conceptualized as "lesbian and gay" issues, and of its logo, two gold lines on a blue background that only barely read as an equals sign. (Although "Equal*idays*" states elsewhere that "the embroidered 'Badge of Equality' lets everyone know where you stand," no text, color choice, or additional graphic actually offers a clue.)[16] The issue itself also failed to mention the continuing controversy over its call in April of that year, with the gay Christian evangelical Metropolitan Community Church (MCC), for a "Millennium March on Washington for Equal Rights." The ad's model, stylish aura, and resortlike setting, however, seem to illustrate the point of critics who charged HRC and MCC with planning, as Barbara Smith wrote, "another march on Washington organized by conservative and moderate white forces that have the single-issue agenda of petitioning the establishment to extend a few gay rights."[17] (As my research assistant Jason Goldman discovered, many political organizations sell merchandise that might be considered far more disturbing. One example: "The NRA Infant Bib" at the National Rifle Association's Web site store, which features the letters *N*, *R*, and *A* on children's toy blocks. To accommodate boys, girls, or, I presume, prebirth uncertainty, the bib is available in blue, pink, or white trim.)[18]

– A chart in the 1998 appendices to the document colloquially known as the Starr report that summarizes the relationship between President Clinton and Monica Lewinsky in parallel columns documenting, by date, their personal contacts, phone contacts, and gift giving.[19] Among many fascinating features, besides the implication that gifts somehow confirm sexual interaction, is the contrast between the promise and denial of easy access to the chart's meaning. On the one hand, the chart suggests truth laid bare, notably by means of its plain visual format, clinical-sounding language ("brief direct genital contact"), and meticulous corrections—apparently it matters that Monica "now believes she sent the package to the President containing sunglasses, an erotic postcard, and a note about education reform on October 16, 1997" rather than a week later.[20] On the other hand, the chart requires much supplementary material in order to interpret it: some taken-for-granted explanations (the phrase "gummy 'boobs'" refers to candy); some common new information (the Black Dog is where Bill shopped for Monica while on vacation with Hillary); and some points that I wish were more commonly discussed (like how the chart, although based on Monica's testimony, records Bill's orgasms but not Monica's, thus pushing toward the reading of Bill as primarily being serviced).[21]

– The 1999 QVC home-shopping collection "Jewels of Unity" from Cicely Tyson. Tyson located the inspiration for her line in the sight of Nelson Mandela's former jail cell on Robben Island,[22] a site that has actually inspired various forms of commercial activity. In December 2000, one could "Spend New Year's Eve on Robben Island—and celebrate the joy of our African heritage" by paying R350 (about $70) per person to participate in "a dinner and dance celebration at the Maximum Security Prison Hall." The price included "two half-hour ferry rides, a tour of the prison, interaction with an ex-political prisoner, a welcoming cocktail, a sumptuous full-course dinner and complimentary Cape wines."[23]

What you make of Ellis Island depends on where you've been, where you think you're heading next, and what you're comparing it to: family photographs, Colonial Williamsburg, yesterday's tour of the Stock Exchange, school on the other days, Ellis Island in texts and pictures, some or none of the above, and more besides. While I abandoned plans for other extended "trips in shopping," not least because of the enormity of each topic,[24] my initial explorations affected my perspective on Ellis Island in several crucial ways.

First, because each topic offers the easy joke, they highlighted for me how easily criticism can engender ridicule and how little it takes to send criticism and ridicule sliding among, or between, human, material, and ideological targets. As Yemi Toure reminds us on the Web site "Hype: Monitoring the Black Image in the Media," Tyson deserves the "greatest respect . . . for an unbelievable lifetime of principle and accomplishment." We aren't justified in trashing Tyson, no matter how dubious seems her foray into QVC—although, as Toure suggests, one needn't be so kind about the station's misspelling of "Robben Island" on the press release.[25] (This misspelling, in turn, followed the press release into several newspaper stories written from it, in a telling indication of what sometimes passes as a sufficient news source.) As scholar-activist Leslie Hill points out, we should also consider the packaging of dining, dancing, and "interaction with an ex-political prisoner" in relation to the current labor situation for many former political prisoners; limited opportunity must affect why some now give tours at the prison turned heritage site.[26]

We need also to discriminate when we trash the scene purportedly captured in the chart in the Starr report. Once we start parsing Bill's definition of sex or picturing him up against the wall, pants unzipped, cigar in hand, a host of interpretive models encourage us to view the sex acts as bad or the actors as worthy of humiliation for engaging in them; it takes work to avoid supporting sexual censure. It takes vigilance, too, not to imply in critiques of products, images, or sites a matching criticism of their users. I may disrespect, for instance, the racial politics that direct disproportionate resources to Ellis Island as opposed to other heritage sites. Yet I don't want to disrespect people who travel there to honor their heritage—or, for that matter, who take away a snow globe—and I don't want to attribute to them, without careful study, values I perceive in their sponsors or purchases.

Second, scanning various product sites together helped me to pinpoint a certain conceptual habit, largely derived, I'm sure, from my training as an art historian, that was hampering my ability to formulate my project. No matter how interdisciplinary my work, no matter how guided by activist interests, I tended to think in terms of organizing around objects: asking questions about them; bringing material to bear on them; analyzing how they are produced, consumed, and interpreted and what they represent, typify, or betoken. But with these topics, the two models of looking from the objects out or from out back to the objects simply could not accommodate where I wanted to go. Nor could alternating between one and the other. As Irit Rogoff suggests, both approaches reflect academic paradigms that unproductively "dictate a relation between theories, contexts, and objects."[27] Indeed, I needed to unstick the connections. I didn't exactly want to explain gummy boobs or the "sporty equality look," and some of the issues they raised shunted them to the side; the objects couldn't further illuminate the issues. The same was true with the Ellis Island placemats, museum displays, and videos. They sent me to areas of inquiry that couldn't fully be mapped onto categories of object, such as souvenirs, books, and photographs, or categories of issues about objects, such as production, consumption, and interpretation, although those issues, as I outlined them earlier, remain crucial to my study.

The objects did, however, both at Ellis Island and in the other contexts I perused, share a certain knotting of issues that can be abbreviated by four words: sex, money, products, nation. I will introduce these topics briefly here as they pertain to Ellis Island.

SEX

By the term "sex" I refer to topics signaled by two common uses of the term. The first, as used in the phrase "biological sex," involves categories such as male and female and related issues concerning gender. I have already indicated some representational issues in use at Ellis Island (and, of course, in dominant circulation elsewhere) concerning sex and gender, like the apparent gendering of the "huddled masses" on souvenirs and the inattention to ways that sex and gender cannot be adequately mapped onto binary categories such as male/female. Gender is not, however, just a matter of inanimate representations. These appear at a site marked by a gendered, and raced, division of labor: light-skinned ferry personnel, virtually all male; dark-skinned sales people in the gift shop, primarily female, with white bosses; rangers more often male than female, more often white than not. How the gendering of work, people, and representations affect each other is a significant issue here.

One interesting matter in this regard lies in the recurring tales of the heroic son and his worshipped mother that figure both at Liberty Island and at Ellis Island. At Liberty Island, one learns that the sculptor Frédéric-Auguste Bartholdi allegedly gave the statue his mother's face (although, as I discuss in chapter 4, some say that the first model for Liberty was, instead, a black woman). At Ellis Island, Lee Iacocca's desire to honor his immigrant mother reputedly was the deciding factor in one contested issue about the restoration: whether to replace the stairs that immigrants had climbed to the registry room as medical personnel, performing what became nicknamed the six-second medical inspection, looked for signs of physical or mental impairment. While architects wanted to replace the stairs for their historical significance, Park Service officials argued that for historical accuracy, the stairs, which had been torn down while the building remained in use, should not be replaced. By some accounts, pressure from Iacocca, moved by Antoinette Iacocca's intense memory of the stairs, helped the architects trump the Park Service officials.[28] Given the disdain with which female influence is often viewed, the circulation of this story may owe as much to an urge to discredit the son, whose role has indeed been criticized, as to the mother's influence. In either case, however, gendered bonds figure importantly in making meaning.

Whether these intense bonds are sexed in the other common use of the term is, of course, another matter. And while I don't plan to psychoanalyze Bartholdi or Iacocca, I will argue that sex in this sense of sexuality and erotics needs to be surfaced and reimagined around Ellis Island. I do not mean here that everything about sex lies deeply buried, or even necessarily buried at all. As I discuss in chapter 1, sex certainly pops up here and there. Tour guides state that commercial and polygamous sex were grounds for the exclusion of migrants, and, not surprisingly, sex sometimes comes up as an issue among visitors. On my trips to Ellis Island, I overheard a fair amount of interactions about sexual relations.

> "You haven't even apologized for last night."
> "Let's just have a good time."
> "I want to talk about it now. Emma, Emma, give me something to prove you love me, give me a sign."
> (An annoyed peck follows—hardly a good sign.)[29]

Sex often appears, too, around topics of great importance at Ellis Island, like ethnicity and nation, with which sex increasingly and publicly cohabits: as, for instance, debates over "gay rights" put sexual orientation into a civil rights framework, or as presidential sex stands as a potential measure of fitness to govern, or as one's stance on abortion seems to operate as a sign of broader political affiliation.[30]

At the same time, however, sex, if not banished or banishable, seems flat and obscured both at and with regard to Ellis Island. Erotic complexity remains largely unelaborated, even unconsidered, which looks remarkable if one considers that Ellis Island's busiest years coincide with the inversions and perversions portrayed (as such) by people like Freud, Havelock Ellis, Picasso, and Mallarmé. Besides, considering its current crowds and fame for teeming masses, the site seems oddly unembodied. How it might be reembodied is one subject I examine here.

As I suggested earlier, part of my initial horror about the snow globe must tap into ubiquitous notions that money taints, demeans, cheapens, diminishes, or profanes much that it touches. In the arts, the ability to make money from one's work can raise suspicion about its quality. Selling may signal selling out—unless the purchase price is huge, in which case it may, paradoxically, confirm transcendent value or pricelessness.[31] With sex, "for free" has a nearly unshakeable place among the criteria for "legal," "moral," and even "meaningful," despite the important role of money in creating moments deemed legal, moral, and meaningful within the same cultural contexts. Gifts of jewelry are seen to express a depth of feeling gauged by their economic value: "a diamond is forever." (Baldly trading jewelry for sex, however, is alleged a wholly differentiable move, sleazy and contrameaningful.) Standard romantic trappings can be pricey, too: the getaway, the lingerie, and sometimes even a little spare time all cost money. So do some pleasures: as a group of working-class SM dykes noted in the zine *Brat Attack*, a certain class privilege is required to rip someone's clothes off without a care for replacing them.[32] Charges regarding money's taint frequently concern commodification, seen as especially vile when it seems to involve mining the sacred for moneymaking products, such as the Disney World T-shirts, seen for sale in 2000, that sport a mouse symbol formed from a yin-yang design.

Immigrants in a snow globe certainly suggest commodification. When I mention my trinkets people often asked me if I was writing about their commodification, and that idea is certainly what grabbed me first. But its hold on me diminished over time, both emotionally and intellectually. This happened partly because I'm disinclined to align myself with purveyors of the other charges I mentioned above; the more I rolled it around, the more I felt myself to be rolling around with the purity police. (As I discuss further in chapter 3, critiques of commodification are often implicitly justified by appeals to sexual shame and disgust for sexual commerce.) More important, I came to question commodification's primacy among relevant economic issues. Putting commodification first among the economic practices directly related to Ellis Island souvenirs suggests that the marketing of certain people's history, people primarily now labeled white, matters more than the working conditions of people, primarily of color, laboring in poor conditions to produce these goods or selling them in low-paying seasonal jobs. Besides being unacceptable, this assignment of relative value, along with the enshrinement of the site, depend on other money matters that demand study, including SOLEIF's fund-raising (Lee Iacocca is himself a book-length economic topic) and the resulting situation, presented by most tour guides as an obvious good, that "no tax dollars" went into the restoration.

In addition, charges of commodification often imply the intrusion of monetary exchange and economic value into a previously unsullied realm. In the process, as Miranda Joseph explains, they often set up certain identities, communities, and activities as separate or as respite from the market.[33] Yet the roles of money and commodities at Ellis Island cannot even be said to have been hidden; they figured prominently long before the Stroh Brewing Company spent $3 million in the early 1980s to become the official beer of the Statue of Liberty and Ellis Island restoration.[34] Financial status determined whether arrivals even landed on Ellis Island. Most migrants traveling on a first- or second-class boat ticket were processed on the boat; only the others were automatically ferried to Ellis Island. In addition, economic incentives contributed to the policing of migration. Since the U.S. government billed the steamship companies for expenses and for the return ticket when their passengers were detained or sent back, the companies had a stake in ferreting out people who would be refused entry under, for example, laws prohibiting prostitutes, anarchists, and certain people deemed mentally or physically unfit. During many periods, migrants had to display a certain amount of money, at one point $25, to prove they weren't "liable to become a public charge" (a precedent approvingly cited in 1996 by proponents of restricting benefits to immigrants under "welfare reform"). Further, if the migrants were solo females they usually needed to produce a supervising family escort, supposedly to safeguard them from being lured into the business of selling sex.

At every phase, there were visible brand names. American Express ran the money exchange. For some immigrants, a giant flashing Lipton sign competed with Liberty for attention in New York harbor.[35] In addition, as I found in the text of a 1998 calendar titled *The Best of JELL-O*, "As immigrants passed through Ellis Island in the early part of the 20th century, they were often served a bowl of JELL-O® gelatin as a 'Welcome to America.'" According to one oral history fragment presented in the museum section on food, it was not actually a gift for all immigrants, as the Jell-O "Fun Fact" might seem to imply, but a weekly treat much fought over by detainees, who got more skilled in procuring it as their detention wore on. Study is needed on the role of money, as well as on the role of how money is represented and why people often think commodification is the most important issue to consider in regards to money and Ellis Island.

PRODUCTS

Ellis Island: The Official Souvenir Guide: both the name and the object itself show how some standard categorizing may fail both descriptively and critically.[36] Go here; get in this line to purchase your memories. The directive language of "official" and "guide" grates against the notion of a "souvenir" as a memento picked for personal resonance by an individual who will use it mentally to revisit, sometimes to narrate, distinctly personal experiences, feelings, or memories.[37] Yet as many scholars have argued, experiences, feelings, memories, and our understandings of them, no matter how personal or unmediated they are commonly apprehended to be, are indeed externally informed and transformed.[38] Besides, the guidebook is of physical as well as imaginative substance. It is a material object just as much as a snow globe is. Like the snow globe, "made in China," it even bears the mark of production outsourced to Asia. Along with cues, like listing the book's designer, that invite readers to infer an intellectual, artistic, and artisanal refinement beyond what "©1991, 1994 by Aramark Sports and Entertainment Services, Inc." might suggest, the copyright page states that the book was "printed and bound in Korea."[39]

The guidebook and snow globe share something in their manufacture, and perhaps in their use as well. Following standard gift shop geography, although some guidebooks live among the trinkets, Ellis Island's store has distinct places for books and for decorative objects, suggesting products of a different order: one set of objects inviting a deeper look, the other easily taken in; one set of objects to derive information from, the other to ascribe meanings to. But who's to say how they function once purchased? A snow globe might catalyze research. A souvenir guidebook might never be opened. Both or neither could lead from "oh, yes, I've been there" on numerous paths, long or short, straight or bent, shallow or profound, more or less idiosyncratic, and more or less attached to the generating source.

I use the term "product" here to designate certain core matters of study, which might loosely be categorized as "material products" and "products of interpretation," both to emphasize certain features about them and to engage certain connections among them. Most important, I want to keep at the forefront the fact that products of both types are, in fact, products, and that it matters how, of what, and by whom they are made.

All objects at the Ellis Island site are products of interpretation and labor. The language tree of "Ethnic Americanisms" in the "Peopling of America" exhibit, for instance, comes from numerous sources: the many-sourced beliefs of its designer(s), and design approvers, that it is reasonable to illustrate immigrant effects on U.S. language in terms of words added to English, itself an immigrant language actually (or, to quote a great poster designed in 1978 by Yolanda López, "Who's the Illegal Alien, Pilgrim?"[40]); the common use of trees among various symbols that lend the sense of organic growth to cultural processes; the work of people who harvested, bought, acquired and built with the wood. Photographs, wall plaques, and other objects can all be similarly described. I use "product" to keep the work of production in focus.

By starting from the general category "products," I want also to avoid presupposing the explanatory value of certain habitual divisions among products—such as manual/intellectual, visual/textual, for sale/not for sale, material/nonmaterial—and to leave room for others that might be more fruitful here. For example, creating a category limited to products that one can purchase at Ellis Island emphasizes their status as commodities when, as Arjun Appadurai suggests, an object's status as a commodity (as something that can be exchanged, usually for money) may be just one phase in the social history of the object that is not always the most relevant one— even, I would argue, at the store.[41] Such a grouping also implies a contrasting set of products to be had for free, but to what extent can anything at Ellis Island productively be understood that way, considering, just for starters, that it costs money to get there?

Similarly, while a division between material and nonmaterial products highlights the physical boundedness of some products as opposed to others, it can also obscure features of boundedness that occur on both sides of the divide. Frequently repeated historical tidbits—like the one, presented to provoke gentle, sympathetic laughter, about how immigrants, when first offered bananas, often bit into the unfamiliar foodstuff without peeling them—can be as canned in content and presentation as immigrants in a snow globe. So, too, can personal histories: as Susan Stewart states, the "personal-experience story" can be "most impersonal in its generic conventions" for interpreting and describing experience.[42] A little more permeable, but surprisingly not much more, are many people's souvenir-buying habits. Some never buy anything at tourist sites on principle, regardless of their experience at the particular place. Others "always" buy a particular thing, such as a shot glass or "a sweatshirt for my granddaughter," or have a more generalized but no less regular buying habit. When I asked one woman how she'd chosen which magnet to buy, she told me that she always picked something that best represented the experience, "a memento." It seemed, though, that she cared little to remember Ellis Island, which she'd hoped would be more like a theme park or boardwalk.[43]

NATION

In the early 1980s, SOLEIF had to trade on public familiarity with the Statue of Liberty to pull in the funds to restore Ellis Island. Even in 1987, the foundation's own annual report explained Ellis Island by way of a migration site with greater name recognition and prestige than Ellis Island itself, although, the text suggests, diminishing stature: "Ellis Island is the Plymouth Rock of full-grown American Democracy. The Mayflowers that once landed here with their human cargo sailed from ports around the world. Millions of immigrants were channeled to this tiny island in New York Harbor—only to spread again across the continent and into the very fiber of American life."[44] Today, thanks in no small part to the foundation's highly publicized fund-raising, Ellis Island had become a frequent point of reference for other migration sites. An article in the *Denver Rocky Mountain News*, titled "Story of Refugees from Mexican Revolution Unfolds on DIA [Denver International Airport] Wall," quotes the muralist Judith Baca on the "huge migration through the Ellis Island of the Southwest, El Paso." The *Portland Press Herald* identifies "Ellis Island South" as a popular term for a town outside of Atlanta from which many resettled Somali refugees are relocating to Maine.[45] Neither article does more than mention the name Ellis Island, which has become shorthand for immigrant arrival sites, and, often, for the status, attention, and/or resources that such a site deserves. "The Mr. Olympia of American counties—which became a 98-pound weakling during the early 1900s—is back on Muscle Beach," states another article, claiming that "Los Angeles has regained its title as America's Ellis Island" by again becoming the nation's fastest-growing county thanks to migrations from other states and countries.[46]

To reference Ellis Island, however, is not necessarily to support its enshrinement as "the Plymouth Rock of full-grown American Democracy" or its legitimacy as a symbol or paradigm of "the Peopling of America." As one of the creators of NuSouth—a clothing line based in Charleston, South Carolina, that features the Confederate flag rendered in an African liberationist black, red, and green—tells GQ, "The South—that's our Ellis Island; that's how we came into this country." Implicit in his statement is an opposition rather than a parallel; another location, not Ellis Island, emblematizes his personal and collective migration history.[47] At the museum that was once the immigration station that operated from 1910 to 1940 on Angel Island, near San Francisco, tour guides emphasize the inappropriateness of its nickname "the Ellis Island of the West," since excluding immigrants, particularly those barred under the Chinese Exclusion Act of 1882, was its primary purpose.

Presumptions that Ellis Island can stand for U.S. nation building through migration are both widespread and embattled. They are also wrapped up with presumptions about what "nations" are in general and about particular nations seen in comparison or contrast, including those associated with ethnic origin or homeland.[48] The sources, adherents, and contents of those presumptions are as varied, and sometimes as weirdly put together, as the metaphoric gestures in the foundation's description of human cargo spreading (like butter, like ants, like germs, like fluids?) into the fiber of American life.

SEX MONEY PRODUCTS NATION

In June 2000, Eric McCormack, famous for being the guy who's not gay but plays a gay guy on TV in *Will and Grace*, emceed a benefit at Ellis

Island for amfAR (the American Foundation for AIDS Research). According to amfAR's Web site, the event, called "Honoring with Pride: An Evening on Ellis Island," honored "gay and lesbian pioneers in the fight against AIDS."[49] According to the *New York Times*, McCormack's suit came from Banana Republic, and the guests, including "James Dale, the telegenetic Boy Scout" of Supreme Court fame and former New York governor Mario Cuomo, dined in the registry room on a "medley of salmon, chicken, and filet mignon . . . served upstairs under a vaulted ceiling decorated with the AIDS memorial quilt."[50] Big donors amid ghosts of poor immigrants; gay pride on ethnic pride's staging ground; products homemade and outsourced; "pioneers" and "Banana Republic": one central argument of this book is that this event makes absolute, if knotty, cultural sense. Like the "great new sporty equality look," the dinner dance at Robben Island (or at Alcatraz, which has them, too), and the deployment of "criminal justice" tools to snare presidential semen on a Gap dress, it is among many contemporary scenes where practices and representations concerning money, sex, products, and nation come together, in ways both transsituational and situation specific, that merit activist critical attention.

WHAT'S NEXT

The chapters that follow consider the coming together of sex, money, products, and nation around various topics connected to Ellis Island. In chapter 1, "Breeders on a Golf Ball: Normalizing Sex at Ellis Island," I engage the normalization of sex at Ellis Island in two ways. First, I consider representations and absences around sexuality that have become normalized. Looking at the much reproduced photograph of a man, woman, and child who stare over at the Statue of Liberty, for instance, I address, among other matters, how the idea that breeders make heritage is constructed to be taken for granted. In chapter 1 also I work to normalize the engagement of sex, both generally and regarding "queer" sexualities in particular, in studies of Ellis Island's past and present. On this matter, a central research question comes from the limited resources about sex, normative or otherwise, regarding Ellis Island, and the more general challenges of getting at sex "in the flesh" from and through inanimate documents, artifacts, and texts. Looking at a range of material about the site, I argue that studying sex at Ellis

Island requires strategies of embodiment, with attention to the particular bodies inhabited and to the complexity, messiness, and contradictions of sexed bodies in their historical specificity.

In chapter 2, "Getting Dressed Up: The Displays of Frank Woodhull and the Policing of Gender," I use the situation and circulation of the case of Frank Woodhull to consider the relationships of representation to power, surveillance, and policing. Appearing at Ellis Island in 1908, Woodhull faced possible exclusion from the United States when he was forced to admit, on being confronted with a medical exam that included forced disrobing, that although he had presenting himself to the authorities as male, his body signaled the sex identity suggested by his former name, Mary Johnson. Besides considering the procedures, differentially imposed in relation to factors like race and economic status, that operated to regulate gender at the border, I address practices of categorization, like the popular term "passing woman," that also, I argue, work to police gender.

After examining sex and gender at Ellis Island I move to the Statue of Liberty. Much of the fund-raising to restore Ellis Island was accomplished by putting the statue forward as the primary beneficiary of SOLEIF's efforts, although it did not get most of the money; less than a third of the $277 million in funds raised that Iacocca announced on 1 July 1986 went to restore the statue.[51] Thus a study of the money involved at Ellis Island needs to consider the money's implied destination. In chapters 3 and 4 I study meaning making about sex, money, race, and migration as they circle around the restoration of the statue and the events of Liberty Weekend, the three-day extravaganza that took place around 4 July 1986 to celebrate and unveil the restoration. Chapter 3, "The Traffic in My Fantasy Butch," takes off from a recurring practice of describing allegedly dubious fund-raising practices as the prostitution of Lady Liberty. I look at this imagined scandal of sex meeting money in relation to other matters about sex and about money where, I suggest, the outrage might better be directed. These matters include the Supreme Court's un-Libertylike ruling, right before Liberty Weekend, to uphold state antisodomy laws challenged in *Bowers v. Hardwick*; and the story of the twelve-year-old refugee who couldn't keep the prize she won in a Statue of Liberty essay contest because its cash value threatened her family's eligibility for public assistance. In gloriously Reaganesque fashion, narratives of regal benevolence camouflage economic inequity.

In chapter 4, "Green Woman, Race Matters," I look at various takes on how, or even whether, the Statue of Liberty has relevance for African Americans. Against the promotion of the statue as a symbol honoring the United States as "a nation of immigrants" two primary arguments emerge: first, that the statue, like those who would describe the United States as a nation of immigrants, ignores and disrespects people whose ancestors were transported by force; and, second, that the reading of the statue as an immigration icon ignores or suppresses the statue's full or partial genesis as a tribute to the end of slavery. I also engage in chapters 3 and 4 the methodological problems encountered in using a relatively linear style of analysis to describe how meanings knot and pile up. I argue for a strategy that, instead of advocating for one particular reading, works to address meaning making by excavating its foundations, conditions, ingredients, contexts, and alternatives.

Chapter 5, "A Nation of Immigrants, or Whatever," continues my examination of fund-raising by studying SOLEIF's "nation of immigrants" money strategies for Ellis Island, especially the extremely successful and ongoing project of the American Immigrant Wall of Honor. In both chapters 4 and 5, in light of the issue of fund-raising, I am especially interested in the race politics attending the representation of these monuments as heritage sites of broad public relevance, and thus worthy of a massive share of heritage funding, by virtue of their relation to immigration and to each other. I argue that SOLEIF's success at raising money—"more than $450 million (and counting!)," as stated on its Web site in a text written in 2000[52]—resides partly in the contradictions and lack of clarity about whose heritage SOLEIF is marshalling resources to honor: Ellis Island immigrants, all immigrants, all migrants, all people who now claim the United States as home, or all who identify with the concept that gets described in phrases like "the spirit of America." My goal here is not to indict the foundation or the museum for its focus on Ellis Island, which in many ways is as obvious as it is understandable, but to ask how claims for a grander focus serve to obfuscate the disproportionate channeling of resources to the heritage of people of whom most are generally considered white. In addition, the mix of pride, disdain, and confusion generated by the Wall of Honor—an increasingly common hybrid of donor plaque as historical record—raises interesting issues about the role of money in various understandings of what constitutes reputable history and meaningful encounters with it.

Chapters 6 and 7 undertake several "trips in shopping," although not quite the ones I first imagined. In chapter 6, "Immigrant Peddlers," I consider some of the players, objects, and economics that factor into the movement of souvenirs by looking at the sales scene at Battery Park, from which ferries travel to and from Ellis Island. People who expect immigrant vendors to be part of the outdoor scene in New York will find many at Battery Park. Some operate illegally. Others—much more highly capitalized than their use of pushcarts might suggest to the nostalgic—appear courtesy of the City of New York Department of Parks and Recreation, which authorizes, regulates, distributes, and profits from the placement of pushcarts there, making over $3 million from Battery Park concessionaires, for instance, in the fiscal year ending in June 2000.[53] In concert with other city agencies, including the police, the Department of Parks and Recreation also acts to back up the notion that immigrants running stationary souvenir stands, in certain gesture-to-the-past locations, enhance the image of the city, while temporary migrants selling from suitcases (usually, in Battery Park, dark-skinned men often from Senegal) do not. In chapter 6 I consider how various players in managing the image of "immigrant vendor" work to reinscribe inequities connected to race, national origin, and access to capital.

Chapter 7, "Product Packaging," pops in and out of the gift shop in two sections that look at a messy set of relations among vending, migration, tourism, labor, and incarceration. The first section, "Flexible Production," considers the disjuncture at the gift shop between increasing multicultural savvy, on some matters at least, and a certain matter-of-factness about the exploitation of labor involved in the manufacture of many souvenirs. Among other matters, I study mystifications tied up in the "made in" labels, which depend partly on conceptions of migrants and places of origin. That is why, even in a store where most visitors can be presumed to think that "made in China" refers to a factory location, not a designer's nationality, marketers can still expect "made in Ireland" to signify "authentic expression of Irish culture." The second section, "Eat Up," begins with a souvenir placemat and follows one of its photographs, depicting women and children eating at Ellis Island, across the hall to the snack shop, to which a sign with the same photograph formerly directed visitors. In the vagueness of the photograph, along with the even more vague gestures by the snack shop toward food of the past, appear, I think, the limit points and contradictions in setting up Ellis Island, a site of detention, with tourist amenities. Who wants to eat, smell, or relive detention food? As important, who wants to sell it to you? In looking at food and food representation at Ellis Island past and present, along with Aramark's own recent ventures into detention cooking, I examine the elisions regarding incarceration in the transformations and uses of Ellis Island as a tourist site.

Finally, chapter 8, " 'Decide an Immigrant's Fate,' " is named after a Park Service program for Ellis Island visitors, which has visitors act as a 1910 board of inspectors hearing the appeal of an immigrant about to be excluded for having unknowingly violated contract labor laws. Considering the continuing and, it seems, increasing notion that the status, safety, residence, and rights of immigrants may justifiably depend on the whims of policy-makers, border policers, and some subset of the public with a firm hold on who gets to count as an "American," the politics of inviting visitors to imagine that they can decide who gets excluded or deported merit examination. At the same time, however, the effects of museum programming cannot fully be judged by positing interpretations from an abstract of its script. With its changing cast of rangers, actors, and audience participants, the program offers a great opportunity to consider what people bring to and take from the production of history. Overall, throughout this book I hope to offer artifacts, interpretations, and politics that can add productively to the mix.

SOME COMMENTS ABOUT TERMS AND METHOD

Because significant bodies of literature have been devoted to many of the topics I consider here—Ellis Island, heritage tourism, immigration history, sexuality studies, ethnicity studies, commodity culture, visual representation, global capitalism, to name a few—an introductory literature review is not appropriate. I will comment on my sources, issue takings, inspirations, and debts as they become relevant to the particular topics under discussion.

Before proceeding, however, I would like to discuss several presumptions that I work from as well as certain features of my approach, particularly those involving my interactions with the visitors and workers connected to Ellis Island.

What You See, What You Get. Much of this project is based on looking at people, live or in photographic media, and I often describe them using phrases, such as "white man," that suggest visible, fixed, and discrete categories of identity. I presume, however, that such categories are neither fixed nor discrete, nor, even according to dominant norms, necessarily legible visually. When I describe someone I see as "white," for instance, I mean to indicate that I perceive visible characteristics that conform to dominant norms for people currently considered "white." I do not mean to indicate that "white" (or any other racial term) actually designates a biologically distinct category. Nor do I mean to imply that I am sure I have accurately assessed by eyeballing how the person would categorized herself or himself, what the person understands possessing "whiteness" to be about (are only "good Christians" eligible?), how the person has been categorized by others, or how the person would have been characterized in other social, historical, or administrative contexts.

Similarly, when I describe someone I see as a "man," I mean to denote a person whom I perceive to present himself, more or less consciously, in accordance with visually accessible cues that generally signal "man." I do not mean that he necessarily has the array of genitals, chromosomes, and/or hormones often taken to determine the biological sex "male" (or that all people fit into one of two discrete categories "male" and "female"); that he presents gender cues that match (rather than, for instance, camouflage) his own understanding of his sexual or gender identity; that he has the same understanding of his sexual or gender identity (in terms of an overall label or its ingredients) that he used to have or that others (including me) have; that he considers "he," "his," "man," "male," or "masculine" appropriate to describe him; or that he believes that he fits into either "man" or "woman."[54] I also presume that even if transgender discontinuities—e.g., a person assigned "male" identifies as "female"—most obviously signal complicated gender engagements, gender is still complicated, constructed, and usually in process even for someone who starts life amid confident declarations that "it's a girl," and goes through life consistently feeling female, presenting as female, and being regarded as female.

Whether particular categories of identity exist, whom/what they designate, and how they are deployed vary over time, across cultures, and among individuals. In various contexts, for example, "Asian" may designate a continent of origin or a race, refer to a majority or a minority, or be deemed usefully inclusive or inexcusably vague. As I discuss later, it is also important here to note that categories and their contents shift in relation to geopolitical relocation.

Talking Points. Although I do not record extensive interviews in this book, I do make use of oral commentary. Isolated research offers limited insight about what events, objects, and experiences might mean to people besides the researcher. (I sidestep here the question about how much one can learn even about oneself this way.) My first visit to Ellis Island, it is safe to say, had some features in common with many visitors—including, for example, my rather happenstance decision to go there. The more I visited, however, the further away I got from being anything like a one-time or several-time visitor. Just knowing in advance where to find the good bathrooms and how much it would cost to buy lunch set my days apart. I took many tours and "decided the immigrant's fate" sometimes twice a day. I saw multiple viewings of the $3 (later $5) play and the free movie, *Island of Hope—Island of Tears.*[55] How many visitors could manage even to sample all the educational fare? I studied enough material, both on-site and off, to notice, eventually, that the same image graces coloring books and speculum displays (a photograph, which I discuss later, of a migrant woman, partly undressed, undergoing a medical exam). I traveled enough in the footsteps of my ancestors so that after a while I thought nothing of it: the "stairs of separation," where migrants were routed according to admission or rejection, felt like any old stairs to me. I spent more money than most at the gift shop and, by virtue of multiple trips, got to perform certain shopping activities that rarely happen with tourist-site purchasing: I could comparison shop (for books primarily, since few other locations sell Ellis Island memorabilia); "sleep on it" before purchasing (do I actually need to own the new fancier snow globe with the polyresin model of the administration building?); and go back, because I was going back anyway, for things I later wished I had bought. I also had the distinction of being able to refer to notes (at least, I'm virtually the only person I saw taking them).

I note these discrepancies to indicate that the range of material and experiences I brought to Ellis Island, including my numerous encounters with the site, differed increasingly from those of most people. I absolutely do not intend to imply a contrast in interpretive depth between the mere visitor and the informed critic or scholar—the former reacting and the latter analyzing, the former simple and the latter complex. Such a contrast, I believe, perpetuates one of the most egregious errors of cultural, activist, and educational work: the tendency to flatten out the motives and interpretive habits of a hypothesized public, often with the implication that the person doing the hypothesizing is ever so much more complicated and aware. In *Barbie's Queer Accessories*, I argued that "both children and adults act as editors, cultural critics, theorists, and text makers."[56] I still believe that. This is one of the reasons why I include my own contexts and practices as a visitor/consumer at Ellis Island; I don't want to set up consumers and critics inhabiting separate bodies. This is also why I opt when possible for the less academic of my own vernaculars. My goal is not to feign a lack of training but to avoid, as much as possible, supporting the perception of a gulf in value that associates "real" theory with fancy words and fancy degrees above all. In addition, because I view my writing as activist work pursued both inside and outside academic environments, and with people who are and are not academics by trade, I strive to write in a manner that can be read without undue struggle in various contexts. This does not mean, however, that I seek to offer simplified interpretations or solutions.

I assume that visitors to sites are critics and theorists. But I learned at Ellis Island that few people were acting as critics and theorists about what first interested me: the representations on the souvenirs. In my study of Barbie, most people I talked to had given the matter some thought before I came along; just mentioning the doll often generated unsolicited comments about her personal or social meanings. In contrast, when I asked people about images on gift shop souvenirs, I could usually tell that my questions introduced a previously unengaged topic; they were also least likely, of all my questions, to yield an interested, or interesting, response. That discovery did not deter me from offering here my own analyses of pictures on products. It did deter me, however, from claiming either that my analyses function to illuminate consumer responses or that my impulse to perform them corresponds to frequent consumer practices.

I looked to other visitors, then, partly to gauge the extent to which my interests and interpretations were shared, and partly to discern patterns among the nonhuddled masses at Ellis today. I also sought out various employees in attempts to learn about the site and about working at it. With both visitors and employees, I used two basic listening devices: eavesdropping and interviewing. The first, which could also more formally be termed a component of "participant observation," enabled me to hear the voices of more people than I could interview, and to do so independently of an interview context—responding to me wasn't in the mix. Therein was also a disadvantage. I couldn't do some things possible in interviews, like requesting clarification or contributing to the conversation's direction, or asking people to repeat themselves (did you say your kid was "Chaim" or "Harrison"?). By exercising choice in approaching people to interview, I could also compensate for another disadvantage of eavesdropping. Since the loudest voices usually belonged to men, lurking diversely with regard to gender was often quite difficult. In both situations, I was also limited to English, with the occasional use of French, which also restricted the demographic scope of my analyses. While I tried, if not systematically, to study a diverse group of visitors, I could not range as far as I would have liked in terms of nationality, place of residence, and ethnicity with respect to people living both outside or inside the United States for whom English is not a primary language.

Besides things I couldn't do, there were things I strove to avoid doing. I didn't want to be unintentionally threatening or to generate suspicions that could seriously impede my ability to continue my activities. I forestalled some problems by introducing myself to relevant staff people; the gift shop manager knew I wasn't spending hours in the store as a shoplifter or competitor. Some misconceptions, however, seemed trickier to protect myself against. For instance, it's difficult, especially these days, for strangers to approach kids without looking like predators. So I rarely talked to kids without adults present, nor did I hang around school groups unless I saw a lot of random adults in the area. On my mind more, I wanted to avoid looking like a spy for management. One of the first employee conversations I heard involved two employees complaining about their conversations being reported to the boss. It reminded me that listening to workers can be interpreted as threatening, just like talking to writers can be risky. I tried to avoid any activities that might put jobs at risk, or suggest that even more surveillance had been added to already monitored days.

All in all, I spoke to a lot of people. Aside from a few longer, scheduled meetings with, for example, museum and city administrators, most of my conversations were on-the-spot interviews. I approached people for different reasons: they were performing a job or activity I wanted to know about; they were carrying packages from the gift shop; they'd said, done, or displayed something that interested me (a follow-up to lurking); or they just happened to be standing nearby, so why not? Since my project changed a lot, and since, at any phase, a detailed explanation of the project seemed ill suited to engage people in discussion, my approach to initiating conversation varied. I often introduced myself to visitors by saying that I was writing about tourist souvenirs or what people bought at heritage sites. This self-presentation was honest (although the context and extent of that topic changed for me over time), and it seemed appropriately short and understandable. Later on, I sometimes told people that I was studying the experience of visiting Ellis Island, or the role of money in tourist sites, especially when that most accurately reflected what I wanted to talk to them about. Certainly, such descriptions were only partial, but any description would be. Besides, I had to start somewhere, and I often learned what individuals considered necessary background information only when they asked for it.

As time passed, my approaches also reflected what I'd learned from my own successes and failures, although I couldn't always figure out what was and wasn't working. During one difficult week in which I had to disentangle myself from conversations with two men whom I expected to see daily— one very anxious to know where I was staying and another who wanted to "fill me with his enlightenment"—I nicknamed this problem "cleavage or credentials?" (the former metaphorically rather than physically descriptive). What had gone so wrong that day? What had gone so right the day before when I'd had a great interview with a park ranger at the Statue of Liberty? Was it my skimpy summer clothing, my college professor job, both, or neither—and what else? It was difficult not just to discern what constituted credentials to different people—that I am a teacher, fellow tourist, descendant of Ellis Island immigrants, writer, Jew, person who has also seen Epcot Center—but also sometimes to judge what people were interpreting from my self-presentation. The FtM director Jed Bell commented, when I told him about my day with the two difficult men, "Think how much harder those encounters would have been [both to have and to interpret] if you couldn't tell whether they were reading you as male or female." As his comment reminded me, people are always decoding each other, more and less consciously. When days or events went noticeably well or badly, I tried to figure out why, and to work within the range of options that I considered ethical and acceptable (dropping an outfit that seemed to repel, ok; dating the souvenir vendor, not ok).

I also tried to check my own biases. For example, I was initially annoyed by a white woman in her thirties who snarled about cheap trinkets, insisted that prices had to be bargained down, and sniped at her husband about the way he was dressed. Seeing her later, however, I suddenly began to soften when I noted the dark hairs over her upper lip that she had done nothing to remove or minimize.[57] Suddenly she seemed less shallow, and I started to fill in the blanks more sympathetically, imagining that maybe decent politics rather than haughtiness might explain her hostility to the souvenir shop and figuring that her clearly energetic kids must have been tiring her out. As a result of this and other such encounters, I attempted to keep an eye on what colored my own views.

Once engaged in on-the-spot interviews, I did not proceed from a prepared list of questions but rather took cues from the first responses I got. Initial questions about a purchase, for instance, might lead to others about the objects, the visit, and/or other material that emerged as relevant. By attending to people's directional guides, I learned more about how they contextualized, theorized, and otherwise interpreted what they were doing, and about what they considered worthy of discussion. I didn't, however, merely go with the flow. I introduced new topics or tried to redirect the conversation, especially if I thought that my questions had come across as intrusive or seemed to shut down someone's willingness to talk—one notable conversation stopper was my curiosity about the Park Service police. Sometimes I shared personal information or anecdotes that seemed likely to keep the conversation going. For instance, I approached one man with a rainbow camera strap bearing an enamel pin with the logo, also in rainbow, for the

Millennium March on Washington—because, as I told him, he was one of the few people I had seen at Ellis Island displaying products designed to signal gay identity. When I asked him if he'd gone to the march, I added that I'd gone to the one in 1993. I did this partly to signal that I was safe to talk to, not a basher or converter fishing for a target. I didn't trash the march's genesis, mention that I'd spent the past year intoning "the millennium, it's Christian," or discuss my nonfondness for rainbow gear, which I tend to associate with the idea that expressing one's politics through symbolic commodities constitutes effective and sufficient activism. As it turned out, however, his disappointed characterization of the march, "We're Here, We're Queer, and We've Got Credit Cards," belied my expectations, which were somewhat contradictory in any case considering how thrilled I was to encounter at Ellis Island the very rainbow accessories I was ready to judge him for. Meanwhile, also not so consistent, he critiqued march goers who apparently came to shop while wearing a march product.[58]

WHAT I GET, WHAT YOU GET

I give the anecdote above because it exemplifies the process, benefits, and limits of my on-the-spot interviews. Our conversation took shape as we both continually sized each other up, filtering more or less deliberate features of the other person's self-presentation through our own histories, beliefs, stereotypes, and values. We made decisions about what to share or withhold, and whether to continue or quit, for various reasons: personal safety or comfort; relations with others, present or absent; senses of pleasure, duty, or payoff. In general, I found that some people enjoyed the chance for conversation while others merely tolerated me. Some jumped at the chance to be written about—"Honey, if we talk to this lady we can be in a book!"—while others prefaced their comments with concerns about confidentiality.

My own decisions also involved matters of professional, personal, and political ethics related to my project. Some, which I discussed earlier, concern my on-site efforts to present myself honestly and to attend carefully to the working conditions of employees. Other decisions came up later during my writing, especially those involving issues of anonymity. To protect anonymity I changed people's names, unless I was presenting material that they had offered in an official capacity. I also altered details or presented composite figures when I believed that certain details might make someone identifiable. As a result, unfortunately, at certain points I have had to omit pieces of information, particularly about gender and skin tone, even when they seemed to be integral factors in the subject under discussion. I believe, however, that I have enough material in recountable form to present important points on those matters convincingly.

I want to add one final exemplifying feature of my conversation with the rainbow guy: what each of us presented was no neat package of words, objects, and apparent values, and the package was a different one than might be presented in different company or at another time. I began this chapter by describing my changing engagement with the Ellis Island snow globe. How I understand both the snow globe and my own encounters with it has changed over time and in response to different modes of reflection; until I started writing, for instance, I didn't see the connection, which now seems obvious, between my initial articulation of disgust and the lust for objects that still makes me tingle. I presume, then, that people's objects and experiences, or what they would choose to say about them, may have looked different to them later—just as the books and articles I read might have been written differently later.[59] What I present here, then, is not an account of what Ellis Island visits or products mean, in any static sense, to me or to others. Rather, it is more like a tour that I have constructed to bring attention to facets of Ellis Island that, I believe, invite critical reflection about politics, pleasures, and justice.

ONE

BREEDERS ON A GOLF BALL:

NORMALIZING SEX AT ELLIS ISLAND

At Ellis Island, corporate, government, and private sponsors contribute to a celebration of immigration at a time when "celebrate" is rarely the operative verb concerning immigrants. Who, then, are these immigrants worthy of honor? A partial answer is simply, to be blunt, that Ellis Island immigrants are either dead or old, and thus are unlikely to be suspect in contributing to current situations for which people hostile to immigrants often, and inaccurately, hold them responsible: scarce jobs, overcrowded classrooms, "terrorist" actions. But some immigrants who did not pass through Ellis Island to the United States are also dead or old. Why are Ellis Island immigrants celebrated, which of them, and what, as perceived or presented, about them in particular? The specifics matter here because actions, ideas, and policies concerning immigration, ranging from anti-immigrant violence to government restrictions on immigrants and immigration, are never as universally conceived or applied as they are sometimes purported to be. They emerge from and enforce dominant values—values that come partly, if through complex and transformative routes, from cultural representations concerning immigrants.

In this chapter I undertake some of the "who" questions from the starting point of sexuality. Even a cursory look at the issue indicates that values about sexuality have long affected U.S. immigration. Laws barring prostitutes were among the first federal immigration restrictions,[1] and while homosexuality stopped constituting grounds for exclusion in 1990, the current bars on "same-sex" marriage prevent many couples from making use of marital and family unification options. The policing of sexuality and sexed bodies does not cease after the acts and procedures of entry. To the contrary, perceptions about sex have often contributed to determining the duration of one's status as "alien." A law of 1910 ordered the deportation of any alien convicted of involvement with prostitution at any time after entry.[2] That one could have arrived at the age of two and then be deported decades later, as if having been admitted under false pretenses, suggests an underlying assumption, manifest as well in other contexts, that some sexual practices were basically congenital to certain, foreign, peoples.[3] A more recent example involves the perception of Haitian immigrants as carriers of HIV. This perception was bolstered in 1983 by the Center for Disease Control's labeling of recent Haitian immigrants as a "high-risk group," and the Food and Drug Administration's subsequent decisions (despite the CDC's removal of Haitians from the list several years later), first that Haitians who had arrived in the United States after 1977 could not donate blood, and then, in 1990, that all Haitians were barred from doing so. While the initial consideration of Haitians as a distinct group depended partly on the idea that they did not fit into the sexual category—"homosexual"—that signaled risk (all this reasoning bound up in the problem of using identities rather than acts as indices of risk), race-coded characterizations of Haitians as sexually, and otherwise, deviant certainly fueled their stigmatization.[4]

This situation also highlights two other points relevant here: the role of sexual characterization in the broader process of defining admissible bodies; and the way that power informs, besides the ability to look or expose, the ability not to do so, or what Eve Sedgwick calls the "privilege of unknowing."[5] As Sedgwick argues, the truism that "knowledge is power" obscures how power often enables people to choose ignorance (it is the U.S. president who needs to speak only one language), especially when knowing might unsettle dominant ideas and structures. With regard to AIDS and Haiti, Paul Farmer explains, this privileged inattention contributed to the erasure of the likelihood that far from originating in Haiti, AIDS appeared earlier in North America, and that much of its early appearance in Haiti was a result of sex tourism.[6] Privileged sexual unknowing has continued to impact both the definitions and treatment of migrants. Examples abounded after the events of September 11, 2001; for example, the idea that all Arabs in the United States are terrorist suspects because good Muslims will gladly blow up airplanes to get to the sexual extravaganza of waiting virgins in the afterlife.

Regarding sites like Ellis Island, then, with explanations of past and present migration on offer, both the treatment of and silences around sex demand study. Yet while several writers have insightfully situated representations of and at Ellis Island in relation to the politics of contemporary ideas and policies,[7] what is present or absent about sex has attracted little attention. Some of the likely reasons, which I discuss later in this chapter, include the lack of information, readily available or through digging, about migrants with nonnormative sexual identities and practices that might make the absence of their representation conspicuous; a certain aura of reverence about the site—for heritage, hard times, ancestors—and, perhaps, habits of avoidance about imagining elders as sexual, which, combined with the often somber tone of scholarly writing, may make polite discretion or silence seem appropriate or unremarkable. As I discuss in the preface, I aim in this book to dislodge the naturalness of sexual discretion and silence regarding Ellis Island, partly because sexual discretion and silence make possible presumptions of normativity. At issue here, too, more generally, are the challenges of getting at sex "in the flesh" from and through inanimate documents, artifacts, and texts. In this chapter I undertake strategies of embodiment, with attention to the particular bodies inhabited and to the complexity, messiness, and contradictions of sexed bodies in their historical specificity.

LOOKING FOR SEX

While I will argue that there is much about sex at Ellis Island to be surfaced, pulled from obfuscation, and reimagined, I begin with a point that may at first seem contradictory: sex at Ellis Island is present everywhere. By that I partly mean something simple that nonetheless merits articulation precisely because of the overriding discretion I mentioned above: people travel with their sexual histories, fantasies, beliefs, and, sometimes, partners. Immigrants did then, tourists do now. So, too, do Ellis Island employees—and, of course, Ellis Island researchers. My own first trip to the site had a lot to do with the hot date I was on. In later trips, I overheard a fair amount about other people's sexual relationships, and the topic also popped up in interviews, although not at my deliberate instigation. I refrained from asking direct questions about sex for reasons ethical, professional, and strategic: I wanted, and for my own protection needed, to avoid what might be perceived as sexual harassment; I needed to conform to "human subject" guidelines about what questions are reasonable to ask, which certainly did not include everything I wanted to know; I was on the lookout for conversation stoppers that would also foreclose discussion about other topics of interest to me. Nonetheless, even when I interviewed people about their purchases, their work at the site, and other matters, sex was, surprisingly often, just around the conversational corner. My asking one visitor where he lived, and revealing where I taught college in response to his similar questions, led him to volunteer his pleasure that his daughter had chosen a school that still had parietals—including those rules against "opposite-sex" overnights that provide peace of mind to some people who presume their children's heterosexuality.[8] When I interviewed the employee who, relevant here, wanted to "fill me with his enlightenment," our conversation turned, faster than Bill, to Monica, via an interesting trip through the New York Police Department, the Diallo verdict (in which four white cops were acquitted of murder after shooting forty-one bullets into an unarmed black man), and Sinead O'Connor (the singer famous for ripping up a photograph of the pope).[9] Both conversations, though highly idiosyncratic, well represent the frequent closeness to the surface of sexual topics during events and conversations that ostensibly concern something else.

A bit less explicitly, but sometimes as obviously, sex informs other matters, too. Sex contributes to metaphorical language, more or less felicitous, like the following description on the Web site of Ellis Island's primary fundraising organization, the Statue of Liberty–Ellis Island Foundation, Inc. (SOLEIF): "Ellis Island, our most potent symbol of the American immigrant experience, had become sadly disheveled. Again the American people responded with passion—and with funds."[10] This example, of course, with its gender extravaganza of disheveled potency, also concerns how sex in the sense we connect to gender informs description, and how sex in each of those senses informs description in relation to the other. Sex lingers often, too, with concepts of great importance at Ellis Island, like ethnicity, race, and citizenship, which have been so frequently linked to sexual matters, if in various forms of connection and to varying degrees of visibility, that they hardly show up sex free anymore. One set of examples among many come from queer politics. Both pro- and anti-queer positions have often been articulated in terms of civil rights models: in arguments about whether queers constitute a so-called minority group, like people categorized by race and/or ethnicity;[11] in the addition of "sexual orientation" to antidiscrimination codes and assorted lists of identity-based categories that affect the distribution of power and resources; in right-wing assertions that queers (supposedly all white) want "special rights" that will hurt African Americans (supposedly all heterosexual) by somehow depleting a finite supply of available rights;[12] in the analogies made often by proponents of gay marriage between their project and the overthrow of laws forbidding interracial marriage. While my examples might suggest primarily that people often think about sexuality through ethnicity and race, my point is also that sexuality, now prominent on the identity-and-rights scene, doesn't merely depart when it's not the focus. As Lauren Berlant astutely points out, sexual matters also increasingly define citizenship: "Now everywhere in the United States intimate things flash in people's faces: pornography, abortion, sexuality, and reproduction; marriage, personal morality, and family values. These issues do not arise as private concerns: they are key to debates about what 'America' stands for, and are deemed vital to defining how citizens should act."[13]

Sex is everywhere at Ellis Island, but, one might say, it's not really out of the closet. Wall plaques and tour guides rarely discuss sex, except to mention the exclusion of prostitutes and polygamists and, occasionally, to call up those unfortunate female immigrants who discovered on arriving that while their husbands or betrotheds were earning money to send for them, the men had also learned to lust after women more modern than greenhorn. Sex is not much present in the flesh either. In 2000, while paging through a visitor sign-in book called the Millennium Registry, I saw a September entry that stated, "Thank you—for the sex!" I thought about whether the entry might refer to on-site sex with a lover, although it could just as easily be junior-high-type goofing, like the nearby "love, peace, and hair-grease." Other entries in the registry ranged from "Free Tibet!" and "Vote or Liberty is Lost" to homages to the site itself, including the tantalizing "My grandmother was conceived here!"[14] Despite the likelihood that the "thank you" message did not actually betoken sexual activity on-site, I tried to imagine, with some pleasure, where the writer might have had a sexual encounter without getting busted. (According to a ranger who worked there at the time, no one had been recently caught in a sexual encounter, and he had heard tell of nothing previous to his tenure.) Restroom stalls, a standard location for semipublic sex, offered one possibility, especially for two people who look like they belong in the same bathroom, and a few have relatively little traffic. My casual research—asking around, checking out Web sites— suggests that none of the restrooms at Ellis Island are celebrated cruising sites, but that can't possibly mean they've seen no sexual action. Otherwise, spaces at Ellis Island are largely open, frequently visited, and/or conspicuously monitored by rangers and park police. Maybe that's one reason I saw little that one might term "making out," not even much open affection. Another reason might be that people are affected by the shrinelike, sanitized aura of the place: "Too clean" and "not appropriately smelly" were two comments I heard often.[15]

So, perhaps the test of a historical site's engagement with sexual issues isn't whether it facilitates visitors' on-site sexual activities. Besides, while many people associate sex with the sacred, and while I would hardly separate sex from the experience or contemplation of hard times, family history, or politics, I certainly understand why many people would not consider their Ellis Island visit an appropriate or exciting occasion for a quickie, even if they are among the many who come with no reverent mission. But I bring up here the possibilities for physical sexual activity to underscore why even sex talk stands out. I do so by conjuring sex for pleasure, with allusions to various partnerings, to suggest why it must be noted, rather than taken for granted, that when hints occur that sex ever happens, they generally take the form, to put it a bit crudely, of breeder signs.

BREEDERS ON A GOLF BALL

A typical example of a breeder sign can be found on the souvenir golf ball, made by Spalding, that I purchased at the Ellis Island gift shop (figure 5). The picture on the ball comes from an undated photograph (figure 6) that is frequently used to illustrate or symbolize Ellis Island. The photograph shows three figures, seen from the back, whose identities, like that of the

FIGURE 5. Ellis Island golf ball. Purchased at the gift shop in 1999. (Photograph by Paul Heroux)

FIGURE 6. *Ellis Island Immigrants*, early twentieth century. (Courtesy of the Ellis Island Immigration Museum)

photographer, are unknown today. The figures stand together, if not intimately, staring across the harbor at the Statue of Liberty. Their clothing and relative sizes suggest them to be a man and woman with a child between them. The man's cap and solid stance, like the woman's kerchief and solid body, with broad hips and thick waist, are common elements in the visual vocabulary of turn-of-the-twentieth-century European immigrants. The image appears repeatedly in books about Ellis Island and has appeared on various products available at the gift shop. In 2000, it showed up on the golf ball, on a postcard titled the "New Americans," on a sports-team-like pennant, and as one of many photographs montaged onto a souvenir placemat. By summer 2001, one could also buy the image on a plaque, a commuter cup, and a miniature baseball bat, where it was superimposed on a stars-and-stripes motif (the abbreviation on the bar code economically states "flag imm bat"), or enjoy a huge version of it while standing in line at the snack shop across the hall from the gift shop.[16]

What accounts for the image's popularity at Ellis Island? The fact that it is in the public domain must be one reason; users easily can acquire permission to reproduce the image for the mere purchase cost of the photograph. But plenty of equally unencumbered photographs never make it to being depicted on souvenirs or the museum walls. The choice to use it matters, and derives largely, I think, from the ability of the image to emblematize the "nuclear" family: mother, father, and offspring.

My contention here may seem pretty obvious: of course the configuration is supposed to represent a procreative unit; of course the image is safe and popular for a tourist site, especially one about heritage and ancestry. Yet precisely because the meaning and popularity may seem to go without saying it is important in an effort to articulate the work that goes into producing them, beginning with the idea that procreative ties underpin kinship. In *Long Slow Burn*, Kath Weston, using the highly apt phrase "procreative ideologies of kinship," emphasizes that beliefs that genealogical relations constitute the fundamental basis for kinship neither reflect some natural or universal law of affiliation nor remain static in form or proponents. The idea of "kinship-as-genealogy," she notes, nonetheless remains "resilient," despite increasing challenges, both within and outside the academy, to procreation-centered notions about what makes a family.[17] This is a crucial idea to remember in thinking about Ellis Island. When tour guides ask, "Does anyone here have a relative who came through Ellis Island?" or when visitors come to find their ancestors, both of which happen very frequently, the general idea in mind seems to be a family tree rather than, for instance, "kindred spirits" or a "chosen family," to use a once-common queer term for the intimate communities built to be present at the holiday table—sometimes defined in contradistinction to one's not always as welcome "family of origin." At least, every single elaboration on ancestors that I've heard at Ellis Island involves blood-and-marriage ties, which is where my own thinking began, too; I certainly thought first of my grandparents. But the mother-father-child unit need not be presumed to occupy an exclusive place at the core of heritage structures.

Neither does the picture on the golf ball need to be presumed to represent such a grouping. For one thing, even if the outfits of the adult figures conform to the early-twentieth-century garb associated with men, for the figure on the left, and with women, for the figure on the right, we should not simply assume that photographs always easily yield up the sexual attribution, identity, or anatomy of their subjects. I once heard a tour guide at Ellis Island say, "Back then it was cut and dried, you were a man or a woman. None of the Jerry Springer hi-jinks of today." But evidence remains of several migrants who got busted at Ellis Island when it was discovered that their gender presentation did not conform to the sex suggested by their bodies. One such migrant, Frank Woodhull, is the subject of the next chapter; others must have gotten through without being detected, especially since the medical inspection at Ellis could be cursory if migrants didn't appear suspicious.

Besides, even if gender identity were relatively "cut and dried" for the adults figured in the photograph, admittedly a likely possibility, they easily could be related in some other way than as the biological parents of the child standing between them. They could be siblings, cousins, or in-laws, with one or neither as the child's biological parent. They might have ties of friendship or acquaintance that are longstanding but not genealogical. They might be new acquaintances or even strangers—given the man's slight distance from the others—whose fleeting contact is belied by the photograph's long afterlife. With no information about the people depicted beyond this single photograph, and, moreover, with little information about the photograph, much remains conjecture.

A number of factors, however, encourage, or at least fail to discourage, a mother-father-child reading. The man's distance from the others, along with the child's proximity to the woman, can simply be seen to reflect women's primary role in care giving and child rearing. The general aura and representational trend at Ellis Island, as I have been suggesting, do not provide a context in which the adults' apparent lack of intimacy would stand out. More important, perhaps, they do provide a context that supports and promotes the dominance of procreative family ties. Of course, most visitors don't need Ellis Island to see procreative ties, emblematized by parent-child lines of descent, as an important feature of social organization, but they will certainly find them represented here. Tours, live and canned, often conjure visitors' relatives as an audience hook—this is where your ancestors might have walked, and so on. Featured texts in the gift shop, like *Ellis Island Interviews*,[18] which on its cover shows the photograph I have been discussing, offer no hints that the never married may have been otherwise affiliated. The on-site theatrical production, "Embracing Freedom: The Immigrant Journey to America," which is performed about four times a day during the tourist season, features a contemporary mother telling her teenage daughter, who is petulant about having to move because of dad's transfer, about great-grandmother Sonya's immigration with her parents. Kiosks all around the site invite visitors to search for the records of relatives who came through Ellis Island—research that they can pursue further at the "American Family Immigration History Center," opened in 2001, which hosts a databank of passenger lists for ships that brought immigrants to New York during the Ellis Island years.

Meanwhile, Lee Iacocca talks about his immigrant parents in fundraising and publicity materials both on the site and away from it, and, as I discuss extensively in chapter 5, the continuing campaign for one of his biggest fund-raising successes, the American Immigrant Wall of Honor, also makes breeder ties a central issue. Indeed, the emphasis is on parents, children, grandparents: nonparental cross-generational relations don't show up much anywhere around Ellis Island—either as objects of reverence or of study. Nor, as I suggested earlier, does one find either nonprocreative models of sexual affiliation, or models (involving either pairs who might procreate with each other or other sexual groupings) that imply sexual purposes or pleasures beyond making babies. The immigrants on the golf ball, apparent parents who don't touch, typify well what is available.

WHAT IS MISSING

If Ellis Island seems relatively dry now, what would be involved in bringing sexuality onto the current and historical scene in all its fleshliness, its pleasures, and its queerness and variety? By "queerness and variety" I refer here not just to homosex categorized by sex/gender identity—men together, women together—but to all sorts of sexual identities, practices, and tastes that often have been labeled queer, perverse, "outside the box." One strategy, of course, involves drawing attention to hitherto unpublicized or underpublicized material. For instance, in the papers of William C. Williams, the Ellis Island commissioner of immigration about whom I will say more later, there is mention of a fascinating case of "two immigrant girls" who were caught "exhibiting a filthy and obscene photograph to other immigrants awaiting inspection" in 1900 (the ages of the "girls" are not mentioned but judging from the common uses of the term at the time and the apparent absence of parents, I surmise them to be in their late teens or early twenties and probably unmarried). The assistant commissioner of immigration at the time, Edward F. McSweeney, ordered the girls to go before the Board of Special Inquiry, the administrative panel that decided the cases of would-be migrants who were about to be refused entry. But then, as McSweeney wrote to his superiors, the photograph disappeared in " 'some mysterious manner wholly unaccounted for.' " The picture turned up later, however, during an investigation by Williams in 1903, in which had been retrieved several boxes of public documents that the departing McSweeney had tried to spirit away under the label of personal property; the incident was covered in the press about McSweeney's subsequent arrest for document theft.[19] Documented stories like this one indicate a more complex sexual life at Ellis Island than historical narratives usually suggest. Indeed, the evidence that women circulated sex pictures—and maybe sold and/or enjoyed them—testifies to female pleasure and agency in sex representation that still remains largely unheralded, with women portrayed far more often as only potential victims in relation to pornography.

The fact that much more must have been going on with migrants through Ellis Island, internally or interactively, seems strikingly obvious given the sexual diversity famously portrayed by writers, artists, and sex researchers during Ellis Island's busiest years. Yet Ellis Island immigrants, stolid and solid, seem often to be conjured as absolutely separate from sexual variation. It can hardly be true, however, that only those patients committed to print by Freud had sexual aims besides the penis-in-vagina act or that the U.S. artist Marsden Hartley traveled to Europe to fetishize his German officers while uniformed inspectors at Ellis Island remained devoid of sexual charge to all who came before them.

What is missing in the Ellis Island accounts becomes visible, too, in the 1981 film *Ellis Island*, which was made by the composer, choreographer, and filmmaker Meredith Monk. A site-specific piece made at Ellis Island before it was restored, the film suggests the processes of flattening that occurred in the documentation of immigrants, which it accomplishes by using black-and-white short segments that stage performers, dressed as immigrants, in near stillness as if they are posed within or for photographs. One sequence shows individual immigrants standing against a backdrop while a hand uses a magic marker on an invisible surface right in front of them to measure and mark their features. The number written across one woman's forehead, the circle around another's nose, and the text "Serb" written across one man's face all call up the physiognomic practices, then labeled scientific, of racial and ethnic profiling; as they also suggest, acts of profiling, often conceptualized as the identification of racial, ethnic, or national types, also work to constitute and define the types they are often presented as identifying only.

Other sequences evoke less-sinister dehumanizing. A woman in a large group of immigrants lined up for a picture briefly breaks her pose to brush an invisible bit of something off the lapel of the man next to her. Both the particular gesture, as she banishes the residue of daily wear, and the act of stepping out of and back into photographic nonmovement underscore how temporary and unrevealing may be a photograph's "frozen" moment. As I pointed out earlier about the image of breeders, photographs often reveal less about their subjects than might at first seem forthcoming. Scenes throughout the film in which only people's eyes move and sometimes moisten work to similar effect. In one sequence, pairs of people face each other with vivid emotion animating their faces. Even with extremely subtle movement, this fullness of expression brings the evidence of rich, if opaque, content to the characters' proximity, energizing the space between them.

I do not intend here to posit a contrast, advocated either by the film or by me, between the flat opaqueness of still photography, or of text, and a greater reality or truthfulness that an ascent toward three dimensions necessarily brings. The film (of course also viewed as a two-dimensional surface image) is explicit in offering contemporary performance about the past rather than a pretense of "you are there." Similarly, the scenes representing the present that are interspersed among the immigrant scenarios read as performed rather than captured; these, all in color, include a visitor's tour and the path of a uniformed guard. The performance element may be clear partly because the setting and actors throughout remain clearly contemporary—both "immigrants" and "the tour guide" stand before the peeling paint of the same long-neglected building—which also helps to set up the alternation between color and black-and-white as a contrast in representational modes rather than one between "living color" and "dead history." For me, one of the film's most striking features is that it refuses to identify a representational medium or tactic with a special claim on the ability to do what consumers and presenters of history often name as an ideal: "bringing history to life." It does, however, eloquently invoke the losses that attend distancing from embodiment, by which I refer both to the physicality of bodies and to the specific people who inhabit the bodies that often appear, for reasons more and less benign, as vague figures or types.

How, then, to use an appropriate colloquialism, can the study of Ellis Island be "fleshed out" regarding sex? Part of the challenge here attends any analytic writing about sex. As the collective called Kiss and Tell so well conveys, in explaining why the group combined sex theory and sex stories in *Her Tongue on My Theory*, the disappearance of bodies, lust, and pleasure when analysis begins is significant, unfortunate, and all too common, even when people are writing about sexually explicit performances or have subjects of study willing, as the group's name indicates, to volunteer information.[20] With Ellis Island, as I suggested above, a certain reverence, discretion, and disinclination may block sex as a topic, and the available resources are limited in numerous ways: historical documents say little; interview protocols prevent certain directions of questioning with living individuals. Nonetheless, it is possible, I believe, to glean from the available resources both some guidelines and some historical specifics for embodying the study of sex at Ellis Island.

BODIES IN MOTION

Two recent texts make crucial points about the study of sex in relation to migration. In "Diaspora Politics, Homeland Erotics, and the Materializing of Memory," Louisa Schein discusses people's relations to the places they see as "homelands" and then argues that the "complex of desires that saturate the figure of the homeland" needs to be linked with the "corporeality of eroticism" because transnational relations are made not just in sexual metaphor but also in practices.[21] As Cindy Patton and Benigno Sánchez-Eppler emphasize in their introduction to *Queer Diasporas*, such desires and practices themselves may shift as the people involved with them do. After noting that many approaches to sexuality assume that "what the body and psyche have" are either socially located in one place or transportable as is to other sites, they argue, to the contrary, that sexuality is "on the move": "When a practitioner of 'homosexual acts,' or a body that carries any of many queering marks moves between officially designated spaces—nation, region, metropole, neighborhood, or even culture, gender, religion, disease—intricate realignments of identity, politics, and desire take place."[22]

Much in the history of Ellis Island immigrants supports Patton and Sánchez-Eppler's point about acts and bodies marked both queer and straight. One such realignment for migrant men, as George Chauncey details in *Gay New York*,[23] might also have included sex with men, widely available in a number of immigrant neighborhoods, sometimes in distinction from sexual practices in their countries of origin, and of interest especially, but not only, to men who migrated alone with the intention of returning to where they came from. Another realignment among migrant men, which I mentioned earlier, can be found in those tales of shifting tastes in women. A 1906 *New York Times* piece labels "very common" the situation of women unclaimed at Ellis Island by the sweetheart who arrived before them, and since women could not enter the United States except in the company of a husband or male relative, such women, as the article states, had to return home.[24]

Those women who didn't face abandonment on entry, however, might nonetheless have contended with previously unencountered models of desirability. A fictional account of the unwanted greenhorn wife appears in the 1896 novella "Yekl: A Tale of the New York Ghetto" by Abraham Cahan, the well-known socialist writer who cofounded the *Jewish Daily Forward* in 1897. The tale dramatizes the visceral changes in the migrant Yekl, bent on being the Americanized "Jake," regarding his wife Gitl. His disinterest in her grows to nausea despite a well-meaning neighbor's attempt to update Gitl's appeal by forcing off the traditional headwrap and wig—called inappropriate in New York even for "a Jewess of her station and orthodox breeding"—that had dismayed her husband when he picked her up at Ellis Island.[25] In Jake's eyes, the "voluminous wig of a pitch-black hue," her "inky little eyes," and the darkening under the ocean sun of her "naturally dark . . . complexion" lent his wife the "resemblance to a squaw."[26]

The use of "squaw," a racial stereotype associated with Jake's new continent of habitation, to describe what makes his wife newly distasteful suggests, too, how sexed bodies on the move were raced, at the same time that racial categories, understandings, and practices were on the move as well. Suggestive also is Jake's perception that Gitl's "naturally dark" coloring left her only a wig and a suntan away from appearing to belong to an inferior dark race, a perception that translated in immigrant communities like the one fictionalized by Cahan into bodily practices as well as attitudes. One such set of practices involved the removal of body hair. From the last decades of the nineteenth century onward, increasing negative attention turned to what was considered excessive body hair, which was labeled with the medical term "hypertrichosis" in 1877. As Rebecca Herzig explains, excessive hair was often associated with immigrant populations and was considered a problem endemic to people of certain ethnicities and an impediment to a promoted ideal of smooth, white skin. Hair removal technologies were thus frequently marketed to migrant women.[27] Cahan's *Jewish Daily Forward* included such promotions. A short piece from July 1915 offers "Four Rules for Women." After advice about keeping the home clean, feeding one's husband, and avoiding complacency merely for having snagged him, the piece describes what to do "if you've been cursed with growths of hair on your throat, cheeks or upper lip": "Go immediately to your druggist and for one dollar buy Wonderstone."[28] Racial transformations occur on and to bodies, not just in attitudes or apprehensions about them.

THE REGULATION OF BODILY ENCOUNTERS

While Ellis Island accounts are generally discreet about physical presence, save for the occasional invitation to imagine the smell of thousands of immigrants newly arrived from steerage, several tidbits about immigrants encountering unfamiliar people at Ellis Island call up the fullness of close looking and proximity portrayed in Monk's film discussed above. One often retold story, also included in the Ellis Island Immigration Museum audio tour narrated by Tom Brokaw, relates that many European immigrants saw a black person for the first time at Ellis Island. Narratives of such encounters from the other side are harder to find—perhaps because European immigrants formed the vast majority, but just as much, I suspect, because racial difference is more readily popularized as the spectacle of dark people rather than the distasteful odor of white people. One example, however, appears in the oral testimony of Ayleen Watts James, which visitors may hear on an audio loop if they pick up a phone in a display called "The Last Hurdle." James, who arrived from Panama with her mother in 1923, recounts that after having spent a year making them new clothes for the journey, with "handmade lace and all," her mother was horrified to find herself surrounded by Europeans filthy from their long voyage, and tried, sobbing, to pull herself and her daughter away from them.

These accounts may bespeak unprecedented diversity in a chaotic crowd, but it is just as important that migration laws and sites have long functioned to regulate and control which bodies encountered each other in the United States and how they did so, sexually and otherwise. For instance, the Page Law of 1875, the first federal law designed to exclude "undesirable immigrants," barred, along with convicts and contract laborers, Asian women understood to be entering the country to work as prostitutes. As a law restricting commercial sex work, the first of many such laws linked to migration, the Page Law constituted a regulation of sexual interaction and a regulation of labor that is important to mark as such rather than merely as a ban on activities presumed to belong to the category "sin" or "crime." The law was also intended to control the sexual behavior of white people, seen to be under threat by contamination from sex with Chinese prostitutes.[29] Like all other laws and understandings concerning Asian immigration, the Page Law also contributed to understandings and self-understandings of European immigrants and "natives."[30] In addition, with scientific racism backing up "the common perception that all Chinese women were likely to become prostitutes"[31] the Page Law was used as an excuse to bar virtually all Chinese women.[32] The resulting gender imbalance, at best before 1920 little better than ten to one,[33] bears, of course, on the issue of whose reproductive practices are valued; any portrayal of an easy flow of heritage along progenitor lines elides the differential access to the making and maintenance of such ties. As I discuss further in the next chapter, bodily encounters between immigrants and inspectors at migration stations also depended on racialized distinctions.

DEMOGRAPHICS, DESIRES, AND CONTRADICTIONS

The migrants' chances of entering the United States depended not only on where they entered and the categories, such as gender and race, to which they apparently belonged but also on the particular people who inhabited the positions that affected them. From 1905 to 1909, for instance, the commissioner of immigration was Robert Watchorn, whose work history included labor organizing. The man who both preceded and succeeded Watchorn, William C. Williams, commissioner from 1902 to 1905 and then from 1909 to 1913, was, in one newspaper profile's social shorthand, "a Yale man" although we can't be sure what any such shorthand accurately predicts or describes.[34] The picture of Williams that emerges from his policies and his papers, which include administrative documents, correspondence, and newspaper clippings, indicates both the value and the limits of using broad demographic categories to flesh out historical understandings, sexual and otherwise.

In brief textual references and museum tours Williams appears primarily as a reformer on behalf of immigrants, for which he does deserve real, if very qualified, credit. He issued a directive upon beginning as commissioner that "all immigrants were to be treated with kindness and consideration."[35] He went after concessionaires who were found to be shortchanging, and he demanded also that "milk shall be furnished to all young children upon the mother's request."[36] He fired employees deemed to be participating in corrupt practices, like Assistant Commissioner McSweeney who pocketed the "filthy and obscene photograph." Less often reported now, however, is Williams's work to reduce the number of immigrants entering the United States, particularly from southern and eastern Europe, whom he considered of inferior stock. As he freely indicated, this was the goal behind his well known but now insufficiently explained 1909 directive that all would-be immigrants needed to show that they had funds of at least $25; newspaper clippings from summer 1909 show the particular application of this directive to exclude Jews. Williams also took other avenues to promote his cause. One clipping hand-marked "1904," probably from the *Lewiston Journal* [Maine], recounts Williams advising the Maine State Board of Trade to seek "frugal, faithful, honest, industrious" people from northern Europe to populate their state rather than the "class of immigrants . . . unfitted to till our soil," namely people originally from "southern Europe," whom recruiters from Maine might make the mistake of hiring from the big cities.[37]

Although Williams's demand for overall courtesy might seem contradictory to his unapologetic exclusionary maneuvers, these qualities might well be comfortably situated together if the former is understood as an aspect of paternalism or noblesse oblige that might induce this "Yale man," who lived at the University Club, to step away from a lucrative law practice for two stints in this modestly compensated position. Yet his actions did not always clearly read as logical extensions of his class position. In summer 1902, he caused a stir by insisting that first-class and second-class passengers, who were allowed to be processed onboard their ship, had to answer the same roster of questions posed to the lower-class ticket holders who had to disembark and be ferried to be processed at the Ellis Island facility. (The first-class and second-class passengers also generally received more cursory medical inspections, based on the general disinclination to indispose the affluent and the assumption that they were more likely to be healthy.) Williams justified his policy by arguing that undesirable immigrants, such as "criminals, procurers, prostitutes, anarchists, persons suffering from dangerous contagious disease . . . and insane persons" might "readily have the means to travel in luxurious quarters."[38] Numerous papers reported the outrage of affluent people affronted by the indelicate questions. A writer in the *Chicago Tribune* opined that perhaps a skilled diplomat or the commissioner himself might be able to ask "a matron of obvious respectability and means if she were a polygamist, a cripple, or illiterate, black or white." (This last item on the list, which does not represent an actual question posed, is a highly telling invention that speaks to the racial categories under threat and maintenance with immigration.) But, the text continues, "The Tribune thinks they would be bold men, even if gifted with disarming politeness, who would put such questions under such circumstances."[39] Thus Williams emerges here as a traitor to his class.

Or is social status the only operative referent? A 1909 headline concerning a related Williams affront, his decision to stop using female boarding officers to conduct inspections of the women traveling first or second class, attributes his insensitivity to a different lack of inculturation: "Commissioner Williams, Ungallant Old Bachelor That He Is, Is the Culprit."[40] The implication that Williams neglects the deference due women of a certain breeding because of his unfamiliarity with or lack of affinity for women in general invites some interesting speculation about this "millionaire bachelor."[41] Intriguing also in this regard is a 1905 letter from James R. Sheffield that begins with the salutation "My dear Billy," and offers what the author calls "a weak attempt to put into words some of the things I feel," that in "affectionate pride in your achievements, I yield to none of your friends."[42] Addressed to Williams's residence yet sent on letterhead from Sheffield's law firm and signed formally "James P. Sheffield," the letter is a hybrid of public and private even in its declared route. The effusive language with which Sheffield states that "what has lain very deep on [his] mind and heart" is Williams's noble service to his country makes Sheffield's expressed interest in Williams's job performance at Ellis Island look a bit like a pretext to lubricate personal relations.

This letter interests me less, however, for what it might covertly express about the sexual practices, liaisons, or desires of its sender or recipient (although I am certainly interested in the homoerotic possibilities) than in what it signals rather baldly: the place of the erotic in matters not ostensibly about erotics at all. (Did George W. look more desirable to Laura, or does he imagine that he does, in positioning himself against "the evil-doers"?) The role of the erotic is often not easy to figure out. Even more information about Williams's life as a "millionaire bachelor" would likely leave much room for speculation about his contacts, tastes, and practices, those times when desire caught him up in ways that did not match any erotic profile that even he might reasonably deduce, and the precise relation of all of these to his work as commissioner of immigration. As Anne McClintock details in *Imperial Leather*, and as Elizabeth Stephens gorgeously articulates in "Looking-Class Heroes: Dykes on Bikes Cruising Calendar Girls," sexual beliefs, ideas, representations, desires, and practices may be profoundly structured by, as well as contribute to structuring, dominant power relations regarding race, gender, economic status, and nation, and, simultaneously, manifested in highly idiosyncratic ways.[43]

Sexual beliefs, ideas, representations, desires, and practices are also changing, often contradictory, and frequently inconsistent. I referred earlier to sexuality "on the move" as people themselves migrate. As important are much more short-lived, local, and microsituational vagaries and variations, of which my own engagement with Ellis Island frequently reminds me. Primary among my contradictions are those concerning souvenirs. I noted earlier the lack of queer-themed souvenirs in the gift shop, although what really would their presence fix? After all, even if one could buy a T-shirt at the Ellis Island gift shop that read "I love my gay ancestor who came through Ellis Island," the tag, like that of other T-shirts available there, would probably say something like "assembled in Honduras of U.S. components," indicating the chasing around the globe for cheap labor and probable disregard for working conditions characteristic of current capitalist practices known as "flexible production."[44] Indeed, the slogan might be viewed to abet the conditions of its appearance; as Rosemary Hennessy argues, queer-friendly products and corporate policies like domestic-partner benefits often function to deflect attention "from the exploitative international division of labor" that the same companies depend on.[45] Such queer friendliness might also deflect attention from economic inequities visible at the site of purchase. At the gift shop, T-shirts cost almost half a day's pay for the person at the cash register, whose base pay, $5.25 an hour in 2003, wouldn't buy the $10 ferry ticket that tourists need to get to the island. There is no simple "We're Here, We're Queer"—to borrow from a chant used in the early 1990s by the direct-action group Queer Nation. Who is "we," where is "here," and what is "queer" are all issues complicated by directions of global production, labor, tourism, and migration. Also relevant to this point are the corporate contributions to gendered, racialized, and ethnically and nationally differentiated economic disparities that affect, in the first place, which queer or pro-queer people have the resources to do things like get to Ellis Island and buy a T-shirt.

Progressive souvenirs. I don't really believe in them unless the conditions for their production and sale depart from the current norm, and unless I have confidence that their purchaser doesn't see buying stuff, no matter how steeped in "clean clothes" or "fair trade," as their primary activist activity. Nonetheless, as I described earlier, I was thrilled to see a guy with rainbow gear at the ordinarily rainbow-dry Ellis Island, and I fell for my Ellis Island snow globe, which doesn't even offer me pleasing surface politics. To the contrary, with its U.S. flag trumping the other flags, the globe reminds me of the sometimes perilous affinity between imperialist chauvinism and expressions of pride in roots elsewhere. I totally understand internal disjunctures of politics, purchases, and pleasures every time I look at the globe, touch it, or shake up the snow because something besides imperialism still gets to me every time. Indeed, the erotics of glitter and fluids, animated by memories of the sexy occasion on which I got it, work against my dry analysis of its motifs. I do not recount my own contradictions to imply that precisely those can be attributed to others, but rather to jog readers to call up their own examples, which, I would argue, we all can. Sex, sexuality, erotics, and pleasure are not readable from products, politics, categories of identity, or even seemingly juicy historical documents in any simple way.

CONCLUSION

William C. Williams isn't more complicated than anyone else, employee or migrant, who spent time at Ellis Island; neither is a book writer or a guy with rainbow gear. We can just learn (a little) more about some people. So I would not presume to posit the message, about sex or anything else, that most visitors take from Ellis Island. Even with discrete individual objects of seemingly obvious content, consumers contribute to the production of diverse meanings, which of course becomes even more complicated at a huge site where even what people encounter varies greatly. Yet it is important to consider what people can encounter, not least because dominant representations and elisions at Ellis Island recur at other immigration heritage sites, with heterosexual units, implicitly sexual because they are pro-creative, constituting the primary sexual reference. At the Johnstown Heritage Discovery Center, which invites visitors to take on one of eight fictional individuals representing immigrants to western Pennsylvania, the characters' lives proceed largely by this model as visitors learn, after registering their own vote on immigration, how their character would have fared with or without (depending on their vote) the ability to relocate. Thus, for instance, the one character also represented on souvenirs, a twelve-year-old orphan boy (significantly quite like the heroic lad featured on Ellis Island souvenirs), either has his descendants endow a scholarship in his name for Johnstown High School seniors or dies during "the severe Polish winter of 1915, . . . 22 years old, unmarried and without family." The Museum of Work and Culture in Woonsocket, Rhode Island, which features the history of French Canadian immigrants (and has the wonderful feature of presenting a clear, highly visible explanation of capitalism as a root cause of social inequality), uses for its logo a sculpture on the museum's grounds, Robert Lamb's *The Spirit of Woonsocket* from 1977. In the sculpture a man and woman join hands as the woman's other hand rests on her slightly protruding abdomen (oddly protruding only on her right) to suggest pregnancy. At San Francisco's Angel Island, which lacks a dominant logo, the image on the sign directing hikers to the immigration station, also repeated once inside the station, shows, in an interesting variation, an adult woman with a child along with two other children set slightly apart. Given the hugely disproportionate number of Chinese men living in the United States by the time Angel Island opened, however, such an image might well be considered to figure the reconstituting of a family unit.

It's easy to imagine some well-intentioned reasons for highlighting a procreative family unit in heritage visuals. One might want to counteract stereotypes of immigrants as sexually deviant. During the Ellis Island years, for instance, representations often attributed to immigrants what were deemed the evils of prostitution. In the 1910 novel *The House of Bondage*, a U.S.-born girl of "peasant stock," who has been born to "a race in which motherhood is an instinctive passion," is seduced into prostitution by a Jewish "alien" named Max.[46] Even if the novel posits capitalism as the primary foe, of which Max, too, is a victim, certain people, generally migrant and/or darker skinned, seem throughout the novel somehow congenitally more prone to participate in prostitution. So, too, runs such a notion in popular opinion about nonfictional prostitutes, in spite of evidence such as that presented by Timothy Gilfoyle, in his study of commercial sex in New York City from 1790 to 1920, that according to the available statistics, most prostitutes of the period were native born.[47] However, Gilfoyle's point isn't that the perception of immigrant participation in prostitution was wholly fabricated, but that the proportion of migrants in prostitution was exaggerated, in part because of prejudice against migrants (and prostitution) and in part because immigrants were often involved in the most visible forms of prostitution. (Think here of how current perceptions about consumers of drugs like cocaine and heroin are skewed by the greater visibility of drug use by people who are poor.)

A more complete accounting of migrant sexual practices might well include representations of stigmatized practices, including commercial ones, especially given the number of young working women amenable to "treating," or dating for some kind of remuneration.[48] A more complete accounting might also include other public relations nightmares. Kate Simon's memoir *Bronx Primitive: Portraits in a Childhood* recounts her experience with two "newer greeners," more recent immigrants, who came to live with her family. Each developed a habit of getting into her bed, which she shared with her brother, and using her sexually. The man she despised and helped to get rid of. The woman, who masturbated against her thigh, made her feel "more curious than menaced": "She was as greedy for pleasure as she was for learning English. Of course I knew what she was doing, but I had never known it to be on someone else's thigh; a pillow, a towel, a hand, but a thigh? Maybe that was the way they did it in Poland and I wondered who her partners had been."[49] Note here also Simon's presumption that sexual desires and practices beyond procreating within marriage are not new information conveyed in the modernity of the "New World." People masturbated in Poland; bring that assumption to picturing the huddled masses.

My point here isn't to comment on Simon's division of adult sexual intrusion into malevolent and benign, or to set myself up as judge of the savory, but to note that available nonfictional accounts of sexual practices and experiences include much that many would consider unflattering to the image of immigrants. And negative images about sexuality had and have real consequences for migrants. The image of immigrants as sexually deviant and diseased, living in social and spatial arrangements different than what Nayan Shah terms "models of respectable domesticity" were, and remain, frequently deployed against them: to bolster arguments for exclusion or deportation; to deflect attention from economic exploitation that, for instance, forced immigrants into the overcrowded residences that they were demonized for inhabiting; and to justify various forms of prejudice and mistreatment.[50] It's understandable, then, that well-meaning people might opt for omissions.

Yet huge costs attend using the procreative-domestic unit as a criterion, a strategy, or a logo for immigrants. At Ellis Island, for instance, migrants traveling alone and identified as unmarried women could not be cleared to enter the United States alone. They either had to leave Ellis Island in the company of a male relative who, supposedly, could be trusted to protect single-women kin from entry into prostitution, or they had to prove intent to marry imminently, including giving evidence of a candidate. Sometimes couples were forced to marry on the spot, or, according to La Guardia, were escorted to city hall, to be married by an alderman who sometimes grabbed a few jokes or a little extra cash at the immigrants' expense.[51] Women outside the domestic-procreative unit were stigmatized, including all women identified as prostitutes, and subject to discriminatory policies as a result. (Since most Ellis Island narratives present the exclusion of prostitutes as a matter requiring no scrutiny or evaluation—not surprisingly since disdain for commercial sex workers is generally presumed reasonable—I should make explicit that I do not find the stigmatization of prostitutes to be an acceptable component or side effect of migration policy.)

Making the procreative-domestic unit iconic obscures the effects, on people who don't conform to the image, of moves to enforce its norms or even to deploy its image. Nayan Shah and Jennifer Ting both discuss, for instance, how harmful material, ideological, and analytic effects attended attempts by activists and historians to secure respect for Chinese Americans by emphasizing their increasing adherence to heterosexual domestic normativity: Shah writes that Chinese "bachelors" were excluded from hard-won public housing after having been evicted from buildings razed to make room for it;[52] Ting discusses how scholars foreclose the study of sexuality by locating "deviant heterosexuality," among other nonnormative practices, in the past.[53] The situations they discuss also raise a point nicely articulated by Cathy J. Cohen in her article "Punk, Bulldaggers, and Welfare Queens." She writes that "many of the roots of heteronormativity are in white supremacist ideologies which sought (and continue) to use the state and its regulation of sexuality, in particular through the institution of heterosexual marriage, to designate which individuals were truly 'fit' for full rights and privileges of citizenship." That is one reason why, as Cohen emphasizes, "the radical potential of queer politics" (to use the subtitle she ends with a question mark) depends not only on attending to acts and identities outside the category "heterosexual" (what fits within that category being also, of course, subject to definition and change), but also to people who "may fit into the category of heterosexual, but whose sexual choices are not perceived as normal, moral, or worthy of state support."[54] I add here "perceived sexual choices," to which the requirement to marry may also respond, as frequently under judgment and regulation, too.

Ellis Island's breeders on a golf ball exist within a larger context in which not looking very carefully—in various manifestations ranging from ill-informed stereotyping to polite discretion to willful blindness—characterizes much about sex representation, although, or sometimes because, sex is central to immigration exclusions and inclusions. As I suggested at the beginning of this chapter, to sidestep sex as an issue of study, contest, and change is also to obscure the extent to which the crossing of national borders routinely serves as an occasion for the policing of sexuality and sexed bodies. At Ellis Island, promoted and supported by private, corporate, and government resources as the primary U.S. immigration heritage site, sexual elisions abet exclusionary policies by anchoring a presumptive sex/gender normativity in an admirable state of back-then. I have suggested here strategies for embodying Ellis Island with the physicality, specificity, and complexity of its historical cast of characters partly to complicate that dominant image of celebrated immigrants (and immigration commissioners), who for two important reasons are not well described as icons of a delightful simplicity unsullied by the "Jerry Springer hi-jinks of today." The first reason is that nothing was so simple. Second, that alleged simplicity, with sex seen primarily as an instrument for procreation, should hardly stand as delightful.

At the same time, attention to the policing of sexed bodies demands attention to something else besides: that despite its reputation and sometimes function as an important activist tool, the activity of making visible is not by definition and in every instance a liberating political maneuver. The ability to show, to hide, or to expose depends greatly on power differentiated partly by matters of gender, race, money, national origin, and citizenship status. Related to the last of these is a requirement in the current process for acquiring long-term residence in the United States today, when application for any such status includes a physical examination "to include complete disrobing."[55] In the next chapter, I consider in more depth the case of Frank Woodhull, who was almost rejected for entry at Ellis Island when the impending requirement of forced disrobing impelled him to admit that the sexual identity suggested by his clothes did not match the one suggested by his body.

TWO

GETTING DRESSED UP: THE

DISPLAYS OF FRANK WOODHULL AND

THE POLICING OF GENDER

Until I noticed the picture of a bra floating next to the lyrics of "Underneath your Clothes" in the booklet accompanying Shakira's 2001 CD *Laundry Service*, I thought that I had been reading against what Shakira had in mind. I had been struck by the following lines in the chorus:

> Underneath your clothes
> There's an endless story
> There's the man I chose
> There's my territory[1]

I saw these lyrics as words to a trans (transgendered and/or transsexual) lover: maybe to someone whose clothes and body signal differently regarding sex and regarding gender, maybe in ways known only to intimates, maybe meeting the speaker's desire in the specificity of what makes an "endless story" of those clothes over that body. Since I still don't know what to make of the bra—drag? discard? laundry? the speaker's? belonging to the "man [the speaker] chose"?—I will refrain from guessing whether on that particular associative path I met up with an intended subtext.[2]

However, I'm quite certain that I did not meet up with an intended subtext when my thoughts traveled from "there's the man I chose/there's my territory" to the issue of the coercive policies and practices of the state. Certainly, Shakira's lyrics draw meaning from the metaphoric language of political and colonial conquest. Yet the territory in the song is the body, not the body politic, and a one-way conquest does not fully characterize the relationship suggested. Other lyrics describe possession as mutual ("When the party's over/We will still belong to each other") and the speaker as equally possessed: "Like a lady to her good manners, I'm tied up to this feeling." Loving as owning or belonging can be fully suspect, yet bonds can be delightfully perverse as well. As important, the speaker in Shakira's song never describes the body underneath the clothes, nor does the speaker take or request access to it. This is part of what makes me want to interpret her words as anticoercive, "transfriendly," and in general sexually open: the lack of presumption about how clothes figure or don't in erotic encounters. You might get undressed, in the active and passive senses of that phrase, but maybe you don't.

Yet no matter how much the lyrics conjure mutual pleasures and belongings, for me they also call up a more sinister set of associations. Essex Hemphill writes, in his poem about the state's intrusion into sexual practices, that bodies are always "occupied territories": "The erogenous zones/ are not demilitarized."[3] The state also assumes power regarding the display of the body. In ways partly determined by matters of gender, race, money, national origin, and citizenship status, state policies and practices affect the ability to choose how and whether to show or hide one's own body or to subject another person's body, dressed or undressed, to scrutiny or representation.

The ordeal of Frank Woodhull reveals how those vectors of power may operate. Appearing at Ellis Island in 1908, Woodhull faced possible exclusion from the United States when he was forced to admit, on being confronted with a medical exam that included forced disrobing, that although he had presented himself to the authorities as male, his body signaled another identity. The details, as most accounts understood them, are summed up in a notation handwritten onto a photograph taken of Woodhull by an Ellis Island employee: "Mary Johnson, 50, Canada, came as 'Frank Woodhull.' ss 'New York'—Oct 4 '08. Lived 30 years in U.S. Dressed 15 years in men's clothes" (figure 7).

Woodhull's story was scandalous at the time. Reports began running in the daily newspapers on the second day of his detention, which turned out to be his last: he was released to enter the United States that evening. Woodhull now appears at Ellis Island hiding in plain sight. A banner show-

FIGURE 7. *Frank Woodhull*, 1908. (Photograph by Augustus Sherman. Augustus Sherman Collection, courtesy of the Ellis Island Immigration Museum)

ing Woodhull's head from the photograph taken on his arrival hangs from the ceiling of the American Family Immigration History Center—minus any identifying text—thus seeming to make its placement there someone's queer in-joke. Much more forthcoming is Woodhull's appearance in *Ellis Island: The Official Souvenir Guide,* where his image from the same photograph appears on a page with pictures of Emma Goldman, Irving Berlin, and Al Jolson, along with the following informative caption: "Faces of the less-well known tell interesting stories as well. Ellis Island staff member Augustus Sherman, who photographed the gentlemanly 'Frank Woodhull' . . . in 1908, found that the Canadian immigrant was born Mary Johnson—and had dressed in men's clothing for fifteen years."[4] Ironically, then, the souvenir guide invites readers to remember something they likely wouldn't have knowingly encountered, and wouldn't have encountered at all before Woodhull's photograph began hanging from the ceiling.

In this chapter I use the situation and circulation of Frank Woodhull to consider relations of representation to power, surveillance, and policing. Although the souvenir guide attributes the photographer's knowledge to a simple process of discovery—Sherman "found that" Woodhull had been "born Mary Johnson"—the circumstances of Woodhull's appearance before Sherman's camera were far from benign or simple. After looking at the conceptions and practices that brought Woodhull before the Ellis Island medical inspectors, as well as examining the implications for gender conformity in the inspectors' ability to require disrobing, I discuss representations of Woodhull that circulate in text and image. These representations also contribute to the policing of gender presentation and possibilities—not the least, I argue, by portraying Woodhull as female in essence, as if Woodhull necessarily is, as written on the photograph, Mary Johnson, and by choosing to follow state authorities rather than Woodhull's own preference in referring to Woodhull as "she" and "Johnson." Throughout, I am interested in how Woodhull gets dressed up (in both of the readings of that phrase—I dress myself up/someone dresses me up) for the public.

According to contemporary newspaper accounts, Woodhull arrived at Ellis Island on 4 October 1908. Before proceeding, I want to underline two ways in which the state already features in what I have just recounted. First, Woodhull became of interest to newspapers, and consequently an object of their representation, because he ran into trouble with border inspectors. Second, Woodhull wound up at Ellis Island due to the state's perceived right to define the identity and effects of the status "alien," which have not been as fixed as common uses of the term might suggest. For instance, popular accounts of Ellis Island processing generally use "alien" to describe new immigrants seeking to join the U.S. population, an account sometimes modified to acknowledge return migration—a frequent enough intention of migrants despite the common image of "America" as the beacon of a permanent future. Yet people with other relations to residence in the

United States have been subjected to treatment as "aliens," as Woodhull's case epitomizes. When he landed at Ellis Island, Woodhull was neither new to the United States nor was he someone who had made multiple entries but considered another country his primary home. Although perhaps he considered himself a lifelong Canadian (I found no evidence either way), at the time he was detained at Ellis Island he had been living in the United States for thirty years and was returning from a visit to France.[5] Ironically, considering the function of Ellis Island today as a pilgrimage site for heritage seekers, Woodhull seems to have been on such a pilgrimage himself to France, having saved up enough money to visit "the little village where her ancestors were born."[6] (A note on pronouns: For reasons on which I elaborate later in the chapter, I have chosen to use "he" to describe Woodhull in accordance with how he presented himself when not under the surveillance of the state. However, I keep as is the pronouns of the sources I quote because the disjuncture they mark between Woodhull's intended self-representation and the representation of him is an important part of the evidence that the sources offer.)

The consequences of "alien" status are neither always obvious nor consistently applied. One matter that might be variously construed, depending on the politics of officials, was a nonresident's date of entry. That date mattered because the criteria for exclusion changed over time and because some restrictions on migrants extended for a certain time period beyond entry. For instance, border laws denied entry to would-be migrants who were deemed "liable to become a public charge"; at the time Woodhull was detained, a migrant once admitted could within the next three years be deported for becoming a public charge. Thus, significant power accompanied the right to define what constituted the beginning of one's sojourn in the United States. (That power was deployed against George Fluti in the late 1950s, when officials tried to deport him for homosexual acts based on laws codified after he was first admitted to the United States but before a little two-hour jaunt to Mexico.[7] Fluti's case went to the Supreme Court, where he lost.)

The fact that Woodhull had to undergo inspection at Ellis Island as if entering for the first time, then, reflects no simple process of categorization but rather a series of decisions about "alien" status that could put migrants subsequently on one side or the other of the line separating insider from outsider, depending on the issue at hand. For wealthier migrants coming into New York, mixed categorization—"alien" on one matter, insider on another—sometimes began immediately. After a policy change enacted by William C. Williams in 1902, migrants traveling in first class or second class, and thus processed onboard their ships, had to answer the same list of questions asked of passengers processed at Ellis Island. Until 1925, however, when the Immigration Service mandated equal treatment, the Public Health Service (PHS) spared onboard passengers the more rigorous medical inspection that occurred in the Ellis Island facility. Amy Fairchild, in her important book *Science at the Borders: Immigrant Medical Inspection and the Shaping of the Modern Labor Force*, explains that class functioned as virtually an inherent biological quality with implications for health, so much so that PHS officials sometimes sent first-class passengers for inspection at Ellis Island when they suspected them, in effect, of not being first-class people but rather masqueraders hiding in first class for the exact purpose of avoiding medical scrutiny.[8]

Woodhull seems to have tried no such ruse. While the caption in the souvenir guide calls Woodhull "gentlemanly," the photograph does not suggest someone trying to dress beyond his means. Some hard-to-read details could reflect bad lighting or garment wear and tear. In either case, however, the photograph could easily read as a migrant of humble origins wearing his best clothing, as many did, to make a good impression with U.S. officials.

Since traveling in a mode above one's station was considered scandalous in itself, one can infer that Woodhull traveled in steerage or third class from the failure of any report to mention his accommodations combined with the descriptions of how he earned a living. Although accounts vary, six of the eight articles on Woodhull that I found clearly place him far from high society.[9] The *New York Daily Tribune* has Woodhull working as a ranch hand. Four others agree that once Johnson became Woodhull, he (although all six would say "she") became an itinerant peddler, some say after a ranch stint. These reports go further to state that he peddled either trinkets and magazines (*New York Post*), trinkets and "toilet articles" (*World*), or "books" (*New York Herald, New York Press*, which described Woodhull's goods as "my little wares"). Accounts also differ somewhat in describing where Woodhull peddled. Taken together, however, they point relatively consistently to a history of travel "all over the Western and Southwestern states" (the *Press*) and an intention to return, if readmitted at Ellis, to his current residence in New

Orleans, where according to the *Post* he sold his wares "among the Creoles." Oddly, one of the two papers that doesn't mention the nature of his work is the *Daily People*, which has boxed quotes on either side of the masthead calling all "workingmen" to international labor solidarity and to see "every class-struggle [as] a political struggle." Perhaps they assumed readers would take his humble economic status for granted.

FORCED DISROBING

Once at Ellis Island, Woodhull got into trouble for an alleged masquerade of a different order when something triggered suspicion during his initial medical examination, although accounts differ as to what.[10] The *Herald* states that "her feminine appearance" caused Woodhull to be detained. The *Tribune* and *Press* name suspected illness: the *Tribune* reports that he was detained for possible tuberculosis; the *Press* reports that "her sunken cheeks and pallid complexion" suggested consumption. These latter types of explanations seem more likely given Woodhull's reported testimony, cited in three other papers (*Post, Press,* and *World*), that in fifteen years of living as male only one person ever caught him passing, to use one popular term for maintaining a cross-sex discrepancy between the gender presentation and the body beneath (*World, Post,* and *Press*), and that was very early on. At a park in San Francisco, the town where Woodhull decided to make the switch, Woodhull encountered a young boy who told him, before running off to play, that he thought Woodhull was a woman in men's clothing. According to Woodhull, apparently, even this doubt was easily remedied. Seeing Woodhull later with his hat back on, the boy indicated that he had changed his mind. One might also find evidence of Woodhull's successful presentation as male in Sherman's photograph, which points as well to some of the specific work involved in passing. The vest and loose jacket, while donned partly, no doubt, to demonstrate general social and economic fitness to enter the United States, added extra layers to camouflage any suspicious protrusions of the chest.

Woodhull's chances of avoiding gender exposure were enhanced, too, by the superficiality of the initial medical check. Nicknamed the six-second inspection for the speed at which medical personnel had to evaluate up to five thousand migrants a day during the peak years, the preliminary exam depended largely on visual scrutiny, although, as Fairchild notes, PHS personnel also used smell and touch. (The common description of this inspection in Ellis Island narratives as solely a matter of eyeballing suggests that visual technologies of surveillance might seem more distanced and therefore more palatable for popular accounts than other forms of scrutiny, even though commanded visual presentation can itself have devastating consequences.) After watching for signs of physical or mental problems as migrants climbed the stairs from the baggage room to the registry room, inspectors marked suspected problems in code with a chalk mark on the migrant's coat.[11] There were codes for suspected heart, lung, and eye problems, mental illness, pregnancy, and more. The exam was intended to flag people with contagious diseases and people with conditions that might make them dependent on the state for support, or those "liable to become a public charge." This second concern, often the primary one, is what made pregnancy, and even general old age, possible grounds for medical exclusion. A judgment regarding indications about those liable to become a public charge often formed the basis of final decisions about entry.

As various scholars have noted, the PHS officials, at Ellis Island and elsewhere, cast their medical gaze, a diagnostic tool on which they much prided themselves, through idiosyncratic filters and common prejudices. One often-cited example involves a doctor who decided that the lack of ordinary sheen on a particular strand of hair on the left side of a woman's head indicated a sign of possible pregnancy.[12] Beliefs that certain "races" were more susceptible to certain diseases, like the idea of tuberculosis as a Jewish disease, also contributed to determinations about whom to pull off the line for further scrutiny. Some prejudices became structurally inscribed in standard procedures at other immigration stations. For example, standard inspections at Angel Island used different and more invasive procedures that were due in part to popular beliefs in the inscrutability of Asians, particularly Chinese. The Angel Island examination included bacteriological tests that required the collection of blood and feces.[13]

One important effect of medical sorting based on expectations triggered by perceived geographic location, economic status, and race—noting that race was understood then to be sometimes coextensive with nationality ("German," "Chinese") or religion ("Hebrew" or "Hindoo")—was that forced disrobing also had a hierarchy of geography as well as a class and race. At

Angel Island, all men underwent disrobing to the waist in front of everyone and complete disrobing behind a curtain; a bit of gender courtesy determined that women had to strip only if under suspicion. Along the Mexican border in Texas, race, class, and citizenship sometimes seemed muddled for many reasons: Mexicans came in many hues, ethnic mixes, and economic positions; there was contest and confusion concerning the numerous Mexicans in ceded territories who had automatically become U.S. citizens with the redrawing of borders under the 1848 Treaty of Guadaloupe Hidalgo and other changes to the border. Policing at that border thus reflected these uncertainties, which complicated ordinary prejudices against immigrants, brown-skinned people, and Mexicans in particular. So did the fear that other migrants, particularly Syrian or Chinese, might use typical Mexican clothing to pass as Mexican "peons."[14] Immigration examinations therefore frequently required complete disrobing. Beginning in 1917, after changes in U.S. immigration laws prompted a regularized procedure in El Paso, Mexicans had to remove their clothing every time they crossed the border, bathing while their clothes were washed. George Sánchez documents the migrants' experience of the procedures as a humiliating treatment, likening people to animals. A number of people, he writes, "tried to avoid the baths by taking special care to be clean and well-dressed in order to persuade officials to waive the requirement."[15]

Implicit in these various procedures are ideas that the body underneath one's clothes is authentically raced as well as sexed, if possibly sometimes still opaque on the body's surface. Yet forced disrobing did not merely reflect divisions and boundaries; it also worked to create, alter, instill, and police them. Fairchild argues, largely persuasively, that a major point of the medical inspection at Ellis Island—which she compares to the then-emerging medical exams for the military, life insurance, and employment—was to prepare people for industrial labor, just as a major point of exclusion was to exclude people unsuited to labor: "The public nature of the immigrant medical exam was the source of its very strength, making it a vector of power: it served to communicate industrial values and norms in a public setting, and demonstrated the power to enforce them by sending back a token number of immigrants." Thus, several dimensions of visual exposure functioned to discipline and classify migrants even when they were fully dressed: inspectors examined migrants; migrants watched each other being scrutinized; and migrants saw themselves "on the line," in new groupings and in mass procedures that might well approximate the working situations of their future.[16] By many accounts, disrobing epitomized and magnified the humiliation of subjection before state authority. Whatever the complexity of psychic effects, forced disrobing functioned as a hostile display and a deployment of power.[17]

GENDER STRIPPING

There is one policing function that accounts of forced disrobing generally fail to mention. Forced disrobing worked to enforce sex and gender conformity by revealing whether the sex suggested by the visual appearance of someone's body matched the sex suggested by that person's clothing. I assume this function to be a by-product rather than a goal of forced stripping, aside from its service to the more general goal of ferreting out information that clothing might conceal, even though Woodhull's story wasn't wholly unique. Other cases occasionally surfaced of migrants who passed. Eithne Luibhéid notes in *Entry Denied* that the sexologist Havelock Ellis as well as the commissioner of immigration at Ellis Island from 1931 to 1934, Edward Corsi, wrote of individual cases.[18] The migrant that Corsi mentions, who had been detained under the name "Alejandra Veles" despite claiming to be a man, apparently arrived long before Corsi's tenure, near the time of Woodhull's appearance. The Veles narrative appears in a chapter in Corsi's book called "A Picture of 1907" as an incident told to Corsi by Frank Martocci, who had worked as an interpreter for Italian-speaking migrants, like Corsi and his family, coming through Ellis Island in that year.[19]

Although the chapter doesn't specify exactly when "Alejandra Veles" came through Ellis Island, and although the interpreter's monologue seems more literary device than transcript, the text nonetheless documents the presence of such cases as part of the available lore.[20] So, too, does the headline of a newspaper clipping in the William C. Williams papers, probably from around 1902: "To Deport Saxon 'Murray Hall': Otillie Castnaugle, Who Came Here as a Girl, Will Be Sent Back in Men's Clothes."[21] Hall was a political organizer in New York whose death in 1901 garnered much press attention when he was exposed as having a female body.[22] Indeed, an article called "Women Who Have Passed as Men" that appeared in *Munsey's Maga-*

zine in 1901 stated that "wherever newspapers go, people have been talking of the strange case of Murray Hall."[23] Ellis Island inspectors, of course, formed part of that public "wherever newspapers go."

The Castnaugle headline also suggests, however, an understanding of individuals like Hall or Castnaugle in terms of an exception rather than an epidemic, and as people to be found through fortuitous discovery rather than as people to be on the lookout for. Marian West, who wrote the *Munsey's* piece, suggests the same by offering an interesting collection of explanations about why, in her estimation, her female contemporaries "do a great many things that were undreamed of by their grandmothers, but dressing up in men's clothes and going out into the world to seek their fortunes is not one of them": more career opportunities; new obstacles like the telegraph that make it harder to hide; a greater refinement and "less openness" of speech that prevents a "decent woman" from "accustoming herself to mingle on equal terms with men"; and a clearer, less poetic vision of war, which seems less like an appealing adventure when "we have grown too reasonable not to recognize some of its absurdity."[24]

I found nothing to indicate that a different perception of the frequency of such practices guided the PHS, which seemed to have had no prior planning for such discoveries, or at least no clear policies, laws, or procedure to deal with Woodhull. According to the *Herald*, officials could not figure out where Woodhull, once detained, should sleep: "As Miss Johnson could not be placed in the detention room for men, despite her attire, and for obvious reasons could not stay in the building assigned to women," he was given a private room in the hospital. (Actually, the reasons are not so obvious. Why did what was deemed merely the spectacle of maleness render Woodhull an inappropriate cohabitant with women? Did suspect desires associated with cross-dressing have anything to do with it?) The Board of Special Inquiry did not know what to do with him either. When Woodhull appeared before the board to plead his case, he was referred to the commissioner of immigration, Robert Watchorn. Thus it was, in the language of the *World*'s headline, that "Officials at Ellis Island Find that There Is No Law under Which Mary Johnson Could Be Deported."

That language, however, also points to another crucial aspect of forced stripping that might seem to be to the side of logic: no matter how accidentally Woodhull's gender ruse came to light, no matter how undeveloped were mechanisms to deal with it once discovered, the discovery nonetheless put him immediately at risk for exclusion. This is partly because officials might presume, as the headline implies they did, that a law against such gender transgression must surely exist. Precedents indicated that officials sometimes acted on that presumption. Otillie Castnaugle was sent back for being deemed a man in woman's clothing, and the person Corsi called Alejandra Veles was released only on his promise to leave the country.[25]

Officials also had recourse to some vague categories for exclusion, such as "moral turpitude," which as Jane Perry Clark explained in 1931 was a very elastic category. Defined in legal terms to include actions "contrary to justice, honesty, principle, or good morals," it covered theft, perjury, and various sexual acts performed outside of marriage. The category had been, however, understood differently depending on where and by whom it was interpreted; states differed, for instance, on whether sex outside of marriage yet without cohabitation constituted adultery.[26] One might think here of Michael Hardwick, of *Bowers v. Hardwick* (which I discuss in the next chapter), who was arrested for sodomy when a police officer entering his home allegedly for another reason came upon him having sex with a man. The analogy lies not just in happenstance but also in the context of surveillance that made such happenstance possible, and in a certain lack of clarity and disagreement about if, when, and concerning whom punitive action should be taken.

Woodhull, then, had to defend himself in terms of policies both solidly and vaguely on the books. Press accounts suggest that he did so by defining his gender presentation as a desperate measure taken to avoid the sorry situation that was also the primary or underlying basis for many exclusions: becoming a public charge. Several papers named dire circumstances personal to Woodhull. He was orphaned without support at the age of twenty (*Tribune*). He was afflicted with rheumatism that prevented him from continuing with farm housework, which also "left her hands with big muscles and masculine looking and her feet also bigger," thus making it easier to pass (*Daily People*). In addition, "Nature had blighted her with a thick black mustache and an unusually low toned voice" (*Tribune*), or, according to the *Herald*, she possessed "a faint down which, she says, has been the bane of her existence." (The *Times*, interestingly, says that Woodhull had been "endowed," by "nature," with "a mustache of proper proportions," the language suggesting the benign order of things rather than issuing any judgments like "blight" or "bane.")

But part of Woodhull's dire circumstances was understood simply in terms of being (identified as) a woman. The *Times* quoted Woodhull portraying his work possibilities—since rheumatism prevented him from undertaking housework opportunities—as a choice between freedom and death: "Men can work at many unskilled callings, but to a woman only a few are open, and they are the grinding, death-dealing kinds of work. Well, for me, I prefer to live a life of independence and freedom." The *Press* displayed Woodhull hinting at moral and legal choices. "'You all know,'" it quotes Woodhull as saying, "'that at the best it is hard for a woman to make a livelihood honestly at the present time. . . . I have done so as a man.'" The common use of "honestly" as shorthand for "not as a prostitute" indicates the knotting of values that put sexual commerce and perjury under the umbrella of moral turpitude, although prostitution had its own clear, explicit, and, in fact, highlighted place on the list of exclusions. "Honest" work then protected Woodhull against three excludable offenses: prostitution, moral turpitude, and becoming a public charge.

The strategy worked: Watchorn admitted Woodhull into the United States, where he crossed into New Jersey and boarded a train back to New Orleans. Woodhull lucked out, perhaps, by arriving under Watchorn's appointment and not during the two tenures of William C. Williams, who was known for judging on the side of exclusion when it came to human irregularities. Watchorn had a history in labor and labor activism, including a stint as secretary of the United Mine Workers, which perhaps made him more sympathetic about Woodhull's stated need to make a living.

Less crucial, however, than the specific content of what Watchorn had in mind is the fact that a lack of conformity between Woodhull's gender presentation and the attribution that inspectors would read off his body made him vulnerable to expulsion and dependent on the particular people who inhabited the positions of power that affected him. His chances also depended on where he entered and on the categories, such as gender and race, to which he apparently belonged. As a white person of northern European descent coming from Europe to Ellis Island, Woodhull had a fairly good chance of slipping through Ellis Island undetected because at Ellis Island only those triggering suspicion on visual inspection had to disrobe. People with female-to-male incongruities like Woodhull's had no hope whatsoever of getting through at Angel Island or, as monitoring there expanded, at certain checkpoints along the Mexican border.

In analyzing various dimensions of the state's power over Woodhull, ranging from the matters of forced stripping that had particular repercussions for him to the definitions of "alien" that affected all migrants, I have been using texts about Woodhull as sources of information, along with Sherman's photograph of him and texts about others identified as gender deviants. But these sources, of course, cannot stand as transparent or neutral indicators of what happened. They represent, publicize, transform, and perpetuate understandings about gender rules that contribute to both policing and self-policing for sex and gender conformity. In the next section, I shift my focus to scrutinize the disciplining activities of the informing representations.

DRESS FOR THE PRESS

"Mary Johnson, Who for 15 Years Posed as a Man" (*World*); "Trousered Woman" (*Post*); "Woman Wore Disguise" (*Tribune*), "Dons Man's Clothes to Make Living" (*Daily People*): my agglomeration of headlines about Woodhull indicates a first and primary representational move that brings him into a certain gender conformity. In using the name "Mary Johnson" along with sex designators like "woman" and "she" and words like "disguise" and "posed," the newspapers present Woodhull as someone whose authentic sex is female. They have some reason to do so, since this assessment appears to agree with Woodhull's own understanding of his identity, at least as shown by his reported claims to have adopted a male persona for utilitarian reasons. This is most dramatically rendered by the *Tribune*, which gives the following account of what happened when Woodhull was called for further examination:

> The woman tried hard to control her nerves, but when the surgeon said, "I shall have to ask you to remove your clothing, Mr. Woodhull," Miss Johnson wept.
>
> "Oh, please don't examine me!" she pleaded. "I might as well tell you all. I am a woman, and have traveled in male attire for fifteen

years. I have never been examined by a doctor in all of my life, and I beg of you not to make an examination now. I know a woman is treated with respect in this place and I ask that you send a woman to make the examination. Surely this consideration is due me as an honest and respectable woman."

The *World* also quotes Woodhull asserting female essence in relation to his story about a boy discovering his identity: "'I have the woman's natural instinct for children, but I found them keen of observation and had to fight shy of them thereafter in order to hold my secret.'"

These presumptions about "Miss Johnson" do not, then, appear to go against Woodhull's wishes. Nor do they appear to reflect hostility or enact censure. To the contrary, the texts in which they occur are largely sympathetic to him. None question his explanation that he became Woodhull to get work, nor do they question the type of work he did: Should a woman be traveling all around that way? Did women thus disguised take away jobs from men? (Perhaps the latter was not an issue because Woodhull worked as an itinerant peddler rather than in industry.)[27] Nor, even if a taste for scandal got his story to the papers in the first place (the headlines that appear near the Woodhull story in the *World* include "Embryo Lawyers Fall upon Sleuth Who Intended to Make an Arrest" and "Locked Up for Killing His Baby Step-Child"), did they speculate about other scandalous matters that might damage his case, such as his sexual proclivities. If Woodhull lived as a man did he take up with women? This phenomenon was not unknown to the press; Murray Hall, for instance, "Had Married Two Women," in the words of a *New York Times* headline, and apparently also had many women on the side.[28] He was not the first such scandal, nor the only one regarding masculine people identified as female sexual partners of other women; the "'mannish lesbian,'" Lisa Duggan emphasizes, was "ubiquitous in published sources of many kinds by the early 20th century" in the United States.[29] The articles on Woodhull don't stir up trouble, and the one in the *Tribune*, written before his case had been decided, even helpfully sum up his fitness to enter the United States according to the standard criteria routinely applied: "Miss Johnson has more than enough money with her to entitle her to escape the 'public charge' clause of the immigration law. The officials consider her a thoroughly moral person, her health cannot cause her deportation, and it is generally believed that she will be allowed to leave the island provided she adopts clothes befitting her sex." Although the final phrase suggests judgment in the term "befitting"—and fails to predict the outcome since Woodhull was sent on his way, according to the *Post*, "to all outward appearances the 'Frank Woodhull' that she had named herself"— it doesn't condemn Woodhull for having adopted male garb.

Given that the "she-ing" of Woodhull matches his own presentation of a core identity as reported in respectful contemporary accounts, it might then seem here that I am the disrespectful one in persisting to use "he" and "Woodhull." But I choose to use the male designation not to promote an opposite assessment that Woodhull somehow is, in essence, male, but rather to challenge certain habits of naming, categorization, and analysis for reasons involving both respect and intellectual inquiry.

My first reason is that even though Woodhull isn't alive to be affected personally by my choices, I draw on the principle that I try to follow in relation to living people by referring to Woodhull in accordance with his own preferences. From the evidence available, he preferred the male address. Even more, for the fifteen years prior to being stopped at Ellis Island, he had actually courted, worked hard to generate, and depended on male address, and he hoped to resume male presentation on leaving. His utterance "I am a woman" may have invited people, as it may still, to see a disjuncture between his gender identity and his gender performance, but it does not address the question of how he wanted people to address and refer to him ordinarily.

Furthermore, given the context in which he uttered "I am a woman," who could say confidently that the phrase represented Woodhull's own perception of an authentic gender identity? Woodhull presented himself as a man except when state authorities confronted him with an order that would unmask him. What he said under duress and at risk of exclusion cannot, I think, be viewed as necessarily more a truth than a strategy—and strategy it must certainly have been regardless of its truth value to Woodhull. How was he to save his skin, his livelihood, his home, and, perhaps, his life? The order to disrobe shook even people who did not anticipate being unmasked as a gender deviant, and Woodhull had something at stake that they didn't. He had reason to fear that authorities might either exclude him for violating sex and gender norms or force him to conform to norms that he believed to threaten at least his livelihood. To call Woodhull "she," I believe, is to align oneself with a state that polices gender normativity and against the right of people to name their gender identity and gender presentation. Therefore, even if Woodhull perceived himself to be "Miss Johnson" in essence, I do not want to join the state in stripping away his chosen presentation.

One might argue, I realize, that if Woodhull did perceive himself to be fundamentally Mary Johnson, he might have preferred to be remembered or historically recorded after his death as Johnson, or as Johnson who passed as Woodhull, when, as it were, he no longer needed to make a living. But, as I state above, I don't find his explanation to Ellis Island officials to be decisive. Without certainty, I'd rather follow the best guide I have, and to indicate, by using "he" instead of but in proximity to the "she" in texts, that there is, indeed, a decision to be made.

My second reason for referring to Woodhull as male is as follows: I want to denaturalize the representation of gender in accounts both about Woodhull and about other people who during the first decades of the twentieth century, and earlier, were raised as female and then decided to live as male. The term "passing women" that is now often used for them reflects an understanding of their sexual and gender identity like the one that newspapers offer about Woodhull. They are women masquerading as men to get the advantages that men had: opportunities for work, travel, adventure, battle, and/or, sometimes, female sex or marriage partners. Indeed, "passing women" have gotten a great deal of attention. Jonathan Ned Katz, who popularized the term, devoted a large section of his 1976 *Gay American History* to "Passing Women: 1782–1920." The San Francisco Gay and Lesbian History Project produced *She Even Chewed Tobacco: A Pictorial Narrative of Passing Women in America*, which was offered in the early 1980s as a slide presentation, video, and article.[30] In Woodhull's time, Bram Stoker, the author of *Dracula*, included a section called "Women as Men" in his 1910 book *Famous Imposters*, in which he attests to prior and contemporary knowledge of them: "We have read of very many cases in the past; and even now the hum-drum of life is broken by the fact or echo of some startling revelation of the kind."[31]

"Passing women" also received attention in fiction, including, notably for my project, a novel by the popular mystery writer Nevada Barr, who is well known for a book series involving a National Park Service ranger named

Anna Pigeon; one novel, *Liberty Falling*, is set at the Statue of Liberty and Ellis Island. Although her book-cover biographies and her Web site don't mention it, Barr, before undertaking the Pigeon series, wrote a novel, called *Bittersweet*, about two nineteenth-century women who live together and become lovers after they move to northern Nevada and one adopts a male persona.[32]

By now, the term "passing women," defined through narratives of disguise, has gained enough currency among people interested in gender and women's history such that many of them, I have discovered, presume the term and concept accurately and adequately to cover virtually the whole of female-to-male trans movement for the nineteenth and early twentieth centuries. I noticed this phenomenon when telling people about my work: for example, frequently, if I said something like, "I'm writing about this guy who got into trouble at Ellis Island when he was discovered to have been raised Mary Johnson" the response to me would use "she" pronouns for Woodhull and mention the term "passing women." I heard this type of regendering from a number of people whom I knew to have considerable sophistication about gender history, theory, and contemporary debate, although, significantly, not people who identified themselves as transgendered beyond the level of, say, butch. Their comments generally seemed intended as a gentle or tacit correction. At least, no one asked me about my usage in any way that might suggest I had caused them to reflect about their own. Typically, they simply met my every "he" with "she" as we talked back and forth until I interrupted the flow to explain that I actually knew of "passing women" and had made a deliberate choice to avoid validating three habits of interpretation: referring to "passing woman" by terms that denote their original sex attribution, which implies that first identity necessarily to be more authentic or true; prejudging Woodhull to be a "passing woman," which elevates his account under state scrutiny to primacy; and using "passing woman" as a catch-all term for anyone in the not too recent past who lived as male after starting life with a female sex assignment.

I want to emphasize before proceeding how much I value and admire the material I cited earlier, notably Katz's book and *She Even Chewed Tobacco*. These sources present extremely useful documentation of the historical richness of gender expression, proffered at a time when female masculinity was buried more than claimed in some (but, of course, far from all) gay, lesbian, and feminist circles. However, with the explosion of trans activism and writings in the last decade a different mindfulness is now possible. To jump to the label "passing women" now, I believe, is to flatten out, obscure, and naturalize the processes by which gender comes to and through representation.

Consider, just to begin, how much interpretive process hides in one tiny phrase given in the caption in the Ellis Island official souvenir guide about Woodhull being "born Mary Johnson." A common device for denoting someone's first surname, most commonly used for a married woman's "maiden name," the born + name formulation collapses a series of identifying actions, based on social, political, and cultural values, into a natural essence. Woodhull wasn't born Mary Johnson. He was born, given a sex assignment, and then named according to the norm that a first name should ordinarily convey gender and, most likely, that the last name should indicate descent from the father. Once Woodhull had been given the name Mary, any introduction of him or reference to him invited a person thus informed to mobilize gender-specific expectations, and Woodhull himself to learn them.

I do not intend to suggest that the caption writer had some nefarious purpose to conceal gender inscription. I see instead a taken-for-granted convention with an appealingly low word count, and I'm actually quite impressed by what gender directives the caption omits. It is the only text I've encountered that doesn't "she" Woodhull; its avoidance of pronouns altogether seems to be a good strategy for such a short account. (I also like the caption for the photograph of Emma Goldman, "[a] powerful speaker and activist . . . deported from Ellis Island in 1919 at the height of the Red Scare," which manages succinctly to signal irrational prejudice as the cause of much action against immigrants.) My point is that texts about Woodhull do not merely reflect or recount Woodhull's sex and gender but rather work, in small and large ways, to produce and reinscribe understandings about sex and gender, both that of Woodhull and of others.

This is certainly true for the newspaper accounts. The *Tribune*'s narrative that I quoted above, for instance, underscores Woodhull's confession that "I am a woman" by describing his spontaneous reversion to female emotional behaviors: faced with imminent discovery, "Miss Johnson" weeps and pleads. While the text doesn't explicitly call the behaviors feminine, readers who missed the point could deduce it later from the text's description of Woodhull after "the nervousness of the examination had passed": "With the unfeigned ease of a man, the woman tilted back her Fedora hat well over her black short cropped hair, thrust her hands deep down in the side pockets of her trousers, and [began to speak] slowly and forcefully." The *World*, which quoted Woodhull on his womanly affinity for children, genders tears explicitly: "Now that her secret is out, Miss Johnson fears she will now have difficulty in earning her livelihood, and when the thought came to her yesterday, one of the first of womanly qualities came forth—tears." In ways enhanced by the metaphorical and physical possibilities of tears, which may suggest a truth within the body that involuntarily issues forth, these texts ascribe an innate quality to male and female sexes by affixing inherent and opposing gender attributes to them.

Or do they? The idea that Woodhull manifested the *"unfeigned* ease of a man" (if he didn't feign it, then was it natural maleness?) is just one comment hinting that Woodhull and perceptions of him disrupted the rigid gender binary implied in the dominant explanation of Woodhull as a women in disguise. The *World* describes Woodhull as "timid" in voice but with masculine characteristics from both nature and nurture: "Of angular, masculine build . . . [she] walks with a mannish carriage and steps firmly and solidly." Woodhull's mustache, of course, also challenged gender binaries in the texts like those of the *Tribune, Times,* and *Herald* that consider it of biological genesis. The *Daily People*, which has Woodhull "wearing a mustache," offers indirect testimony that assigning a correct sex to Woodhull involves more than name and pronoun shifts. Besides the ambiguity of "wearing" regarding whether the mustache was artificial, the article devoted a third of its relatively few column inches to explaining Woodhull's large feet and "masculine looking" hands as the happy by-product of disabling rheumatism. To root Woodhull in the category "female" a fair amount had to be explained, or rather explained away. Stoker may be the best of those who explain away the general phenomenon of people raised women but presenting as men: he went through many convolutions to explain, regarding those earlier crossings to male for soldiering or piracy, that "a nature that took new strength from the turmoil of battle" nonetheless revealed "some self-sustaining, self-ennobling quality in womanhood."[33]

If these texts suggest cracks in the explanation of gender-crossing as masquerade, the story that Corsi recounts about Alejandra Veles departs from it almost completely. According to this narrative, Veles, who told an Ellis Island medical inspector that "she would rather kill herself than wear women's clothes," had been impelled toward male clothing as a child with an intensity suggesting a primary identification rather than a costume:

"Alejandra Veles" was the daughter of a cultured Englishman who had married a wealthy Spanish woman, and then had been sent to represent his government in the Orient. The girl had been born in the Far East and, when a little child, for some reason or other unhappy at being a girl, she had insisted on dressing as a boy. Although her parents did all they could to discipline her, she would tear her dresses to shreds. She defied all control and finally was allowed to grow up as a boy.

At the age of fifteen she deserted her parents and started drifting. She came to this country and for two years worked as a hustler in a New York stable, after which she went to the West Indies and bossed men around, nobody ever suspecting she was a girl. Her father, frantic and at his wit's end, had provided his lawyer [whom Veles sent for upon being detained at Ellis Island] with a liberal sum for the girl's support. Was there anything she wanted, she was asked. "Yes—give me two plugs of tobacco and a pipe."[34]

This passage should not, I think, be taken necessarily to offer a more transparent access to Veles's understanding of his gender than do texts about Woodhull offer about their subject, not the least because of distance from the source. The passages purport to represent what Veles's lawyer, hired by Veles's father, told migration inspectors, as remembered by a translator at the site several decades later when he recounted the tale to the book's author. It would be remarkable if changes didn't occur, as they ordinarily do, in repetition over time and space. Besides, each of these narratives had aims to secure, from holding the interest of listeners or readers to the more instrumental aim implied for the core narrator, Veles's lawyer. According to the translator (and hence according to the author), Veles sent for the "very prominent" lawyer when "threatened with arrest for her defiance of the rules" (again, this is the threat of rules inconsistently specified or known). The lawyer then told Veles's "amazing story," which occurred "after he exacted a pledge that the girl's identity would not be revealed," but before he secured Veles's release. He traded a seductive narrative, it seems, for his client's release and privacy.

The lawyer rescues the client: this narrative, like Woodhull's, takes shape under threat from the state. At the same time, it locates this gender exoticism outside the state. Originating in the child of two Europeans sojourning in the twice-mentioned "Orient" and "Far East," Veles's gender deviance is expelled from the United States when Veles is released on agreement to leave the country. Gender variance is thus as alien as the "aliens" who can be admitted, excluded, and policed through border control because of it. (So, too, a bit, with Woodhull, at least as implied by the *Press* and *Herald*, which almost invite readers to blame the problem of Woodhull on Canada, with the *Press* citing Woodhull's claim that "hundreds of women in Canada are wearing men's clothes in order to earn an honest living, simply because they are obliged to do so." Unemployment for women, however, is fully U.S. homegrown. Woodhull continued, "A woman of my age can get no employment in the United States, especially if she is not strong.")

The texts I have presented about Woodhull and Veles do not offer enough evidence to assess how authentically they represent Woodhull's and Veles's understandings of their own gender identities. Both the texts and their content represent strategic as well as descriptive moves, with all the constructing and transformation that both strategy and description entail. The stories that emerge from them, separately and in relation to each other, offer reasons simultaneously to believe and to suspect them. Veles had the money to live the way he wanted, so maybe he didn't need to camouflage. Then again, maybe what the money most relevantly bought him was Scheherazade-by-proxy for a lawyer. Woodhull's story gets backing from the number of others who seem to have the same one, people now referred to as passing women. But maybe so many people put forth that story because it worked to get them out of trouble. As the trans activist and author Leslie Feinberg emphasizes in *Transgender Warriors*, in challenging the notion that the oppression of women can fully explain what is termed passing as male, so many accounts that remain "were made under duress in front of police and magistrates." Besides, Feinberg reminds the reader, passing is very difficult ("how many could live as male for a decade or a lifetime?"), some men passed as women (so could escaping oppression explain everything about moving in the other direction?), and it is insulting to view individuals as simply a product of their oppression (a tendency that Feinberg succinctly glosses with "Gee, thanks so much").[35]

In Woodhull's case, does an economic explanation really make sense? As Jed Bell put it, if Woodhull lived as male only for employment, why did he travel as male when he wasn't trying to work, especially given the consequences he risked by presenting himself to border inspectors as male?[36] True, appearing at Ellis Island as a woman alone could cause different problems, but Woodhull was well beyond the age associated with the prohibition against letting females enter unescorted lest the innocent be lured into prostitution. (Another question then comes from all these questions: if many economic "passing women" explanations bear the evidence of being told under duress and/or don't cohere easily, shouldn't we also be asking why they remain so appealing later?) Besides, who is to know what Woodhull might have said if he had money for a fancy lawyer? "Give me two plugs of tobacco and a pipe"? How many people now remembered for taking on a male public identity in order to earn a living might have described themselves differently under different economic circumstances?

And how many such people, or people living unhappily as women in accordance with their original sex assignment, would have understood or described themselves differently if available representations, nonfictional or otherwise, did not relentlessly "she" the female-to-male presenters in narratives of masquerade? In 2003, several people on a trans education panel that spoke to one of the courses I teach talked of having recently figured out their trans identities partly by finding like-identified people on the Internet. In addition, Feinberg's novel *Stone Butch Blues* began serving as a similar catalyst on its publication in 1993.[37] As people repeatedly testify concerning how they come to understand their identities, regarding gender or other matters, available representations matter a lot. They matter not because people have a gender identity that developed prior to and remains unaffected by encounters with culture—identities already fixed that cultural products then help us recognize. To borrow again the phrasing used about sexuality by Patton and Sánchez-Eppler in *Queer Diasporas*: sex and gender identities, whether trans or not, are "on the move,"[38] forming and altering in relation to movements and to encounters with people, products, representations, and with laws and labels designed to police, inform, and sometimes please.[39] Even sex/gender identities experienced as fixed, and even attributes that might justifiably be called biological in origin—like Woodhull's mustache if he grew it rather than attached it—are only apprehended through culture as gendered in particular ways. Medical technologies and concepts, themselves produced and called up through social understandings, along with terms like "secondary sex characteristic," filter perceptions of how, for instance, facial hair signals regarding sex, which, in turn, factor into how people identify themselves and others.[40]

These identifications are also historically specific. As Joan Scott explains in her classic essay "The Evidence of Experience," although people's accounts of their own experience often seem like a foundational truth on which interpretations can be grounded, they are "discursive constructions of social and political reality" formed in "complex, contradictory processes." Thus, "experience," she writes, "is at once always already an interpretation *and* something that needs to be interpreted."[41] Nicholas Rose, discussing "human technologies"—"hybrid assemblages of knowledges, instruments, persons, systems of judgment, buildings and spaces, underpinned at the programmatic level by certain presuppositions about, and objectives for, human beings"—suggests, too, how regulatory institutions contribute both to particular understandings of the gendered self and to "regimes of the body which seek to subjectify in terms of a certain truth of gender, inscribing a particular relation to oneself in a corporeal regime: prescribed, rationalized and taught . . . and enjoined by sanctions as well as seductions."[42] In other words, the medical inspector's sorting by sex at Ellis Island is one of many disciplining practices, specific to place, time, politics, and social context, that contribute to gendered identities and behaviors.

So I don't posit that among all those "passing women" are people who were in essence genderqueers or boydykes or trannyfags who would have figured that out if only these terms in use now were available then. I do, however, think that we can transfer from the present, first, an expectation of nuance and variation among people suited, at least in some ways, by particular labels, and, second, the assumption that gender identity and expression were more nuanced and varied than any one term or narrative can characterize.[43] Regarding "passing women," the evidence for my first point appears clearly in texts about them, which show variation on many matters, including the elements of utility and pleasure, diverse in portion, content, and combination, in their male presentations. Woodhull, for instance, indicates something of both concerning his clothing in making a point attributed to him by the *World* and the *Times* that exemplifies the historic and material specificity in which gender is perceived, performed, and policed, here in early consumer culture: " 'A woman is a walking ad for jewelers, milliners, and dry-goods stores. See this hat, for instance,' pointing to her Fedora, 'I have worn it for more than three years and it is still in good condition. It can be cleaned and brushed carefully and made to look well. How many hats for a woman in a year? One for each season at least—four!' " (*World*); "They [women] live in the main only for their clothes, and when now and then a woman comes to the front who does not care for dress she is looked upon as a freak and a crank" (*Times*).⁴⁴

Sources also indicate, however, that the term "passing women" could not possibly successfully have encompassed everyone involved in female-to-male gender identity or expression during Woodhull's time. The concept of "passing women," as the term that came to designate it well represents, implies that there exists exactly one perception among female-to-male presenters of the relation of their gender expression to authenticity and masquerade: none of the former, all about the latter. Certainly, some people looking for a category legible to themselves or others must have found themselves insufficiently housed there, just as some people today have their gender identities misread according to prevailing models or equations. (A parallel example from recent years concerns contemporary presumptions, among people with a certain degree of gender savvy, that female sex assignment + facial hair = FTM, or female-to-male transperson, on hormones, although many other possibilities, and sex/gender identifications, might possibly explain the combination.⁴⁵) Veles seems to be one example of such a person, and while, as I said above, I don't take Corsi's account as an exact rendering of Veles's own gender or sexual identity, I do think that it is likely to be evidence of understandings of female-to-male gender diversity, in representations of and by people so identified, that extend beyond passing women.

I have been working in this section to denaturalize the "she-ing" of Woodhull by exposing some of the representational work involved in making his gender come out right. "The unfeigned ease of a man," the mustache: things get noted that might, but don't, serve to challenge the idea that a female sex assignment at birth indicates what people so identified fundamentally are and remain, an idea enfolded into the term "passing woman" that guides subsequent accounts of people whose stories look like Woodhull's. How their stories might look, to themselves or to others, under different circumstances, conceptual frameworks, or regimes of authority cannot really be known for sure.

What can be known is that the stories appeared because the practices of border policing got Woodhull into gender trouble that the publicity about him threatened to enhance, given his need to appear convincingly male rather than male-costumed, and that made him dependent on the will of authorities in terms of whether he became a spectacle. Fortunately for Woodhull, the authorities helped him sneak away as Frank Woodhull via a boat to New Jersey, thus, according to the *Post*, "disappoint[ing] a large crowd gathered at the Battery" in New York. Woodhull's exit, it turned out, was quite timely because by the next day he would have been easier to spot owing both to the *Post* article reporting his getaway and to the *World* piece featuring his photograph by Augustus Sherman. In the next section I consider the photograph as it characterizes, circulates, and, again, polices Woodhull's image.

NOW YOU SEE HIM

The specific operations of power that brought Woodhull to be photographed by Augustus Sherman are not clear. Sherman worked as a registry clerk at Ellis Island from 1892 until 1921, and then as a personal secretary to the commissioner until his death in 1925. He took many photographs of migrants on Ellis Island, and he is especially known for the photographs of migrants in the costumes of their countries of origin that now circulate widely in Ellis Island histories; a number of them, for example, are reproduced in the souvenir guide. Sherman also produced photographs of people that, at least as they are currently grouped in the Augustus Sherman Collection, whether Sherman or subsequent catalogers dictated the groups, seem to compose a collection of freaks. They include: a woman with a fifty-five-pound Russian baby; "Peter Meyer—57. . . . A wealthy Dane in search of

FIGURE 8. *Wladek Cyganiewicz Zybszko*, 1918. (Photograph by Augustus Sherman. Augustus Sherman Collection,
courtesy of the Ellis Island Immigration Museum)

pleasure"; a "Russian Hebrew . . . vegetarian"; "tattooed German stowaways
deported May, 1911"; a body builder, "Wladek Cyganiewicz Zybszko . . . Aus-
trian—Pole," shown from both the front (figure 8) and the back, seated on
a stool flexing; and "Marcel Derova, 29, 'Nostris'" (figure 9), who is also
posed seated to reveal his solid muscular form. The portrait of Woodhull is
also included in this group.

Sherman photographed primarily, it seemed, for his own pleasure and
interest. Several photographs, like those of the muscled men mentioned
above, suggest an order of pleasures that most likely were far removed from
his job description. Zybszko, dressed only in tight athletic underwear, poses
for Sherman's view from the front with his fists framing the large bulge

FIGURE 9. *Marcel Derova* (undated). (Photograph by Augustus Sherman. Augustus Sherman Collection, courtesy of the Ellis Island Immigration Museum)

in his shorts, implying its hardness by their proximity. His thumbs grip the band of his shorts, as if ready at any time to remove them. The image of Derova, fully naked, barely follows decorum; a dark shock of pubic hair draws the eye down to the base of the photograph, which is cropped just high enough to conceal his penis, but low enough to show his thighs. The homo-cheesecake look of these photographs might also point to why few details are known about the life of Sherman, who is described in the American Park Network's biography as "an inveterate bachelor" who "took pride in being well dressed."[46]

Most of Sherman's photographs, however, imply desires more suited for Ellis Island's official stamp. The array of photographs marked with handwritten notations like "Holland" or "Serbian Gipsies" suggest an interest in classifying and categorizing that is much in line with Ellis Island inquiry. So do the notations on the photographs of Woodhull, the vegetarian, and the "wealthy Dane," which offer viewers information that the visuals either deliberately camouflage or could not be presumed to yield up. As I discussed earlier in the chapter, differentially applied legal and medical inspection procedures at Ellis Island built on beliefs that the clothed body that migrants presented for initial view offered a surface legible only to the trained visual reader—but sometimes not even then, as in the cases of migrants perceived to have personal or, for instance, racial characteristics that signaled them to be duplicitous or inscrutable.

I turn here for a moment to the writing of Alan Sekula about the instrumental uses of photography in the late nineteenth and early twentieth centuries. Writing in "The Body and the Archive" about the development of photographic systems to identify criminals, he points out that these systems responded just as much to ideas about what photographs couldn't reveal as to ideas about what they could: "Contrary to the commonplace understanding of the 'mug shot' as the very exemplar of a powerful, artless, and wholly denotative visual empiricism, these early instrumental uses of photographic realism were systematized on the basis of an acute recognition of the *inadequacies* and limitations of ordinary visual empiricism."[47] While migrants photographed at Ellis Island were not generally seen as criminals—I take up in Chapter Eight, however, the sanitizing required to downplay Ellis Island's function as a place of incarceration—Sekula's insights are relevant here. They identify concepts about evidentiary photographs that match up with those that underpin the Ellis Island inspection process, which also accommodated both belief in the revelatory properties of the professional gaze and the presumption that such gaze required supplement.

Sekula writes, too, that "roughly between 1880–1910, the archive became the dominant institutional basis for photographic meaning. Increasingly, photographic archives were seen as central to a bewildering range of empirical disciplines, ranging from art history to military intelligence."[48] His argument that we need to see the connections and interdependence between the photographic systems developed to abet policing and those designed for less apparently regulatory inquiries resonates with Sherman's photographs partly because they bear important relations to policing. Sherman's intention is often described in terms of ethnic pride and diversity: "That is the lesson in Augustus Sherman's photography: that together, we make a nation."[49] But the images cannot be fully separated from the scientific racism in criminological schemes to identify racial types with propensities to crime and disease—especially considering the role of stereotypes in informing, to various degrees, the work of Ellis Island inspectors, as well as Sherman's habit of designating most of his subjects by "race" but not name.

In addition, the photographs owe their existence to the detention of their subjects for border policing, an originating circumstance that must have had varied and numerous effects, beginning with the migrants' assessment of whether posing for Sherman was a command performance. Given the occurrence of these photo sessions at the scene where authorities subjected them to scrutiny, examination, and a judgment with momentous consequences, it is hard to imagine that all migrants approached for photographs would understand or trust that posing for a portrait was optional—no matter how it was presented, which, importantly, remains unknown. The photographs themselves suggest varying degrees of volition on the part of the sitters. Zybszko looks like a career poser, happy enough to be doing it again. The German stowaways, photographed nude, at least as much as the photograph shows from their arms folded over their chest upward, look far from pleased, whether due to being importuned to pose or to the thought of their imminent expulsion. In other photos, the migrants in ethnic finery or clothes worn from travel manifest sometimes more, sometimes less, apparent enthusiasm for the process.[50]

Where Woodhull fits along the spectrum of consent might be surmised by the mug shot aura and grim expression. Yet the photo still yields up no firm answers regarding his consent or contribution to the image. Did Woodhull pose for the photograph before or after he learned of his (re)admission to the United States? The photograph appeared in the newspapers on 6 October, suggesting that the notation on the photograph, "ss 'New York'— Oct. 4 '08," might signal simultaneously the dates of Woodhull's arrival and sitting. In either case, he might have felt obligated to humor Sherman. What did Woodhull contribute to his appearance in the photograph? For instance, his hat shades his eyes. Why? Perhaps this was partly Woodhull's doing. For him, as several different press stories indicate, the hat had long functioned as protection; he considered it key to his successful presentation as male. Pulled low now, it shielded his eyes, at least, from yet another inspecting gaze. On the other hand, Sherman chose the camera angle, positioned his camera, possibly gave Woodhull some directions ("look here," "tilt your hat"), took the shot, and made choices in developing the picture.

Whatever the portions of intention and consent in the occasion and details of the sitting, Sherman did, however, have the last word in crucial ways. Presumably, he chose this particular image among others he had taken and developed, thus keeping or discarding effects that could have corresponded, or not, to the intentions of either of them. The photographs also could have corresponded, or not, to what Sherman or Woodhull thought that Woodhull looked like or felt. As Lizard Jones testifies, based on her work in the group Kiss and Tell, accidents of lighting and such might totally distort appearance or mood; an event that participants experienced as fun might look sinister and scary.[51] So while we might read a tepid consent or grim exhaustion on Woodhull's face, which makes sense given the circumstances, his look reflects at least partly the vagaries of the medium filtered according to Sherman's practice.

Besides ultimately determining how the circulating image looked, Sherman most probably exercised control through two actions to which Woodhull hardly seems likely to have consented since they undermined his ability to return to the United States as male: by scrawling Woodhull's female origin and story across the top of the photograph (at least the one Sherman kept for his own archive) and in the distribution of the photograph to several newspapers. Did Sherman intend to sell it to the newspapers all along? I don't know. According to the American Park Network biography, he occasionally provided photographs to the National Geographic Society and to the government for reports, but I did not find evidence of Sherman as a frequent peddler of migrant oddities to daily newspapers. To ascertain whether Sherman had a little business going, I tried to find out whether some other photographs, such as those of the muscled men or the vegetarian, appeared in local newspapers around the dates on the photographs. After some research, it appears that they did not.[52]

Once the papers had the photograph of Woodhull, captions like "Miss Mary Johnson" (*Post*) continued to affix to Woodhull's image the tools for reading his gender presentation as a scandalous disguise. In so doing, they underscore the concept that his presentation could be best conceptualized as masquerade and scandal, which, as I have been arguing, should not be taken for granted. Compare Woodhull's story to Bram Stoker's chapter in *Famous Imposters* called "The Bisley Boy." It considers the validity of the "tradition," which Stoker finally judges improbable but not impossible, that the adult known as Queen Elizabeth I was really a man who, as a child, had been substituted for the girl Elizabeth after she died under the care of a governess.[53] This case, were it true, would be a scandalous imposture. Compared to the idea of a boy substituting for a girl who had actually inhabited a different body, not to mention one destined to inherit the crown, the case of one person's shift in gender expression seems far less dramatic. The whole notion that such a shift constitutes pretending to be somebody else testifies more than anything to how rigid, fixed, and binary female and male sex and gender identities are often understood to be.

Moreover, the "can you believe?" tone of articles on Woodhull belies the evidence that many people born with female gender assignment wound up living as male. Evidence exists in the agglomeration of so many similar one-of-a-kind stories and in the occasional commentary on their recurrence (including by Stoker). Evidence also exists in Woodhull's success up to that point, which invites speculation about how many people whose clothes thus disguised their bodies passed every day, both through Ellis Island or in the ordinary movements of daily life that people undertake apart from state scrutiny, at least in terms of patent intervention. Woodhull's accounting of his gender identity precisely under that state scrutiny calls us, as I have argued, to question the portion of strategy in his own account of passing for utility only. No matter how he understood his identity, however, he most clearly understood how he wanted to live: as male. Sherman and the others who describe Woodhull as "she" worked to take that away from him.

NOW YOU DON'T

Representation is political. What gets represented, and when, where, and how it does, depends on and affects relations of power. That is why the publicity about Woodhull at the time functioned in some ways like the silence about him functions now. Printing Woodhull's story and photograph, especially with the insistence on him as in reality Mary Johnson, publicized a norm of gender conformity, and, in a sense, a norm of gender nonconformity, given the predominance of the "passing woman" as an explanatory narrative. The effects of that publicity cannot, of course, fully be specified. Some who encountered Woodhull's story might have found their presumptions of essential identities confirmed; others may have found hope, a good plan, or an identity or a kindred enough practice from which to take strength. One effect on Woodhull, however, can be specified: running his name, story, and, sometimes, picture threatened his ability to live as male, and, consequently, as he attested, his livelihood.

Now long dead, Woodhull gets little attention, even though such attention poses no harm to him and could arguably benefit others by interrupting the presumptions of sex and gender normativity that, as I discussed in the previous chapter, inform most representations of Ellis Island. Instead Woodhull hangs from the ceiling next to Marcel Derova, aka "Nostris," each of whom is flipped backward and dequeered by being reduced to a headshot. Woodhull bears no explanatory narrative. Derova bares no naked body. Although Derova's lack of clothing may be suggested in the contrast between his naked shoulder and Woodhull's suited one, the cropping forestalls an invitation to consider the context in which his thumbs subtly pull apart his thighs for Sherman, the "inveterate bachelor" widely praised for immigrant portraits that are most famously all about the clothes.

One might argue in Derova's case that the American Family Immigration History Center is no place for a naked guy. Maybe so. But only prejudice explains why there is no place for Woodhull's story. The American Family Immigration History Center is all about interesting personal stories: finding them through research, composing them for one's "family history scrapbook." Yet from the exemplars provided it appears that the "American family" story is the one where the part about the uncle who used to be the aunt, or the uncle who had other men pose naked for him, somehow gets left out. The center's inaugural brochure images well the family-with-closet concept. The central photograph on the cover, which shows the center's main room, actually includes a substantial part of the Woodhull banner, and a bit of Derova's banner next to it (figure 10). As a result of their cropping, however, the banners fail to complicate the progenitorial model liberally sprinkled across the eight inside pages. There, images include four

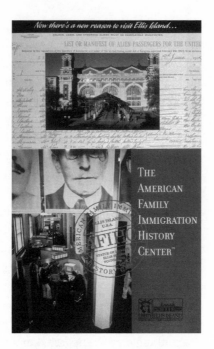

FIGURE 10. Cover of a brochure advertising
the American Family Immigration History Center,
2001. (Photograph by Kathryn Lattanzi)

groupings implied to be mother, father, and two children; variations in skin tone among, but significantly not within, the groups suggest the Center's multiethnic, multiracial appeal. Also depicted is the "Wedding Anniversary Memory Book" available for purchase at the online gift shop. (It's shown behind a baseball cap decorated with an image of the U.S. flag and the words "Ellis Island/Freedom's Gate": sex, money, products, nation.)

Derova's missing body cannot fully be explained by understandable propriety. It needs also to be considered in the context of other images that raise issues of bodily display, which are not always handled with propriety as the guiding principle. One such image is a photograph that depicts female medical personnel examining a female immigrant, seen from behind, whose bare shoulder indicates that she has been required partially to disrobe (figure 11). A large blow-up detail of the image, which appears fre-

FIGURE 11. Photograph of migrant women undergoing medical inspection at Ellis Island (undated). (Courtesy of the Ellis Island Immigration Museum)

quently in Ellis Island histories, is displayed at the Ellis Island Museum in the room devoted to medical inspection. The caption states: "For a woman who had never been touched by a man other than her husband, being examined by a male doctor could be traumatic." Note here, of course, not just the presumptive heterosexuality but also the presumption that heterosexual arrangements are always wanted and benign, outside the realm of traumatizing touch, and the implication that the touch of one man somehow authorized another's.

The point of the caption as a whole is partly to demonstrate the sensitivity of Ellis Island authorities, who, in 1914, hired women doctors; the photograph, which has only female medical personnel, illustrates or symbolizes this sensitivity.[54] Yet one might find as well a certain, if unintended, invitation to voyeurism and violation, especially given two other items on display

FIGURE 12. Display at the Ellis Island Immigration Museum showing a photograph of migrant women over a display case showing surgical and medical examination instruments. (Photograph by Sallie McCorkle)

in the medical inspection room. The first is the display for which the image provides a backdrop: a collection of "Surgical and Medical Examination Instruments," with a "Graves vaginal speculum" at the top left-hand spot in the case (figure 12). The second is another wall plaque that paints the spectacle of just how innocent, and therefore vulnerable, a migrant girl might be, this one through a text from La Guardia's autobiography. The wall text states:

> One case haunted me for years. A young girl in her teens from the mountains of northern Italy turned up on Ellis Island. No one understood her particular dialect very well, and because of her hesitancy in replying to questions she did not understand, she was sent to the hospital for observation. I could imagine the effect on this girl, who

had always been carefully sheltered and had never been permitted in the company of a man alone, when a doctor suddenly rapped on her knees, looked into her eyes, turned her on her back and tickled her spine to ascertain her reflexes. The child rebelled—and how!

If that last sentence seems oddly to interrupt the portrait of a naive girl positioned and repositioned to give access to multiple assaults that she is helpless to fend off, it is partly because the plaque omits the sentences that originally followed: "It was the cruelest case I ever witnessed on the Island. In two weeks time that child was a raving maniac, although she had been sound and normal when she arrived at Ellis Island."[55] Maybe the designers of the exhibit dropped the end of La Guardia's quote to give the girl some agency; the idea that she revolted could conjure up spunk if it isn't named lunacy. Whatever the intention behind the editorial decision, however, there remains an interesting effect: the truncation of all the lurid details precisely at the point when they begin to allege that the deployment of state-sanctioned power can cause permanent harm.

I find interesting, too, that the producers of the *Statue of Liberty and Ellis Island Coloring Book* considered appropriate for inclusion a line drawing based on the photograph of the girl.[56] Also interesting is that a photograph of partly stripped men (figure 13) gets less play: no coloring book page, no big blow-up printed for a wall display. Not only is the photograph more forthcoming than most images of medical inspection in signaling, if discreetly from the back, the extent of exposure that fuller inspections required, the photograph also suggests the medical gaze to be varied, to be possibly more complicated than just all business, and to be, maybe, sometimes queer. The inspector in the back seems to stare directly at the penis of the migrant seen from behind whose arm positions suggest he is pulling away clothes to show what inspectors require him to show. The inspector's look seems disinterested enough, but in its disinterest it throws into relief the turning-to-look head of the migrant in the back, next to the vision chart in Hebrew letters, and, most attention grabbing, the expression of the medical inspector holding a reflex tester, who looks like he's been caught in some act by the photographer. His face, though belonging to someone in authority, issues a reminder that both of these photographs exist because migrants were at the mercy of Ellis Island authorities. Sherman's portrait photographs might

FIGURE 13. Photograph of immigrant men undergoing
medical inspection at Ellis Island (undated). (Courtesy of
the Ellis Island Immigration Museum)

have an element or more of consent involved, but it is hard to imagine any
version of these inspection scenarios in which something like "Mind if I
take your picture?" could function, were anyone to utter it, as a meaningful
solicitation of consent.

CONCLUSION: CLOTHES MAKE THE MAN

The article mentioned earlier on Otillie Castnaugle, the "Saxon 'Murray
Hall,'" concludes with an anecdote about the shock that her unmasking
caused a fellow passenger:

> On the voyage to this country Otillie's main friend was a Hebrew, who
> is to be deported, too. The latter never doubted that Otillie was a Ger-
> man woman coming to this country to seek work. The Hebrew was

seated on a bench in the detention pen yesterday morning when a door opened and Otillie, dressed in the suit of male attire given to him by Uncle Sam, was led in by a guard.

"Ach!" he said as he looked in astonishment at Otillie. "What a strange country. She was a woman yesterday. Now they make her a man. Take me away!"

This story, obviously told for laughs, makes gentle fun of the "Hebrew" for, significantly, his immigrant naiveté about trans-sex presenters, as opposed, by implication, to the reader in the know who recognizes the reference in the headline.

But the Hebrew, I think, was onto something. In effect, the state did make Otillie Castnaugle a man. As with Woodhull, she lived as one sex until she was stopped by official practices that presumed the truth of sex to be displayed, transparently readable, underneath one's clothes. The officials then had the power to judge their fates. Woodhull got through but Castnaugle did not; her story of having been raised from birth and baptized as a girl apparently was not adequate to sway the officials. Assuming the truth of the report that they forced Castnaugle to return home in men's clothes, the incident testifies also to the power and desire sometimes to enforce gender codes even beyond the denial of entry to people who deviate from them.

I have been working in this chapter to specify the series of state policies, conceptual habits, and representational maneuvers that have contributed to the policings of gender that caught Woodhull at the border in 1908 and that render him now the guy too often without a story in a place where stories abound. I have been trying, too, both in practice and interpretation, to suggest some alternative approaches, beginning with the principle that when the names and pronouns assigned to people do not match the ones of their choice, the latter should be the default mode. This an act of respect that makes analytical sense. In the case of neither Woodhull nor Castnaugle does sufficient evidence exist to consider anatomy the best guide to their gender identity. But the risks and pain they faced from unmasking publicity are absolutely clear, as, significantly, they seem also to have been to the agents of representation who "she'd" Woodhull and "he'd" Castnaugle. From this perspective, the politics of terms like "passing women" need another look, and so do the stakes in hanging onto them.

In looking at the various facets of Woodhull's situation, I have used the word "policing" in various relations to force: I refer both to direct regulation and to the promotion and articulation of gender norms that made it difficult to live outside of those norms. In a sense this double use is appropriate in part because the two forms are interdependent: Woodhull made the papers because the border authorities considered his alleged masquerade a problem; it looked all the more out of the ordinary when the press made a scandal of each case of passing, rather than another piece of evidence that gender norms and restrictions weren't working. Yet it is still crucial to avoid collapsing different levels of policing. For one reason, being ordered to take off one's clothes by migration gatekeepers is simply not the same as hearing that one ought to be wearing a dress. For another reason, as I will argue later in this book, mystifications and metaphors around the operation of force are part of the topic to be studied. In the next chapter, however, I consider a realm of sex and perceived criminality from which Woodhull successfully distanced himself as I turn to metaphors about the Statue of Liberty's virtue that attach her to prostitution.

THREE

THE TRAFFIC IN MY FANTASY BUTCH

It is obvious to me that the Statue of Liberty is one hot butch. Her out-fit, I know, doesn't really suit her. Yet there is something sexy about the way her butchness shows through anyway. You can tell, for instance, de-spite all that drapery, that her hips would never swing side to side. She'd stride or saunter and then plant her feet in that I'll-move-when-I'm-ready way, alert for any encroachment yet confident that no one would dare to try. Liberty is the kind of butch who makes her muscles evident without ever looking like she's showing them off. Her calves are visibly stunning. Her torch arm, thrusting high for over a century now, cannot be anything less than spectacularly endowed (figure 14). As suggested in figure 14, the photograph with the guy standing small in her flames, Liberty seems to in-vite all comers to become well-rewarded size queens.[1] Those fingers, nicely rough in some places and smooth in others, look strong and flexible holding the torch, which, if you think about it, is one serious power tool—an activist power tool, wielded for liberty. Imagine what else she might be wielding, thrusting, planning. The designer of the New York Liberty team logo offers one possibility, as Liberty, in characteristic WNBA butch glory, punches her flames-turned-basketball into the air. Once you get into that erotic space, the possibilities abound.

I proffer this vision and invitation against a different direction in butched-up Liberty that has gotten much more play than the likes of my butch Lib-erty since the events of September 11, 2001. Liberty, it has been suggested to me, had shrunk over the years as vertical majesty migrated to other parts of the New York skyline; it wasn't so big anymore, or even such a big deal.[2] Now Liberty is taller and tougher so as to enable her stand in for, and avenge,

FIGURE 14. *Charlie DeLeo, Keeper of the Flame, on Top of the Statue of Liberty's Flame, July 1994.* (Photograph by Vincent Di Pietro, National Park Service, Statue of Liberty National Monument)

the missing World Trade Center towers, which themselves, it sometimes seems, have changed in conceptual size, beginning to loom larger once physically demolished. The most benevolent type of post-9/11 butch, Liberty can be seen in a sign purchased for me from a New York City street vendor in late 2001 (figure 15). Designed to hang from a car's rear window, with the plastic diamond shape and suction cup retained from the genre's "Baby on Board" years, it features the phrase "America Stands Tall" superimposed on an abstracted stars-and-stripes motif and next to an image of the statue. The thick, elongated letters of "Tall," while ironically downscaling the statue, convey the will to endow Liberty with phallic oomph and stature.

Two widely circulated cultural products put Liberty's torch arm to more sinister thrusting. In the lyrics to the 2002 song "Courtesy of the Red,

FIGURE 15. "America Stands Tall," decoration for an automobile rear-window display, 2001. (Photograph by Robert Diamante)

White and Blue (The Angry American)" by Toby Keith—"The Statue of Liberty/Started shakin' her fist," while Uncle Sam added names to his list (presumably a hit list) and "Mother Freedom" prepared to ring her bell—each action is a herald of revenge against the unspecified enemy who, having "sucker punch[ed]" the nation, must face the consequences: "You'll be sorry that you messed with/The US of A/'Cause we'll put a boot in your ass/It's the American way."[3] If the boot's destination seems to place Liberty's fist on the path to sexualized revenge, such connections are less understated in an image (which soon after 9/11 was found easily on the Web) that shows Liberty giving the finger with the text "We're Coming, Motherfuckers" written in the blue sky next to her arm.[4] The finger and the phrasing, suggesting that the (perverted) fucker will become the (still, if differently, perverted) fucked, makes Liberty the symbol and agent of a punishment marked implicitly here, but explicitly elsewhere, in the sodomizing vengeance genre popular at the time, as feminizing, homosexualizing, and, consequently, humiliating.

How does popular culture contribute to constructing, circulating, and validating normative ideologies of citizenship? As Jasbir K. Puar and Amit S. Rai point out, post-9/11 vengeance imagery in popular culture pointed to contradictions and consistencies both within and between registers of representation and practice. Made during a period in which the United States was also being depicted as feminist and gay-friendly in relation to Afghanistan, depictions of vengeance as the fag making or fag bashing of bin Laden and others came with a documented increase in violence against queers, especially queers of color, that the visual and textual rhetoric could well be considered to incite.[5] Worth noting, as well, is how much "We're Coming" was on target. "We" were indeed coming, with impending U.S. invasions that depended for popular support partly on the same elision of geographic or political specification—not that more cogent connections would have justified them—on which the legibility of "motherfuckers," "sucker punch," and, in fact, "we" also depended. I note these connections not to suggest direct causality, as if image x propelled action y, but to suggest ways that "dominant structures, practices, and effects," as Lawrence Grossberg puts it, "circulat[e] around and determin[e] each other."[6] Popular culture demands study, then, because it informs about actions, policies, and practices that inform it as well.

In this chapter and the next I consider the knotty meanings about sex, gender, sexuality, money, race, nation, migration, and U.S. citizenship that pile up around the Statue of Liberty during the years around 1986. As an important year for both the ceremonial and legal construction of U.S. immigration systems and ideologies, 1986 included Liberty Weekend, a three-day extravaganza centered around the Fourth of July to unveil the statue's centennial restoration. My interest in this topic arose when I noticed the use of sexual metaphor to attach the taint of seedy commerce to the activities of the Statue of Liberty–Ellis Island Foundation, Inc. (SOLEIF), which oversaw the restoration of both monuments. Among its various money-making strategies, SOLEIF sold sponsorships and product licenses that many viewed as ill-suited to ennoble the statue's image. Stroh's, for $3 million, became the official beer of the restoration; Eveready turned the torch into a flashlight.

Other licensed products included Liberty Edition Harley-Davidsons, the now-famous crown of green foam, and "Spirit of America Air Freshener" in the shape of the statue and "impregnated with a 'fresh citrus flavor.'"[7] In the context of this commercial activity arose a recurring practice, in a wide variety of sources, of describing the allegedly dubious fund-raising practices for Liberty's restoration by saying that she had been prostituted. As I continued my research, I came to see this scandal of sex meeting money at the body of immigration's so-called "lady" as obstructing the view of other matters about sex, money, and race circling around the statue's centennial that truly ought to be considered scandalous but frequently don't seem to be. I consider two such matters in this chapter: the Supreme Court's un-Libertylike ruling, right before Liberty Weekend, to uphold the state anti-sodomy laws challenged in *Bowers v. Hardwick*; and the story of a 12-year-old refugee who was not able to keep her prize in a Statue of Liberty essay contest because its cash value threatened her family's eligibility for public assistance, an irony spun as the occasion for regal benevolence not for critiquing economic inequities. In the next chapter I consider a third matter: the burial, under the official rhetoric linking Liberty to the "tempest-tost" immigrants through Ellis Island, of the likelihood that honoring the abolition of slavery was one inspiration for the statue.

My goals in this chapter involve both process as well as content. One problem with presenting a relatively linear argument about how meanings knot and pile up is that the form of the argument belies its content.[8] Here, while nonetheless advancing an argument that, I hope, readers can follow easily, I tweak the linear flow with variations in some features of academic writing that ordinarily remain standard. The tone changes, as does the relation to sources, the degree of investment or detachment, and the play of invention and analysis. Thus, for instance, a fictional scenario that imagines Liberty taking charge of her own relation to sex work abuts a more formal exposition of the ideological premises involved in picturing Liberty in sexual commerce. In addition, by offering extended comments on a few topics in the mix around Liberty's restoration instead of trying to catalog them exhaustively, I intend to advocate for an approach that, instead of arguing for one particular reading of an icon (the statue is a hot butch) or for a fixed list of indispensable referents, excavates the foundations, conditions, ingredients, contexts, and alternatives to such meaning making.[9]

Henry Giroux suggests that perhaps more significant than how audiences interpret cultural products may be the way that "some ideas, meanings, and messages under certain political positions become more highly valued as representations of reality than others—and, further, how these representations assume the force of ideology by making an appeal to common sense while at the same time shaping political policies and programs that serve very specific interests."[10] As Susana Peña documents in her work on gay men who came to the United States from Cuba during the Mariel boatlift, policies and programs are only part of the issue. Regimes of visibility and silencing, promulgated by the state, the media, individuals, and communities, make histories that affect people's lives in extremely varied ways, from defining criminality to internalizing codes of behavior.[11]

BUTCH LUBRICATION

Because I began this chapter by contrasting my taste for Liberty's erotic charms to the dominant habits of using her butchness to endorse sexualized violence, I want to emphasize before proceeding that I am far from the only person to associate her with erotic pleasures. Of course, takes on Liberty are often hard to read. Who is to say what's going on when people extol the Lady? What does it mean, for instance, that when the game show *Family Feud*—"100 people surveyed, top five answers on the board"—asked people in 2000 to name something associated with the statue, 58 chose the "torch" ahead of "New York" (15), "freedom" (10), "Lady Liberty" (6), and "Ellis Island" (5).[12] Does it mean that 58 people see the flaming torch like I see it, or that the only people who conceived of her first as one glorious female saw a Lady above all? Yet among numerous indirections in expression are hints of Liberty's turned-on fans. Terms like "in love" or "my girlfriend" that might reflect erotic fantasy come up not infrequently in immigrant narratives, and little eruptions occur in odd places. In the quite staid *Dear Miss Liberty*, a collection of letters sent with donations for the restoration, the author of a prose poem suddenly tells his "beautiful Lady" that "Your freedom is the sweetest, most succulent fruit that any being of this earth could ever hope to pick."[13] In *The Cat Who Escaped from Steerage*, a children's novel about immigration through Ellis Island, the grandmother mistakes Liberty for a woman indecently on display in her nightgown.[14] Although the scene's humor hinges on the idea that Grandma, entrenched in the Old World and frequently confused lately, is offended by the slightest hint of sexual display (an idea underpinned, no doubt, by stereotypes of old people as nonsexual), I like to think of her instead as hip to Liberty's erotic charge.

Liberty has other queer fans, too. In *Icky and Kathy Find Liberty* (1999), a short film by Kathy High, pubescent twin girls, turned on by the Statue of Liberty, masturbate together. A cartoon at the beginning of *Betty and Pansy's Severe Queer Review of New York* invites readers to "Take Liberty from Behind." Depending on how or if one codes anal pleasure—does it have a bit of a fag aura no matter who is doing it?—this invitation could be seen as one confirmation from another direction of my sense of Liberty's sex/gender queerness.[15] (I realize here that one might also interpret "take" to imply nonconsensual force, but given its common appearance also to describe or invite consensual sex I want to leave room for a reading of anal penetration to signal other than the rape, degradation, and punishment that it designates in the examples I cited earlier. Homohatred cannot be permitted to evacuate possibilities of pleasure.) Another sex/gender queering comes from a queer punk T-shirt that I heard about, which pictures Liberty lifting her dress to show a penis underneath, along with, below her base, the title *America's Hardcore*.

Yet I tend to find my erotic appreciation of Liberty as butch to be far to the side of common readings. Many people apparently mistake her lack of feminine wiles for sexual disinterest, abstinence, or, at least, decorum. These people often view her as matron, mother, or spinster ("Miss Liberty"), drawing, it often seems, on the unhappy traditions in which those figures lack sexual content. Others register her masculinity without knowing quite what to do with it. A few immigrants believed what they heard when told that they were seeing Christopher Columbus.[16] A more recent observer, noting Liberty's lack of "feminine qualities," called her "gender neutral," "an armed non-woman with whom men would certainly prefer not to mess."[17] Marvin Trachtenberg, whose monograph on the statue was revised for the centennial, also imagined her ready to take on manly men, although it's unclear whether he envisioned her as comrade or lover. In boldly claiming to know what "the nineteenth-century eye would undoubtedly have imagined beneath Liberty's thick antique drapery," he saw viewers envisioning "a characteristic academic nude . . . large boned, massively curved, substantial and severe, with few traces of delicate femininity, altogether a fit companion for the iron men who dominated the age." To illustrate his hypothesis, Trachtenberg reproduces a painting of a naked woman, representing "Truth," who stands with her weight shifted so that one hip juts dramatically out to the side.[18] What could he be thinking? Liberty doesn't move her hips that way.

Knowing that few see what I do doesn't diminish my appreciation. Erotic taste is diverse, and that is good. Besides, in watching others flail around I can simply revel in my talents as a connoisseur of butch. I also understand the challenge of getting beyond Liberty's dresslike garb as well as ubiquitous cultural directives to keep the scary unruliness of sex from tainting models of political virtue, or what Linda Zerelli calls "the risk of the female body set loose in the public sphere."[19] (To these ends, Liberty was deliberately designed with the disheveled, décolleté barricade-charger in Delacroix's famous *Liberty Leading the People* [1830] as an antimodel.) For those who have been told that Liberty's sculptor Frédéric-Auguste Bartholdi modeled her, at least in part, after his mother Charlotte, other taboos may be at work.

FOR SALE

My sense of Liberty as a commanding activist babe is not shaken by something that would seem to shake others: the knowledge that time with Liberty or her image can be purchased, a phenomenon frequently described when it is criticized, particularly around the restoration, in terms of prostitution. In 1983, early into the restoration project, Michael Kinsley, a *New Republic* commentator, punctuated his argument in the article "Liberty Deflowered" that the restoration should be paid with tax dollars instead of corporate dollars by asking "Who wouldn't pay a dollar a person to keep Miss Liberty from becoming a high-priced corporate tart?" Two years later, Garnet Chapin, then a recently fired employee of the Department of the Interior who had worked for the director of the National Park Service as liaison to the Statue of Liberty/Ellis Island project, imagined her working the streets. Commenting on the unseemly competition among corporations for sponsorship spots, he stated: "If she's sold to the highest bidder, it's not unlike a whore who's being pimped on the sidewalk." A *Washington Post* piece, commenting on corporate sponsors using Liberty's image in advertising, argued more vaguely that "the price for survival should not be her virtue."[20] In the Left press, the *Nation* also hinted at sexual sales in giving its exposé on the restoration financing the title "The Selling of Miss Liberty," sacrificing feminist basics—shouldn't the *Nation* by 1985 be addressing Liberty as "Ms.?"—so as to invoke a maiden turned out.[21]

One other direction in prostitution metaphors involves a dirty joke played for serious. Trachtenberg, derisively labeling feminists "perhaps the most unthinking" of all the statue's appropriators, counts among what makes Liberty an unsuitable feminist icon that "for a fee she is open to all for entry and exploration from below."[22] Barbara Babcock and John Macaloon then revived Trachtenberg's point in the early 1990s. While they criticize his attack on feminists in their essay "Everybody's Gal" (named after Reagan's term for Liberty), they nonetheless grant "the reality" of the access situation that he describes, noting that as a result "it is possible to view Liberty as a prostitute, although she seems to be a mother."[23] Unlike Trachtenberg, Babcock and Macaloon don't seem to think that working as a prostitute affects one's feminist credentials. But for their conceptual space to remain generous toward Liberty, while also seeing her as open for business, depends, further reading suggests, on understanding Liberty to be without agency where money for her services is involved. They pick up on this theme later when they go on to describe their own feminist interpretive project as something of a small consolation for collective helplessness in the face of female victimization: "Clearly, we cannot control the traffic in women, and it is obviously futile to struggle against female objectification, but we can do something about the interpretation thereof."[24] They also borrow another writer's term, "statuary rape," as a lead-in to a paragraph on the trying of "her dignity . . . in the name of raising money to repair the ravages of time and to celebrate her birthday."[25]

Meanings about sex and money pile on, inform, and alter meanings about sex, money, and more. They also depend on what's already available —in the air, in the media, in the archive, in various sense-making contexts. The motif of Liberty turned prostitute came easily, it seems, to many people, some of whom made it into a wide variety of print sources. Consequently, it came to me easily later; not looking for it at all, I found it all over. I also found repeated coverage of the related matter about those who would pull Liberty into the realm of the trashy by making unseemly use of her image or bringing tasteless extravagance and inappropriate entertainment to her party, like three hundred Jazzercizers and two hundred Elvis impersonators.[26]

My goal here isn't to condemn these texts. I could hardly do so unhypocritically; I can't resist the material myself. I'm fascinated by the decisions made by Hamilton Projects, SOLEIF's licensing representative, which turned down requests to license Statue of Liberty lingerie, whips and chains, pet collars, toilet seat covers, caskets, guns, knives with blades over three inches long, and a pictorial tribute in a pornographic magazine to "Love in America," but then did approve snuffboxes, barbecue grills, fishing rods, shower curtains, dart boards, and swizzle sticks.[27] These lists virtually compel promiscuous dissemination and invite luxuriating in what remains to be imagined: the objects, many now out of production; the rationale for inclusions/exclusions, alternately obvious and odd; the people charged with deciding. Liberty on the patio with snuff but no kink—or was there kink on the patio for the people in licensing? In 1985, Mrs. America (the kink on the patio?) rode with Liberty's old torch, along with a giant picture of Liberty's head formed in flowers, on the Hilton Hotels float in the Tournament of Roses parade.[28] The details of Liberty put out for profit can support the conjuring of many scenarios.

But some of them are more common than others. Interestingly, for instance, the uses of the Liberty-turned-prostitute motif, despite coming from various political positions, nonetheless turn on certain shared conceptions. Trachtenberg's sarcastic attribution of Liberty's spread-skirt policy to her own bad politics and Kinsley's warning that Liberty could "becom[e] a high-priced corporate tart," which suggests a woman needing rescue from her own bad impulses, both envision Liberty participating in sexual commerce perhaps by choice, but if so unthinkingly. The other examples I cited all invoke Liberty as a victim who is acted upon only: abused, pimped, trafficked. Why not imagine a scenario more like the one I create as follows:

> Liberty wants to treat herself to some body work and a big party for her 100th birthday. Thinking about how to raise money, she considers the options available to a woman with limited vocational training or credentializing degrees: "I need to protect my hands and wrists if I want

to keep holding that torch, so jobs with repetitive chores like typing and minute assembly work are out. I don't want to work in the snack shop downstairs. Maybe I'll go back to sex work. I know I'm good at it. Besides, last time I chose this form of labor, I found it enjoyable on the best days, and, on many of the worst, more tolerable than my earlier job in the sweatshop. This pays better, too. If I can't make what I want that way, I'll model for ads. I hate standing around under those lights, but I can make a bundle in a few hours."

This scenario, I admit, involves selective labor realism. Besides throwing in an anachronistic allusion to repetitive stress injury, I enabled Liberty knowledgeably to assess the job possibilities she was rejecting within a range constricted by gender and class oppression—and, in contrast to the fallen-woman stereotypes, to consider sex work as a temporary pursuit—yet did not require her to articulate how those would affect the work she chose to pursue. But my point is partly that all the sex talk above is selective, even when invoking purportedly literal truths. The "reality" simply is not that "for a fee" some "she" is "open to all." For one thing, such a statement evades the simple fact that the fee alone to get to Liberty Island, now $10 per adult and $4 per child, prohibits access to all. It also obscures the additional resources that are required, all of which vary according to location, work flexibility, transportation needs, field trip money and so forth as well as in terms of the social and economic inequities that differential access to them may indicate. Nor was the reality ever that all people, once at Liberty Island, had equal access to the inside. After the events of September 11, 2001, the National Park Service closed the statue's interior to all visitors. Before that, entry was effectively limited to people who could deal with waiting in line outside, possibly for several hours and in difficult weather. Further, getting all the way up in her required the ability to climb stairs.

If open access to Liberty is not factually true, neither is it metaphorically as transparent as the "reality" would suggest. While the meaning of all the scenarios I presented is obvious, they all depend on both metaphorical transfers and ideological premises. The metaphorical transfers include entering a representation of a woman is like entering a woman; selling a reproduction of a statue of a woman is like selling the statue of a woman is like selling the sexual services of a woman; the statue, being inanimate, is like a helpless person. The selectivity of metaphor making stands out here when we consider that the statue, weighing over 450,000 pounds, might well be imagined as a person who could dictate the terms in any interaction. It takes a lot of work to view this huge figure as wholly victimized. The ideological premises include the idea that the sale of sexual services is generally bad—dirty sex paid for with dirty money; that it degrades the person providing the services and/or is permanently transformative (once a prostitute, never again, or simultaneously, Miss Liberty); that it is more degrading and transformative than any other sort of labor one might perform no matter what the working conditions; that one would have to be forced or deluded to do it, or, at least, to choose to do it and remain a sympathetic figure worthy of aid if circumstances warrant it; that it is more about morality than labor rights.[29]

I wrote my own tale of Liberty's entry into sexual commerce to highlight, by proceeding from some contrasting assumptions, the connective work required to make sense of the commerce narratives I cited. This work generally goes without saying partly because it entails the marshalling of certain dominant attitudes about sex work. Some of these attitudes have found life in immigration laws. Laws against the immigration of prostitutes date back to 1875, and in 1910 prostitution became one of the first and only crimes for which an immigrant could be deported at any time after arrival. As Wendy Chapkis points out in her discussion of the Trafficking Victims' Protection Act of 2000, current laws still pit sexual agency against virtue. The definition of which migrants are covered under the act depends precisely on valuing a lack of sexual agency or foreknowledge; no matter how badly one might have been misled or treated, any consent to enter the sex industry disqualifies migrants from assistance.[30]

But while these attitudes may be widely intelligible and easy to grab for, that doesn't make applying them to Liberty's money matters a simple production. Besides depending on ideas about sexual commerce, images of Liberty defiled by certain commercial transactions turn on various understandings about gender, sex, and sexuality; about various economic players and practices; and about the nation for which the Statue of Liberty is meant to stand. Is Liberty a hot butch or Lady Liberty, and what constitutes either of these? Is Lee Iacocca a hero or a slimeball? Is it OK to have an official hot dog (Oscar Meyer) of the restoration? Is government funding cleaner than private funding? What makes them dirty? Are they ever clean? Is sex ever? Are women ever?

Can personifications of U.S. ideals ever be conceptualized as having sexual agency—for free or otherwise? Lauren Berlant, who sees a "pornographic structure" as well as sometimes sexual content in the political deployment of female icons existing to be used as desired, suggests that gender-coded passivity, partly projecting as immobility in the case of the Statue of Liberty, is key: "When the body of the woman is employed symbolically to regulate or represent the field of national fantasy, her positive 'agency' lies in her ability to be narrativized."[31] (Or, as Mobil Corporation puts it in an essay-style Liberty Weekend ad titled "Confessions of a Lover," which portrays Liberty as something of a high-toned serial monogamist with exacting standards, "She is a silent figure, yet based on eloquence."[32]) Maybe, then, to the extent that Liberty's gender functions as a stable ground for narration—which, I have argued, is not always the case—metaphorical habits work against interpreting Liberty, or her allegorical sisters, as grabbing the sex that serves her for pleasure or profit.

One might argue, however, slightly differently, that such gender-coded passivity concerning figures like Liberty is a metaphorical habit that requires work to sustain. Jacqui Alexander points out that because the state uses the heterosexual nuclear family physically to reproduce and ideologically to legitimate itself, and because "loyalty to the nation as citizen is perennially colonized within reproduction and heterosexuality," women's sexual agency and erotic autonomy—frequently "cathected onto the body of the prostitute and the lesbian"—carry a threat to the national order.[33] In writing about state practice in the Bahamas during the last decades of the twentieth century, Alexander demonstrates the complex work of the state to censure and contain such autonomy, even sometimes within the alleged purpose of bolstering women's rights within the heterosexual family.

In the United States, one example among many supporting the applicability of Alexander's point lies in the early and continuing legislation, mentioned above, against the entry of prostitutes. Another example, from the period of Liberty's restoration, can be found in the Immigration Marriage Fraud Amendments (IMFA), passed in November 1986. The IMFA was designed to curtail a practice, which the INS alleged but did not demonstrate convincingly to be rampant, by which immigrants contracted marriages with U.S. citizens solely to take advantage of the spousal reunification policies that enabled them to bypass quota restrictions and that shortened the waiting period for citizenship.[34] The congressional hearings on the IMFA repeatedly reaffirm "the value placed on [heterosexual] marriage and the unity of the nuclear family" (4) in immigration law without ever justifying why benefits should accrue to people who can demonstrate such ties. They imply in the process that people who don't have these ties are less desirable or less worthy neighbors and appropriately disadvantaged in seeking long-term residence or citizenship. The hearings also recapitulate the opposition, which underpins much immigration policy, between virtuous women who violate social and sexual norms only as victims without agency—lured into marriages by "smooth-talking aliens" (14)—and evil women who manipulate sexual and social arrangements for their own profit.

How these categories and the issues at stake are racialized, ethnically marked, and economically specified comes through in the examples in the report of the congressional hearings. One example involves "sham marriages between illegal Pakistanis and welfare mothers" (16). A derisive expression for women needing economic assistance, connoting profligates or fools in sex and thrift who sometimes deliberately reproduce for a bigger government allotment, the term "welfare mothers" could also safely be expected to call up images of black women despite statistics to the contrary about who received assistance under the program Aid to Families with Dependent Children. Another example concerns a woman, a U.S. citizen of Indian descent, who enters into an arranged marriage, "in keeping with the common practice in India" as Alan Simpson, the senator running the hearings, glossed the situation. She then discovered that her husband, a resident and citizen of India, married her only to bring over his own family and "build the empire," a phrase Simpson reiterates several times to underscore the horror of such an invasion.

While both parties in this case might be described as racially and ethnically similar, Simpson's comments imply that we might view the wife's distress over "the empire" to signal the whitening and civilizing effects of U.S. citizenship. Asians, he explains, in one of many allusions by various hearing participants to the notion that "immigration marriages often barely resemble the common interpretation of a nuclear family" (10), have a different understanding of family than the " 'cohesive family' or 'nuclear family' " in the minds of the "American citizen" (42–44).[35] In consenting to an arranged marriage but horrified and victimized by her husband's empire building, the woman is marked by her relation to family formations as both Asian and not Asian, alien and citizen, although her hold on citizen seems much less stable. This is hardly surprising given the dominant racial politics in which U.S. citizens with darker-than-labeled-as-white skin, regardless of links by birth or tradition to areas outside the United States, frequently struggle to exercise the rights of citizenship. However, the woman's status is further enhanced, I would argue, by her apparently comfortable premarital economic status. This arranged marriage is not for love, but it is not (apparently) for money either. The disinterest in poor women shown by the IMFA's architects may be seen in the disastrous consequences of the law's enforcement provisions for immigrant women rendered vulnerable to abuse by economic dependence on their husbands; the law has already been amended several times to try to lessen this effect.[36]

As the IMFA hearings underscore, the oppositions that separate the good women who support the nation from those, threatening virtually by definition, who act as independent sexual agents depend on values and practices concerning sexuality, economics, race, and ethnicity. While I have been focusing in this section on Liberty's gender, in the next sections I consider incidents and issues around the statue that indicate how the traffic in Liberty both occludes and depends on homophobic, classist, and racist structures.

BAD PARTY

On 30 June 1986, just before Liberty Weekend, the Supreme Court issued its decision in *Bowers v. Hardwick*. The decision upheld the rights of states to criminalize what the decision called "homosexual sodomy" although the Georgia law upheld by the Court indiscriminately banned all acts involving "the sex organs of one person and the mouth or anus of another."[37] (As Janet Halley points out, heterosexuals are excused from the verdict primarily by silence—that is, the decision's refusal to mention them.[38]) A national ruling against the right of adults to engage with each other in private consensual sex acts clearly has relevance to the weekend's theme of the ideals of freedom, rights, and liberty, especially since the United States was being promoted in conjunction with Liberty Weekend as the primary place to enjoy these ideals. Indeed, Chief Justice Warren Burger oversaw a ceremony designed to signal just that on 3 July, several days after his absolutely superfluous concurring statement to the Bowers decision; it was added solely, he said, "to underscore [his] view that in constitutional terms there is no such thing as a fundamental right to commit homosexual sodomy."[39] Officiating at Ellis Island, he administered the oath of citizenship to several hundred immigrants from about a hundred countries, representing thirty-one states, which they recited simultaneously with tens of thousands connected by satellite TV or audio hook-up from forty-four other sites, including the Orange Bowl.[40] The Bowers verdict itself got major coverage, and if writers covering the weekend needed a nudge to note the gross irony of its timing, activists provided it without hesitation. On 4 July, thousands of people (estimated at six thousand by the *Advocate*) marched in protest from Greenwich Village to Battery Park, the site of part of the Liberty Weekend festivities. Signs like "Miss Liberty? You Bet I Do" and "Lady Liberty, Light the Torch for Us, Too," made the connections visible.[41]

Yet the case's relevance to Liberty Weekend received little attention in the mainstream press. Articles in the *New York Times* about protests against the verdict cited less-pointed connections,[42] and only a few articles devoted to Liberty Weekend mentioned it at all. After I was reminded of the verdict's timing by a text on gay activism that I was reading outside the context of this project,[43] I searched the Lexis-Nexis database for July and August 1986, using the keyword "Liberty" along with either "gay," "Hardwick," or "sodomy." I found only six articles, four of which appeared in one paper, the *Los Angeles Times*. Of the six, only one, in the "opinion" section, is an article about the case, which, without mentioning Liberty Weekend specifically, explains the "subtle cruelty of the timing" involved in releasing the verdict just before Independence Day.[44]

The other articles, which very briefly mention the demonstration against the verdict in more general accounts of Liberty Weekend, show little interest in the liberties under assault. There are none that use the key terms "consenting," "private," or "adult" that are necessary, especially given the homophobic conjurings commonly evoked by putting "homosexual" and "sodomy" together, to convey the decision's reach and limits. Two articles in the group don't even mention antisodomy laws: the *Toronto Star* misleadingly describes "yet another Gay Pride demonstration" among the downtown spectacles and amusements, while a *Los Angeles Times* piece lists "monitor[ing] a gay-rights demonstration" among police tasks for the weekend, along with finding lost children, responding to accidents, and "coax[ing] drunk spectators off rooftops."[45] Far from addressing or even naming the protestors' charges alleging state-sanctioned antigay bigotry, the writer portrays a social landscape in which police function as benevolent agents of the benevolent state, saving children and drunks from themselves, and the public from gay activists. And while two articles cite activist invocations of liberty, all nonetheless present the protests primarily as evidence of the general social good: "The crowd was tolerant"; "Police said the protest was broken up peacefully."[46]

These snippets, among other omissions, fail to indicate that all was not peaceful toleration. David Deitcher writes in *The Question of Equality* that "revelers responded to the estimated six thousand queer activists in their mists by bloodying a few noses," "hurling . . . verbal abuse," and tossing a few firecrackers at them. Nor, of course, do they question whether the protest not disrupting the party should be considered good news.[47] "Liberty Shocker: Highest Court Calls Consensual Sex at Home Illegal but People Party on Anyway": Where is that headline? On 2 July the *New York Times* did run an editorial against the decision, which it titled "Crime in the Bedroom." But the article declined to mention Liberty Weekend, an omission that can be seen as commission given the editorial under it about the symbolism of the Fourth's tall ships and fireworks. Even more relevant was the editorial one day later that, in praising the Supreme Court decisions upholding affirmative action and the voting rights act, calls them an important civics lesson for Reagan on Liberty Weekend.[48] Apparently, the lesson of *Bowers v. Hardwick* is supposed to be that (homo)sex belongs off to the side of Liberty. Of course, however, that dismissal defines Liberty as well.

SWEET POVERTY

Ought-to-be-scandals about money also appear as passing tidbits of good news in the literature on Liberty's restoration. Four letters in *Dear Miss Liberty* explain the sender's small contribution in terms of financial problems related to aging: can't find work; cost of retirement home; life on fixed income made more difficult by job-related loss of vision; and ". . . you under-stand. I am now 91," as if it should go without explanation that old age brings hard economic times.[49] In the context of this book where the primary crite-rion for a letter's inclusion is clearly that it be "heartwarming," these state-ments come off as evidence of love for the statue rather than of inexcusable inequities.

Another story about economic inequity that gets folded into touching sentiment concerns a twelve-year-old girl named Hue Cao. A refugee from Vietnam, she was Hawaii's winner in the nationwide state-by-state essay contest on "What the Statue of Liberty Means to Me" (a contest named, to add one emotion-tugger to another, after Christa McAuliffe, the school-teacher killed in the explosion of the space shuttle Challenger). After Hue Cao won, it turned out that she couldn't keep her prize, a $9,000 new car, because having resources above $1,500 would make her family ineligible to continue receiving public assistance. Moved by the story, the state com-mittee auctioned off the car and started a scholarship fund for her with the money. President Reagan congratulated her personally by phone, someone else bought her family a 1980 white Skylark valued at $1,499, and a rich donor paid for her family to stay at a fancy hotel on Liberty Weekend. Then, introduced by Henry Winkler, "the Fonz" from TV's *Happy Days*, she read her essay at the unveiling ceremony.[50]

Unlike the protests about *Bowers v. Hardwick*, which received only brief, trivializing mainstream press coverage in relation to Liberty Weekend, Hue Cao got a lot of media coverage. The issue here is what kind. Like the image of Liberty as a prostitute, which regardless of a dominant interpretive trend could be spun in various and divergent ways, the tale of Hue Cao is inter-esting partly for the range of economic analyses it could easily support. For example, it might well be interpreted to epitomize the gross inequities of capitalism. Some people struggle to subsist, while some have the money to put up others in expensive hotels (or earn $23.6 million a year in com-pensation, as Iacocca did from Chrysler in 1986).[51] Or it might be seen to highlight the failure of "Reaganomics," which gave tax cuts to the wealthy in 1981 and 1982 on the theory that the benefits of economic opportunity for rich people would "trickle down" to everyone. The situation of being too poor to accept free stuff is a perfect illustration of the structural barriers to this hypothesized flow of resources that the term "trickle down" implies to be natural. The spectacle of a heroic refugee on welfare also intrudes into the cast of characters put forth for Liberty Weekend. As the historian Mike Wallace points out in his essay on immigration history at the two sites, the "Reagan/Iacocca" reading of immigration history presented for the occasion has immigrants—including those who might now be characterized as refugees—making it on their own, with the implication that currently struggling residents of the United States, new migrants and otherwise, should be able to pull themselves up without aid, too.[52] During the same year that the Immigration Reform and Control Act, which Reagan signed on 6 November, inscribed several measures to restrict immigrants' eligibility for public assistance,[53] Hue Cao's situation advances the notion, with the emotional nudge of melodrama, not just that public aid for new residents is appropriate but also that current policies to dispense it may even be too stingy.

That these interpretations don't make it to the daily newspapers can be attributed to a number of factors. The first factor is Hue Cao's own interpretation of her current situation, represented in her prize-winning essay:

> My family and I are from Vietnam. After the war ended, the Communists took over and they were very cruel, stern and ill-tempered. They took away our freedom, and worst of all, they could kill anyone. . . . In 1979, we escaped on a small fishing boat, and I remember how crowded it was before a Navy ship saved us. The Americans provided us with food, shelter and clothing. We wanted to live in America, a land where there is liberty and justice. Every time we saw a picture of the Statue of Liberty, my mother would tell us that she is America. America is a place that lends a hand to those in need.[54]

Hue Cao's sense of herself as fortunate is certainly justified and completely understandable, if also ideologically convenient for right-leaning political-economic interpretations. Her linking of communism, privation, and indiscriminate murder, on the one hand, and America, relief from need, and freedom, on the other, lines up nicely with the common misconception that capitalism is the required economic system of democracy. Her ideas obviously appealed to Hawaii's contest judges, who picked the essay over two thousand other entries.

In addition, the dominant themes of Liberty Weekend, besides that mentioned above about immigrants most appropriately struggling to make it, beckon away from interpreting Hue Cao's story as an illustration of inequity. The idea, also dramatized in the big naturalization ceremony, that the United States stands in relation to other countries only as a place of shelter from them or as a model of freedom for them also finds expression in narrations about Hue Cao, which offer no clue that the United States had any role in Vietnam other than to receive its refugees. The idea that rich people make up with gifts for what the government withholds fits right in with restoration rhetoric, too. At the time, the restorations were touted as the epitome of Reagan's "public/private partnership" idea. Tours and texts about both Ellis Island and Liberty Island still frequently explain that "no tax dollars" went into the restorations, with no hint, usually, that the value of privatizing the care of national monuments might be contested—not the least because, as a number of people have argued, sponsorship affects the histories told.[55] In addition, although a portion of the restoration donation narrative, far greater than the portion of the restoration money, concerns poor people sending their pennies, much of the funding narrative builds on the idea that sufficient resources for the social good lie in the benevolence of rich people and corporations willing to step in where the government can't, won't, or thinks it shouldn't have to.[56]

These themes are specific but not unique to Liberty Weekend; they appeared, and continue to appear, in other contexts. As Amber Hollibaugh puts it, narratives of idealized greed and "manipulative 'pity'" predominate in mainstream histories and media as opposed, for instance, to accounts of "collective struggle against injustice or oppression" (think, too, of the underreported Bowers protests) or detailed, respectful accounts of the "too-often-forgotten, ridiculed lives most people lead."[57] Dorothy Allison writes, on a similar topic, about the draw and erasures of the "romanticized, edited version of the poor" that dominate cultural narratives.[58] Add to these dominant themes and characteristic omissions the obfuscating pathos that often attends gifts from the rich to the poor, as if small windfalls could be a solution to problems caused by the inequitable distribution of resources, and it is easy to see how the wonderful fortune bestowed on one fortunate individual might be the winning spin about Hue Cao.[59] (Her story is one of many in the genre of queen-for-a-day economics that is so nicely parodied in the movie *Bring It On* when the cheerleaders from an underfunded "inner-city" school full of black and Latino kids need money to attend the national cheerleading championships. After refusing the corporate philanthropy that a rich, white cheerleader from the predominantly white public school has squeezed for them from her dad, they get their money during "Wish Day" on the "*Pauletta Show*" [Pauletta being in appearance and style a parody of Oprah]; the cheerleaders know that their economic power lies, at best, in determining who gets to be the hero of their weepy public relations moment.[60])

"LIBERTY LOVE BOAT"

In 1997 Liberty's thrusting torch arm was chosen for the cover of R. L. Jones's *Great American Stuff: A Celebration of People, Places and Products that Make Us Happy to Live in America*. In the section on the statue, right before Jones lists her impressive measurements (torch arm: forty-two feet tall), he ponders her official title, *Liberty Enlightening the World*: "She can certainly enlighten us Americans, if we let her, by reminding us of who we really are. And for the rest of you folks huddled somewhere out there on the planet, are there any among you who long for liberty? If so, then we welcome you to join our nation of open-spirited and independent-minded people. There are no racial or religious requirements. All you have to do is want to be American and to unite with us in our quest to build a better world free of superstition and the chains of the past. We'll leave the light on for you."[61]

I don't think it is necessary to comment extensively on the U.S. chauvinism in this passage, although I do enjoy its unintended virtue of stripping a certain rose-coloring sentiment from related representations like the simultaneous mass naturalizations at Ellis Island and the Orange Bowl. I want, instead, to set it against one more Liberty sex work scenario, this one staged in the year after Jones's book came out, by the performance artist and sex worker Annie Sprinkle, with organizational support from Performance Space 122, which was hosting a run of Sprinkle's show *Herstory of Porn*. The announcement, headed "Ahoy! Artists and Sex Workers Unite!" invited people to participate in the "Liberty Love Boat," a "Columbus Day Cruise to the Statue of Liberty to celebrate Freedom of Creative Sexual Expression," and to denounce sexual censorship, including zoning laws generated under the regime of New York Mayor Giuliani to banish the sex industry (especially where Disney might want to set up shop).[62] As Sprinkle recounts, the two hundred people who showed up, "most in 'wild' clothes or costumes" and some with signs, were immediately surrounded by police in cars, boats, and helicopters: "It seemed that because of the way we were dressed, they assumed we were going to bomb the Statue of Liberty." Police also refused to allow even what they perceived as tokens of nonviolent protest: "Although we had a permit to gather and to do a photograph, they said that if we held up our signs they would arrest us. (We would need a different permit for that.) We explained that our signs were photo props not protest signs. That didn't work. We opted not to get arrested and be relatively cooperative." The group circled the statue, passed around the megaphone, and took turns doing their "performances, speeches, rituals." Tourists, Sprinkle writes, were "shocked or delighted," some asking to pose with their families for pictures: "The Goddess of Freedom smiled down upon us."[63]

I have been working in this chapter to identify some of these understandings and silences that contribute to dominant meaning makings about Liberty. As my last two examples can emblematize, accounts of Liberty as available to everyone come up against evidence of exclusionary criteria. Signs saying "Get Sex out of the White House and Back on 42nd St. where it Belongs" (this was the year of the Starr report) or "Support Your Local Porn" herald for some a danger to Liberty, but not too dangerous for the tourist scrapbook, in a way that laws against consensual sex often do not.[64] My purpose in assembling this somewhat idiosyncratic collection of topics circling around the statue material is not to propose one new reading—add these and see exactly this—as much as to suggest how meanings depend on a complex of views and practices that bring gender, sex, money, and race to bear on immigration narratives. I do, however, want to popularize the idea of adding these specific topics to the mix. When people regard Liberty and her big party weekend, I want this material to be as easy to come by as the comments I found all over about Liberty as a victimized prostitute: the gendering of immigrant worthiness; the heterosexualizing of citizens in Chief Justice Burger's trip from Bowers to Ellis; and the situation of being too poor to accept the benefits that allegedly trickle down from the rich.

In the next chapter I turn to one more topic that belongs front and center, which I am far from alone in putting forward: the antislavery activism of Liberty's gift makers. Although *Great American Stuff* offers a relatively common nicety in announcing that there are "no racial . . . requirements" for migration (just a willingness, apparently, to bow to declared U.S. supremacy), its even more common maneuver lies in its author's call to "you folks huddled somewhere out there." By invoking, without naming, Emma Lazarus's "huddled masses," Jones contributes to a tradition of poetic cliché that, in turn, contributes to a tradition that makes of welcoming immigrants the meaning of the statue that goes almost without saying. Comments like these, I will argue, are raced less by a declaration of open arms than by sliding away from the subject of skin.

FOUR

GREEN WOMAN, RACE MATTERS

In his 1984 best-selling autobiography, Lee Iacocca made heavy use of metaphor in describing the organizational problems he encountered when he first arrived at Chrysler Corporation, the company he became famous for saving by securing a controversial federal loan guarantee (or, in the phrasing of critics, engineering a bail-out). After looking around to see "what kind of fraternity" he'd joined, Iacocca found it simultaneously "in a state of anarchy" and "like Italy in the 1860s, a cluster of little duchies, each one run by a prima donna." It was an unstable edifice: there was "no cement in the organizational chart," plus "when the secretaries are goofing off, you know the place has dry rot." Meanwhile, "guys" who apparently "didn't believe in Newton's third law of motion—that for every action there's an equal and opposite reaction" were, consequently, "working in a vacuum." Thus, while "people in engineering and manufacturing almost have to be sleeping together," "these guys weren't even flirting!" Nor did they realize that "you just can't run a big corporation without calling some pregame sessions to do blackboard work."[1] College, government, construction, science, gay sex, and sports all can be found in a two-page span in the book.

As Iacocca's pile-up of clichés well illustrates, the way things go together, or should go together, may be at once seemingly obvious and difficult to specify. In his text, the work of making smooth-looking linkages appears not only through what he finds in disarray but also through what he can take for granted: that "guys" and guy institutions like fraternities and football constitute the primary agents and reference points for corporate structures; that he can use a metaphor of homosex flirting without having readers understand him to be either endorsing homosexual activity or positing the homosocial interactions he seeks as in any way homoerotically formed.[2] Both the connections and their components depend on long-developing ideological, material, and structural formations.

The same is true for the two monuments that became one of Iacocca's next big projects: the Statue of Liberty and Ellis Island. From one angle, their connection is straightforward and plain to see. They have been conjoined as a matter of record since 1965 when President Lyndon Johnson used the 1906 Antiquities Act, which empowers presidents to act by proclamation to create national monuments of significant federal property, to declare Ellis Island part of the Statue of Liberty National Monument.[3] By that point, the thematic logic of their pairing had long been established, and today it is standard fare, often referenced in shorthand through Emma Lazarus's much-memorized poem "The New Colossus."[4] Written in 1883 as part of a fund-raiser for the statue, and inscribed on a bronze plaque on its base, the poem is often used as well to explain Ellis Island and the link between the monuments. To summarize by using some of the poem's most-recited phrases, Ellis Island processed the "huddled masses," the "wretched refuse . . . tempest-tost" that the statue, "Mother of Exiles," "[lifted her] lamp . . . beside the golden door" to welcome. This was the reading emphasized in the 1980s, when the Statue of Liberty–Ellis Island Foundation (SOLEIF), led by Iacocca, oversaw the fund-raising, restoration, and the attendant pomp for their reopenings.

Yet neither the individual monuments nor their connection bear meanings as longstanding or fixed as the easy recourse to poetic cliché might suggest. The smooth surface is misleading. Again, things are more knotty, more twisted and troublesome, and for "knotty reasons both clear and opaque," to borrow apt phrasing used by the artist William Pope.L in a different but related context regarding how people collaborate in fraught inheritance.[5] Most simply with the poem and monuments, the timing is off. Although the phrase "huddled masses" may fittingly caption numerous photographs of migrants approaching, filling, and waiting to be processed at Ellis Island, the poem appeared almost a decade before the migration station at Ellis Island opened. And although Lazarus wrote the poem with one group of immigrants particularly in mind—refugees from Russian pogroms, who would later contribute to Ellis Island's overflow—the connections between the statue, the poem, and the welcome of immigrants did not arrive with Ellis Island.[6] Indeed, as John Higham notes in describing the history of these linkages, the poem was so little known in the first decades of Ellis Island's operation that one immigrant writer suggested in 1906 that someone ought to write a poem about how the statue inspired immigrants.[7] The idea of the statue as a beacon for immigrants, long popular with immigrants from "Old World" countries, did not really burgeon in popular lore, textbook teaching, and Park Service narrative until the 1930s and 1940s, when the poem, too, became standard fare.[8]

In this chapter and the next I consider the sometimes uneasy sometimes overly easy representation of the Statue of Liberty and Ellis Island as paired immigration icons, focusing on the period after the advent of SOLEIF, which greatly contributed to the publicizing of the monuments' conjunction, not the least by using the already famous statue to enhance the name recognition of Ellis Island. I am particularly interested in the race politics that have attended the representation of these monuments as heritage sites of broad public relevance and thus worthy of a massive share of heritage funding by virtue of their relation to immigration and to each other. In this chapter, I look at various takes on whether and how the statue has relevance for African Americans. Against the promotion of the statue as a symbol honoring the United States as "a nation of immigrants" two primary arguments emerged: that the statue, like those who would describe the United States as a nation of immigrants, ignores and disrespects people whose ancestors, transported by force, could not and, importantly, should not, be described as immigrants; and that the reading of the statue as an immigration icon ignores or suppresses the statue's full or partial genesis as an tribute to the end of slavery. I argue here that while one might reasonably doubt certain claims raised sometimes to bolster the latter argument, more important is how the discrediting of those claims is used to relegate a plausible inspiration for the statue to the (race marked) category of urban legend.

I begin, however, by looking briefly at another set of connections that may well deceptively appear smooth: the relationships between SOLEIF and the monuments for which it raises funds. As I will suggest, questions about what the sites honor, played out partly in representations of the monuments' meanings, are complicated by the often mystified paths and structures through which the resources to fund them travel.

The following text appeared in 2002 in SOLEIF's twentieth-anniversary newsletter: "Twenty years ago, in 1982, President Ronald Reagan asked me to head a citizen's group to raise funds for the restoration and preservation of the Statue of Liberty and Ellis Island. The Statue of Liberty–Ellis Island Foundation was soon founded."[9] This text suggests an author in the know about SOLEIF's beginnings, whether the author is, as indicated, Iacocca, or, more likely, the person who wrote "About the Foundation" on SOLEIF's Web site, a text dated 2000 that this one closely approximates. It is all the more interesting then, that the passage does not readily yield up the facts. A different, and well documented, story emerges in the two most detailed accounts of the foundation's beginnings: "The Selling of Miss Liberty," a 1985 *Nation* exposé by Roberta Brandes Gratz and Eric Fettman; and the 1993 book by F. Ross Holland, *Idealists, Scoundrels, and the Lady: An Insider's View of the Statue of Liberty Project*. A meticulous record keeper, Holland was involved with the restorations as assistant director for Cultural Resources for the National Park Service until 1983 and then, after he retired, as director of restoration and preservation for the foundation.[10] According to both sources, the events transpired more like this: In 1982 President Reagan, announcing an appointment made not by him but by the Department of the Interior, of which the National Park Service is a part, named Iacocca to head not the Statue of Liberty–Ellis Island Foundation but the Statue of Liberty–Ellis Island Centennial Commission. Then, with Iacocca's approval, the Statue of Liberty Foundation, Inc. (incorporated in 1981 under the impetus of Richard Rovsek, president of Westport Marketing Group, and involved more with corporate sponsorship than the phrase "citizen's group" might suggest) moved to add Ellis Island to its name and become the primary fund-raiser for the project.

Why tweak the story of origin? Sure, one could, if pressed, defend the truth of the printed account. The text doesn't actually specify that Reagan proffered the very first invitation to Iacocca; certainly he might have said something like "Mr. Iacocca, will you do us the honor?" in the ceremony announcing the already formed commission. Nor does it technically identify SOLEIF as the citizen's group founded; it invites the reader to infer that connection from the succession of sentences. One might also argue that in this slick transition across the punctuation mark from the unnamed "citizen's group" to SOLEIF, the text economically highlights the organization that really matters. Both critics and fans of the man and the foundation generally agree that Iacocca basically ran SOLEIF as soon as he took over the commission, if unofficially, before the foundation elected him president in 1984, and that SOLEIF, not the commission, was the prime mover in the restoration. As Gratz and Fettman note, the commission, packed with celebrities and business people rather than restoration experts, had always been ill suited to direct the show and never really tried to do so. Even by late 1985, they indicate, the commission, although legally required to meet quarterly, had hardly met and had never touched its staff budget. A *Washington Post* piece of 1986, which noted baseball commissioner Peter Ueberroth, the industrialist Pierre DuPont, and Bob Hope and his wife among the commission's members, concurred about its virtual inaction.[11] Interestingly, while *Liberty for All*, Iacocca's 2002 coffee-table book on the Statue of Liberty restoration, says "President Ronald Reagan asked me" twice within the first three text pages, he does name the commission as his appointment. But he then links the creation of the foundation to his discovery that "government panels . . . really can't do much of anything—but give advice! They can't solicit money [maybe not in the way he wanted to], sign contracts [?], negotiate [?] or do a hundred other practical tasks."[12] Apparently, however, the commission did not give advice either.

But the fact that one can coax truth value from SOLEIF's story of origin does not make it less misleading. So why write it that way? Several answers seem plausible. It is more prestigious to have been tapped for leadership by the president than by his underlings—even more so, perhaps, now that time and his illness and death have cast Reagan as a more sympathetic character. The origin of SOLEIF in the mind of Rovsek, previously best known around the White House for running the annual Easter egg rolls, hardly matches up. That genesis is even less appealing if you know that in 1984 the foundation fired Rovsek for acting in conflict of interest; he had contracted his firm to get corporate sponsorship for the restorations, often from clients that Westport already had or would subsequently pursue for more business.[13]

Getting rid of the commission offered diverse benefits as well, partly to Iacocca who got fired from it—although when that news was fresher, Iacocca began his 1989 book *Talking Straight* with his account of the firing, which also concerned conflict of interest. Secretary of the Interior Donald Hodel saw, Iacocca quotes, " 'potential of future conflict or the appearance thereof' " if Iacocca continued to chair both the organization raising the money and the commission that, Iacocca stated, "recommended how to spend it."[14] The commission's erasure also banishes a matter described rather mildly in a *Washington Post* subheadline, "Statue of Liberty's Public Panel Overshadowed by Private Group," as well as with clearer disapproval by the *Nation* authors, who attacked "the downgrading of the role of the commission, a public body operating under a Federal mandate, and the unauthorized takeover by a private group that is legally accountable to no one."[15] Without the commission in the picture, the foundation's ascendancy might look like a product of government intention.

But SOLEIF's prominent role might well appear to be government approved, even without the benefit of narrative disappearing acts, for the same reason that SOLEIF's ascendancy cannot actually be described in terms of a private body overshadowing or taking over a group in a wholly separable public realm. The term governmental does not necessarily mean fully "public," especially when the terms "public" and "private" are used as the articles mentioned above use them: with a "public" that designates "government" against a "private" that designates or connotes "for-profit" (as opposed to designating, say, "home"). With Ellis Island, that particular public has never banished that particular private. Recall that when Ellis Island processed migrants, the government contracted private businesses, including American Express, to provide diverse services, such as money exchange, and to perform certain government functions, such as feeding detainees. Now, think about the Reagan years. To call a private takeover of government functions "unauthorized" suggests a government disapproval that hardly suits the administration. To the contrary, as Holland points out, the Statue of Liberty/Ellis Island project was considered a flagship of Reagan's much-touted "public-private cooperation."

Holland compares Reagan's "public-private cooperation" with George H. Bush's subsequent "thousand points of light"; both were ubiquitous yet vague directives that few knew how to execute.[16] With the restoration project, the combination of vagueness and new permissions created a lot of space for both conflict and profit. Iacocca and SOLEIF maneuvered around that space in all sorts of ways, most amusingly, perhaps, during Iacocca's stint as a self-declared antiprivatization activist. After getting fired from the commission, Iacocca called a press conference to charge that he'd been dismissed for opposing a government plan to privatize most of Ellis Island. When people had submitted plans for the rest of Ellis Island (the part restored for the Ellis Island Immigration Museum being just a fraction of the island's 27.5 acres) the government, he said, favored a proposal calling for a luxury hotel and a convention center. Although the luxury hotel idea had apparently been dead for several years, and although the "ethnic Williamsburg" proposal that Iacocca was said to prefer seems unlikely to have been imagined as a not-for-profit endeavor, Iacocca managed to raise outrage on his and the island's behalf in the name of antiprivatization.[17]

The irony of this posture, of course, lies in Iacocca's more usual public role regarding commercialization: defending SOLEIF against charges of sullying the statue by licensing undignified products with her image and selling various corporations the status of official sponsor, which included the right to use that status in advertising and marketing. Both SOLEIF and Iacocca got a lot of attention for some of these practices because they were relatively new as well as suspect. Corporate sponsorships may today seem ubiquitous, wholly mundane, and of tedious longstanding, now that even LGBT pride events may have "official sponsors" (witness the "Bud Light/*San Francisco Chronicle* main stage" at San Francisco Pride 2000). But sponsorships first gained major attention during the 1984 Olympic Games in Los Angeles, a year after American Express patented the term "cause-related marketing" and launched its first such project on a national scale: donating a penny to the Statue of Liberty restoration project for every use of its credit card, producing a total of $1.7 million for the statue and even greater savings in tax deductions for the company.[18] (Twenty years later, in 2003, the company launched a similar campaign to raise money for the security upgrades required for the statue after it was closed in the aftermath of September 11, 2001, so as to "reopen Lady Liberty" so "you can see up close what our country is made of."[19] There are interesting echoes in this phrasing of both the sexualized access language regarding Liberty and the proprietary voyeurism regarding medical inspections that I discussed earlier.) During the restoration project, SOLEIF was recognized for helping to make common practice what SOLEIF's executive vice president Stephen J. Briganti called a "marriage between proper commercialization and philanthropy" and what an American Express representative, with a laudable refusal to mask a profit motive but perhaps an overblown claim to public service, termed "marketing in the public interest."[20]

As I discussed in chapter 3, many complaints about advertising the Statue of Liberty in these ways focused on the notion that commercialization made unseemly, undignified, and demeaning use of the statue. Critics of "cause-related marketing" in general warned that it would diminish corporate philanthropy, not just the reputation of its more virtue-laden objects. If a corporation could use its giving to generate direct payback, as opposed to the less-certain payoffs of making a good impression through publicized good deeds, why give donations outright at all?[21] Further, with SOLEIF another set of issues emerges about marketing, or fund-raising, in "the public interest": Which public? For both the statue and Ellis Island, the identity of that public has been variously represented both by SOLEIF and by other interested (or disgusted) observers.

GREEN WOMAN

The statue was in between two green phases on Liberty Weekend, with the first hundred years of copper patina cleaned off and the next batch waiting in the weather. But on one level green suits the Statue of Liberty quite well because much race talk around her follows phrases that posit colorblindness as a virtue: "I don't care whether you're white, black, red, blue, green or yellow." One example of that position in literal proximity to Liberty can be seen in the *New York Times* editorial mentioned above, where Reagan gets a Liberty Weekend "civics" lesson from the Supreme Court on Affirmative Action and voting rights. "America," the editorial states, "not only aspires to be a color-blind society, it remains committed to achieving it."[22] Yet if, as this editorial also admits, seeing race is key to fighting racism—one reason among many that one might question failing to see race as the ultimate goal—then statue talk is all the more notable for the skin talk that seems repeatedly to get dismissed.[23]

I say dismissed rather than missing deliberately because skin talk certainly exists and is often easy to find. As Juan Perea points out, race issues appeared early in the statue's history, during the initial fund-raising and inauguration when people protested that Liberty hardly raised her torch for everyone. In 1885, for instance, Saum Song Bo, in "A Chinese View of the Statue of Liberty," criticized the appeals to Chinese people in the United States for contributions to the statue's pedestal fund, given the harsh treatment of Chinese people already living in the United States and the denial of liberty inherent in the Chinese Exclusion Act of 1882, which prevented many other Chinese people from entry.[24]

Related comments attended Liberty's centennial. In *Enacting Political Culture: Rhetorical Transformations of Liberty Weekend*, David Procter documents the extensive commentary in the black press about whether blacks have been included or excluded in the freedoms extolled as American on Liberty Weekend.[25] This issue also got enough mainstream publicity that David Wolper, who produced the extravaganza—and whose previous credits include the sitcom *Welcome Back, Kotter*, the Los Angeles Olympics, and, notably here, the landmark miniseries *Roots*—was called on to stress that "blacks, too, were immigrants to this country." (A generous reading of that comment would be that Wolper was referring to black people who chose to migrate as opposed to lumping enslaved blacks brought to the United States into the category of immigrant.)

Jim Haskins, then in the position of vice director of the southeast region of SOLEIF, also took on the charges. The author of many books on black history for adults and children (the latter including *The Statue of Liberty: America's Proud Lady*, published in 1986), Haskins showed more respect than Wolper for those who argued that it was negligently thoughtless, at best, to declare the United States a nation of immigrants—a rhetorical move that subsumes forced transport for slavery under voluntary immigration. In a June 1986 piece in *U.S. News and World Report*, Haskins admits a basis for why "some black leaders" declined to support the restoration campaign from the position that "blacks came through the back doors of America—the slave markets of New Orleans and Savannah—not Ellis Island." He also notes the "common saying among blacks that she [Liberty] has always had her back to us." But, he states, tweaking the words of Lazarus, even though "the newest Afro-Americans—Haitians, West Indians, Africans and the wretched refuse of other black countries' teeming shores," are now likely to come through Kennedy Airport, not by boat, those immigrants who saw the statue from the plane "must have felt the same swelling of hope as did the shipbound immigrants from Europe."[26]

Hey, "black countries" have teeming shores with wretched refuse now, too, just like the Europeans did before. In arguing that the poem can newly be applied to black immigrants, Haskins points to something frequently camouflaged by the unmarked language ordinarily used to describe Liberty as the welcomer of immigrants; that is, that this dominant device for explaining the statue's meaning as the "Mother of Exiles" welcoming "huddled masses" is rarely racially neutral. Its racial specificity depends partly on the particular immigrants that the poem is generally considered to reference: Ellis Island immigrants, associated primarily with European origin and with groups either already then (e.g., German, English) or later (Irish, Russian, Jewish) generally considered white.[27] Race content also emerges through the dominant statue-poem-Ellis trope by virtue of what it erases: the possibility, which Haskins discusses, that the abolition of slavery was a big part of what inspired Edouard de Laboulaye, the prime mover behind the statue, to propose it.

BLACK STATUE

It is only in *U.S. News and World Report* (suggesting, perhaps, some editorial hedging on the magazine's part rather than the author's assessment) that Jim Haskins describes the celebration of abolition as merely a possible motive. In *America's Proud Lady*, he names it as a definite motive, but one that, he notes, "most people do not realize."[28] He repeats his certainty in an essay on his Web site: "In *The Statue of Liberty: America's Proud Lady*, I state that the impetus for the creation of the statue—and its presentation to the United States of America by the people of France—was the abolition of slavery in the United States. . . . At first, she held a broken chain in her other hand, to symbolize the broken chains of bondage; later, Bartholdi decided she should hold a tablet, inscribed with the date of the Declaration of Independence, and that a fragment of chain would be on the ground, as if she had already thrown it there."[29] Haskins's confidence about his assertion makes sense. The dinner party at which Laboulaye reputedly first proposed, in the presence of the sculptor Bartholdi, to offer the United States a monument to liberty at its 1876 centennial (the project took an extra decade) occurred in 1865, the same year in which the Civil War ended and in which Laboulaye both organized the French Anti-Slavery Society and spearheaded a project to present a commemorative medal to Mary Todd Lincoln. It is hard to imagine that a mere coincidence of timing links the genesis of the statue to the liberty from slavery on which its creators labored. To the contrary, the link seems so solid and causal—at least in terms of revealing part of the statue's origin and intended meaning—that its virtual absence from the staging of Liberty Weekend seems inexcusable.

The primary purpose of Haskins's Web site essay, however, was not primarily to publicize race silence or race content about the statue's relation to slavery. Rather, it was to distance himself from two further claims about the statue's racial inspirations that had then recently found wide circulation through an anonymous e-mail message on the Internet. The first claim in the message was that "the Statue of Liberty was originally a Black woman . . . because the model was Black," which, the e-mail claims, can be verified by looking at two early clay models in the Museum of the City of New York. The second claim was that the statue was commissioned to honor, as the e-mail puts it, "the part that Black soldiers played in the ending of Black African Bondage in the United States." The e-mail attributes at least this second point to Haskins, via a book that the e-mail appears to claim that Haskins wrote: "In a book called 'The Journey of The Songhai People,' according to Dr. Jim Haskins, a member of the National Education Advisory Committee of the Liberty–Ellis Island Committee, professor of English at the University of Florida, and prolific Black author, points out . . . what stimulated the original idea for that 151 foot statue in the harbor."[30] To that, Haskins had a simple response: "I have never written a book entitled *Journey of the Songhai People*."

Haskins's rebuttal seems straightforward enough: it is true, easy to prove, and uncomplicated. But it is actually not at all transparent because of what it omits: that there in fact exists a book called *Journey of the Songhai People*. It was written by members of an Afrocentric organization, the Pan African Federation Organization and published in 1987.[31] As far as I can tell, virtually everyone who uses the fact that Haskins did not write the book to discredit the claims in the e-mail also fails to mention the book's actual existence; only the relatively sympathetic article "Was the Statue of Liberty First Conceived as a Black Woman?" that appeared in *Black History Magazine* takes a different approach by saying that other sources mistakenly credit the text to Haskins.[32] An acknowledgment that the text exists puts the e-mail's claim in a different light by raising the possibility that the e-mail's author is mistaken or sloppy rather than wholly fraudulent or delusional, perhaps accidentally misattributing authorship rather than inventing fake sources. A look at the book suggests something different still: that the e-mail's author intended not to misattribute the book but rather to repeat the book's statement, which the e-mail repeats almost verbatim, that Haskins did make the argument.[33] (In other words, the e-mail author intended to convey that in the book *Journey of the Songhai People*, the authors state that "According to Dr. Jim Haskins, . . .")

Of course, this information doesn't necessarily enhance the e-mail author's reputation. In the worst interpretation it makes the author a sloppy plagiarist, especially because while the e-mail implies, again not necessarily intentionally, that perhaps only the comment about Haskins comes from *Journey of the Songhai People*, virtually all of the text following that comment is almost a direct copy of the book. Alternately, the author might be judged an unintentional plagiarist with a loose interpretation of the rules of citation. Still other possibilities emerge from the format of this essay as a much copied e-mail: its original author might actually be one of the book's authors; someone formally or informally authorized to disseminate that material (from the Pan African Federation Organization, for example); or someone with better citation habits but whose text was revised, in the manner of a game of telephone, as the e-mail circulated.

I give all of these possible interpretations in order to introduce the following argument: the responses to this e-mail are deeply raced on many levels. If I am a person who knows of its textual source, I can understand its misrepresentations as sinister, negligent, or accidental. I can choose, or not, to understand its citational inadequacies in relation to "college kids these days," which has racial content depending on whom one envisions those college kids to be, or through an implied recourse to "human nature." Haven't we all received or transmitted a message that inevitably lost something in the transmission? Depending on my choices, I work to credit, discredit, isolate, or universalize the source of an allegation about neglected black history, the look of which has already been greatly transformed by the attribution to Haskins of *Journey of the Songhai People*. The argument now appears to come from a black man given credentials by the (white-dominated) mainstream—he is a "member of the National Education Advisory Committee of the Liberty–Ellis Island Committee, professor of English at the University of Florida, and prolific Black author," in the e-mail's words—rather than from a cultural and intellectual tradition operating outside it, from a book cited in a preface to it as "a masterpiece of Afrocentrism."[34]

This relocation, however, did not deter one of the e-mail's most prominent and widely quoted commentators, Barbara Mikkelson, from invoking suspect Afrocentrism to denigrate the theory. Mikkelson, as coeditor of the *Urban Legends Reference Pages* Web site, is often cited in the press as an authoritative debunker of prevalent myths. On the Web site she wrote a long essay dismissing the content of the Statue of Liberty e-mail.[35] This essay provides a great example of the contrast between the rhetorical trappings of objectivity, beginning with the site's purpose of delivering truth behind rumors, and the highly subjective use of sources. Despite including a bibliography that is long enough to signal more than cursory research, and a point-by-point analysis of the e-mail's main arguments, Mikkelson neither includes nor even acknowledges the existence of *Journey of the Songhai People*, which would direct interested people to the longer version of the argument. I don't think this is necessarily a sin of commission: I can easily imagine her presuming the title to be utter fabrication because Haskins's disclaimer invites such a reading and because she is so hostile to the e-mail author in general. "If knowledge is power," she begins her assessment after reproducing the e-mail, "then willful misinformation is the work of the Devil. The Dark Prince must have happened upon a pair of idle hands—it's the only possible explanation for the preceding bit of e-lore." Mikkelson's failure to mention the book may reflect the same raced and rage-enhanced lack of care suggested in the unfortunate use of "the Dark Prince" as a nickname for the devil in the context of dismissing black contributions to U.S. history.

I do not give Mikkelson even that much benefit of the doubt concerning another omission: her failure to cite the opinion of Richard Newman, identified as "a research officer at Harvard University's W. E. B. DuBois Institute for African American Research" in a widely circulated Associated Press story about revisiting the Statue of Liberty's origin that appeared in newspapers around 8 February 2000.[36] This article focuses on the most immediately plausible of the e-mail's claims, that "Lady Liberty may have been intended, at least in part, as a monument to freed black slaves," and recounts Newman's assertion that the claim has a longstanding and academic pedigree: that "it is widely believed [a bit of editorial hedging there?] in academic circles that Laboulaye meant for the statue to honor the slaves, as well as mark the recent Union victory in the Civil War and the life of Abraham Lincoln." (Recall that one such long-standing believer was Haskins, whose texts on the matter date from 1986.) Mikkelson must have known of this Harvard-linked opinion, although most of her piece must have preceded the AP article. David Emery, whose text about the matter for the "Urban Legends" section of About.com ("Dateline: 02/09/00,") appeared right after the AP story, gives Mikkelson "kudos for the earliest efforts to prove the rumor true or false" and quotes her extensively. But whereas Emery picks up the reference to Newman, the reference is ignored in Mikkelson's text, which is first marked as "updated" five days, and subsequently three years, after Emery's text.

In contrast, Mikkelson gives significant attention, 172 words to be exact, to someone who a decade earlier had advocated for revising the history of the Statue of Liberty: Leonard Jeffries, the controversial promoter of Afrocentrism who was then chair of the Black Studies Program at the City College of New York. Linking the alleged "canard" to Jeffries, Mikkelson reminds readers of Jeffries's anti-Semitism and other apparent manifestations of unreasoned prejudice and "erroneous, racially-biased statements," including "the notion that AIDS was invented by 'rich white folks' plotting against people of color, and that CCNY is controlled by a secret Jewish organization called 'The Cabala.'" To add further authority to her dismissal of him, she then cites the shocked ridicule of Jeffries in the *New York Times* in 1991.[37]

I do not intend here, of course, to reverse Mikkelson's maneuver: to use Jeffries to enhance by association the challenges to the race content of the statue's origins. My purpose instead concerns the race content of Mikkelson's own representational strategies, despite her own frustrated assertion that the attribution of race content is the problem. "What seems to have eluded Jeffries and others," she admonishes, "is that whatever the color of the person who served as the model for the Statue of Liberty may have been, the statue itself is colorless. It does not represent a particular color of person any more than the Michelin Tire Man does" (a worthy comparison to be sure). Yet as Manning Marable states, making a reference to Jeffries is by now a standard device for discrediting claims about the neglect of black history and about African American studies in general.[38] Mikkelson's invocation of a theory about AIDS that is sometimes presented as a conspiracy theory foolishly believed by black people, who, in turn, are often portrayed as the most sympathetic audience for "urban legends," reminds us that ascribing the label "urban legend" to a theory may itself involve a race-coded dismissal.

Meanwhile, Mikkelson skips the guy whose Harvard affiliation represents the (white-formed) pinnacle of academic credibility, and finds a way to reroute Haskins, too. Haskins's disdain for the black soldier and black model theories makes him essential to her essay, but she doesn't much care for his views on the connection to slavery. So she suggests that the broken chains he mentions might just as easily symbolize other new freedoms: "Broken chains fit the statue's theme, whether the message of liberty gained is applied to America's independence from Britain, France's then recent struggle with Prussia, or the freeing of African Americans from slavery." She then suggests how one might go along with Haskins's claim that the end of slavery was the "impetus" for the statue: "Possibly France did not feel America deserved a monument dedicated to freedom as long as a significant portion of its population was enslaved. That is not to say the Statue was dedicated to the abolition of slavery (else Liberty's tablet would surely have been emblazoned with the date of emancipation, not the date of its formal break from Britain), but that this happy change of affairs inspired some of those behind the gift to support the project." Mikkelson's point about the date may bear consideration, although it can be handily dispensed with if one entertains the possibility that Laboulaye wanted to honor the end of slavery with the gift of a statue commemorating the U.S. centennial. This is one of those points, like how one interprets the e-mail's citation failures, which shows how politics may attend awarding the benefit of the doubt. But the rest of Mikkelson's statement looks primarily like a convolution of logic designed to hang on to the one black scholar she found who could give credential to her view.

FADE TO IMMIGRANT

The failure of Mikkelson and Haskins to direct attention to the possibility of reading *Journey of the Songhai People* doesn't necessarily hurt the cause of the author of the anonymous e-mail on the role of black influence on the statue. Some of the claims found in *Journey of the Songhai People,* including an argument about blacks having the most evolved hair to protect the most evolved brain, provide a less-than-ideal context for considering its more substantive arguments.[39] The contentions about the black soldiers and black model seem difficult to back up and are ill served by the book's illustrations. A line drawing depicting "the original model of the Statue of Liberty," I suspect, would fail to convince skeptical readers; the difference between the rendering of Liberty's nostrils and lips and the view offered by a typical photograph of Liberty's face suggests artistic distortion to invoke African descent.

Nonetheless, the book offers, as shown in the following text, an assessment of the Statue of Liberty centennial events that is right on target in alleging that it was a controlled media event, underwritten by big business, that was scripted to emphasize European immigrants and to ignore any connection to the events of the Civil War:

> During the summer of 1986, a nationwide celebration of the Statue of Liberty took place in the United States, and was widely televised over ABC network as the world watched the ABC production. The ABC production coincided with the big business financing of the renovation of the century-old Statue. The whole celebration had to do with the landing of European immigrants in America, their feelings, their emotional ties to the Lady in the Harbor, how they felt, and what it meant to them. No mention was made to our knowledge about the real reason for the Statue of Liberty—the celebration of the winning of the war by Black soldiers.[40]

As I discussed in chapter 3, SOLEIF, despite promoting the idea that the statue was refurbished through small donations from a loving public, drew much of its funding by soliciting corporate sponsorship. Some of this funding was hard to miss since it came with advertising rights that companies like American Express, Stroh's, and Oscar Meyer were quick to make use of; other corporations, like the U.S. Tobacco Company from which Iacocca solicited $10 million,[41] did not get the same publicity for their money. Money was also raised by SOLEIF through the sale to ABC of the television coverage rights to Liberty Weekend. The sum of $10 million was paid by ABC for "exclusive broadcast rights," which set off a conflict about the commodification of broadcast news after it was revealed that ABC planned to offer CBS, NBC, and CNN only nine to ten minutes of footage, which was to include Reagan's relighting of the torch and the massive naturalization ceremony led by Chief Justice Warren Burger on Ellis Island, but not, for instance, the appearance by French president François Mitterand, which is arguably different than the appearance of entertainers like Frank Sinatra, or the awarding of Medals of Honor to twelve naturalized citizens.[42] Eventually ABC handed over Mitterand but kept the medal ceremony for itself.

The argument that Liberty Weekend was predominantly focused on immigrants finds one element of support, among many, in the fight over the coverage of ceremonies about them. More evidence exists in the sheer volume of immigrant narratives in the coverage linked to Liberty Weekend, which the *Songhai People* catches with its description at once humorous and weary in its repetitiousness of the focus on immigrant emotions: "Their feelings, their emotional ties to the Lady in the Harbor, how they felt, and what it meant to them." Meanwhile, the silence in the mainstream press testifies to the absence of publicity regarding even the point asserted by Haskins, that the end of slavery in the United States provided the impetus for Liberty. So, too, does the argument Haskins cites, in order to counter it, that the statue has no relevance for black people whose ancestors' passage wasn't voluntary.

What I want to emphasize here, however, is not the merits of this particular source, *Journey of the Songhai People*, although I find the trashing of it significant and inappropriate, but the erasures in which it has been enmeshed. These erasures persist despite the increasing challenge to address them in the years since the statue's restoration. Evidence of significant and by now long-standing, if circumscribed, attention to the black Statue of Liberty appears in Haskins's annoyed comment on his Web site about the Museum of the City of New York receiving inquiries for "the past dozen years," and in Mikkelson's essay, which locates Jefferies's public enthusiasm for the idea in 1991. By 2000, the e-mail had generated enough publicity that the National Park Service agreed to look into it, ABC news and an AP story had spread it in the mainstream press, and McDonald's saw enough of a market for the image to put coloring books with a black Statue of Liberty in some of its Happy Meals.[43] In addition, no matter how plausible one deems the argument about the black soldiers or the black model, there is really no reason to question whether Laboulaye—chairman of the French Anti-Slavery Society, as sources on the statue ranging from *Songhai People* to PBS indicate—saw the abolition of slavery as one reason that he wanted to present a statue to the United States that would honor, as the school books say, the friendship between the two nations. Information is also readily accessible that the statue was not originally about immigrants.

Thus, every immigrants-only reading of the statue needs to be understood in relation to the absence of readily available and credible material tying the statue to slavery. This absence constitutes just one element in the racial profiling of those on whom Liberty smiles, which may change in various contexts, depending on matters such as the racing of immigrants, often perceived as dark themselves, and on other circumstances. On 20 December 2001, for instance, the day Liberty Island reopened after the events of 9/11, Al Roker said on the *Today* show that the statue "welcomed immigrants on the way to Ellis Island from 1890 to 1954," a description in notable contrast with Katie Couric's identification of "Lady Liberty" on the *Today* show episode of the previous Fourth of July as a "symbol for millions of immigrants." Couric had vaguely suggested Liberty's continuing and general welcome, although, interestingly, the remark introduced a story about white U.S. parents adopting equally light-skinned Siberian children. Roker's comments, in contrast, implied that the welcome of immigrants ended after Ellis Island closed, and consequently before the subsequent influxes of non-European migrants, who are now labeled dark and dangerous increasingly on the surface of discourse and policy. Clearly, with the *Today* scriptwriters, telling omissions that whiten the statue, besides the absence of abolition, concern the particular migrants presented.

RETURN TO SCANDAL

In the book *Seeing a Color-Blind Future: The Paradox of Race*, Patricia Williams suggests an affinity between silences about sex and about race: "In a sense, race matters are resented and repressed in much the same way as matters of sex and scandal: the subject is considered a rude and transgressive one in mixed company, a matter whose observation is sometimes inevitable, but about which, once seen, little should be heard nonetheless."[44]

I want to posit something related to this statement but also a bit different regarding the statue's relation to sex, race, and scandal. In the last chapter I suggested that the scandal of Liberty as a hooker stood in the place of certain matters about sex and money that ought to be considered scandalous but frequently are not. Into the struggle over whether the statue is fundamentally white or black (or "colorless," as Mikkelson chastised "Jeffries and others" to realize) I want to place something that is often considered scandalous but shouldn't be: the reality of racial mixing. Liberty's history, like much about race, simply isn't just black or white, for a number of reasons. The first reason is that people beyond those often designated by the terms "black" and "white" are involved. I have indicated earlier several instances involving issues and people beyond those categories, like the connections made to the Chinese Exclusion Acts in the 1880s and the case a hundred years later of the Vietnamese refugee Hue Cao, who won an essay contest about the statue but was not able to keep the car she won without jeopardizing her family's public assistance. The second reason is that terms like "black" and "white" imply only fictively the ability to place people in wholly separable groups. Whites and blacks, slaves and immigrants, people of European descent and people of African descent—the groups often set in opposition to each other in debates about Liberty—cannot actually be presumed to be wholly distinct. Nor can narrations about them. "In what public discourse," asks Toni Morrison, "does the reference to black people not exist?" Among her examples she cites the presence of black people as referents in the framing of the Constitution, in battles over the enfranchisement of people disenfranchised on diverse grounds, and "the preeminent narrative that accompanies (if it does not precede) the initiation of every immigrant into the community of American citizens."[45] Regarding racial mixing, an example comes from Liberty's sculptural parentage. Whether or not a black model posed at any stage it remains known—if, very significantly, unheralded—that Liberty most immediately descends from a proposed statue commemorating the opening of the Suez Canal that Bartholdi, in the late 1860s, tried to get the khedive Isma'il Pasha of Egypt to commission. The models for *Egypt Carrying the Light to Asia*, a colossal figure of an Egyptian peasant woman in traditional dress holding a lantern, look not quite white but quite like the statue.

The third reason is that ethnic and racial groups have pasts and presents that form and transform in relation to each other (and to others, of course). I offer below one example of these mutually forming connections that also demonstrates, both in its content and in the manner through which I began to consider it, how the politics of racing the Statue of Liberty may be fraught with the politics of racial conflict today. During my research, a Statue of Liberty scholar, trying to hand me a tip, said, "Emma Lazarus's father made his money in sugar refining and you know that money's not clean," referring to the dependence of the sugar economy on the plantation labor of enslaved people. "That's really interesting," I replied. "So why didn't you write about this?" I didn't get much of an answer. But the answer lies, I presume, in the ugliness that might result from calling a Jewish poet-hero a virtual slaveholder, especially in light of the recent inaccurate accusations that Jews constituted the primary actors regarding slaveholding.[46]

I understand wanting to avoid being the bearer of that message about Emma Lazarus, even though the information raises complicating issues worthy of discussion, including many concerning race attribution, money, and dirt. Plantation money is not clean, to be sure, but when are Jews or their relationship to money ever considered clean? Or blacks or their relationship to money? As Anne McClintock points out, concerning the "Victorian dirt fetish," the nineteenth century witnessed an increasing attention to dirt, which she links to a "poetics of surveillance" regarding the transgression of social boundaries. Concepts of " 'dirty' sex" (including masturbation, prostitution, and deviations from heteronormativity) and " 'dirty' money" ("associated with prostitutes, Jews, gamblers, thieves") mapped sex and money onto naturalized racial distinctions that connected dark skin itself with dirt.[47]

Neither Lazarus nor her family's money can be viewed as having, or maintaining over history, a secure hold on the notion of "clean." This is one reason, perhaps, that the fact that Lazarus was Jewish is not so well known. At least it doesn't seem to be well known, according to the highly informal polling I did by querying friends, family members, the audiences in talks I gave, and so forth. Many people did not know, even if they could name her as the author of the "huddled masses" poem or were very big into the "did you know Lou Reed was Jewish?" type of pride activity that is gently satirized (and perpetuated) through venues such as Adam Sandler's Hanukkah song. Although information always drops out in the transmission of popular history (the poem's phrases without the poem, the poem without the author, the author without her history), the lack of publicity concerning Lazarus's Jewish identity is worth noting, both because it links her to a large group of Ellis Island immigrants whom the poem is understood to invoke and, especially, because her interest in penning the poem was directly related to her involvement with the plight of Jewish refugees fleeing pogroms in Russia.

At the same time, if dirty money binds Jews to other people judged to be racially inferior, partly because Jews are perceived as dark and with the result of making Jews appear even darker, it hardly authorizes any equations among Jews and other racialized groups. Plantation money betokens the enslaving of people who functioned thereby as commodities and capital, with circumscribed relations to commodities as well.[48] Using reviled money or capital, being reviled for having money or capital, or spending money to abet or participate directly in practices that are, justifiably or not, reviled—none of these are equivalent. Nor do perceptions of dirty money play out the same way across categories of suspects among people not enslaved. As Regina Austin persuasively argues about the contemporary United States, blacks are routinely considered suspect, sometimes criminal, both for having money and for virtually every way they might use it: buying, selling, engaging in entrepreneurship.[49] The accusations, discussed in the previous chapter, about "sham marriages between illegal Pakistanis and welfare mothers" in the hearings for the 1986 Immigration Marriage Fraud Amendments offer another example of how dirty money is specified racially, as well as in relation to sexuality, race, and nation.

GREEN MONEY, RACE MATTERS

The symbology of money as clean or dirty, and the race content of that opposition, are certainly two elements in the knotty mess of meanings surrounding the Statue of Liberty that bear on issues of race. But the statue raises a far more direct issue regarding race and money. Money, whether symbolically clean or dirty, constitutes a resource that the spender who spends in one place will not have to spend in another. The Statue of Liberty restoration depended on corporate, private, and government money. Thus different readings of the statue change the answer to the following important question: Whose heritage were these resources being marshaled to honor? Ronald

Reagan could say that Liberty is "everybody's gal," but the universal rele-vance falters when boosters promote the statue in terms of "America" as "a nation of immigrants." This narrowing can be considered especially galling since it ignores not only the fact that the United States is not wholly a na-tion of immigrants but also the information that could publicize the statue's relevance to people whose ancestors came to the United States through the Middle Passage.

This issue about resources is even more complicated regarding the Statue of Liberty, however, because much of the money raised for the statue was not merely going into a monument publicized in relation to Ellis Island; it was actually going into Ellis Island. When SOLEIF began its campaign, Ellis Island had a much-lower level of name recognition than it does today. According to Holland, an early study by SOLEIF showed that 20 percent of people recognized Ellis Island, whereas 75 percent recognized the statue.[50] Thus SOLEIF, charged with funding the restoration of both monuments, quite logically focused its campaign on the statue (also the monument with the first centennial year) in its early fund-raising, promoting the Ellis Island connection as it went along but emphasizing the statue as being what the money was for. "Official sponsors" generally focused on the statue, too.

The result, as some critics have suggested, is that many people who do-nated to SOLEIF with the intention of contributing to the statue's restora-tion might have been surprised to learn that most of the money raised was going to Ellis Island. Less than a third of the $277 million raised that was announced by Iacocca on 1 July 1986 went to restore the statue.[51] Thus, the issue is not just that people were encouraged to see the statue as welcom-ing immigrants but also that whatever vision of the statue might have in-spired someone to donate to her cause—immigration icon, testimony to the end of slavery, gracious lady, hot butch, abstraction of Liberty, America, freedom, whatever—the money went largely to the cause of honoring Ellis Island immigrants.

One might think, then, of SOLEIF's general disinterest in the connection of Liberty's history to the abolition of slavery as, in one sense, all for the best. The emphasis placed by SOLEIF on the statue's importance for immigrants winds up gesturing, if sideways, to where most of the money raised for the statue went anyway: to restore an immigrant processing station. Trumpet-ing the end of abolition as a core referent would have mystified the actual money path, and, consequently, prevented some donors from putting heritage money where they want it to go. I do not presume here that African Americans would not want to honor immigrants, or that people who want to honor immigrants would not want to honor abolition, or that people of African descent never voluntarily migrated to the United States. I presume simply that it might be galling for anyone to believe oneself donating to one heritage project and find one's money serving another, even if one might want to contribute to that other one, too.

But that version of all for the best is far from good because the "nation of immigrants" narrative rests on appalling erasures and on the very disturbing if tacit premise that the "nation of immigrants" can be called everybody's history while slavery and abolition constitute black history, of interest and constitutive relevance for black people only. The treatment of subsequent debates over the importance of Civil War history and the racial identity of the statue's model further perpetuates this notion, especially when commentators choose to invoke as a primary proponent one of the most discredited Afrocentrists. Claims about neglected history concerning black people come to look like the machinations of a special-interest lobby, with all the connotations attached to the term about selfish priorities impeding the common good. One might argue, to the contrary, that it is the erasures of abolition from the genesis of the statue that constitute the work of just such a special-interest lobby. How lovely for white people if the inconvenient history of slaveholding does not have to mar our celebration.

What happens when the centennial bash is over? Since the biggest twist in the money path up to that point was the rerouting to Ellis Island of many donations made with an eye on the statue, one might expect that SOLEIF's subsequent fund-raising strategies would be relatively direct: raise funds about Ellis Island for Ellis Island. Instead, the slippages between migrants and immigrants play out in a different way, along with competing claims about whether the Ellis Island Immigration Museum is a museum about Ellis Island or, as the canned announcement on the ferry to Ellis Island calls it, "the American Museum of Immigration." In the next chapter, I turn to these slippages as they are seen to be at work in one of SOLEIF's later projects: the American Immigrant Wall of Honor.

FIVE

A NATION OF IMMIGRANTS,

OR WHATEVER

During my research for this volume, whether chatting up Park Service employees or talking to them in more formal interview situations, I found two sure signs of the tensions between the Park Service and the Statue of Liberty–Ellis Island Foundation, both of which could be expected in light of the foundation's early history with the government. First, when I asked Park Service higher-ups at Ellis Island about the relationship between the foundation and the Park Service, they immediately deflected my question by offering some terse phrase such as "fine" to indicate that there was nothing to tell, or at least nothing to tell me. In fact, this was one of two subjects of inquiry, the other being the park police, that were most likely to generate suspicion about my motives or my "real topic": in order to avoid shutting down the interview I would have to back away from the forbidden territory.

The second sign of tension was evident in the fact that lower-ranked rangers, those in front-line contact with the public, often had a lot to say about SOLEIF. Several of these rangers wanted to hand me leads, including one who jokingly told me to call him "Deep Throat," alluding to the famous and still-unidentified Watergate informant. In general, these leads alleged that the foundation raised money to keep itself in business rather than to support the monuments. Some rangers pointed to the foundation's lack of thrift. Ask yourself, one said, why SOLEIF maintains its corporate office on prime Manhattan property, in high-rent midtown, rather than somewhere less pricey—or rather than simply on Ellis Island. This fact is true; SOLEIF's office is located on Madison Avenue near 41st Street. Another ranger pointed out that SOLEIF does not participate in the Combined Federal Campaign

(CFC), a group of charitable organizations to which government employees may contribute through a payroll deduction. The foundation doesn't qualify, the ranger said, because organizations must have operating expenses of no more than 25 percent to be eligible, and SOLEIF doesn't come close to that figure. The ingredients of this point are true, too. The government has the 25 percent limit, and SOLEIF, which has larger operating expenses than 25 percent, isn't on the CFC list, which includes well over a thousand organizations, national and local, some with goals related to that of SOLEIF, such as the Yellowstone Park Foundation and Friends of the National Parks at Gettysburg.[1]

Implict in these complaints was the question that made the alleged foundation practices seem especially like hoarding: Where was the money going? Not to more renovation: to the contrary, one ranger said, earlier talk about raising money to restore other buildings had faded. Not to the benefit of visitors, whom SOLEIF arguably viewed primarily as the source rather than the beneficiary of funds. One ranger told me that foundation greed almost derailed the American Family Immigration History Center (AFHIC). The Church of Jesus Christ of Latter-day Saints (more commonly known as the Mormon Church) provided much of the labor involved in transferring the twenty-five million names from 3.5 million ship manifests to the AFHIC database.[2] According to this ranger, the Mormons almost pulled out of the project because SOLEIF wanted to charge for all access to the database, while the Mormons, who pursue genealogical information as part of a religious project to baptize after death people who died outside the faith, believe access to genealogical information should be free. (The current situation suggests a compromise: access is now free if done offsite, but there is a charge of $5 for thirty minutes to use the computers at the AFHIC facilities at the museum.)

Further, the money did not seem to be spent to benefit employees; indeed, the rangers often thought that SOLEIF was out to push them aside. Several, for instance, told me that while rangers used to perform in an on-site play, the production then current, *Embracing Freedom: The Immigrant Journey to America*, is fully a foundation production, meaning $5 per ticket for the foundation and fewer labor hours available to rangers. Workers employed by SOLEIF were not all satisfied either. In August 2002, the actors in *Embracing Freedom* voted to unionize, citing among their problems the lack of health benefits, pensions, and respect given to them. Peg Zitko, communications director for SOLEIF, challenged comments that SOLEIF had, ironically enough considering Ellis Island's themes of freedom and betterment, discouraged actors from exercising their rights to unionize. The fact remains, however, that the union vote had to occur because SOLEIF refused the workers' request that it recognize a union without a vote.[3] One actor described to me another problem, this one linked to meeting the expectations regarding costumed employees that visitors might have developed at other heritage sites, like Colonial Williamsburg, or at other tourist venues, like Disney World. Seeing the actor at the snack shop after a show I attended, I asked whether visitors ever followed up on the introductory announcement that while cameras couldn't be used during the play, actors would happily pose with visitors for pictures afterward. They did, she answered, but the actors hated it. With so little time between performances, and much of that time assigned to hawking the show, posing (like answering my questions) made their already small breaks miniscule.

The park rangers hardly saw SOLEIF as their only source of problems on the job; complaints about the foundation were among the many others that concerned the various people and institutions with power over their work environment, including the Park Service and, more generally, the federal government. Yet the complaints also fit with other evidence and allegations about SOLEIF that combine to suggest that now, even more than during the restorations, SOLEIF's interests seem often to float free of the monuments and government body it was founded to serve. Regarding the statue, the issue flared up again in the first months of 2004, when critics blamed SOLEIF for the continuing delay in reopening the Statue of Liberty after the events of 9/11. Why had the foundation embarked on a new fund-raising project for upgrading security rather than using money from its considerable endowment or the money apparently available to award its president over $340,000 in annual compensation?[4] Regarding Ellis Island, additional evidence exists on the Web site ellisisland.org. Devoted almost entirely to the American Family Immigration History Center, the site encourages its visitors to look up immigrant ancestors who came through Ellis Island, to buy documentlike memorabilia to commemorate their finds, and to spend money on celebrating heritage in several other ways. The site does little, however, to generate interest in learning about or visiting Ellis Island. It is, instead, Aramark's Web site, ellisisland.com, that offers significant historical information—along with information, of course, about Aramak's money-making ventures at Ellis Island: on snack and souvenir vendors, or on renting the registry room for charity galas. The difference here, then, is not in motives of altruism but in the fact that Aramark makes most of its money from Ellis Island when people show up at the site.[5] The seeming detachment exhibited by SOLEIF also stands out in contrast, for instance, to the Colonial Williamsburg Foundation, which makes a significant effort to recruit visitors and also reminds purchasers with a message on every receipt for a meal, a hotel room, a souvenir, or an event ticket that their purchase contributes to "the funds necessary for preserving and maintaining the Historic Area."[6]

Yet no matter how detached are SOLEIF's interests, they are, at Ellis Island, simultaneously in your face—at least at the entrance, where costumed actors roam with billboards hawking the play, and computers, kiosks, and information desks direct attention to two of SOLEIF's money makers, the American Family Immigration History Center and the American Immigrant Wall of Honor. In this chapter I consider SOLEIF's contribution to the production of meanings and experiences at Ellis Island by looking closely at the content, reception, and success of the Wall of Honor. Besides discussing the wall's contribution to centering the focus of visitors on personal history, I argue that SOLEIF contributes to proliferating a lack of clarity about the subject of the wall and the museum that has racial content and racial consequences.

HISTORY FOR ONE

I have already discussed two areas of concern raised by critics of SOLEIF's fund-raising tactics: the effects of crass commercialism on Liberty's image, and the long-term transformation of corporate philanthropy by strategies like official sponsorships and cause-related marketing, which invite donors to expect more tangible returns than good will. Lynn Johnson addresses another concern in her 1984 essay "Ellis Island: Historic Preservation from the Supply Side," which was published six years before the Ellis Island museum opened. In the essay she points out that the risks in involving commercial enterprise include more than a distasteful commercialization on the order of "McEllis Island," as a cartoon in the essay puts it, or "Immigrationland," the theme park—a formulation that suggests history and commercialism as separate entities jockeying for position (interpretive programs over here, vendors over there). Instead, she emphasizes, when private money sponsors historical sites, the sponsors affect how history is presented.

Johnson presents this warning even as she acknowledges the appeal of pulling in supplemental funds. Having interviewed David Moffitt, then superintendent of the Statue of Liberty National Monument, she described as "mind-boggling" the interpretive materials and programming that a then-projected $191 million could buy. She also quoted Moffitt's speculation that if some parts of the island were leased for compatible commercial purposes (the "ethnic Williamsburg" idea again), the benefits could extend beyond support for Ellis Island: "'We can then take that money and put it to use in preserving other historical property that might not have the glamour that Ellis Island does . . . places like the Women's Rights Park up at Seneca Falls.'"[7] Moffitt could advance that possibility because of the 1980 National Historic Preservation Act, which, as Johnson explains, enabled the Park Service to recoup for historic preservation money raised from leasing historic structures. By that logic, money raised at one site could help another (arguably the way that much of the money for Ellis Island's restoration was raised), although I can't help wondering how much Moffitt actually envisioned working this new opportunity in the particular way that he mentioned. While the opening of the park at Seneca Falls, designated a National Historic Park in 1980 and opened to the public in 1993, was, in fact, a Park Service project running simultaneously with the Ellis Island project, a professed interest in funneling money to Seneca Falls might well have been a strategic move during an interview with a female scholar perhaps visibly skeptical about some of the Park Service's proposed commercial endeavors.

Whatever the sincerity or smarminess of Moffitt's Seneca Falls reference, on which Johnson doesn't comment, and regardless of what I assume to be Moffitt's genuine dedication to enhancing Ellis Island's educational offerings in the face of shrinking public funds, Johnson still saw risks attending the prospect of private and commercial funding. Working from historian Mike Wallace's argument that history museums have been "'constructed by members of dominant classes, and embodied interpretations that supported their sponsors' privileged positions,'" Johnson saw at Ellis Island a new stage, where "the dominant class control of history is being codified under the auspices of the federal government."[8] The problems that Johnson predicted for Ellis Island include the pressure to recount immigration primarily as a history of noble individuals from quaint traditions who triumph through personal endeavor to achieve the American dream, as well as the omission of political context even regarding the much-emphasized "contributions" of immigrants. As she sums up the issue: "Lee Iacocca has said that Ellis Island should show 'what the immigrants brought with them.' If so, radical political traditions should be valued and preserved just as much as rural handicrafts."[9]

Johnson also points out that the impulse to embrace "ethnic populism — a history of the American Dream as told from the threshold" is "by no means a strictly top-down phenomenon." Witness, she said, people pouring into the Lower East Side neighborhoods where their ancestors lived to experience a "sanitized, commodified ethnic history." Merchants and visitors alike bear responsibility for perpetuating a "noble suffering mythology" about the individual struggling against the odds.[10] As Johnson's comments imply, this concept of the heroic individual as the moving force in social history gains strength when people engage in the study of history primarily in order to understand themselves. According to the research of Roy Rosenzweig and David Thelen, many people study history for such reasons. Surveying people's interest in history in *The Presence of the Past: Popular Uses of History in American Life*, they found that an interest in one's own family history provided the dominant motivating force for studying the past. For many white people especially, family history was also often the main point: they primarily used history to reference or explain their own or their family's past. In contrast, the African Americans and Native Americans whom the authors studied "drew on and constructed a much wider set of usable pasts, building ties to their communities as well as their families."[11] Rosenzweig and Thelen also note that the African Americans often engaged in heritage or history tourism much more deliberately than white people.[12]

The findings described in *The Presence of the Past* may help to explain the multibillion-hit appeal of ellisisland.org. Following a huge publicity blitz on morning talk shows and so forth, the Web site was immediately flooded with people looking for their Ellis Island ancestors: the site received 72,000 hits per second when it opened on 21 April 2003, and 2.5 billion hits total in its first year of operation.[13] At the site, SOLEIF's emphasis on people finding "new insights into their family's pasts—and into themselves" would seem to strike just the right note. The activities and products SOLEIF offers to investigate and honor ancestors address visitors primarily as individuals who act as individuals, buy for individuals, and research individuals, with individuals implied to be connected to social systems primarily as parts of family units: branch out to the family in order to return to the self. Not even the basic information about Ellis Island, or much of that about immigration, encourages people to think outside that loop.

PAYING FOR POSTERITY

In its physical context at Ellis Island the American Immigrant Wall of Honor achieves an effect similar to the Web site to the extent that finding the names of family members becomes a dominant activity. A park ranger I interviewed in September 2000 told me, with just a bit of annoyed exaggeration, that the question that visitors most frequently ask him (after "Where's the bathroom?") is "Where is the Wall of Honor?"[14] I was not surprised by his statement because I had already seen the attention received by the wall, both from the people who knew of it before arriving and those who learned of it on-site. The Wall of Honor is a large steel structure made of conjoined arced panels inscribed with the names that people paid $100 to have inscribed there (figure 16). The $100 also buys an "Official Certificate of Registration," indicating the honoree's name and country of origin, and a place on the list on a special Web site.

A fund-raising idea by Iacocca, the wall turned out to be more successful than anyone predicted. By the time of the museum's opening in 1990, the first list of names, according to Holland, was inscribed on copper plates placed on top of the sea wall around Ellis Island. So many people participated, however, that SOLEIF decided to continue the fundraiser.[15] By 1993, the names were displayed on a freestanding steel structure placed on the grounds behind the administration building. This structure initially contained panels 7–484; two more sets appeared in 1995 and 1998 (485–579 and 581–650). A brochure I first picked up at the museum in 1999, and then in 2000 and 2001, announced the "new Millennium edition" across the bottom right-hand corner, a next set of panels to be added by the end of 2001.

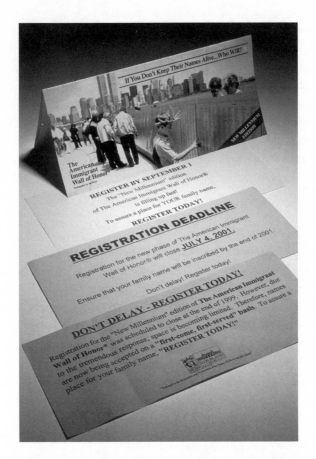

FIGURE 16. Pamphlet and inserts for the American Immigrant
Wall of Honor, 2000. (Photograph by Robert Diamante)

The brochure I picked up in 2002, updated to account for the 2001 opening of the American Family Immigration History Center, specified that the
wall already had more than 600,000 names. The financial statement produced by SOLEIF for the fiscal year ending in March 2002 indicated that the
wall continued to attract interest and had raised over a million dollars during that year as well as in the year before.[16] The Web site, wallofhonor.com,
stated in May 2003 SOLEIF's intention to add the newest list of names by
the end of that year.

Visitors, donors, Ellis Island, the wall: connections among them vary.

Many of the wall's donors no doubt gave money with no intention or expectation of ever seeing it, or with intentions that remain unmet. Some donors, surely, would have visited Ellis Island regardless of their participation. Others come to Ellis Island primarily to see the wall, often to look up the names they paid for. One such family I met lived not so far away on Long Island, but had never thought of traveling to Ellis Island until a visiting grandmother wanted to see her parents' names.[17] She'd learned of the opportunity to inscribe the names when a friend had shared material she'd gotten in the mail "a long time ago" when the wall started. While she didn't remember much else about the early solicitation, a few people told me, including a cousin who had her parents (my great-aunt and-great uncle) inscribed, of getting a letter from Lee Iacocca. The sense of personal contact — "I got a letter from Lee Iacocca" — and even the very memory of it testifies to Iacocca's fame and influence in the 1980s.[18]

Among those engaging with the monument also include interested visitors to Ellis Island whose prior connection to the wall consists merely of hearsay, as well as those who first learn of it after arrival. Visitors may easily happen on it while walking the grounds, eating at the outside tables, or looking out of certain windows, and tour guides occasionally (but, interestingly, not so often) point it out. In addition, much has been done to draw attention to the wall's existence in the first space that visitors enter, formerly the baggage room. A staffed booth with information about adding a name to the wall stands to the right near the entrance doors. A bit farther ahead, relatively directly, a bank of computer terminals beckon that enable one to search for names on the wall and directions for their location. Both the wall and the computer bank get a lot of attention from visitors, partly because many people, initially or throughout their visit, assume that either (or both) the wall or computers list the names of all immigrants passing through Ellis Island rather than paid-for honorees.

Where does this misunderstanding come from? In my hours of observation (less impressively called eavesdropping) at the wall, the computer banks, and SOLEIF's information desks, I noted that many people came to Ellis Island presuming, or got the idea innocently enough, that a list of all immigrants existed somewhere. Maybe they had encountered a description, on-site or in advance, about how inspectors scrutinized ship manifests, the lists with passenger information. Or perhaps they saw "registry room" given on the floor plan and thought that registry records would be there, or at least somehow accessible. Or they had heard about a wall of names or saw it, and drew a logical, if erroneous, conclusion. For anyone expecting a list of migrants, the wall and its computers offer the likely visible candidates. Before the opening of the museum's American Family Immigration History Center, where visitors can, for a fee, search a database of Ellis Island immigrants, the wall and the computers appeared to be the most likely candidates. Indeed, they still remain the most immediately visible, since AFHIC is off to the side and one needs to get further in to discover the many kiosks now advertising it.

Confusion must also come from the knowledge and understandings concerning other walls of names. Probably the most famous referent is the Vietnam Veterans Memorial in Washington, D.C. that was created by Maya Lin. Both historical and comprehensive, it lists all known U.S. military dead from that war. Unveiled in 1982, and thus a likely inspiration for the Ellis Island wall, the Vietnam Veterans Memorial has had steady fame and, since 1996, renewing regional attention through a traveling half-size replica sponsored by the Vietnam Veterans Memorial Fund (VVMF). This replica, called "The Wall that Heals," has traveled to one hundred locations, with each visit involving word-spreading activities including fund-raising. The program for the Lewiston, Maine, exhibit in 2001, on the replica's fifth trip to Maine, lists over two hundred sponsors ranging from individuals to "Simone's Hot Dog Stand" to veteran's groups to bank and supermarket chains.[19] (Cosmic connection factoid: The *Urban Legends Reference Pages*, home of Barbara Mikkelson's essay against the black Statue of Liberty, also includes a page, "last updated 26 March 2003," debunking the rumor, "collected on the Internet, 2002," that "Target stores do not 'support veterans.'"[20] The page alleged that a local Target store refused to contribute to bringing the exhibit to town. Interestingly, when I checked the VVMF web site in May 2003, Target appeared as a major sponsor of the traveling exhibit; it was not so listed on the 2001 program I studied.)

In addition, lists and walls with some claim to historical record and with a cost for adding material to them seem to be popping up all over. I offer two examples. In 1999 it was announced that Troy Perry, of the Universal Fellowship of Metropolitan Community Churches, more commonly known as MCC, would officiate at a massive commitment ceremony for "same-sex" couples. Called "The Wedding: Now More than Ever!" it was to be held in April 2000 in conjunction with the Millennium March on Washington, the much-contested rally for lesbian, gay, bisexual, and transgender rights. Anyone could participate in "The Wedding: Now More than Ever!" for free. However, for $25 couples would get "a limited edition, personalized certificate of participation suitable for framing" and inclusion in the "permanent Historical Archive."[21] Notice here how the discourses of economic and historical value run into each other, with neither making enough sense even though both resound with familiarity. "Limited edition" suggests a value-increasing strategy of deliberately making supply fall short of demand, but what could the demand be here? Who wants someone else's relationship document? "Historical Archive" connotes a source of information that future interested parties might research. How "historical" is a record of an event that includes only the event's paying customers?

The Wall of Tolerance project, a fund-raiser for the Southern Poverty Law Center, plays similar signs of import in a different order. This offer, too, involves a certificate. But instead of serving as a reward for participation, it functions as a kind of advance, designed partly to make the project seem historic in the first place. The certificate arrives in the mail with a letter that begins, "Mrs. Rosa Parks and I [that is, Morris Dees, cofounder of the law center] would like to honor you by placing your name on the Wall of Tolerance." The certificate comes in various sizes, depending, I imagine, on how much money they deduce the recipient might be good for. I received two mailings, with slightly different renderings of my name suggesting different mailing lists. One, which measures 5 by 6.5 inches and is printed on glossy but ordinary paper, appears to be the downscale model. In its perforated-edge attachment to the order form it resembled an ad insert. Further, its photographic close-up of a waving U.S. flag framed by a narrow, gold fleur-de-lys type border provide a common mishmash of dignity signs whereby the trappings of aristocracy jazz up signs of democracy.[22] The other certificate, 7 by 9 inches, with an affixed gold-colored seal and a mechanically embossed blue border, showed greater aspirations of being "suitable for framing." The text on both certificates states: "The undersigned co-chairs do hereby authorize that the name of [your name here] be placed on the Wall of Tolerance Honoring those who are leading the way toward a more tolerant and just America as Founding Members of the National Campaign for Tolerance[.]

Authorized this __th day of _____ 200_." Whereas "The Wedding" offer was about making history, the Wall of Tolerance certificate appears to certify participation in past events that should count as history, with the additional authentication of Rosa Parks, a recognizable historic name.

But here, too, money pulls history toward something else, even if one sets aside the question about how one's presence on such-and-such mailing list, which so often reflects a record of purchase more than anything else, indicates behaviors and actions. As it turns out, after I check the box next to "Place my name on the prestigious Wall of Tolerance in Montgomery, Alabama, as official recognition of my role in making America a more tolerant and just nation" I must then check that "I understand I must be a Founding Member of the National Campaign for Tolerance to receive this honor," and then indicate my pledge and include my check, of, ideally, at least $35. Again, one must pay to go down in history. Further, one must pay immediately to go down accurately. The three solicitations that I read — which were dated a year apart, from 2001, 2002, and 2003 — each inform the receiver that to "ensure that [my] name is registered correctly" I should return my completed "Authorization Form" so that arrives "no later than 30 days from today."[23]

The Wall of Honor at Ellis Island, then, has referents and analogs, to which the brochures allude by claiming it to be "the largest wall of names in the world" (size queen). These referents and analogs could easily contribute to confusion. (Alternately, they could contribute to clarity. I overheard one conversation in August 2000 at the outdoor tables near the wall in which a woman suggested to her kids that maybe if they searched the wall they'd find their great-grandfather, who came over by himself on a boat at age thirteen. Her son, who appeared to be about eight or nine, looked over and replied, "Is that a wall for donors?" His frame of reference got him right to the point.) Visitors might also misinterpret the wall to fulfill expectations that they derive independently from it: the migration process involved paperwork so there must be a list; immigrant admission to the United States is important to history, the nation, to me, so putting the list on a monument would be appropriate.

But SOLEIF's own presentation, both on paper and on the ground, itself contributes to confusion. For one thing, there is a certificate involved with wall donations, too. The certificate, which comes with every name purchased, is made in diploma-like form with centered lines that vary in the size and appearance of their lettering and, at the bottom, the reproduced signature of Iacocca and the seal of SOLEIF. The text reads as follows: "The Statue of Liberty–Ellis Island Foundation, Inc., proudly presents this Official Certificate of Recognition in The American Immigrant Wall of Honor to officially certify that [name] came to the United States of America from [country] joining those courageous men and women who came to this country in search for freedom, economic opportunity, and a future of hope for their families."[24]

Unlike "The Wedding" promotion, SOLEIF doesn't advertise the certificate as "limited edition": one can order as many duplicates as one wants (for $5 a piece in 2002). But the idea that one must act now to be on the winning side of scarcity appears in a succession of pamphlet inserts regarding one's very inclusion, or at least one's timely inclusion, in the historical record itself: "Don't Delay—Register Today! The registration for the 'New Millennium' edition of the American Immigrant Wall of Honor was scheduled to close at the end of 1999. However, due to the tremendous response, space is becoming limited. Therefore, names are now being accepted on a 'first-come, first served' basis. To assure a place for your family name, 'Register Today!'" Like the multiple mailings for the Wall of Tolerance, the Wall of Honor publicity reveals a rolling emergency deadline: "Register by September 1 [2000]. The 'New Millennium' edition . . . is filling up fast!" "Registration for the new phase . . . will close August 5, 2001." Here is yet one more instance where promotional language works against history, implying that historical record has only so much room.

This is not to suggest that promotion or fees always work against the recording of history when they are anywhere around it. My great-uncle Lester's 1916 circumcision certificate advertises the many services offered by the *mohel* who performed the circumcision and the local "wine and liquor store" with which he was affiliated. (At the top are crossed flags of the United States and Israel: sex, money, products, nation.) The contrast between this certificate and the certificate signaling inclusion on the Wall of Honor suggests also how sanitized and only artificially decommercialized artifacts commemorating the past may be, in comparison to artifacts of the past that they commemorate.

As my comments above may suggest, these pamphlets with their inserts are easy to make fun of. The play to a fear of scarcity calls up the much-parodied sales pitch of the car dealer or the local appliance dealer screaming out "prices for one week only" in low-budget TV ads. The echo of the cheesy hypester undercuts SOLEIF's pretense to be able to offer a document of authentication, which is suspect in any case. On one level, the certificate reminds me of a conversation I heard on a supermarket line during the heyday of Ricky Martin's "Living la Vida Loca." "You know," the woman behind me told another in disgust as they surveyed his multiple appearances on the magazine rack, "Ricky Martin is officially bisexual." What could the source of such certification possibly be? Similarly, what is SOLEIF authenticating? The words "to officially certify" suggest a process of verification and an authority to offer a seal of witness to that truth. Yet the actual process for getting that certificate reveals that SOLEIF will hand it over for the mere submission of a name along with $100. No independent verification happens.

I want to put a brake on the ridicule here, however, for the reasons I discussed in the introduction. It is easy to send ridicule or criticism sliding from material to human targets, from products to their users. I want to be vigilant in not doing so, most importantly and simply, perhaps, to avoid ridicule altogether. But were ridicule acceptable, little justifies it in this particular situation. What is funny or foolish about desiring to honor in a public way people important to one's own history, or to have the names of those people included in a historical record? Or even one's own name? Eileen Myles, in her nonfiction novel *Cool for You*, offers the following comment: "Why can't I record everything down like my life counts, like I'm the Queen of England or Bobby Vee, and that way I can be safe and not have to wait to die to be important." In this comment presented as a memory from "half my life ago" Myles invokes a common connection between being of consequence and being recorded, between counting and being counted.[25]

In addition, if the discourse around related commemorative projects is any indication, the genesis and popularity of such monuments may be connected to a perception that recognition for individuals is actually under siege. The Southern Poverty Law Center's Web site states that "The Wall [of

Tolerance] will show that individuals, not government or organizations, are responsible for the progress of the past, and the vision of a future America where all people are treated with respect, justice, and fairness."[26] The implication here that one must pick either individual or social forces as agents of history appears also in the controversy over a proposed exhibit for the Smithsonian Institution's National Museum of American History. In 2001, the Catherine B. Reynolds Foundation promised $38 million for an exhibit, tentatively titled "The Spirit of America," that would feature up to one hundred individuals of great personal accomplishment. Reynolds was to help choose members of a selection committee to pick honorees; some such honorees, she said, might be Jonas Salk, Martin Luther King Jr., Sam Donaldson, and the figure skater Dorothy Hamill. In 2002, however, after much conflict over both the exhibit and the role of donors in exhibition planning, Reynolds withdrew her donation and implied that the dominant ideologies of history at the museum undermined the recognition of individual achievement: "Apparently, the basic philosophy for the exhibit, the power of the individual to make a difference, is the antithesis of that espoused by many within the Smithsonian bureaucracy, which is 'only movements and institutions make a difference, not individuals.'"[27] In her rage, Reynolds presented precisely the preference for history as a tale of individual achievers that Lynn Johnson predicted could cause trouble for an Ellis Island funded by rich people, corporate philanthropy, and commercial enterprise.

I don't raise these positions in order to endorse them; far from it. Reynolds pushes an explanation that benefits the rich by, just for starters, supporting the idea that there should be some rich people: if individuals can triumph over hardship through perseverance, then they deserve to be at the top and needn't trouble themselves with people below, who in order to advance need merely their own perseverance, not resources or social change. The Wall of Tolerance promotion, while digging at the insufficiencies of governments and organizations in a manner with which I sympathize, seems nonetheless, in the process, to back up the questionable idea that racism and other forms of prejudice might be eradicated without systemic transformations. At the same time, however, in expressing a need to retrieve individual recognition these positions provide a clue, perhaps, about the popularity of these monuments.

No one who has written an acknowledgments piece to include in a publication has any right to scoff at the impulse to record in public the names of people important in one's life. I would not want to criticize such an impulse in any case, and there is a reason besides decency to avoid being slippery with derision: the transfer in target often inappropriately transfers the characteristics under criticism. The Wall of Honor offers a great example regarding the interest in historical accuracy. The disinterest by SOLEIF in making the wall a historical document is clear from the single criterion for inclusion—payment—as well as some of the features of the product, like the apparent practice of recording a person's name once on the wall for every time someone initiates a donation in that name. I deduced this practice from some obvious cases of duplication. I'm willing to believe that more than one Meyer Kaufman came through Ellis Island, maybe even one for each of the five listed (panel 218), but the arrival of three different people named Julia Walsh Keeney (panel 219) seems doubtful. Other practices, too, testify to a low priority on accuracy, like the limit, described in the solicitation brochure, of forty characters maximum per entry (unless one donates "$1000, $5000, or $10,000," which buys two lines "specially placed") and the policy to use only "English language alphabet letters . . . with no accent marks," this last suggesting as well that the low priority on accuracy has an unequal distribution in effect.[28]

In contrast, the visitors, information-seekers, and potential name buyers that I encountered often showed much more interest in historical accuracy, an interest that stood out all the more when it ran up against SOLEIF's different standards. After all, many of the people approached the wall, booths, or computers looking for information and evidence about family history. The wait for a computer on busy days owed much to the erroneous belief of many visitors that the computers had data about immigrant arrivals. Standing in line myself, I heard this misperception voiced often. Thus would arise the researcher's dilemma about whether to trade observer for participant, kindly sparing misinformed visitors the aggravation. I refrained often enough to see how much time one could spend on the computer without figuring out the nature of its data: I found out that the answer is a lot of time. A senior undergraduate in one of my courses told me in 2003 of a trip to Ellis Island when he was in high school during which his father spent frustrated "hours" trying to find family names; I didn't see hours of labor at Ellis Island, but I did see a lot of frustration among numerous people finding few emerging clues at the computers themselves. Even figuring out that the inclusion of a name requires payment didn't always fully debunk the notion that the wall offers some kind of historical information. One of my colleagues, fully engaged in historical research of her own, was a bit jolted when I pointed out that one could easily register the name Mickey Mouse. Although she'd figured out that names were paid for, partly because the wall included some of her relatives processed at Ellis but not others, she had never quite considered the implications of payment being the main element of the process.

Then again, I don't think my colleague's impulse to trust in an implicit truth criterion is so far off base. From the standpoint of what donors do, if not what SOLEIF allows, her lack of suspicion seems appropriate. Needless to say, I can't prove intention regarding every name donation; I couldn't track them all even if I wanted to. I also know just from my own family that people have various reasons to prefer mystifying the past to transmitting an accurate historical record. In the 1980s, for instance, the woman we knew as my grandfather's younger sister revealed herself to be his older sister when pride in her own longevity surpassed a desire to shave a few years off her age. While working on this book, I was informed of another secret buried in order to sustain the first one: that contrary to the story of my grandfather as the intrepid young man who initiated the family's path to America, his older sisters had come through Ellis Island first, sending money back for his passage. (I wonder how many other accounts that the man came first conform more to gender norms than to fact.) Surely, and especially as coming to America through Ellis Island becomes increasingly heroicized and iconic, some names placed on the wall to represent such a passage reflect varying degrees of myth or fiction. Nonetheless, there is no more reason to doubt the source material behind a name that few people would recognize than to doubt that "Antoinette Perrotto Iacocca" came to the United States from Italy, as the sample certificate, using the name of Iacocca's mother, attests. To see that name as somehow more guaranteed is to buy into the idea that fame itself lends some people, like Iacocca, a certain authority to validate history simply by naming it.

Furthermore, I overheard people much more determined than SOLEIF to abet historical accuracy regarding the list of names on the wall. Questions asked of personnel at the booth, for instance, sometimes revealed a search for guidance about protocols for historical documentation that potential donors presumed to exist and intended to follow. One woman asked a SOLEIF staff member what to do if someone's name was spelled one way in the old country and another way in the United States. She seemed a bit taken aback when he spoke nothing of documentary standards; he told her to pick the spelling she was most comfortable with.[29] As her comments suggest, a willingness to pay for inclusion does not necessarily signal disrespect for or disinterest in historical accuracy—any more than paying for sex or art necessarily fixes those experiences, services, or products in particular relation to authenticity and value.[30]

Compare this woman's concern to the slick handling of the wall's relation to information in a 1999 venue for its promotion, Martha Stewart's annual Christmas special. Called *Martha Stewart's Home for the Holidays: The Family Tree*, the 1999 edition, which aired 8 December on CBS, used family heritage as an overall theme. It showed viewers how to archive family recipes for the next generation, mail family cookies, make Aretha Franklin's family ham, put photographs of ancestors on ornaments, and, or so one segment would seem to suggest, find ancestors at Ellis Island. The scene begins with Stewart explaining to two nieces that "tracing your roots can be an incredible adventure," leading perhaps to "forgotten links to royalty or just some ordinary people coming here from Poland in the early part of the twentieth century looking for a better life." One of the nieces then jumps in to show that they've already discovered an instance of precisely the second hypothetical in their very own family: "Well, you know, we actually did some research, and we went to Ellis Island, and we discovered that your grandmother, Helen Krukar, came directly to Ellis Island." "Oh wow," Stewart interjects, reaching for a framed certificate from SOLEIF, "this is the certificate." She then reads the certificate, filled in with her grandmother's name (which she corrects to "Helena") and place of origin, and adds, "What a wonderful gift, a beautifully framed commemorative certificate that honors my grandmother's arrival in America in the early part of the century." She ends by saying more generally that viewers can "search the Internet for links to family members," and that Ellis Island "will soon have a great Web site that will let you search for your relatives among the millions of immigrants who arrived there." This final statement, for careful listeners, locates the provision of genealogical information only in Ellis Island's future. The clear implication of the whole, however, is that such information was already available there, rather than what the nieces could actually have discovered: that someone paid to put the grandmother's name on the Wall of Honor, a monument that, interestingly, the segment fails to mention.[31] In fact, the segment fails to mention that money factors in at all. Stewart says of the certificate, "This is so nice of them to give us this; how great!"

I do not hold SOLEIF wholly responsible for the misrepresentation in Stewart's Christmas special. Although the segment approximates nothing so much as an infomercial, with a prominent product placement and celebrity testimonial, the celebrity is Stewart, the testimony occurs on her show, and it well suits her own thematic emphasis there, and periodically elsewhere during that year, on family (and sometimes ethnic) heritage.[32] (Looking at her next Christmas special, *Martha Stewart's Christmas Dream*, I suspect an unconscious retreat from going ethnic: "This year I want to make everything white," she says, and proceeds to assemble white food, decorations, flowers, and birds.)[33] Yet if responsibility ought plausibly to be apportioned between Stewart and SOLEIF, or between Stewart's people and SOLEIF's people, the segment's relation to misrepresentation typifies SOLEIF promotions in the way that it mystifies the nature of what is on offer: history or commemoration.

ABOUT WHOM

Stewart's segment does not, however, mystify the issue about which SOLEIF always seems a bit cagey: not just whether the wall offers history but whose history it offers. On this matter, Stewart's framework is simple. Ellis Island ancestors represent a subset of family history; you might learn of Ellis Island ancestors, or honor them, at Ellis Island. Ironically, while for some people the appeal of registration might be enhanced by the sleight that makes Stewart's SOLEIF certificate look like evidence of immigration through Ellis Island, it simultaneously thwarts another, contradictory, SOLEIF sales pitch: that the wall is for everyone. The brochure I picked up in 2000 states that the wall represents "virtually every nationality," and also includes "those who endured forced migration from [?] slavery," and "our earliest settlers, the American Indians." The revised brochure I picked up in 2002 claims that inscription on the wall is meant to be for anyone who has "an American story," "whether they arrived in America on the Mayflower, were part of a forced migration, or just came over on a jet plane." Like De Beers trying to expand the consumer diamond market with new traditions such as the "diamond anniversary ring," this later brochure offers new suggestions about appropriate occasions for registration: "pay tribute to someone who has just become a citizen" or "even inscribe your own name as a thank you to an America that has been good to you."

Yet much works against this promotional contention that SOLEIF holds in equal esteem everyone among this diverse array of solicited participants. The first issue is in the name *Immigrant* Wall of Honor and the wall's placement at its particular immigration site, which certainly supports the notion of Ellis Island immigrants, even more specifically, as the prime honorees. The primary image for the wall on the Web site wallofhonor.com, suggests the same. It depicts a human time line in front of the wall, in which images of Ellis Island immigrants on the left, taken from black-and-white photographs, give way to contemporary color-photographic imagery of Ellis Island visitors implied to be their descendants: first grandparent types, and then, on the far right, an apparent father and mother, whose little girl excitedly points up at, it would seem, a name on the wall. All of the people bear visual characteristics generally seen to designate people of European descent, in particular those generally considered "white." Racial signalling is complicated, however. The dark hair, dark wardrobe, and grayish skin of the immigrants particularly against the light hair, pale or bright clothing, and pink skin of the visitors, suggests the same racialized cue of "immigrant" as dark that also appears in some souvenirs, like the picture of an immigrant boy that appears on numerous Ellis Island souvenirs. After seeing a souvenir with the image of the boy, several people commented to me, "Why does that guy look Asian?" due to his skin tone and facial shape. By his typifying hat, clothes, and sack, the boy otherwise seemed to signal a turn-of-the-twentiety-century and now-viewed-as-white European; it was as if the artist had grabbed the wrong markers for dark.

My point here is not to condemn SOLEIF for emphasizing Ellis Island immigrants or for using predominantly "white" Ellis Island immigrants to symbolize them. Most immigrants who came through fit into that category, and the museum for which SOLEIF raises money, appropriately enough, focuses on immigrants through Ellis Island. Were SOLEIF and the museum consistently to use that focus and address its raced features, I would be satisfied.

Finessing that focus, however, involves race content and race consequences of dubious effect. To begin, an invitation to inscribe enslaved or native ancestors under the label "immigrant" seems, at best, offensively thoughtless—unless, perhaps, it is accompanied by a defense of new usage, as occurred during a rarely mentioned episode in the history of attempts to refurbish Ellis Island: the July 1970 occupation of the island by sixty-two members of a group called NEGRO, the National Economic Growth and Reconstruction Movement. This group, which had already begun to clean and refurbish the deserted space by the time a helicopter spotted their laundry, intended to create at Ellis Island both a rehabilitation center for former convicts and drug addicts and a monument to immigration. The group left after being discovered, but by August it moved back with the change of status from squatter to invited guest holding a five-year permit from the National Park Service to inhabit and transform the island (although not much resulted). Thomas W. Matthew, NEGRO's president, explained the signs at the site proclaiming that "New Immigrants Are Returning": "There are immigrants to the land and immigrants to the society. European immigrants who were not part of the land were part of the society. Black America is part of the land but we were not and have not been part of the society, so now we are not immigrants to the land but immigrants to the society."[34] Regardless of the merits of this characterization, it shows why some justification is needed to extend the reach of the term "immigrant." No such justification is offered by SOLEIF, and as critics pointed out regarding the Statue of Liberty, simply to call the United States a nation of immigrants is disrespectful rather than inclusive.

In addition, particular racial inequites become obscured through the universalizing of "immigrant" in the context of appeals and explanations that, like much around Ellis Island, emphasize breeder ties. Maybe it is because I began research on Ellis Island at a time when I was dealing with the fallout of becoming the only nonprocreative adult among seven siblings and stepsiblings in my own "family of origin" that I was extremely conscious that the promotional literature for the wall never even seemed to say "Honor your aunt," not to mention "Honor Uncle Sam's longtime roommate" or "those two great old women down the block who everyone knew weren't sisters" or "that femme/butch couple who showed you what life could be like" or "your activist role model." Framed instead in terms of progenitorial relationships in its calls to honor one's parents and grandparents whose names will be viewed with pride by their descendents, the publicity for the wall occludes the distinctions between the enslaved and immigrants precisely concerning the ability to maintain, know, and honor parent/child relations, the disregarding of which, as Hortense Spillers astutely analyzes, was a central practice of slaveholders.[35] As with differential policies regarding would-be immigrants, like the Page Law and the subsequent exclusion acts that rendered Chinese immigration disproportionately male, issues of race and sexuality knot up frequently regarding the ties alleged to be everyone's to have, to access, or to honor at the wall—if one has the $100 to do so.[36]

ON THE WALL, WITHIN THE WALLS

In neglecting to make key distinctions, the promotional material about the Wall of Honor works against the tenuous hold on those distinctions in presentations and representations at the museum itself. Only one exhibit, "The Peopling of America," is designed to situate Ellis Island in the context of other migrations. Despite the unfortunate use of "America" in the title to designate the United States, the exhibit has a number of positive features. The introductory text displayed on the wall explains how statistics reflect the prejudices of the researchers who derived them. Other wall texts demonstrate care not to subsume "peopling" under immigration or all immigrations under an Ellis Island model; another carefully explains the difference between slavery and indentured servitude. Yet the attention to these distinctions makes up a very small part of the exhibit, especially in contrast to some of the larger and splashier three-dimensional displays on other themes, like "A Changing Pattern: Male/Female Immigration Trends" and a word tree of "Ethnic Americanisms."[37]

The word tree suggests something else masked in the "nation of immigrants" idea. In showing contributions to English from other languages, the display suggests that English is the original language of the United States that is spiced up by other, "ethnic" languages. Those other languages look like the travelers, like add-ins that migrating speakers bring with them. Omitted, of course, are the processes of conquest, colonization, and continuing arrogance by which English, itself an immigrant language, attained and maintains its current status as the dominant, official language of the United States. The display itself hints at something irregular in its implied narrative by using asterisks to designate language sources that, while presented as transplants into English, are actually the native ones: "totem— Ojibwa*" versus "coffee klatch—German" and "macho—Mexican Spanish." What the asterisk explodes in the narrative is nicely expressed by Yolanda López in a poster printed in 1981. "Who's the Illegal Alien, Pilgrim?," the poster states, as a man crumples a paper headlined "Immigration Plans" in one hand while pointing like Uncle Sam with the other. Like the text, his headwear, with its geometric designs akin to the style of the United Farm Workers Eagle, links the figure to Chicano and Native American movements, and to the struggles for the rights of indigenous peoples more generally.

The exhibit "The Peopling of America," then, has some problems in its presentation. Yet its biggest problem is that many visitors do not even enter the room where it is on display. Frequently in passing, and also in several stints of sustained lurking, I noticed that the room generally attracted minimal sustained attention and that visitors received little encouragement to enter it. This is a phenomenon that Mike Wallace noted, too, when he visited in 1990.[38] Both the canned voice on the ferry and, sometimes, live personnel advise visitors to visit the second and third floors first, leaving the "Peopling" exhibit to tour only if time permits. Indeed, not just the object of their visit, but also the visitors themselves are sometimes hailed as if defined by this more narrow focus on Ellis Island alone. "You'll be inhabiting history, . . . walking in the steps of our parents, grandparents, and great-grandparents," Tom Brokaw states at the beginning of the audio tour, which, significantly for my point here, may be rented in "English, Espanol, Deutch, Francais and Italiano"—no Asian languages and, again, nothing as multicultural as putting the "ç" in "Français" or the ñ in "Español."[39]

In addition, the park rangers are sometimes less careful than the exhibit texts about offering careful distinctions among various forms of migration and habitation. In *The New History in an Old Museum: Creating the Past at Colonial Williamsburg*, Richard Handler and Eric Gable emphasize that the presentation of history at heritage museums depends partly on how interpreters adapt the historical narratives presented to them as information or directives, a matter complicated by the expectation that interpreters play an active part in putting together their own tours. Handler and Gable describe competing models at Colonial Williamsburg, where social historians recruited in the 1970s to update the dominant narrative advanced constructionist accounts of history that aimed to expose how traditional histories benefit people in power and to induce "complacent Americans" to confront injustice past and present. Yet, as they explain, "social history on the ground tended to comfort visitors' qualms about social injustice or banish a discussion of it altogether." One primary example they considered concerns miscegenation. White interpreters often avoided the topic, many agreed, because it made them uncomfortable or because, as one interpreter from the "all-black" Department of African-American Interpretation and Presentation suggested, " 'they'd just rather not talk the dirt.' "[40]

As I discuss more extensively in chapter 8, interpreters at Ellis Island have a lot of leeway in designing their programs; leeway that is often used to great effect even if it is partly motivated by a budget-driven inability to provide much guidance. In terms of content, interpreters need primarily to cover the basic themes assigned, by Congress, for the area's "Interpretive Themes and Objectives," which gives "the story of immigration as a historical and contemporary phenomenon" rather than the broader notion of "peopling" or migration as the large contextualizing theme.[41] (Again, I am highlighting here the minimal gesture toward other types of migration rather than criticizing the museum for a focus on immigration.) Partly for that reason, perhaps, slavery, from what I heard while attending a range of programs, rarely came up. When mentioned, it often functioned more as a basis for (inaccurate) analogy than anything else. I heard one ranger call indentured servitude "a nice way of saying 'slave,' " and another say that contract labor was "no different than coming here as a slave."[42] While the appeal of the analogies is understandable, especially given the brief time that guides have with visitors, such statements bury significant differences.

I also noticed the term "slave" oddly used to designate something like "subordinate" in the Division of Interpretation's "Orientation Packet #2," which, I have to say, actually offers more useful guidance for teaching than I ever got in graduate school, although the following passage concerning "What the Visitor Expects" is rather infelicitous: "The visitors expect courtesy. As a member of a democratic society he considers himself as good as the next person and places himself on an equal social plane with you, the tour guide. He respects your position and special knowledge . . . but he does not worship or fear you. He, therefore, expects courtesy not as a master and a slave, but as an equal." I mention this passage more for its interest than its influence; I'm sure I lingered over the text more than any intended recipient. Interesting, too, is the reference to the visitor as "he" and the assertion in a preceding paragraph that visitors expect the "full story . . . in keeping with the American idea of 'getting his money's worth,'" another little marker of the perception that access to history sometimes involves getting what you pay for.[43]

The claim that the Ellis Island museum honors all immigrants, all migrants, or even all who "people America" also functions to mask the inequity involved in the concentration of heritage resources at a site that honors and documents primarily white people. What the resources accomplish becomes obvious in contrast, for instance, with the old immigration station at Angel Island, near San Francisco, which operated from 1910 to 1940 primarily to exclude Chinese immigrants in accordance with racist exclusion laws. Ellis Island, open every day except Christmas, has extensive exhibits and a huge staff to manage the site: among the federal workers are park rangers, museum curators, and full-time library staff, in addition to a number of SOLEIF employees and large crews for maintenance and security. Resources also bring publicity, which brings more interest, which brings more resources, in various ways such as licensing fees. Circle Line pays the Park Service to runs its ferry to the site, and Aramark pays, in a percentage of sales, to run the snack and gift shops. The gift shop has enough business so that Aramark employs a full-time buyer for it, who, in turn, increases profits.

The lack of comparable resources for the Angel Island immigration station has numerous consequences, primarily involving access to the site. Because the pier closest to the immigration site needs an expensive restoration in order to be functional, visitors dock about a half hour's walk away. Most either must hike the distance or must be content (and pay about $10) to pass by the immigration station on a tram tour. The building, staffed by volunteers, is open only half of the year for a few hours a day at most; its gift shop, a little shack, is also staffed by volunteers. The issue of money also affects what can be seen at the site. For example, as Lynn Eichinger, president

FIGURE 17. Wax figures used to depict the interrogation of a Chinese immigrant, Angel Island Immigration Station. (Photograph by the author)

of the Angel Island Association, explained on a tour I attended in October 2000, the reconstruction of a scene for an immigration interrogation uses donated wax figures; thus, the interrogator, recycled from the body of an umpire and the head of baseball player Mike Piazza (perhaps unneeded in California after he moved to the Mets), gestures "you're out" in a different realm of signification (figure 17).[44]

To obfuscate the white-centeredness of Ellis Island is to perpetuate a pernicious and prominent form of institutionalized racism in which resources described as universally distributed accrue in practice to white people. Compare the "$450 million (and counting!)" raised by SOLEIF to the $15 million promised to Angel Island's restoration through the passage by voters of California's Proposition 12 in 2000, less than half of what the Angel Island Association estimates would be required for the restoration.[45] The presidential decrees, federal budget, and large private and corporate contributions that have gone into Ellis Island as a heritage site are not really supporting everyone's history. These resources, however, contribute to the predominance of publicity that often makes Ellis Island the subsuming point of reference; Angel Island, much less well known, is often inaccurately called "the Ellis Island of the West." Imagine what would happen in terms of resources and resource-generating publicity if American Express ran a national campaign in which credit card purchases triggered automatic donations to Angel Island, like the project that raised $1.7 million for SOLEIF in the early 1980s or the campaign two decades later for reopening the Statue of Liberty after 9/11. That it is hard to imagine such national attention and work on behalf of Angel Island is precisely the point that I am trying to make here.

CONCLUSION

I have been following, in this chapter and the previous one, a raced path of heritage resources that accrue especially to white people. The Statue of Liberty is promoted as everybody's lady, but her relation to abolition, which ought certainly to enhance that status, is made to look like the self-serving claim of a special-interest lobby. Promotions for the Wall of Honor gesture only half-heartedly beyond Ellis Island immigrants, and largely, it would seem, to expand the donor base; otherwise, a name change would certainly be in order. The Ellis Island museum, in accordance with Ellis Island history, primarily concerns people now considered to be white. Since much of the money for Ellis Island was raised in the name of the Statue of Liberty, the path is a trajectory from "for all" to "for white," except that "for all" functions sometimes already to camouflage "for white"—as signaled by the persistent use of Ellis Island to figure "a nation of immigrants" and the dismissive approaches to the Statue of Liberty content regarding people in the United States of African descent.

If the wall's name and its publicity contribute to these obfuscations, does its format as an agglomeration of individuals do so, too? I argued in chapter 1 that the wall is one of many features at Ellis Island working to naturalize the idea that procreation and genealogy make kinship, family, and ancestors, even in the face of growing challenges to presuming this particular biological core as foundational for those units. As I noted earlier in this chapter, the wall can also be seen as an invitation to keep a focus on the individual in family history. According to Rosensweig and Thelen, white people in general, the primary descendants of Ellis Island immigrants, tend to be all about that anyway. Right there is a reminder that race content informs and comes from approaches to heritage on every level.

Yet it wouldn't be fair, I think, to read a "more about me" focus into everyone who approaches the wall with interest or with cash. Two of my premises in this book are that the contents or processes around each person's approach to the parts and the whole of Ellis Island cannot be read off footsteps or purchases, and that these contents and processes should be presumed until proven otherwise to be at least as complex, as potentially contradictory, and sometimes as convoluted as that of a historian who got totally rerouted on her first trip to Ellis Island by a flirtatious argument about a snow globe. The material I presented above about the disparity between SOLEIF and potential donors on the matter of historical accuracy begins to speak of this complexity.

The wall's focus on individuals may not reflect back to its visitors the initial interests with which they approach it. But that focus affects how the wall might inform people's interests and understanding, as do the race content and race consequences that work to make of Ellis Island immigrants an apt and subsuming norm. In the next chapters, I look further at the perceived and practiced relations among migrants and objects that contribute to shaping the possibilities for interpretive transformations.

SIX

IMMIGRANT PEDDLERS

In late October 2000 I was flying back to Maine from a two-week trip to San Francisco to study the immigration station at Angel Island. In a bag I carried a souvenir that I had purchased at a store called Alamo Flags located on Pier 39, a venue for tourist-geared commerce near the pier from which boats travel to Angel Island and to Alcatraz. The souvenir came from a series of takeoffs on the genre of No Parking signs that indicate parking restricted to certain vehicles or people, like "patrons," residents, or employees. These souvenir signs use national and ethnic identities instead, inserted into the text "Parking for [name] only. All Others Will Be Towed." Among the choices of names displayed were "Irish," "Lithuanians," "Slovaks," "S. Koreans," "Italians," and "Palestinians," one of the latter of which I purchased (figure 18). The second intifada, the Palestinian uprising against the Israeli occupation of the West Bank and Gaza, was then a month underway, and I was struck by the odd resonance, yet full inadequacy of comparison, between the joke souvenir and the grim situation. Hey, that's where I get to park.

In my last-minute packing for the trip home, I discovered that the sign didn't fit into my small suitcase but it did fit perfectly into a flat bag from another gift shop. The bag, made of semiopaque orange plastic, offered a tantalizing yet penetrable visual barrier to the sign's text, and I considered whether I might be setting myself up for trouble. Might a visible sign staking out Palestinian territory, no matter how small the territory nor how humorous the claim, delay my trip if I ran into someone with the too-common habit of translating "Palestinian" as "terrorist"? After concluding that I was insufficiently equipped to make the most productive use of the

FIGURE 18. "Parking for Palestinians Only."
Souvenir purchased in San Francisco, October
2000. (Photograph by Robert Diamante)

media event that unjust detention for the souvenir might cause, as well as realizing, on a decidedly less lofty terrain, that I really wanted to get home, I tried to avoid detection by carrying the bag discreetly through security onto the plane. Later, however, in rushing to make a tight connection I momentarily forgot everything but my quest to reach the gate on time. I raced onto the connecting plane just before the doors closed, holding everything I was carrying in front of me in order to get through the narrow doorway.

There was the orange bag resting right on top of my carry-ons, with the front of the sign flush against its covering. I noticed it just as it was catching the eye of the flight attendant greeting passengers. "What does your sign say?" he asked cheerfully. He got visibly less cheerful as he deciphered the text, while I silently sped through my earlier musings: What if they take me off the plane? I want to go home. But maybe I should just go with the flow. Palestinians should be able to travel without harassment. This brewing incident could make that point. But maybe other people could make it better. Why haven't I been more diligent in reading the many daily e-mails from a Right of Return electronic mailing list that a colleague on the *Radical Teacher* editorial board had been forwarding to me? Why don't I carry the board's phone list? Whom would I call to get me out of trouble: my editor, my dean, my girlfriend? Looking at the flight attendant's face, which seemed to indicate that he was going through his options with equal speed, I decided to try for a quick fix. "I'm writing a book on funny souvenirs," I chirped, as if clueless about the sign's potential to displease, "Isn't this one of the funniest souvenirs that you've ever seen?" "No, it is not," he replied, "But I'm going to let you on anyway."

If finding my snow globe at the Ellis Island gift shop marked the beginning of the project that became this book, it was my experience with the Palestinian parking sign that came to sum up, for me, the key issues involved in studying both the globe and the shop. There are several reasons why the sign works in this way. First, I found the sign in a context where the on-site politics might seem alternately unpleasant and savvy to the same person: a store named after the Alamo—a shrine to white supremacy—that validates Palestinian identity. My airplane experience had a political mix, too. Fresh from my close call at the doorway, I observed with great interest that the map in the in-flight magazine had carefully avoided the erasure of Palestinian land claims that simply labeling a region "Israel" might effect. A notation mark following "Israel" directed attention to a clarification below: "Gaza Strip and West Bank Israeli-occupied with interim status subject to Israeli/Palestinian negotiations—final status to be determined."[1]

Second, the circulation and meanings of the parking sign depend on access to power, privilege, and resources that is regulated along the way, linking the sale and movement of objects to broader issues about the movement of peoples and its representation. In this chapter, I consider some of the players, objects, and economics that factor into the movement of souvenirs by looking at the sales scene at Battery Park. There, migrant vendors mix with people selling or buying a path to the image of their migrant predecessors in vending, as tourists gather on the way to or from the ferry to the Statue of Liberty and Ellis Island. In looking at a range of money-making operations, from the souvenir stands, food concessions, and art stalls licensed by the New York Department of Parks and Recreation to living statues and illegal vending-on-the-go, I discuss how the regulation of vending at Battery Park, in ways that reinscribe inequities connected to race, national origin, and access to capital, is used to promote and to profit from the idea that immigrant peddlers, but only certain peddlers, are a defining element of the New York scene.

Before moving to Battery Park, however, I return once more to my Palestinian parking sign, in order further to introduce some issues about the making and movement of products that are relevant to vending at Battery Park and Ellis Island.

MOVING OBJECTS

Access to power, privilege, and resources—I can also tell my story of the Palestinian parking sign as follows: A professor on a salary that puts me comfortably in the middle class, I was, in fall 2000, on a sabbatical. Sabbaticals are the glorious interludes of time off with pay for research that are available to faculty at decently endowed institutions, which rarely offer anything as good for administrators and certainly not for staff on hourly wage, like food service workers, even though all employees would certainly benefit from extended support for professional development and the chance periodically to get enough sleep. This free (actually, paid) time and some grant money enabled me to fly from Maine to San Francisco to study Angel Island. So did my recourse to deans and editors and a network of friends and allies that time and money helped to nurture (travel to conferences and demonstrations; the ability not to have to hold down more than one job), and that, in turn, helped me to stretch the time and money I had (housing, hospitality, connections).

Consider, for comparison, the greater barriers in getting to Angel Island faced by some eighth graders at King Middle School in Hayward, California, even though they lived only a few hours away from the island rather than across the continent. Jeff Sherman, one of the teachers I encountered leading their field trip, itemized the cost of the trip for me. Since enough parents volunteered to drive and pay for gas, thus eliminating the $800 rental fee for each bus, the trip cost each kid $5.50 for the ferry from Tiburon along with the $2 docent fee, plus anything they were able to contribute to the $9 parking fee for the car they traveled in or for their potluck-style lunch.

Still, these costs proved potentially prohibitive for some of the kids in the school, which Sherman characterized as lower-middle to middle class. He told me about their fund-raising strategies, like running a school store, and the donations from teachers, which were used to ensure that everyone could go on trips like this. A parent reiterated the financial burden: "I usually pay for two or three other kids," he said, "We're all struggling."[2]

The items I could buy at Pier 39 reflected issues of access in other ways. For instance, consider two examples of morbid humor about Alcatraz expressed in sarcastic lists. The first:

> We feel that this so-called Alcatraz Island is more than suitable for an Indian reservation, as determined by the white man's own standards. By this, we mean that this place resembles most Indian reservations in that:
>
> 1. It is isolated from modern facilities, and without adequate means of transportation.
> 2. It has no fresh running water.
> 3. It has inadequate sanitation facilities.
> 4. There are no oil or mineral rights.
> 5. There is no industry and so unemployment is very great.
> 6. There are no health-care facilities.
> 7. The soil is rocky and non-productive, and the land does not support game.
> 8. There are no educational facilities.
> 9. The population has always exceeded the land base.
> 10. The population has always been held as prisoners and kept dependent upon others.

The second:

> ALCATRAZ CONDOS
> Around the clock security
> Panoramic bay view
> Exclusive neighborhood
> Large swimming facility
> Designed to last a lifetime
> No down payment

Which list appears on a souvenir magnet made in China and priced at only $1.99 due to the gross disparities in power that underpin the manufacture of most objects for sale, resulting in minimal pay for making them? It is the second one, of course, with its jokes about prison (a topic to which I return in chapter 7). The first list comes from *The Alcatraz Proclamation to the Great White Father and His People*, issued in 1969 during the Indian occupation of Alcatraz Island. In this proclamation also is the offer to purchase Alcatraz Island from the government for "twenty-four dollars in glass beads and red cloth, a precedent set by the white man's purchase of a similar island [Manhattan] about 300 years ago."[3] The proclamation's list derives humor at the expense of institutionalized racism, critiques of which generally do not circulate so widely.

The proclamation makes the point about circulation, too. So did a text, clearly inspired by it, that had been prepared for an attempted takeover of Ellis Island in March 1970 by what one article described as a group of "militant Indians." Even more rarely discussed in the literature on Ellis Island than is the occupation by NEGRO that occurred several months later, the March 1970 event was foiled by mechanical problems with the group's boat.[4] The two texts assert, over three decades ago, that venues to expose the effects of racism as well as those to enable and promote cultural production by and of Native Americans remained insufficient; each proclamation called for land reuse that would accommodate both critique and creation.[5]

Thirty years later, it is not the mockery of white supremacy but nostalgia for it that gets shelf space, appearing in the persistence of mass-produced souvenirs like mammy dolls and Confederate currency. I found the latter item, along with copies of the deed to Manhattan Island, for sale at the Ellis Island gift shop, among other packets with old textual material, like the Bill of Rights (on pseudo-aged paper). While I would hardly suggest that getting one's message onto cheap trinkets made possible by the exploitation of labor would constitute a triumph in cultural representation, what does and doesn't get popularized in mass circulation remains important nonetheless.

The Alcatraz prison jokes, Confederate money, and deeds to Manhattan at the souvenir shop are symptoms of dominant relations of power; the marketing of nostalgia for white supremacy also contributes to the maintenance of this power.[6] A more localized relation of power likely explains why the Palestinian sign was for sale. When I brought it to the counter, the woman working there asked me enthusiastically if I was Palestinian. I told her that I wasn't and asked if she was (even though my looks made me a much more likely candidate). She was Korean, she told me, but the store's owner was Palestinian. I thus suspect his hand in the availability of that particular selection, which was politically charged enough, especially then, that someone without an investment in the matter might choose to skip it. Two months later Sam's Club faced attack regarding their sale of globes, after a circulating e-mail charged that the globe makers had marked an area "Palestine" (which they had), and omitted any designation "Israel" (which actually they had not).[7]

I suspect, also, however, that the privileges of money and ownership would not have helped the store owner on the plane. My friend and colleague Francisca López, whose speech marks her, in her occasional sarcastic self-denotation, as "a foreigner," thought I was foolish to imagine that my particular words to the flight attendant mattered much, if at all: "That's not why they let you on. They let you on because you sound American." Assuming she is right, which I think she is, I benefited, then, from certain prejudices that affect mobility in numerous ways: those that make "Arab" always the likeliest suspect no matter how many "terrorists" turn out to look like Tim McVeigh; those that, within one week in 2003, triggered law enforcement alerts about two "Middle Eastern-looking" people perceived to look "a little" like men whose pictures were on an FBI Web site and another "who looked like he didn't belong" on a Maine state ferry; those behind the disinterest, within the same week, in triggering any ethnic profiling after a guy named Kilpatrick claimed, while holding people hostage, to be a terrorist in touch with Al Qaeda; those that let people wander around with swords at the Maine Highland Festival or win knives via a ring toss at a carnival in West Virginia, with limits only for those under eighteen (no metal detectors for white people?); those that sent border patrol agents who were trolling Portland, Maine, for illegal immigrants to African, Asian, and Latino markets and restaurants (thus causing organizers to cancel an upcoming Latino health fair); those that change the portability of signs in the parking series, depending on the pride designated.[8] A year after my airplane incident, I noticed the "Italians Only" version of that sign, produced by a different company, on the wall of the Italian Bakery in Lewiston, Maine. I doubt that encountering a passenger carrying such a sign would have troubled my flight attendant. In the words of a 2003 Vermont Supreme Court decision supporting a woman's right to put "Irish" on her vanity license plate, it is "common sense" to recognize some ethnic references as harmless affirmations of ethnic pride.[9]

Maybe so, but even though I recognize the value of the information and sometimes the judgment that everyday usage offers,[10] I'd like a neon sign to flash "danger, danger" any time common sense gets trumpeted as a standard for judging the content or import of ethnic or racial appellations, self-proclaimed or otherwise. For one thing, the use of "common sense" as a legal rationale has a relevant history that impels caution. In *White by Law* Ian F. Haney-López discusses the numerous U.S. state and federal cases from 1878 to 1944 concerning who occupied the category "white" and could therefore be naturalized as a U.S. citizen—"white" being a prerequisite named in 1790 and not fully canceled until 1952. Many judicial decisions, Haney-López explains, often used "common knowledge" as a basis for exclusion.[11] In *United States v. Bhagat Singh Thind* of 1923, for instance, the Supreme Court rejected the argument of Bhagat Singh Thind who sought naturalization claiming to be white because he was, as an Asian Indian, of "Caucasian" ancestry—a criterion that the Supreme Court had affirmed in a decision several months earlier. Instead, the court ruled that the "common understanding" that "unmistakable and profound differences" between the "brown Hindu" and the "blond Scandinavian" should prevail.[12] (That common understanding in the United States, as Haney-López notes, included the standard and misleading use of "Hindu" to mean "from India" although the majority of migrants from India were Muslim or Sikh.[13])

The problem in cases like these, obviously, is not that the court did not help worthy petitioners into the justifiably elevated category of "white," but that, as Haney-López indicates, the enshrinement of common knowledge also enshrines such dominant racial understandings of white supremacy as objective facts in the natural world, making interrogation of them appear to be unnecessary.[14] Sideways evidence of enshrinement over examination may be found, perhaps, in the numerous variations on "common understanding" in the decision, including "common usage," "popular meaning," and "the average man." They suggest a certain kind of overkill, not unlike Warren Burger's superfluous assent added to the *Bowers* decision, that stands in the place of addressing the prejudice and contradictions involved.

Another problem with common knowledge or common sense as a standard is simply that it depends on and perpetuates exclusionary and marginalizing aspects of dominant cultures. For example, "Irish" on a license plate might call up the Blarney Stone or green beer as much as the IRA if not more so. Common knowledge in the United States about the term "Palestinian" doesn't proffer light-hearted lore or American appropriationism. There is no Palestinian equivalent to the humor about how we are all Irish on St. Patrick's Day; the more that "Palestinian" is seen to designate "suicide bomber," the less likely there is to be one.

Yet if common knowledge affects how the harmless and harmful are mapped onto different signs of the foreign in both human and object form, such knowledge also sometimes functions, regarding the foreign, as the knowledge that people aim to strive beyond. Dean MacCannell, in fact, in his canonic book *The Tourist*, states that the desire for insider knowledge is a defining feature of tourism and touristic looking. As MacCannell relates, sites and guides often play to that perceived interest.

I do not want to overgeneralize about tourist aims, however. One interesting counterexample, at least about aims that people imagine others to have, emerged during the 2003 edition of *"Today* Throws a Wedding."[15] As part of this summer series on the *Today* show, the program asks to choose a (heterosexual, no older than thirty-five) wedding couple by voting, on a Web site, among a group of finalists. Viewers may then vote weekly among four choices for various wedding components, like the wedding dress, the bride's hairdo, the reception site, and the honeymoon location. (One year they even voted on wedding-night lingerie, but they no longer seem to feature that particular item.) In the 2003 program, after being invited to choose among the wedding favors viewers rejected choice number 3, a set of binoculars along with a copy of *City Secrets: New York City*, which the cover claims is the "ultimate insider's guide." Like the tackle box filled with toiletries and an array of personalized cookies, choice number 3 lost out to a bag full of souvenirs including the Statue of Liberty foam crown; sometimes a person just wants to cut right to an unsophisticated payoff.[16] In the next section, nonetheless, I consider one feature of touristic shopping that I encountered frequently among Ellis Island and Battery Park tourists that trades in insider knowledge about the foreign: the traffic in fakes.

Common knowledge may not yield up a Palestinian Blarney Stone but, as the following passage from a fashion report suggests, the perception of peering beyond the pale may enhance the appeal of foreign lands, at least when approached with certain buffers.[17]

> Michael Sears and Hushi Mortezaie have long had a following in New York's East Village, where they established their first store in 1997. . . . Their design aesthetic is a potent mix of politics and kitsch, with garish costume jewelry sharing space with provocative items like 'Long Live Iran!' T-shirts and Palestinian flag scarves—all slashed and deconstructed to trendy perfection. The duo veers away from the Persian Punk theme with more elegant items like tiered scarf dresses and ruffled blouses. At a recent show, Michael and Hushi caused a stir among attendees by sending machine gun-brandishing models down the runway wearing traditional Iranian chadors.[18]

In this text, the foreign land is the East Village and the insider knowledge is allegedly up-to-the-minute and equally old news. In *Selling the Lower East Side*, Christopher Mele writes about the area (of which "East Village" is one name given to a part of it) that "for most of its history, representations that characterized the Lower East Side as marginal, threatening, dangerous, or abnormal . . . were influential to the unfolding of local struggle" over, among other things, property. These representations were also integral to a consistent middle-class and upper-class revulsion and fascination with the area and, in turn, to the area's appeal as a "space of authentic resistance": "Put bluntly, the drama of the disenfranchised, struggling to make do and to counter economic and political exploitation enticed avant-garde movements and subcultures to settle [there]."[19] The text on fashion given above speaks to the reader who already knows what it means to have "a following in New York's East Village." But it also addresses the uninitiated, offering enough information for the outsider to make progress toward becoming that person in the know: the East Village is where the politically dangerous, the socially marginal, and the aesthetically outrageous combine to form a "potent" and "provocative" spectacle.

As MacCannell says, however, the location of that desired behind-the-scenes truth, like the distinction between the scene and behind it, might be highly staged. The "back region" may be as viewer geared as the "front region," with cues prompting the perception that one is accessing truths about a place.[20] How, then, can one be sure what one has found or where one stands? The *Full Frontal Fashion* writer posits the "insider" as the one who can spot 'Long Live Iran!' T-shirts and Palestinian flag scarves as a fashion statement. Yet surely many readers construe the writer to be the object rather than the purveyor of insider knowledge: the fool with a false sense of entrée. The text reads like a parody of the offensively clueless appropriator, too steeped in colonizer mentality to see how truly far from getting it phrases like "deconstructed to trendy perfection" make one look. Other readers, in turn, might see standing at that level of awareness as somewhat shallow, too; by now, posers can be, in slang that was dated by 2002, "all about" scoffing at the Disneyfication of diversity. Maybe they don't know anything about the specific politics involved or the complex intentions and relations to Iran of the designer, of Iranian birth though raised largely in the United States.

I spoke to Hushi Mortezaie at his store in fall 2000, on the advice of a mutual friend (notice how easily one can fraudulently intimate her own insider credentials). The friend told me that Mortezaie could offer a broader context for another phenomenon of tiered authenticity that kept popping up in tourism narratives: the trade in fake Rolex watches.[21] According to Mortezaie, the traffic in fake Rolexes and other luxury fakes in New York had a long history of shifting players and meanings. In the early 1980s, the fakes signaled "urban ghetto style" mixed with a commentary on New York living. In the 1990s, "certain fashionable downtown youth" got into older fakes, "fake vintage"; it was from this group that he and "Michael and Hushi" emerged, which featured transformed fakes in some designs. Current buyers of fakes in 2001 included "cheap rich ladies" coming to Canal Street in Chinatown from all over Europe to spend "$180" for fakes they intended to pass off as real; nonwhite immigrants and African Americans buying goods taken from luxury; and various people in the fashion business coming downtown to stores like his and, in essence, poaching "East Village" takes on fakes. Trend forecasters, he said, would "suck up your style" and then sell the information to more mainstream designers. Or stylists would buy things in his store that would then turn up as elements in fashion magazine photographs, generally without credit to him—although, as I started to notice, the coverage and credit lines for Michael and Hushi were steadily increasing.[22] The movement of fakes, then, traversed racial, economic, ethnic, and subcultural groups that were, simultaneously, significantly marked by race, economics, ethnicity, and subculture.

So, too, with the traversals that concerned me. I had become interested in the topic of fakes after one day working my way into a conversation of a group of people on the ferry to Ellis Island who had various pretensions to being on top of fakery and souvenirs.[23] One person in the group, a white man who seemed to be in his fifties, was traveling with his wife and some in-laws, whom he characterized as "good tourists." He caught my attention when I overheard him explaining that he was using a yellow filter on his camera lens to make the sky blue in his pictures; since you're only going to a place once, he told me, you should make it look like the best day possible. (I wondered if his work as a marketing consultant was relevant to this strategy, but he said no.) He planned to use a sepia filter for Ellis Island, as he had at Old Sturbridge Village, to make the photographs look vintage. I learned later from Annette Dragon, a photographer who also worked the retail end of photography, that the practice of giving fake age to photographs, which I'd associated primarily with mass-produced souvenirs like the Ellis Island placemat, was actually quite popular in private use, partly due to relatively newly available forms of technology. The tinting, once "possible only in the darkroom via a smelly chemical process," could now be achieved through a variety of devices including various filters, warm-toned printing papers, tint-prepared disposable cameras, and digital reproduction machines with a "sepia" command.[24]

The man's group entered into conversation with a younger white man, in his early twenties, who was on a year-long trip around the United States and Europe, courtesy of family money. He told me that he'd never bought a souvenir in his life, adding "My souvenirs are up here," as he pointed to his head. Still, he'd undertaken a buying activity that he understood to be characteristically "New York." He showed the group a watch he purchased for $200 from a guy on Fifth Avenue near Central Park that came with a certificate of authenticity and a yellow credit card receipt, both allegedly verifying it as a real Rolex worth $7,000.

The $200 price put the watch in the cost category of the fancier fakes whose customers Mortezaie identified as "cheap rich ladies," but distinguished it, whether real or fake, from the many fake Rolex watches for sale around New York, including at Battery Park, that were easily identified as fakes by the asking price of around $25. Tourist smarts about such watches concern the best deals on obvious fakes, and I once heard a Circle Line ferry announcer warn people away from the Battery Park vendors of watches and sunglasses that they were about to encounter; these vendors, he said, sold their wares at three to four times the price one could find elsewhere in the city (not true).[25] Smarts about the $200 watch, suggested the brother-in-law of the sepia photographer, required experience with the genuine article, like the watch that his father had bought in 1972 from a real Swiss Rolex dealer. The ambiguous phrasing made it unclear about whether he meant "real Swiss" most importantly to modify the Rolex or the dealer; in either case it implied contrast to the jewelry hustlers in New York, which the term "Swiss" is rarely used to conjure. The younger man seemed absolutely unperturbed by the possibility that his watch could be a knockoff. His apparent reserve of discretionary income must be one reason—it wasn't $200 that, thus spent, prohibited other necessities or pleasures. He also seemed to view the whole experience of buying a watch on the street as worth having in any case, no matter the value of the watch.

One would expect, however, that many tourists would not view being scammed out of several hundred dollars to be part of the fun, and the City of New York does not want it to be part of the tourist experience either. Among the various agents of vending control is the Department of Parks and Recreation, which regulates who sells what at Battery Park.

LOCAL COLOR

Immigrant peddlers, immigrants with pushcarts, immigrants selling things on the streets: they have long stood as iconic images of the New York scene.[26] They pop up in the books I mentioned earlier, like *House of Bondage* from 1910 and Abraham Cahan's *"Yekl" and "The Imported Bridegroom" and Other Stories of the New York Ghetto* from the late 1800s. In addition, the primary character in Cahan's 1917 novel *The Rise of David Levinsky* begins his New York immigrant life, like a significant and visible percentage of his nonfictional counterparts, as a peddler, working his way up from a basket to a pushcart.[27] Pushcarts frequently feature later in representations of the past. Hasia Diner, who opines that the Lower East Side has become the "American Jewish Plymouth Rock," notes that photographs of streets crowded with pushcarts have become "classic."[28] Sometimes those images of historic local color are used to generate more sales, to entice visitors, from far away or just uptown, hoping to find their ethnic immigrant roots. A poster for a 1996 Lower East Side festival shows the use of commerce past for commerce present in that area: it superimposes a list of come-ons, including "Relive the Lower East Side of 1900's" and "Hundreds of Vendor [sic]," onto a picture of buying and selling on the bustling streets of yore.[29]

Thus recirculated, such representations also may provide a lens through which to see new immigrants. Vignettes in newspaper articles about the Statue of Liberty and Ellis Island sometimes point to current immigrant peddlers as evidence of the continuing tide. In one New York Times piece on the sights of Liberty Weekend 1986, the author describes encounters with a man "from India" running a newspaper stand and "a Colombian" selling U.S. flags; it is the typical downtown "ethnic collage," he says, in which "the rest of us" can and do easily "pick out new immigrants."[30] Spectacles of past and present reinforce each other, combining to suggest that today's immigrants typically get a foothold now as earlier, by peddling on the streets of New York City, which thus becomes the place long characterized by immigrant vendors.

Such analogies fundamentally misrepresent the degree of transhistorical similarity and even the extent to which "just like before" characteristically governs comparisons. As Nancy Foner notes, for instance, in dominant cultural norms, the "traumatic ocean crossing" may make heroes of immigrants past and unwanted illegals of immigrants present.[31] Vendor analogies rendered in fond tones with quaint images also generally omit hints that public commerce has long had a contested presence. Mele points out that "the commerce of pushcart vendors who crowded the streets of the Lower East Side in the 1920s . . . was characterized as an obstacle to middle-class redevelopment."[32] At the end of the century, perceived problems of untoward commerce continued to concern those focused on image and development, and was being addressed at many levels: the sexual commerce increasingly zoned out, to the pleasure of Disney, in Times Square, as the Dangerous Bedfellows explain in Policing Public Sex; the police and the parks department increasingly brought in, as Mele explains, to "enforce 'quality of life' measures that facilitate middle-class renewal of poorer neighborhoods." Under Giuliani in the 1990s, he writes, "pro-growth policies have been combined with the ardent zeal of public officials (especially the mayor) to put to use new or existing (but relatively inexpensive) policies to 'improve' the city's image, and, consequently, middle- and upper-class property values."[33]

While Mele does not make this comment specifically in regard to street vending, Giuliani's "quality of life" measures included actions against street vendors, who battled from 1998 to 2000 against plans to close to vending up to three hundred streets. Robert Lederman, then president of ARTIST (Artists' Response to Illegal State Tactics), wrote in February 1999 that vendors, largely "Asian, Central American, Eastern European and African immigrants" were daily targets both of police action against those without requisite licenses and of political maneuvering to further limit their possibilities of working legally. Besides trying to designate more and more streets as off limits to vending, the city council was getting ready to vote on a plan, supported by corporations such as Disney and MacDonalds, to institute high-cost bidding for individual slots that would drive most immigrant vendors out of business.[34]

In addition, the two city departments that Mele identifies, the police and the parks department, have been integral to the control of vending images and practices in Battery Park. As I elaborate below, vending there already functioned under a version of the bidding model by the time city council considered instituting it more broadly, and it occurred amid area upscaling. During my research, luxury residences were going up nearby and a waterfront path along the west side of Manhattan was being increasingly spruced up and patrolled. I habitually walked several miles of the lower portion of that path to Battery Park, and once, in 2002, a jogging tourist with a tennis-club well-preserved look asked me how to get to "Ground Zero." After I told her, she decided that the distance added too much mileage to the run she'd begun at her elegant hotel—she'd grab a cab there later. Although she didn't really typify the people I saw on my walks—which more frequently were peopled with locals of somewhat diverse, but seemingly often comfortable, economic status—a goal of the changes was clearly to make people like her feel at ease.

In Battery Park itself, however, image management involved making less of a visibly sanitized upscale than of a discreetly sanitized downscale, with the idea of modest means in the common concepts of "immigrant peddler" helping to camouflage the extent to which access to capital governs the conditions of participation here, too. This is not to say that the parks department worked as a master manipulator of a concept seen by its agents to trick gullible people or to operate at the level of image only. When I interviewed Ronald Lieberman, director of Concessions for the Department of Parks and Recreation, I learned of the benefits that some individual immigrants gained from the department's own understanding of concessions licensing in terms of the upward-aspiring immigrant peddler of the past. Lieberman explained that his department sometimes provided an "almost social function" in terms of "partnering up" with people to help them get started in business. To that end, his office advertised opportunities in newspapers directed to immigrant communities and "could deal with any language" to help walk applicants through a process that might otherwise be too formidable. The process was rewarding, he said, because you could watch a "family business" develop. M and T Pretzels, for instance, started with a few pretzel stands in the 1980s and then moved up to running an ice rink in Central Park, besides vastly expanding its number of pretzel pushcarts.[35]

But this account of the parks department acting as facilitators of immigrant self-empowerment and access to the American dream, no matter how accurately it might describe the department's work with some migrants, needs to be seen alongside the department's general antagonism to unmoneyed migrants who seek to peddle in their parks. This is true even in "Historic Battery Park," so named partly for having been a place where immigrants landed, as indicated in a description of the site in a document for prospective concessionaires.[36] At Battery Park now, of the cash-poor migrants who might most closely correspond to the storied immigrant vendors of the past—who could get into business by spending a few dollars for a license (maybe), a cheap pushcart rental (maybe), and the cost of the goods they sold, bought daily[37]—only those selling art or actually being art get a comparable deal. Living statues, with body and costume in marble white, space-suit silver, or, in the case of the living Statue of Liberty, weathered-copper green, work the park, generally without permit or harassment, for the dollars that people would pay to pose with them for a picture. One pair of performers, a woman from Argentina with a male partner from Colombia, worked all around the city during the summer and in the subways during the winter. The woman told me that they needed a permit only for Penn Station; she thought they were thus generally unhampered because their routine was quiet.[38]

Art vendors enter a lottery for a month-long "artist vendor permit." The permit costs $25, thus requiring less cash in hand but more year-round output compared to the city's 853 "general vendor" permits, which cost $200 for the year but guarantee a longer term of permitted operation.[39] An artist vendor permit allows the permit holder to sell art in a specific designated place; when I was there several paths near the ferry launch site in Battery Park were lined with these artists' booths.[40] (Here is a small example of the macro affecting the micro, or the global affecting the (global) local: when I asked one of the artists why most artists' booths showed a city permit that day but not the week before, she told me that fewer police had been cruising Battery Park then because they had been working the gathering of world political leaders at the U.N. Millennium Summit.[41]) Permits also hold artists to certain requirements. They must sell their own "original artwork" that is "signed by the artist" and refrain from selling "mass-produced jewelry or other mass-produced objects."

Vendors other than artists with permits for Battery Park pay heavily for the privilege and must have sufficient cash in hand even to be considered as possible concessionaires. In 1999, a $10,000 cashier's check or money order had to accompany proposals to the parks department for a two-year contract to operate "two mobile souvenir carts at Historic Battery Park." The check was likely to remain uncashed but the funds nonetheless had to be available, along with the funds to build carts, buy stock, and pay for $1,000,000 worth of insurance against liability and property damage insurance.[42] For the fiscal year running from July 1999 through June 2000, when Battery Park licenses brought in over $3,250,000 for the city, Universal Souvenirs paid $413,550 to run the two souvenir stands. The food pushcarts with pretzels and bottled water, run by the company Lieberman told me about, brought in more.[43]

Being a licensed concessionaire brings restrictions as well as advantages. The parks department dictates in detail the specifications for the manufacture of stands (e.g., "two painted steel spoked wheels, 26" in diameter"), the signage ("Historic Battery Park" in a pre-designed "logotype" on "Glen Raven Mills, Sunbrella 'Pacific Blue'" or approved alternative), and the objects permitted for sale. "The concession may not sell watches, jewelry, or handbags" or "merchandise promoting musicians, entertainers, sports figures, cartoon characters, commercial products, or non-park-related events"; an added warning states that the sale of "counterfeit merchandise" will "result in immediate termination of the permit and seizure of the security deposit."[44] The department also keeps an eye on pricing and encourages the hiring of people who are "members of the local community," two features that suggest the reach but also the convenient distance for higher-ups intrinsic to the practice of subcontracting. For instance, the parks department mandated the availability of some inexpensive products but did not have to bear the onus of their possibly labor-unfriendly origins. Further, although proposals did stipulate access for people with disabilities as mandated by law, Lieberman's office did not generally concern itself with something else that I noticed: that concessionaires predominantly hired males. The parks department also dictated the location of businesses and retained the right to approve the exact relocation of mobile carts due to unusual circumstances, such as the Battery Park renovation project that was warned about in the 1999 proposal form.[45]

The importance of this provision about relocation became clear to me over the course of several years through my conversations with one vendor to whom I spoke often when I visited Battery Park in 2000 through 2002. Originally from Lebanon, he had come to the United States several years earlier to work with his brother, who had emigrated eight years previously and now ran the business. On the best days, he told me in early September 2000, the business could make $15,000 from the stands. A little while later, with construction underway, the park had become less enjoyable and less sales friendly. It was easy to see that this situation was in part the result of the fact that the parks department had relocated the vendor carts by cramming them together in a smaller space. His business fared better under the parks department during the disruption following the events of 9/11 when the Statue of Liberty and Ellis Island were closed and Battery Park was turned over to serve the purposes of the military. I'd wondered from time to time if the city had given a break to concessionaires who had paid a flat fee, or if the vendors had been forced to absorb the costs attending unforeseen lost sales. When I returned to Battery Park in the summer of 2002, I learned that neither had been the case. Instead, he told me, his company had printed up FDNY and NYPD T-shirts and hats, honoring the police and fire departments lauded as heroes of 9/11. He had then moved the stands up to Queens, where the merchandise sold very well.[46]

It did not, however, take the events of 9/11 to bring NYPD merchandise to this man's souvenir stands. Starting in at least 2000, when I first visited his stands, he had carried a supply of NYPD-marked items among the Statue of Liberty souvenirs and other New York memorabilia. I'd noted this right away because of several high-profile incidents that remained big news regarding NYPD brutality toward immigrants, like the cases of Abner Louima, tortured in 1997, and Amadou Diallo, a street vendor himself. Diallo was killed in 1998 by police who claimed to mistake his wallet for a gun; and at the time of my visits to Battery Park in 2000 they had recently been acquitted of murder charges. So my own preconceptions about "immigrant peddlers" did not include the hawking of NYPD items. When I asked the souvenir vendor about it, he told me that the products were very popular and that he "loved" the NYPD. When I responded that I wasn't so happy with them, he repeated that he liked them and said that the "ones down here," in the park, are good.

One reason he might have liked the NYPD is that they occasionally showed up to participate in policing the park in order to expel one source of competition for tourist dollars: the vendors operating illegally about whom the ferry announcer had warned visitors. As Lieberman explained to me, the NYPD sometimes aided the Parks Enforcement Police, which patrolled the parks partly to contain illegal vending, participating as well in the occasional "blitz." Vendors caught operating illegally were issued a summons from the Environmental Control Board, which required them to go before a judge in the regular New York City court system. The judge usually fined them and "confined" their merchandise. It happened often enough to be considered, Lieberman said, part of the "cost of doing business."

Another cost to the vendors, of course, concerned the stress of having to be constantly on the lookout for people who threatened their livelihood. Enforcement personnel, Lieberman told me, sometimes worked under cover, which is why, I learned immediately, vendors might expect me to be affiliated with law enforcement when I asked questions that did not explicitly reflect possible interest in making a purchase. In one of my first attempts to learn more, I approached a vendor selling sunglasses and chains and tried to signal casual, sympathetic interest. He said "thank you," closed his case and left the park. Unlike the artist vendor who simply rebuffed me with a line, "trade secret," when I asked how he got his permit (but opened up once I convinced him I was a writer not a competitor), this man couldn't risk working with me around.[47] After that, I decided not to pursue such inquiries. I wanted to avoid impeding these vendors' livelihoods or adding one more person to their environment that who appeared possibly to police them.

One afternoon, however, I did learn a bit more with the help of a friend who could approach vendors by speaking in Arabic (later moving on to French).[48] When my friend described himself as a fellow Muslim far from his original home, true enough in terms of his origins if potentially a bit misleading about his piety, vendors were often willing to talk to him and sometimes even glad for the conversation. This was one way that we met our own ethical criteria of avoiding harassment and ideally giving a little something back. We also bought a watch from a man who gave us a lot of his time. ("Rolex Genuine Swiss Made" and "Officially Certified" were inscribed on the back.) That vendor, like many who spoke to us, was from Senegal; except for one man who said he was from Jamaica, although my friend and I had doubts, all came from Senegal or Mauritania. The watch vendor had been in New York for ten years, working to send money home. He got his merchandise from someone to whom he then paid a portion of what he made from sales. Like others, he found the work hard, and living in the United States was also difficult. Several women we spoke with said that they couldn't send money home because all of their income went to rent; money also went to the cost of returning home for new visas. Even with the expenses, however, they fared better than they had in Senegal, where they could find no work. One of the women, whose sister worked in France, also "in commerce," knew that it was difficult there, too.

JUDGING BY APPEARANCES

From one perspective, my account of the vending scene at Battery Park is a story of camouflage. The place looks and sounds like the marketscape of yet another generation of immigrant peddlers. To some extent the image fits—once one shifts the term "immigrant" to "migrant," acknowledging that some migrants come intending to leave, an intention often buried now as in the past under the prevailing conceit that everyone dreams of calling "America" home. All over the park vendors sell their products. Few "sound American" in the way that likely helped to get me onto the airplane on my return from San Francisco. I certainly didn't manage to hear the voice of every vendor I saw, but I did at least have my sense of the array confirmed by a living Statue of Liberty. Her portrayer, a woman, originally from Cleveland, whom I took to be in her fifties, frequented the park, using a flirty, Mikado-esque mask to perform a hip-shaking, come-hither torch bearer of greater youth than her herself. I mentioned to her, in a conversation during one of her smoke breaks, that she was the first person working the park that I'd talked to who sounded of U.S. origin. She thought herself rare that way, too, although like the others she was a migrant; she spent much of her life performing in Europe (in many personae but never the Statue).[49] My sense was confirmed also by Lieberman, who said that most of their licensees were immigrants, and by the guy I interviewed over the years at the souvenir stand, who matter-of-factly responded to my question about who worked for him by identifying the workers according to place of origin: seven to nine Pakistanis, four Hondurans, and one Puerto Rican. (They were, he said, all the same in one way: "Everyone needs to take care of their families."[50] Yet another bundle of privileges and presumptions tied to concepts of family; perhaps this comment related to the dearth of women employees.)

But the look of transhistorical continuity over the span of more than a century is deceiving because the peddlers who most correspond to their predecessors referenced in the "Historic" of "Historic Battery Park" are the ones most embattled and disdained. The briefcases from which they often sell their products can well stand for the contradictory features of their situation: the cases are both sufficient to hold their small amount of stock, a modest investment of the sort associated with the storied peddlers of the past, and necessary to enable sudden flight because vending regulations now render them criminals. Meanwhile, protection goes to the pushcarts and souvenir carts backed by large capital investments and stocked to make thousands of dollars a day, as long as they don't offer merchandise that is determined to blur the lines between preferred and unwanted vending. The emphasis in the concession-competition information against watches, jewelry, and handbags—the first two being the staples of illegal vendors at the park, and all three part of street vending all over the city—and the dire consequences to be assessed for selling counterfeits indicate a set of parameters that involve, among other matters, distinguishing legal from illegal vending. Lieberman told me that they checked out merchandise to make sure it was decent quality (but "don't expect Bloomingdale's") and that it didn't look good to sell watches. Yet the looks criterion is subjective and thus arguable (is the standard "I ♥ New York" t-shirt inherently more attractive?) and the parks department's criteria for goods clearly had some give. With artists, for instance, the requirement for signed "original artwork," emphasized along with the requirement against "mass-produced jewelry or other mass-produced objects," did not prevent various artists from selling virtually identical photographs of the city. And while souvenir concessionaires were "encouraged to sell merchandise related to New York City Parks and specific tourist attractions in the vicinity of Battery Park," they were allowed to sell NYPD-wear alongside the Liberty statue souvenirs. Then again, given the integral role of policing in the park, NYPD goods fit the criteria just fine.

So looks can be deceiving regarding the economics under the awnings labeled "Historic Battery Park." At the same time, one feature of the parks department regulation of vending is actually plain to see: the people whose vending doesn't "look good" to the parks department turn out to be that belonging to the darkest-skinned vendors. This fact of the situation can be sidestepped in a number of ways: by decrying the traffic in counterfeits as what looks bad; by invoking the distinction between legal and illegal vending as the operative distinction in the matter; by speaking in generalities about immigrants or immigrant vendors; by categorizing migrants, sometimes simultaneously, primarily according to country of origin; and by attributing correlations between people's origins and current vending activities fully to self-selection, which can only be part of the story. Certainly, when Lieberman noted that Greeks tended toward food vending while people from India and Pakistan more frequently ran newsstands, he was in part making a reasonably grounded observation among many to be made about how workers sometimes follow others of like origin into particular types of work. What is missing, however, is an accounting of matters that need to complicate and undermine the intimation that such labor sorting fully represents some kind of culturally ingrained preference or implied free choice. That doesn't mean discounting the importance of geopolitical origin, which may have a lot to do with reasons to migrate, access to capital, and other factors that bring to vending those migrants with more or fewer resources and that bring many of us into networks circumscribed, to various effect, by likeness.

These factors, however, also include racial identities, as construed and perceived about self and/or others, and racism, which must be named here for several reasons. First, naming such issues of race reveals the Battery Park scene as consistent with a series of policing actions that came under Giuliani's "quality of life" regime. Giuliani was hardly the one to initiate policing vendors, the regulation of whom, as Regina Austin emphasizes, has long been a source of struggle, both within and outside of New York.[51] At the same time, the policies and practices regarding vending under Giuliani's administration fit among many that had the function of "criminalizing the marginal," as Michael Tomasky put it in *New York* magazine in 1998, itemizing initiatives that harmed street vendors, street artists, CUNY students, people needing care in city hospitals, and cab drivers. Many in these categories, as he notes, are "black or brown, powerless, unorganized, on the fringes, struggling for their daily bread, or some combination thereof," and many are also, "by and large the kind of hardworking immigrants Giuliani once celebrated rhetorically, back when he was angling for reelection by a huge margin."[52]

How the confluence of immigrant status and "black" skin could make one doubly a target was illustrated in the situation of Amadou Diallo who pursued characteristic and embattled immigrant work as a street vendor before his death added him to a list of unarmed people, primarily black and Latino, who had been shot by police officers, more often white than not, in what Amnesty International in a 1996 report called "apparently non-threatening or questionable circumstance."[53] Human Rights Watch publicized the issues again in 1998, noting a "racial or ethnic component" in the preponderance of "police abuse cases" in New York.[54] Testimony after testimony that the "quality of life" regime involved increasing harassment and violence against people of color suggest the actions against unwanted vendors at Battery Park to be part of a pattern. This is not to allege that those actions were violent—although I do want to note that I saw several arrests of vendors despite the statements in various descriptions I encountered that issuing a summons was the primary initial action against them —but to situate them within a climate where dark-skinned black people disproportionately wind up on the policed and evacuated side of image management.

Second, given the visibility of this pattern, the politics of failing to name race as a factor suggest complicity with maintaining the pattern. I make this claim on top of another one: that decisions about naming race as a potential factor always have politics, as do decisions about how and whether to link race to ethnicity. These politics vary in context. For example, recall that in the 1923 decision of *United States v. Thind* the "common sense" in separating race from ethnicity was invoked when identifying race by ethnicity (white = Caucasian) was not able to support the logic of exclusion. The decision, in effect, said, "look here." In New York at the end of the twentieth century, it was often failing to say "look here" that supported logics of exclusion and practices of racism—including, allegedly, the practices of the parks department. Just a few months after Diallo was killed (with a newspaper's slant sometimes visible in whether or not its articles described the incident as the killing of a black man by four white police officers or omitted race identifiers altogether), twenty current and former employees of the parks department, all "black or hispanic," filed complaints with the federal Equal Employment Opportunity Commission (EEOC) that the department "discriminated on the basis of race and national origin in assigning and promoting employees." In February 2001, the EEOC ruled that it had found "reasonable cause" to believe that illegal discrimination had occurred. Interestingly, Parks Commissioner Harold Stern, defending the personnel assignments that gave the highest-ranking positions to white people, said, according to an article in the *New York Times*, that "much of the agency's personnel patterns reflected the workers' personal preferences."[55] Again, the attribution of work situations to personal preference places the distribution of labor under the rubric of free choice and self-determination in ways that may obscure other forces involved.

At Battery Park, the image of immigrant peddlers struggling to lift themselves up coexists with and to some extent masks the practices designed to
get rid of them. The migrant peddlers operating legally either have the resources to make a huge capital investment, far beyond today's equivalent
of the dime for pushcart rental, or work as employees for the people who
have the resources. The people most like the migrants of the past in terms
of low-budget entrepreneurship face numerous maneuvers to put them out
of business. To mix artistic metaphors, the peddler image is stage managed.

But the stage managing gets complicated, overlaid, and transformed by
various players, themselves variously framed and self-framing, and by various divisions besides, if informing, that of the separation between the legal
and the illegal. One set of these divisions involves authenticity. The traffic in
fakes and the claims to knowledge about it play across, and shape, various
lines marking distinctions in race, ethnicity, and economic status, and between insiders and outsiders. Earlier I discussed insider knowledge about
fakes as part of tourist smarts. Of interest here also is the proprietary alle-
giance regarding ownership rights that is sometimes expressed by people
hardly poised to lose or profit monetarily. Over the course of my research
I was surprised by the number of people I encountered, like the ferry announcer telling passengers to buy fake watches somewhere else, who articulated a strong position about who got to sell what, even when they had no
stake but perceived righteousness. At Ellis Island, I heard a park ranger tell
a visitor who had inquired about Nevada Barr, former park ranger and author of ranger mysteries such as *Liberty Falling*, that it is "a huge conflict of
interest to make money off what you do for the [National] Park Service"; her
defense of this conjured principle stands out against the modest salaries of
park rangers.[56] At a National Park Service store on Pier 39, I wondered out
loud to a sales clerk, who must have been equally ill-compensated, about
the similarity between a certain set of stylized images on various goods celebrating California national parks and a T-shirt I'd bought at Angel Island
State Park that commemorated the immigration station's new status as a
national historic landmark. Might the same artist have designed them all?
She responded with alarm, explaining that "we" were having a big problem
with copyright because the artist's designs were so popular.[57] As I have been

suggesting in this chapter regarding other matters, many factors may contribute to someone wanting to present themselves as in the know or as important; still, choosing this way to represent oneself as either is significant.

This impulse to police needs to be seen, too, against the increased prominence of policing as an object of carefully scripted representation itself. For example, during September 2000, the month in which I conducted most of my Battery Park interviews, a huge big-budget recruiting campaign for the NYPD touted the merits and diversity friendliness of the NYPD: one ad series among many had the actor Ray Romano pronounce his brother the cop the brave one in the family; another showed a young woman with her arms around a seated grandmother figure along the text, "She will hug the neighborhood the way she hugs me. It's people like Katy Ngan that make our Mission:Possible. Join Us."[58] I encountered these ads, which obviously did double duty working to improve the image of the NYPD, while watching TV, listening to the radio, and riding the subway. Less well funded were the ads, running simultaneously, to call 1–877-PROFILE, the ACLU hotline number to report racial profiling, including being stopped for what has been nicknamed DWB: driving while black or brown.

If I kept running across the impulse and power to police in my various engagements with souvenirs, this is partly because the movement of people and goods is increasingly subject to visible policing—in air travel, under New York's "quality of life" regime, and beyond. The visibility of public relations activities about policing has increased accordingly. These have become so common in some forms that they may pass without remark, like those ubiquitous automated voices that put surveillance forward as a device for our protection, announcing that calls are being monitored to enhance our satisfaction. Does the possibility of grabbing a souvenir and a sandwich at the old detention center belong on this list of contemporary acculturations working to make policing activities that might otherwise seem dubious look instead natural, palatable, or perhaps even pleasing? This is one question I take up in the next chapter, which looks at Ellis Island's tourist amenities.

SEVEN

PRODUCT PACKAGING

Deborah Bright's *Glacial Erratic, Plymouth, MA (Sunrise)* (2001; figure 19) from her *Glacial Erratic Series* offers a wonderful visual meditation on the factors both human and natural that shape perspectives on what she terms "sites of patriotic memory." The site shown in the photo is Plymouth Rock, which "geologically speaking," Bright explains, is a "glacial erratic, a large boulder deposited by retreating glaciers from the last Ice Age."[1] Having been literally relocated, reshaped, and reframed many times over, Plymouth Rock epitomizes why terms like "restoration" frequently fail to do justice to the processes that make historical monuments. Named by a town elder in 1741 as the Mayflower Pilgrims's first 1620 landing spot ("Pilgrim," too, was a later appellation), the rock broke in half in 1774 when about thirty yoked oxen were used to pull it from the shore to the town square; the bottom part stayed behind. Because souvenir seekers kept chipping away at the rock, in 1834 the top part was moved again, this time pulled by schoolboys, to reside in front of Pilgrim Hall within a protective enclosure built for it. The bottom half, meanwhile, was covered, along with some pilgrim bones, by a granite canopy in the 1860s, and, in 1880, the top was returned to the bottom. In honor of the three hundredth anniversary of the Mayflower landing, and courtesy of the National Society of Colonial Dames, Plymouth Rock got a fancier architectural protector in 1921: a neoclassical temple-like pavilion designed by the well-known architectural firm McKim, Mead, and White.

Since then it has undergone repairs and protests, including burial in 1970 during a protest organized by the United American Indians of New England (UAINE). After the organizers of a banquet for the 350th anniversary

FIGURE 19. *Glacial Erratic, Plymouth, MA (Sunrise)*, 2001. (Photography by Deborah Bright, courtesy of the artist)

rescinded an Aquinnah Wampanoag man's invitation to speak once they had previewed the speech's contents, which detailed crimes against the Wampanoag by the arriving Europeans, UAINE declared Thanksgiving Day to be a National Day of Mourning and initiated an annual protest in Plymouth.[2]

Several contrasting presentations of UAINE's protests well illustrate how textual framing sets historical monuments into different-looking scenes. The Internet account published by Plimouth Plantation in 2000 notes that "protesters of one sort or another have used the Rock as the focus for their causes and cast paint, sand and other materials on it which the Town then patiently removes." This text portrays "the Town" as of collective mind and as a benevolent keeper of social peace and visual order. It also makes UAINE appear rather isolated and ineffectual by mentioning only its 1970 protest and stating rather ambiguously that the group "symbolically buried this icon of European immigration," which might imply that the burial did not take material form, and by declaring the rock's continuing meaning as "the symbolic stepping stone from which the American nation strode forth."[3]

In contrast UAINE's Web site indicates that besides burying the rock twice during that first action, protestors replaced the Union Jack on the [replica of the] Mayflower with a flag that had flown over Alcatraz Island during its nineteen-month occupation by Indians of All Tribes, then still in progress, and that protestors had returned every year since. This information links the protest to a broad and continuing movement for Native American rights (which included, as I noted in the last chapter, an attempted takeover of Ellis Island seven months earlier).[4] The UAINE Web site also describes the very unbenevolent response of the Plymouth police in 1997 who used mace and clubs to break up the annual protest and arrested twenty-five people. The settlement with the Town of Plymouth and Plymouth County prosecutors testifies to the official acknowledgment of inappropriate police action. Besides dropping all criminal charges, the settlement included the sum of over $100,000 from the town to fund educational material and historical plaques that expose the unjust treatment of native peoples in Massachusetts; a commitment to make UAINE literature available to visitors alongside other tourist material; and, as UAINE put it, "our right to walk on our own land without a permit on National Day of Mourning."[5]

In a sense, Bright's approach relates to that sponsored by the Colonial Dames much as UAINE's Web site relates to that of Plimouth Plantation. Her view from beach level trades the neoclassical columns—a predictable but, one might argue, questionable cultural device to enshrine a break from Europe—for steel bars that do nothing to mute the purpose of controlling access. Nor do the bars aggrandize the object, which Plimoth Plantation calls "a familiar and homely marker" and Bright likens to a potato. The vantage point from the water, she writes also, "makes the rock appear caged like some animal in the zoo."[6] At the same time, the photographs in the series overall show effects on viewing that cannot be primarily ascribed to human positioning and intervention. Bright explains about the series, which plays off Monet's paintings of Rouen Cathedral in initiating each image on different occasions: "As the tides wash in and out of Plymouth Harbor, they leave their residue: seaweed deposited on the steel bars and displacements of the stone rip-rap that protects the shore from erosion. Changing weather, times of day and seasons of the year create their own sensuous play of color and light on the caged, immobilized rock, restoring the 'grace of nature' to this most unnatural and ambiguously symbolic scene."[7] The photographs, on their own and in series, evoke what exceeds human intervention, even if, of course, they nonetheless are created and seen through it. In *Sunrise* a reddish glare suggests the nowhere-to-hide of incarceration, the bars' shadows stripe the rock itself, and the surface looks scraped and bruised like flesh. In *Dusk* the rock, unmarked by the bars, sits quietly behind them, an undramatic captive with a bad repair job.

This chapter pops in and out of the gift shop to look at a messy set of relations among vending, migration, and tourism. I stated at the beginning of this book that my first physical encounter with Ellis Island entailed a rush to discover whether it had a gift shop that sold snow globes, contrary to my lover's insistence that our Ellis Island hosts would clearly recognize such frivolities as patently inappropriate. Although I won our bet, she certainly had a point that the path from Ellis Island's history to its trinkets could not possibly be seamless. As my research went on, I kept running into images, places, and issues that brought into focus the temple columns and steel bars, as it were, that set up Ellis Island, a place of detention, with tourist amenities.

I have divided the chapter into two major sections. In the first, "Flexible Production," I consider the disjuncture at the gift shop between increasing multicultural savvy, on some matters at least, and a certain matter-of-factness about the exploitation of labor involved in the manufacture of many souvenirs. In the second, "Eat Up," I begin with a souvenir placemat and follow one of its photographs, depicting women and children eating at Ellis Island, across the hall to the snack shop, to which a sign with the same photograph at one time directed visitors. By looking at food and food representation at Ellis Island past and present, I examine the elisions regarding incarceration in the making of Ellis Island as a tourist site. Throughout I argue that images do not lie on top of truths, hiding them more or less, but rather that the packaging matters in terms of both the labors and the looks involved.

New and Different. A great example of the frequent disparity between the politics of representation and the politics of manufacture can be found in the transformations at the Ellis Island gift shop over a period of several years, beginning in 1999, when I first started paying a lot of attention to its contents. My attention, I begin by reemphasizing, separated my apprehension of the gift shop from that of most of its other visitors, although it wasn't wholly different. Like that of everyone else, my gaze was certainly partial—in the senses of being incomplete, only a part, and directed, as in "partial toward." The purchases that people showed me included objects I'd never noticed, or noted with detachment, while I fell for some things that others actively disdained. I interviewed a group of white students from Bristol on summer travel as we sat waiting for the ferry. They told me that they found tourist souvenirs to be completely stupid, excluding the soft yellow taxi one regretted having passed over at the Stock Exchange, but including the snow globes that one woman always bought for her sister as a semi-mean joke about bad taste. To illustrate how foolish and despicable souvenirs generally seemed to them, one mentioned a flashlight resembling the Statue of Liberty torch that they'd seen at the gift shop there.[8] I knew just what they were talking about because at one point I had excitedly grabbed one as a present for my tool-toting girlfriend.

My interests in the gift shop were characteristically partial, but my status as a repeat visitor set me apart, as did my big interest in apparent content: which immigrants were on the magnet, which countries were getting flag decals, which skin colors were depicted on the "Ellis Island: Where Children of the World Come Together" T-shirt.[9] In fall 2000, for instance, I witnessed a conversation among three white teenaged girls standing in front of a document collection display (described in an earlier chapter) with Confederate money and the deed to Manhattan. One girl, picking up a copy of the Declaration of Independence, asked her friends if she should buy it. "No," another replied, "get some candy instead." The first girl readily assented, and they all walked away.[10] I don't cite their apparent attitude as predominant, although the interchange serves as a reminder against making presumptions either about how people group consumer items—Declaration and Constitution or Declaration and candy—or about how, and how seriously, they may take the choices or perceived content of items under consideration. I do think that I was more likely than most people to stop and read all the options in the document collection, and that I was just about the only person to write them down.

A repeat visitor paying a certain kind of attention, however, might notice the changes in the gift shop that suggest, at least in some areas, an increasing and welcome sophistication regarding certain issues about nation and ethnicity. For example, I noted in the introduction how some of the souvenirs I encountered during my first research trip in 1999, like the glittery plaque showing the Ellis Island administration building superimposed onto a flag of Israel, reflected the inadequacies of division by nation-states. The signage at the gift shop did something similar. A seder plate, a kiddush cup, and another plate with "Shalom" written on it stood behind a sign saying: "These Products reflect the heritage of the people from the middle east and are part of the exclusive Ellis Island Gift Collection. Use them with Pride and remember those who came this way." Clearly, "middle east" was a way to say "Jewish," implying a series of equivalences with neither historical nor contemporary accuracy, since "those who came this way" were generally not coming from the "middle east," which was hardly, then or later, summarized by the cultures of Jews alone.

In September 2000 the signage for the plates and cup display changed to a listing of "Favorites" with "Middle East" abandoned for more specificity. One set of products was named as associated with Jewish migrants, with the category distinguished from places or nations: "Many Immigrants from many countries were of Jewish Heritage. Our collection of these products reflects this Heritage." Another sign designated products associated with Egypt: "Egypt is one of the countries on the Coast of North Africa that is represented in this Gift Collection." Besides being noteworthy for its departure from an earlier habit of treating Africa as a relatively undifferentiated entity, the Egypt sign should be noted simply for naming Egypt as part of Africa. As Martin Bernal details in *Black Athena*, the portrayal of Egypt in isolation from the rest of the continent has been one common intellectual habit with the effect and sometimes intention of failing to associate early cultural sophistication with Africa, and by implication, dark-skinned people; a glance at art history survey books from not too long ago shows this practice at work.[11]

I am not saying, however, that all of the signage was stellar. The sign for Kenya, for instance, which states "products reflect traditional African Art on many items to accessorize your home," despecifies Kenya back to Africa in general. Its use of "traditional," which appears also on the China sign but not on the sign about Poland, suggests a mark of the primitive accorded to continents associated with skin considered "of color." Besides, the notion that items reflecting "traditional African Art" would "accessorize your home" might well seem trivializing, even if one doesn't have a separate category or special regard for art with a capital A, or consider it the height of boorishness to pick paintings to match furniture. I also find the text a bit too close for comfort to the pop culture trope whereby cultural production associated with black people appears primarily to serve the pleasure of white people (like when Barry White helps characters on *Ally McBeal* get sexy). Nonetheless, the texts overall showed improvement, if— once again and very, very importantly—with race-marked degrees of attentiveness. I found more than a few times at Ellis Island that material I would have changed or dropped, were I in charge, had been changed or dropped without my help.

Significant, too, are the texts I didn't find, texts like these: "Grab one of these darling shtetl characters and shmear the cream cheese on your bagel!"; "the 'Enola Gay' made history when it dropped the first atomic bomb on Hiroshima, helping to bring World War II to an end"; or "Blame it on Elián—suddenly, Cuban eats are hotter than a Havana heat wave." The first, describing "Fiddler on the Roof [cream cheese] Spreaders" from a catalog called *The Source for Everything Jewish*, presumes the reader's recognition of the source as a like-identified insider. This is like the issue of who gets to call whom a "fag": who can call a shtetl or its characters cute without suggesting bigotry or insensitivity?[12] In general, the gift shop doesn't stock products that may bespeak ill will or ignorance if unlinked to identifiable insider status.

The second text comes from a 2003 newspaper ad for "die-cast models presented by The History Channel®" of "Two of the Greatest American Bombers Ever," which the ad, exemplifying "history" told and sold from power, claims to be "national treasures."[13] While the gift shop is full of souvenirs celebrating and glorifying the United States, with flag paraphernalia and items marked "Ellis Island U.S.A." in ever increasing supply, blatant applause for deadly U.S. violence against, or even power over, people in other parts of the world does not appear. In citing the Enola Gay ad, I realize that I have chosen an example that cannot stand for the typical no-show in any museum gift shop, given the huge controversy in the early 1990s over strategies for exhibiting the Enola Gay at the National Air and Space Museum in Washington, D.C. The fight was so contentious and so highly publicized that, as Steven Dubin points out, it came to emblematize, from many positions, the nightmare politics that may attend museum exhibitions concerning material with widely divergent stakeholders.[14] Thus big reasons already exist to avoid Enola Gay memorabilia, especially if not related to the site. But my point here is that, regardless of those particulars, the Ellis Island shop would not carry it anyway.

The third text, a subtitle in *Glamour* magazine to "Cuban Can-do Dinner," has a cheerful trivialization that frequently appears even more trivializing when commercialization comes into the picture.[15] Elián González, here given the one-name celebrity treatment and the cheery effect of generating a menu craze, is the Cuban child who in 1999 was rescued in the waters off Florida where his mother and stepfather, seeking to defect to the United States, had drowned. He became an object of controversy when his U.S. relatives tried to claim political asylum for him rather than send him back to his father in Cuba. Although, as Sarah Benet-Weiser points out, the press frequently portrayed González with a deifying childhood innocence rarely attached to illegal migration,[16] or perhaps because of that, the traffic in Elián goods was frequently seen to sidestep respect. For instance, eBay pulled from auction the alleged raft on which González traveled, one among many items put up for sale on the site that have generated debates about propriety. Others include memorabilia connected to Pamela Smart, convicted for seducing her teenaged lover into killing her husband, and a bullet-ridden piece of the door in front of which police killed Amadou Diallo.[17] The seller planned, detailed the columnist Leonard Pitts, to use the $41,000 at which he had priced the item ($1,000 for every bullet) to support a memorial for Diallo and a march on Washington against police brutality. Pitts argued that the sale was inappropriate no matter what: "To sell such things—particularly on the open market like a Ping Pong Table or a used car—is to deny them the weight of meaning. To make them common and small."[18] While the standards for unacceptable trivialization certainly vary, and I'm sure many people would point to candidates at the Ellis Island gift shop, there is a certain shying away there from the controversial and contested edges of the breezy and the tasteless.

Buying Experts. Various factors may explain the gift shop's improvements and discretions, including, in some instances possibly, customer complaints or requests.[19] In addition, as Marilyn Halter explains in *Shopping for Identity: the Marketing of Ethnicity*, published in 2000, "ethnic marketing has become an industry in its own right," with professionals specializing in precisely that. Sears, for instance, has a director of multicultural marketing, and companies like Multicultural Marketing Resources, Inc. (MMR) put out publications to help people navigate insufficiently familiar territory.[20] In 2003, MMR's Web site identified the company as the "premier source for marketing executives looking to reach multicultural and lifestyle markets" and for "journalists who cover the latest trends and news in diversity." It also claimed that MMR's *Source Book of Multicultural Experts* served twenty-five hundred marketing executives and eleven thousand journalists looking for information on the various focus periods, like Hispanic Heritage Month (15 September to 15 October), Black History Month (February), Women's History Month (March), and Asian Pacific American Heritage Month (May), as well as "year-round coverage of a diverse America."[21]

That journalists might turn to marketers for sources might seem a bit alarming, with the predicted effects like the one discussed earlier regarding the newspaper coverage of Cicely Tyson's Jewels of Unity collection for QVC, where the repeated misspelling of Robben Island serves as an indicator of the likelihood that QVC's press release was the single source for the item presented as a news story. Yet, as Halter emphasizes, the benefits that marketers can derive from cultural care sometimes give them a strong impetus to move beyond shallow attention. She cites as an example the Bacardi Folk Arts Fair in Puerto Rico. Begun as part of Bacardi's campaign to change its image from Cuban to Puerto Rican (a fact interesting on its own) and to improve its market share in Puerto Rico, the fair became known for "exacting standards of authenticity," developed in conjunction with the government. These standards were so rigid they forced "unofficial cultural vendors," to set up "their own individualized renditions of the meaning of Puerto Ricanness" outside the fair venue.[22]

Halter's comment on the "irony" of a corporation enforcing cultural purity standards does not get close enough to the problems and blind spots in ethnic marketing that the Bacardi case raises, a central one being the concept of cultural purity itself. Many people have justifiably criticized beliefs that certain peoples and cultures remain hermetically sealed within geographic boundaries, developing only in relation to themselves and remaining unmarked by contact, forced or otherwise, from outside; such views are inaccurate characterizations that aggrandize or, more often, primitivize the cultures linked to them. As Doreen Massey notes, for instance, "the quintessential [English] cup of tea could not be sipped without plantations in India, Opium Wars in China and—if you take sugar—a history of slavery in the Caribbean." At the same time, the women she interviewed in the Yucatán, making tortillas the way "bread had 'always' been made," had a picture of the Virgin of Guadaloupe on their earthen walls and were speaking the language of the conquering Spanish; neither the elite nor the indigenous are as culturally pure as they sometimes claim or are claimed to be.[23] This point has relevance for goods like those at Ellis Island displayed and named by country, with terms like "traditional," "craft," and "heritage" invoking fixed roots and discrete groups; those roots, groups, and products bear the results of intercultural contact. The Bacardi example does show, nonetheless, the work that marketers may put into multicultural research and the expertise on which they may draw.

The selections at the Ellis Island gift shop reflect the use of such expertise. Lynn Hand, the buyer whom I interviewed in 2000, after he had been working at the gift shop for two and a half years, specialized in product-by-nation venues; he had come from a similar job as general manager and buyer for the gift shop at the United Nations.[24] Although he did not speak to me in much depth about the specific political niceties that I mentioned above, except for clearly stating "Jewish" as a designation that could not be subsumed under designation by country, the fruits of his particularized experience were clear. At the United Nations, for instance, he had had to negotiate the situation of trying to be representative of the member nations, 185 at the time, when, in his terms, not all were "set up for export." He tried, then, to distribute evenly by continent. There and also at Ellis Island he worked partly through import companies, who handle dealing with customs, and partly via direct import to acquire merchandise chosen to represent the craft traditions of different countries.

Hand's influence also appeared in the array of souvenir trinkets. He commissioned designs and products from various manufacturers, suiting the supply both to trends and his own standards. For example, after I mentioned having seen back scratchers in 1997 and noting their disappearance at a later time, he told me that back scratchers were his "personal peeve" among souvenirs. When they appear in a store they "cheapen the whole place," and thus he had discontinued them on arriving. Other products, he said, just ran their course, like Ellis Island lanyards, hot a few years previously, or the glittery flag plaques, which I'd noticed in shorter supply. Mountain climber key clips, however, were then all the rage, especially with kids.

What he did not use his expertise to do was to involve himself in issues of labor and manufacture. It was clear from our conversation that he understood stocking the gift shop to involve ethical decisions. He told me, for instance, that once a company developed a design for the gift shop, like the immigrant boy hauling his luggage in front of the "Front Doors to Freedom," he felt responsible to buy from that company all of the products that he intended the design to embellish. It was apparent, too, that he also saw decisions about product manufacturing as ethical—or, at least, as politically fraught—thus putting the immediate desires of consumers and the financial success of the gift shop (and thus the job of its buyer, I presume) in conflict with considerations about labor that one might otherwise engage. During the course of the interview, Hand described two goals that affected his choices about what to stock. He wanted to offer some items that people "can buy at a decent price [with a] decent perceived value, not a piece of junk," so that they could "last and be cherished," as well as cheap objects that most tourists, especially kids, could afford. These latter items included snow globes like the one I bought: Hand ordered 5,600 at a time to cover the supply needs for a year. Cheap labor, he explained, although without using that phrase, determined his ability to accomplish the second goal. A key tag priced at $3.99 would cost $9.99 if made in the United States; a T-shirt made in the United States would cost $35. "How many will you sell?"

Concerning Hand's labor interests, what is perhaps as telling as his purchasing decisions is his articulation of the options in terms of an opposition between production inside the United States and production outside, with the United States implicitly standing for higher labor costs and presumed better working conditions. To an extent, despite erasing some of the horrendous conditions in U.S. manufacturing, this opposition does signal relevant issues and actions: production is moved, or phases of it outsourced, to save money on labor and avoid pesky U.S. labor laws, with U.S. manufacturing jobs disappearing as a result. Yet a greater interest in labor activism might have put alternative formulations and strategies closer to the surface. These might include seeing the situation of U.S. workers in manufacturing jobs as interdependent, more precisely than in competition, with that of workers in other countries, or considering activist alternatives to boycotts. Antisweatshop activists have frequently argued against simply boycotting or otherwise pulling business from workplaces with sweatshop conditions, which leaves already struggling workers with no jobs at all. They have demanded instead that companies using overseas production monitor factories and take responsibility for improving them.[25] I do not want to make too much of the comments that Hand didn't volunteer, which might easily be attributed to his assessment of my knowledge base or interests. "Made in the U.S.A." campaigns are prominent enough (presented as matters of labor or patriotism, or sometimes both) that Hand might logically have presumed that concern for U.S. workers alone motivated my question.[26] Still, his frank statement of the bottom line as the primary concern seemed unapologetic.

Trade Secrets. Hand's frankness about the bottom line stands out against other matters about which secrecy reigns in the souvenir industry. After talking to Hand, I noticed that the price tag on many souvenirs had the "made in" information but no hint of the business(es) responsible for their production. As a result, I occasionally found myself using discarded tools from my training in art history, including those such as stylistic attribution that I associated primarily with connoisseurship or with memory cheats for slide tests (like learning to recognize the Madonnas of Hugo van der Goes by their big foreheads but writing in my blue book grander statements about northern Renaissance painting). A souvenir potholder I found at Pier 39 in San Francisco (figure 20) reminded me of the Ellis Island immigrant-boy souvenirs like the tile in figure 21. Each has a teal border, an oval-bounded center image, a place name across the top in outlined letters, and a horizon-

FIGURE 20. Potholder, "San Francisco: The City by the Golden Gate." Purchased at Pier 39 in San Francisco, 2000. (Photograph by Robert Diamante)

FIGURE 21. Souvenir tile, "Ellis Island: Front Doors to Freedom." Purchased at the gift shop in 2000. (Photograph by Robert Diamante)

tal slogan in a shape simulating a metal name plate below; on the potholder, a crab sits between "San Francisco" and "The City By the Golden Gate." The potholder's tag states "Karol Western Corporation." Maybe Karol Western produced the immigrant boy, too, or hired the same designer. Or maybe one designer or company poached another's style, or two companies made use of a decorative device so common in the souvenir business as to transcend issues of plagiarism.

But I couldn't readily figure out the origins of the pieces. The Ellis Island souvenirs were marked only with "Made in China"; some also had certain details of enticement on the packaging—like "Decorative . . . Useful . . . Protects your furniture . . . A lasting remembrance"—but nothing else. Hand never offered the names of companies, but he did tell me that I could learn more about souvenirs by going to trade shows like the Gatlinburg Gift Show in Tennessee. I located a contact number for the show via a Web search, only to learn from the woman on the other end, before she hung up on me, that only retailers could attend. I could, however, she added, easily get the same information from the magazine *Souvenirs, Gifts and Novelties*. Actually, I couldn't easily get either the magazine or information from it. After I tried initiating a subscription by phone, the order somehow disappeared. I only began to receive it after mailing a check and naming my work address for delivery.

Besides, things just weren't the same on paper, even though I found much of interest in the magazine. The March 2001 issue, for instance, included various examples of multicultural marketing research at work: one article showed how retailers might profit from applying feng shui principles to their stores; another article described how "minorities" are likely to spend more on Father's Day than "Caucasians." There was also a fascinating piece called "Economic Trends Worth Watching." It suggested that a "Bridal Bonanza" might result "if the so called 'marriage penalty tax' is dropped" and described a three-way relationship between the military, nationalism, and the "made in" tag that offers a reminder, in retrospect, about how characteristics now often linked to the aftermath of 9/11 actually predate it: "Military issues will be in the news more than any time in the last eight years. A new president always raises the nationalism factor, too. These and other factors will bring a new puff of steam to feelings of patriotism in consumers in every age bracket. It could increase the demand for Made in America merchandise, but prices may make it more talk than action. However, also look for a new wave of anti-Americanism to sweep the globe."[27]

The magazine helped me to see how issues regarding ethnicity and labor were formulated in the industry press. But I had to attend a trade show to get information about issues like price markup, since most companies advertising in the magazine put barriers between readers and prices so as to keep the latter from improperly credentialed information seekers.[28] Fortunately, in 2002 a storeowner friend sneaked me into a show by registering me as an employee. There, I lucked into a discussion with a marketer of novelty golf balls. He told me that he had been underbid to make the Ellis Island golf balls by a nickel a ball, having offered to provide the balls, which sold for just under $3.00 at the gift shop, for $1.05 apiece. Finally, I had some numbers.

Compared to the deliberate secrecy about companies, markups, designers, and other factors in the souvenir business, "made in China" might seem all the more forthright and direct. It is and it isn't. "Made in China" has become a common code phrase for cheap labor, but that is not what it always means at the gift shop. One of the new "Favorites" signs in September 2000 stated: "Most Asian immigrants began their journey to America in China. We offer these traditional Chinese items to decorate your home." The interpretive work involved in the common reading of "made in China" is indicated by its juxtaposition with the use of "made in China," according to the other logic of the "made in" designation prominent at the gift shop. This "made in China," as explained on the "Favorites" signage, is meant to signal that the product represents a cultural expression of Chinese people.

But even though it is generally clear which "made in China" means which, much remains unindicated by the "made in" labels. Neither factories nor cultural traditions are uniform, and "made in" doesn't reveal working conditions or wages in either designation.[29] In addition, one might view the space sharing of the two "made in" designations actually to help obscure labor conditions, by implying contrasts between the handmade and the mass produced, and between the artisan and the laborer, that then are manipulated for various purposes.

Labor language is manipulated a lot these days, especially in texts that fetishize work by hand, which is often described as if it automatically belongs in a realm of old-fashioned care and love of the process even though factory workers attaching plastic hair to Barbie dolls can also be said to be working by hand. For example, an article on wild blueberries in Martha Stewart's *Living* claims that many pickers consider the job "a family affair, a working vacation, a ritual repeated every summer," each developing "his or her own technique and style," for harvesting "by hand." These assertions about the pleasure and art of blueberry picking might obscure the hints in comments about "harvesters bent at the waist" and following the crop, which indicate that the author is describing backbreaking migrant labor.[30] The paper cups holding the Java City coffee that I bought at Ellis Island in summer 2001 state: "*Time.* It's a valuable commodity. At Java City, our time-signature roasting process coaxes the flavor from the finest Arabica beans. We do this process *by hand*—watching, smelling, listening, measuring the progress of the beans until just the right time. And while this extra care takes time, the uncompromising smoothness and rich taste makes [*sic*] it worth the wait." "We" who watch and wait, apparently, do not endure tedious repetition; "we" participate in this coaxing of sensual luxury. But who are "we"? Surely the owners of Java City are not out watching beans grow. The text recalls a point made by Joanna Kadi in *Thinking Class* about learning that when rich people say "I built a house" they mean that they paid other people to do it.[31]

The lure of the handmade comes into product sales as well. The description of the Fiddler on the Roof Spreaders in *The Source for Everything Jewish* states that the handles are "hand-painted polyresin." The point is obviously not to generate concern about the big pressure and little reward for people painting multicolored "darling shtetl characters" that cost $11 for a set of four, but to bring the objects into the realm of the $225 "Statue of Liberty Platter" from the same catalog, which justifies the platter's price by upping the artiness discourse with a named artist and a gesture toward one-of-a-kind originality. "No two [are] exactly alike," although each platter bears "stained glass imbedded with fragments of patriotic and seasonal printed art," including U.S. flags, a portrait of Emma Lazarus, and a poster in English and Hebrew for World War II war bonds, all on "a background of flowers and birds."[32] A related example from the Ellis Island gift shop is a sign displayed in 2003 advertising "Hand Made Crafts from Haiti." In explaining about "pieces for the home," such as small boxes and trays, it states that they are made from "recycled steel oil drums" and that "each piece is hand made, so there will be variations from item to item which is the hall mark of hand made crafts." The text, with a large recycling symbol displayed next to it, uses the markers of the precious and the socially responsible to imply a certain process of making and a situation of the maker that there is no other reason to suppose. (In her novel *Inventing Memory*, Erica Jong has her character Sarah, who came through Ellis Island, remind her great-granddaughter Sara of something similar regarding what donor labels are not forthcoming about: "When you look at the names of benefactors on buildings, notice that they don't engrave up there how their ancestors made the money in the first place.")[33]

I have been arguing in this section that representation belies labor at the Ellis Island gift shop. Representations become more multiculturally sophisticated in ways largely disconnected from the politics of their manufacture, even though signage about place of origin and hand crafting might encourage one to construe certain objects, with no actual justification to do so, as the production of loving hands bearing the gift of culture. One further bit of evidence about the different trajectories of looks and labor resides in the apparent changes from 1999 to 2003 regarding the "made in" criteria for the objects offered as representations of particular cultural traditions. In 1999, those objects were advertised as products of the places they were stated to represent. Meanwhile, the souvenirs generally came from China, although many but not all of the T-shirts bore tags signaling outsourcing and flexible production, such as "assembled in Honduras of U.S. parts." (One mark of flexible production that I've noticed since I started studying souvenir T-shirts is that shirts with the same design on the front may vary in place(s) of manufacture, suggesting the chasing around for a better deal even from one batch to another.) In 2002 and 2003, however, some signage for the culture products indicated a change. In September 2003, for instance, although the store still offered "Traditional *Arts & Crafts* Imported from Russia," other signs advertised "Gifts imported by and inspired from Italy," and "Gifts inspired by the *Emerald Isles* of Ireland." Given the appeal of objects that come from a particular place as a signifier of the place or of the inhabiting people it conjures (think of conversations like this: "Oh, how beautiful," "Thanks, it comes from Indonesia," "Really?!" "Yes, it's batik!"), there needs to be a reason to sell the Celtic Collection, made in China, that I saw in 2002. Maybe a cross-shaped ornament decorated with a shamrock was more exciting than any items made in Ireland. More likely, it is a better deal.

The worse deal for the retailer or consumer, however, does not necessarily signify a better deal for the people who make it. "Handmade" or "traditional" suggests a physical connection between people and objects that is implied to transfer cultural authenticity when the people and products are labeled under a place or culture. But why suppose that the people who painted the little Russian bearded guy "from Russia" available in 2003, who looks like a cross between a rabbi and an old wizard who might teach Harry Potter, have a better situation than the people painting the "darling shtetl characters," even if the former is sold as "traditional arts and crafts"? The lack of necessary correlation between the cost of goods and the wages paid to produce them is obvious from even a casual familiarity with sweatshop labor or the Nike boycott—or, regarding the work by hand invoked in many labels, with the history of trades like sewing and lace making. My point here is not to introduce the concept of labor exploitation but to point to ways in which the representations of cultures, products, and places contribute to mystifying it. In the next section, I consider relations of representation to Ellis Island's history in detention and incarceration.

EAT UP

In 1998, maybe before, at the Ellis Island Immigration Museum, the sign right outside the snack shop included a reproduction of an undated black-and-white photograph showing women and children eating a meal at Ellis Island. Under the image are the words "Ellis Island" in all-caps black print, newspaper style; beneath that, the word "café" is written in delicate blue script. The photograph also appeared in a photomontage on a placemat (figures 22 and 23) that for a few years was on sale at the gift shop: it cost $2.50 to eat on some ancestors. In 2003, the photograph was one of many, including the "breeders" photograph I discussed in chapter 1 (which the placemat also uses), that decorated a wall of the snack shop in a long friezelike montage.

I used to think of this photograph as the Ellis Island antidocument (or, as I elsewhere termed it, the "antilube").[34] So much of eating is always lost in the image of it—the texture, the taste, the smell. This picture dramatizes

FIGURE 22. Ellis Island placemat. Purchased at the gift shop in 1999.
(Photograph by Robert Diamante)

FIGURE 23. Detail of Ellis Island placemat. Purchased at the gift shop in 1999.
(Photograph by Robert Diamante)

what is never on offer by being conspicuously difficult to decipher. The sign on the back of the left wall of the photo is virtually illegible. At best, one can recognize that it delivers a message in more than one language; in some reproductions, you can't even see words. The food on the table is largely unrecognizable. Some kind of bread, some kind of meat. If the aspiration is to "bring history to life," as is the aim of many heritage sites, including Ellis Island, this picture stops short of doing so.[35]

But I now think of this photograph, at least in its location or intended location near actual food, as a superb document, but a document of something slightly different than migrants eating at Ellis Island. Rather, I see it as a document of a certain register of vagueness born partly of the dissonance between Ellis Island's functions as a tourist site and a history that might not best be described as entertaining. This is not to say that visitors might not seek and find both entertainment and education, or seek one and find the other (or both or neither). Nor is it to suggest a vagueness specific to Ellis Island itself. In the business of marketing encounters with heritage, the direct translation of food history seems to be in short supply. When Martha Stewart asked in 1999 "Have you ever tasted a memory?" (the same year that she put the Wall of Honor on her Christmas special) her goal was to sell a cookbook for making *Favorite Comfort Food* better than anything you could possibly remember tasting (like a BLT on a baguette with "oven-dried tomatoes").[36] When Colonial Williamsburg, "where history lives," serves dinner, historical flavor comes largely as a gesture garnished with allusive phrasing and spelling. Or, as the *Colonial Williamsburg Tavern Cookbook* puts it, "Visitors sample foods suggestive of the past but that suit modern appetites."[37] Thus, the King's Arms Tavern, which opened in 1772, as the menu explains, "to accommodate gentlemen customers in the tradition of the leading public houses in the mother country," now offers "the grilled and roast meats that remain the hallmarks of fine British cooking," along with "soupe," "salat," "A goodly stuffed Meadow Mushroom," and some breads and relishes from seventeenth- and eighteenth-century recipes.[38] Even at the scene of voluntary pleasures, history doesn't translate too well into actual food. (Nor, precisely, into the setting, where now, the menu assures us, at the site or in advance at www.history.org: "Rest rooms are located on the second floor.")

Moreover, the people eating in the Ellis Island picture were detainees.

Since Ellis Island narratives, including mine, generally use the terms "processing" and "detention" to describe two separate functions at the site, it is worth reiterating here that everyone processed at Ellis Island had been, to some extent, detained—forced to stop for permission to continue travels from one location to another—and that nothing about border policing should be taken as the natural order of things. At the beginning of her essay "Race, Nationality, Mobility: A History of the Passport," Radhika Viyas Mongia emphasizes that although "the global monopoly of a system of states over the international movement of people seems an unremarkable fact in the present world," even the idea that nationality should signal a "privileged relation between people and literal territory" needs accounting for.[39] Her study of how Canada over the ten-year period from 1906 to 1915 came to require passports for migrants from India shows the series of maneuvers in state, nation, and empire making that may go into a particular form of border regulation, far beyond what the relative straightforwardness and apparent standardization of passage documents might imply. These maneuvers themselves have important layers of indirection. In the example Mongia discusses, as with the U.S. immigration restrictions of 1924, the use of nationality as the official source of classification (we'll take x number of Russians) was partly used to effect racial and racialized exclusions without naming them as such. As noteworthy as all of this indirection and complexity in the development of border patrol mechanisms is simply the existence of geopolitical borders and border patrol mechanism: the very notion that state authorities can say, in effect, "stop here, and we will to tell you if, and how, you may proceed to enter or exit a territory over which we claim jurisdiction." Restriction of mobility need not be the case; the fact that it is, then, should be a matter of study rather than a given.

That said, the migrants in the Ellis Island photo were detainees in the sense of "detention" as it is ordinarily used to indicate the lengthier forced stay associated with being in some kind of trouble. Ellis Island procedures did not include meals for people subjected merely to routine medical and legal inspection—be our guest if you dock at the dinner hour. Migrants could buy food, and, after the reform of Commissioner Williams, get free milk for young children. The people that the government fed in sit-down meals during the peak migration years were primarily would-be entrants to the United States who either didn't make it through the first inspection and awaited further scrutiny or had already failed further scrutiny and awaited a boat returning them to their port of departure. A few in this picture, perhaps, were like the majority fed there later: people who had been admitted earlier but subsequently picked up for deportation.[40]

Little in the chain of responsibility for the food suggests the likelihood of appetizing meals. The government got much of its money to feed the detainees by charging the steamship companies for the meals fed to the passengers they had transported who could not readily prove themselves fit to land. Since the steamship companies paid as little as they could get away with paying and the concessionaires providing the food served as little as they could get away with serving—one notorious concessionaire offered stewed prunes as the main fare—it is safe to say that the mystery-meat look of the photograph serves as an appropriate if uninformative visual for the institutional food served there. (It might also be appropriate to reference here the testimony I mentioned in the introduction that Jell-O was a fought-over weekly treat that longer-term detainees honed their skills at procuring.)

Eating At the Detention Hall: What? Not surprisingly, then, no one at Ellis Island today is trying to sell imitations of Ellis Island food, or even advice on how to re-create it. *The Ellis Island Immigrant Cookbook*, on sale for about $18 at the gift shop, describes the food served at Ellis Island but offers recipes from the immigrants' lives before and after their time on the island.[41] Aramark, today's concessionaire, sells food that gestures to alien eating even less clearly than the photograph, if on a different register of vagueness. The food items are recognizable, and, of course, different from any photograph of food in being palpable—accessible to taste, touch, and smell. As far as I can observe, one can recognize the food's contents as much as one can recognize the contents of any prepared food; its meat is only mystery meat to the extent that most meat these days acquires elements in animal farming or processing of which the contents or effects may remain hidden or unknown.[42]

At the snack shop, the vagueness lies instead in the connections made between food present and migration past, connections clearly intended at the level of allusion only. In the late 1990s, when the snack shop was called a café and the sign outside bore the photograph of women and children eating—which also appeared as one panel between menu items, with the words "All menu items available at any registry" superimposed in capital letters on the bottom—Aramark's menu included a lot of food items that referred explicitly or implicitly to peoples associated with Ellis Island: deli sandwiches on allusive bread ("Jewish rye," "croissant," or "kaiser roll"); dessert from Gretel's bakery (Gretel, like Ronald MacDonald, baked chocolate chip cookies and apple turnovers); and "World's Fare," such as gyros, nachos, pizza, "Greek salad," an "Italian meatball sub," and a fish sandwich. I suspect that the fish sandwich would have been a nod to British "fish and chips," except for the advantage of selling the chips separately as "french fries," wherein Aramark got another national reference and, of course, more potential sales by floating its fries as a side dish appropriate to order with other sandwiches. The menu also included Chablis and beer from eight countries: England, Denmark, Germany, Mexico, Ireland, Holland, Japan, and the United States.[43]

On several different levels, 1999 looks in retrospect like the glory days for facile reference. Beyond Ellis Island, shallow food-to-nation links acquired serious implications in spring 2003 during the fight in the United Nations over the proposed invasion of Iraq advocated by the United States. Even though neither the concept of french fries nor french fries themselves actually come from France, the act of renaming them "freedom fries" became, for some who disagreed with the intention of France to veto the invasion, a rejection of French products that constituted an act of U.S. patriotism. (The name change of the fries at the congressional cafeteria now sometimes gets describe as "an act of Congress," although it was more specifically an act of several members of Congress with access to authority over the eateries.)[44] At Ellis Island, for reasons presumably more mundane, the menu had already been stripped down. By 2002, Gretel's baked goods had disappeared, the only beer choices remaining were Bud or Beck's, and the overarching name for the snack shop had gone from "café" to "food court" (Paris traded for the mall). A Java City side kiosk in the space sold coffee, in the cups I mentioned, along with a few ready-to-serve prepackaged items like sandwich wraps.

These changes, I suspect, can be attributed to practical rather than symbolic matters: simplifying the inventory; streamlining preparation; dumping less popular items; bringing the offerings more into line with those at other Aramark venues like snack shops at colleges, which sometimes feature Java City kiosks, too.⁴⁵ But some changes in the menu seem to reflect more sophisticated thinking—the recognition of the United States as itself multiethnic and as a component, rather than just the big appropriator, of the rest of the world. In 2002 the snack shop's "American Fare" included sauerkraut. "Snacks" included a churro. "World's Fare" included a "BBQ Chicken Sandwich." This kind of menu change might reflect the advances in multicultural marketing that I discussed regarding the gift shop, although one might certainly wonder why it is barbecue that belongs to the world, since barbecue might be considered as generically American as the Fourth of July or a bit racially or regionally alien if one associates it more specifically with black people or the South. But, in any case, multicultural marketing doesn't trump streamlining or sales. In July 2003, the menu, which bravely retained its "french fries," had become simpler still, despite a certain new flashiness: the "Euro Baguette" signage at the Java City kiosk; the "World's Fare" traded for the trendier "Global Fare"; and "American Fare" folded into a "Grille and Deli." Now, however, the beer was just Bud, the churro missing, and the "Greek salad" abandoned for "garden salad."

In none of these incarnations, however, is the Ellis Island food today about the Ellis Island food of yesteryear. Rather, it is about mixing and matching Ellis Island ethnicities with contemporary fast food staples, for a collection of selections that the term "Food Court" well serves, calling up the similar combination produced by mall or campus conglomerations of Sbarro, Taco Bell, and the like.

Eating At the Detention Hall: So What? So what? Why should anyone care that the snack shop serves nachos instead of the beef stew and boiled mutton that was served at Ellis Island, or the borscht, potato pudding, many variations on cabbage, or Good Friday supper ("homemade noodles cooked in milk. . . . served with cooked, dried prunes") that are all featured in the *Ellis Island Immigrant Cookbook?*⁴⁶ There's no reason that the snack shop should offer historic food and the menu can hardly be called duplicitous. Granted, no advance planning can assure the universal or uniform apprehension of what is and is not intended to re-create the past; I once overheard an Ellis Island visitor correct another who had mistaken a fire alarm, which sounded to me like a typical contemporary fire alarm, for a simulation of sirens from the past.[47] But it would be outlandish to blame Aramark for any similar misapprehension regarding its food, or its representation of food.

Similarly, on the placemat it is the caption, not the photograph of eating, that comes close to any suspect claims about re-creating the past. Underneath its central photograph, which is a detail of the "breeder" picture, the text reads in part: " 'The front door to freedom' received today's arriving ferry passengers as it did hundreds of thousands of new arrivals between 1897 and 1938."[48] The comparison implied here seems unproblematic enough if one reads the "front door" literally or superficially to mean the architectural structure; the caption doesn't offer any deeper analogy. It is not really Aramark but rather the Park Service that has tried to take such analogies farther. In 1990, for instance, the Park Service faced proposals to make permanent a bridge built for restoration workers that could have given visitors approaching Ellis Island from Jersey City a pedestrian alternative to the ferry's long lines and $6 price ($10 by 2003). Park Service officials argued, however, that arriving by boat was essential to experiencing the history of the place.[49] In the words of then superintendent of the Statue of Liberty National Monument, M. Ann Belkow: " 'From the moment someone arrives here, I want people to know and feel what others before them felt coming through these doors, walking through these halls.' "[50] Some critics, understandably, thought the Park Service seemed more interested in protecting the profits from its contract with Circle Line Ferry, which at the time had been renegotiated to include a jump in ticket price.

My answer to "so what?" about the food has less to do with the particular snack shop menu or with immigrants depicted eating on a placemat than it does with the cumulative effects of the move toward which is gestured by the mismatch between the real food and the picture food: putting incarceration into the realm of the tourist attraction. In thinking about this matter, I have been influenced by the work of Margaret Stratton, whose photographic series called *Detained in Purgatory* includes images of unrestored sections of Ellis Island along with images of Alcatraz and other former prisons. In her essay about the series, she argues that the "prison as historic monument" functions in part to turn visitors away from incarcerations both past and present. "Modern historical sites," she writes, "do not commemorate past events, but deflect them."[51] While I might modify her formulation to add that historical sites sometimes deflect past events for the purpose of crafting a version to commemorate, much of what exists at Ellis Island supports her point, including the sanitization of the restored environment itself and the interpretive habit of the parallel. How illuminating can it really be to posit the arrival of visitors today as analogous to the forced appearance of migrants for inspection?

Stratton also writes, putting "we" in quotations to highlight the privileged position of people who view prisons only through heritage sites and cultural representations, "It is noteworthy that the only access 'we' have to prisons is to places which are defunct and, subsequently, viewed as sites where historic figures resided or as the location of past events (like massive immigration and selective deportation)."[52] As a result, she suggests, visitors are invited to locate the inhumanities of incarceration in the past and, importantly, are offered no views of incarceration in the present: "The act of looking at the empty prison tells the viewer that barbarity and confinement no longer exist. The lexicon of the grizzled old convict fading into the ghostly walls of the defunct institution assures the tourist that the old prison is a thing of the past. The new institution of incarceration (the High Security Unit) and the new face of incarceration (the young Black or Hispanic man, and increasingly the young woman of color), have no place in this narrative . . . and are invisible."[53]

If the terrified migrant held at Ellis Island for a now discredited reason is the Ellis Island figure comparable to the "grizzled old convict" of Alcatraz, the same point about locating injustice in the past can be made. The unfairly treated migrant is implied to be a person of long ago. Some rangers invite viewers to apply what they learn at Ellis Island to immigration today. Not even these interpreters, however, suggest thinking about contemporary border policing; instead, they encourage reflection about the pros and cons of immigration in general. Museum displays also largely ignore current border apparatus. In the contextualizing exhibit on the "Peopling of America," only a small section concerns migration today, and maybe its most notable feature is how little attention it invites. A loop of videotaped comments by recent immigrants constitutes its primary display. The location of the exhibit makes it easy to overlook and the surrounding din on busy days makes hearing difficult; during several stints of prolonged lurking I saw few people stopping or lingering. Those who do study the video will not find information about border patrol; the hardships that immigrants discuss occurred to them in their countries of origin.

Yet today news abounds that the detention of immigrants is not a relic of the past. Just one example that could serve as a fruitful basis for comparison concerns the situation of two men from Haiti who, placed in detention on arrival in October 2002, remained there for months even after being granted asylum in early 2003. The parallels with Ellis Island detentions are numerous: the very fact of detention; presumptions about the men based on their nationality rather than personal history, since only applicants for asylum from certain countries await decisions imprisoned; and the effects on credibility of difficulties in presentation that might be better attributed to innocent causes. In one man's case, government lawyers cited inconsistencies in his dating of events that the judge who granted asylum ascribed to the man's inability to read or write.[54] This aspect of the man's situation recalls the story recounted by Fiorello La Guardia that I mentioned earlier about the girl detained as possibly unfit to enter the United States after her uncommon rural dialect led to a "hesitancy in replying" that officials considered suspect.[55] Reports that detention diminished the migrant's mental state in each case suggest issues that merit careful attention. Many other parallels arise in the wake of the Patriot Act, passed in October 2001, which "permits the Attorney General to incarcerate or detain non-citizens based on mere suspicion, and to deny re-admission to the United States of non-citizens (including legal, long-term permanent residents) for engaging in speech protected by the First Amendment."[56] The cases of some migrants detained at Ellis Island might well be considered precedents for such detentions. Think of Frank Woodhull, threatened with expulsion after thirty years of residence, Emma Goldman, deported for expressed anarchist political views, or the many more held routinely on suspicion of one thing or another.

As important, detention as a live issue was present during Ellis Island's restoration, or, more precisely, it could have been. In spring 1986, Arthur C. Helton opened an opinion piece for the *New York Times* noting a certain irony of timing: "A dedication ceremony will be held next week in the small town of Oakdale, in central Louisiana. The subject will be immigration. The ceremony is not, however, a preview of the national rededication of the Statue of Liberty and Ellis Island scheduled for July 4. Rather, it is to commemorate the opening of the largest immigration detention center in the country."[57] Helton, then "director of the political asylum project of the Lawyers Committee for Human Rights," points out that detention for migrants had been revived in the 1980s, after humanitarian concerns, among others, had led to the decline of the practice. Liberty Weekend's massive naturalization ceremony at Ellis Island, then, which set welcome as the primary parallel, failed to encompass all of the material of analogy that might make for fruitful thinking about migration and incarceration. Detention and debates about it did not go away after that. The imprisonment at Guantánamo Bay of asylum seekers from Haiti who tested positive for HIV, a highly publicized and protested practice, spanned the period of 1987 to 1993 when the "Peopling of America" and Ellis Island's interpretive programs in general were designed, honed, and debuted.

Programming could but doesn't cover the then-and-nows or now-as-thens of incarcerating migrants. So, too, with the gift shop. I raise this point even as I imagine some readers thinking here, "What do you expect? A book section full of material like the ACLU's report called *Insatiable Appetite: The Government's Demand for New and Unnecessary Powers after September 11?*" After all, the Ellis Island gift shop is located in a government-run national monument. It is operated by a concessionaire, Aramark Corporation, that has benefited greatly, as I discuss below, from privatization, for which the regime championing the Patriot Act has also served as a great advocate. True enough. Yet I think that it is important to pause once in a while to articulate the source of fulfilled expectations, in this case that combination of government oversight and private commerce, that has always characterized Ellis Island. Besides, I've learned through visits to other gift shops of the existence of more subtle possibilities. At the United Nations gift shop, for instance, I discovered in 2001 the book *Stand Up for Your Rights* available for $9.95. The cover identifies it as "A Book about Human Rights Written by and for the Young People of the World" produced as a project of "Peace Child International" and presented by *World Book Encyclopedia*—hardly a badge of the card-carrying Left or liberal sort. The book uses the "Universal Declaration of Human Rights" adopted by the United Nations in 1948 as a framework for discussing the goals and realities of human rights. Articles 13 through 15 include the right to freedom of movement within the state one inhabits, the right to leave and return to that state, the right to seek and enjoy asylum from persecution, and the right to have and change one's nationality.[58] While a political framework centered on individual human rights has justifiably been challenged for emphasizing the individual rather than the social collective as the basic unit of social organization and object of activism, my point here concerns the availability of material that addresses freedom of movement regarding borders. Options exist.

Eating At the Detention Hall: What Else? Ironically enough, once incarceration is on the table another path emerges from the photograph of women and children eating—a path that leads to Aramark, which has provided food service for prisons in a number of states involved in trying to save money by privatization. From the accounts of complaints against the company, one wouldn't want to see what Aramark has served at prisons any more clearly than one can see the food in the photograph of Ellis Island. In Ohio, which declined to renew its contract with Aramark when it expired in 2000, an inspection team wrote in January 1999 that "'the sanitation levels were inexcusable'" even after Aramark had been charged to address the problem.[59] In Florida, which hired Aramark in 2001 despite knowing about the concerns in Ohio, corrections officers recorded hundreds of food incidents between February and May 2002, according to a report in the *St. Petersburg Times*, whose staffers had reviewed the daily logs. Besides including repeated concerns about matters like cleanliness ("'horrendous,'" maggots, spoiled chicken soaked in vinegar to get rid of the smell) and quantity (Saltine-size pork servings, too few portions to go around), the logs featured several unfortunate menu items. One Hernando County prison served "a spaghetti dinner using chili con carne from the previous week and creamed chipped beef from the day before. The cream sauce was washed off and the beef reused."[60]

Besides detailing the problems with prison food service under Aramark, the article in the *St. Petersburg Times* exposes an attitude about prisons that is also relevant in this context. "Take any cross-section of Floridians and poll them about prisons," the article begins, "Few would care that, on one day last February, lunch at the Madison Correctional Institution featured a particularly soupy batch of sloppy Joes," which, it turned out, had been diluted by skimping on the meat, eliminating the called-for vegetables, and adding ketchup and tomato paste to stretch the supply. The issue, according to the article, concerns not treatment of the incarcerated, even though they live "in a world where eating is perhaps the day's only pleasure," but that discontent with food can spark protests that put corrections officers in danger.[61]

How do the content and coverage of Aramark's prison food relate to Ellis Island? While the topics I have assembled here can make for a lovely conspiracy theory about historical narratives silenced to protect a profitable licensing agreement that benefits both Aramark and the Park Service (which gets a cut of Aramark's on-site profits), I don't intend to posit it. I suggest instead something both less and more sinister: that the ingredients I've assembled do not specifically cause each other but epitomize and contribute to a certain business as usual. Here, in part, I mean "business as usual" as a figure of speech. Push just a little around Aramark and find prisons. Look just a little at contemporary migration and find the same. This is partly because prisons and imprisoned migrants are increasing and increasingly visible. But I also use the phrase "business as usual" more literally, too, not only because prisons are, as is frequently mentioned, a growth industry, but also because a particular form of doing business, privatization, underpins everything I've discussed here. Recall that the restorations of the Statue of Liberty and Ellis Island were hailed from the beginning for fulfilling Reagan's directive to pursue "public-private cooperation." Aramark's entrance into prisons, as well as other public institutions like schools, represents one more set of moves by federal and state governments to abandon functions that were previously deemed public responsibilities—often under the argument, made especially by Republican elites, that for-profit businesses can perform the tasks more cheaply and effectively. It's hardly surprising that, as the *St. Petersburg Times* reported, "Aramark and its top executives gave thousands to Republican campaign accounts for the 2000 elections, including Bush For President."[62]

Nor is it surprising that what got Ohio to kick Aramark out of its prison cafeteria was predominantly a better offer, although the better offer itself merits enthusiasm. One effect of outsourcing service provision is often less-favorable working conditions for employees in terms of pay and other issues. Aramark, which in 2003 offered $5.25 per hour base pay at Ellis Island—under $11,000 per year calculated by a forty-hour workweek—has faced various charges regarding discrimination and labor conditions. In

2001, the year Aramark began in the Florida prisons and posted annual revenues that topped $7 billion, the company faced protests about working conditions by dining service workers at George Washington University; a complaint at High Point University from a manager who stated that he had been forced to fire disabled employees; and a class action race discrimination lawsuit on behalf of black workers in three divisions at the Presbyterian Medical Center in Philadelphia.[63] According to an item in *Ethnic Newswatch*, Aramark workers in Detroit called the Philadelphia suit "no shock," noting a job distribution with predominantly white managers in a predominantly African American workforce that resembles, at least from what one might discern by looking around, the situation at Ellis Island.[64] In Ohio, the labor activists prevailed. Aramark lost its contract with the Ohio prison after Local 11 of the Ohio Civil Service Employees Association (OCSEA), the labor union representing Ohio state workers, "contracted in" by submitting a less-expensive bid for the job than did Aramark and two other contenders, the Canteen and Wackenhut corporations.[65] The successful challenge to what OCSEA's press release called unsubstantiated propaganda about the cost savings of privatization and the return to a labor force with union representation surely constitute good news.

Yet whether engagements with Aramark's prison food reflect or, occasionally, challenge the business as usual of privatization, mainstream publicity about them manifests a highly disturbing feature that today is just as ordinary: a disinterest in the well-being of the incarcerated that apparently needs neither justification nor even a camouflaging murmur of concern. Why should Floridians care about prison inmates? Only if it affects the safety of nonprisoners. Why should we rejoice at the booting of Aramark from Ohio's prison system? Only because of the benefit to workers and the money saved for the state.

If I Can't Eat. Entertainment and education are not mutually exclusive. Neither, I argue, are pleasure and politics, even though I've attached some sour links here to items presented to please. I agree with one of Ellis Island's most famous deportation-bound diners, the activist Emma Goldman, who had quite a few words, if not quite those printed on T-shirts, for the boy who told her that "it did not behoove an agitator to dance. Certainly not with such reckless abandon anyway."[66] To put it a bit differently: If I have speculated that tourist amenities lighten up the place partly lest the smell of incarceration kill your appetite for the swirly chocolate-and-vanilla "low fat softserve," my goal isn't precisely to turn your stomach either.[67]

Instead, my point is similar to the one I made in chapter 3 about how the meanings of Liberty Weekend were partly constituted, and should partly be constituted in retrospect, through the evacuation of protests against the Supreme Court decision that had just been made in *Bowers v. Hardwick* to uphold what the court rewrote as a ban on "homosexual sodomy." I argue now for bringing issues about labor and incarceration to a trip around the tourist amenities, for taking them home, and for reconsidering the politics and practices of historical analogy. Your ancestors, your history, your "nation of immigrants": Ellis Island is all about generating involvement through identification. Cues for sympathy and empathy matter.

Of course, cues don't determine what visitors actually come away with. Even setting aside the question of whether historical empathy works, the matter of how intentions relate to effects in educational and other processes always depends on many variables in execution and interpretation. I take up this issue further in the concluding chapter when I consider a Park Service program called "Decide an Immigrant's Fate," which invites visitors to take the position of administrative gatekeepers who determine whether would-be immigrants stay or go.

EIGHT

"DECIDE AN IMMIGRANT'S FATE"

During most of my research at Ellis Island I used my observations of and discussions with other visitors primarily to get a sense of how much my own interests and interpretations matched those of others at the site: whether people cared about the pictures on souvenirs (not so much); whether they found the Wall of Honor as confusing as I thought it might be (fairly often). In this final chapter, I undertake a more sustained study of people at the site, at least the beginning of such a study, by looking at "Decide an Immigrant's Fate," a Park Service program that is staged sometimes twice a day during the busy season. The program re-creates a 1910 hearing of the Board of Special Inquiry (BSI), which considered the cases of would-be entrants to the United States who had been marked for possible exclusion during the preliminary medical and legal inspections at Ellis Island. Ordinarily, a ranger runs the program, an actor from the on-site play "Embracing Freedom" plays the migrant, and audience volunteers are recruited to play the panel of administrators who constituted the board. Over three different periods, September 2000, June and July 2001, and August 2002, I attended the program about thirty times altogether.[1] Of all of the programming available at the site, including live tours, the audio tour, the movie, and the play, I was most drawn to "Decide an Immigrant's Fate," at first by some implications of the melodramatic title. What does it mean to try to hail visitors by inviting them to imagine themselves with the power to make or enact immigration policy?

On the surface, the prospect of such an invitation seemed pretty scary, and the context made it increasingly so. I first thought especially of the parallels between the let's-pretend about "deciding an immigrant's fate" and the all-too-nonfictional practices that put human rights up for votes and bad legislation: Should queers get protection from discrimination? Should immigrants get health care? In the aftermath of September 11, 2001, terms like "evoke" and "parallel" that suggest teasing out metaphoric threads and highlighting isolated, if plentiful, cases seemed absolutely inadequate. Since 9/11, evidence has proliferated of a widespread belief that deciding which immigrants stay or go, which have access to what rights and services, and which spend a lot of time incarcerated and/or otherwise harshly treated is justifiably subject to the whim of policymakers, immigration officials, and some subset of the public considered to be fully credentialed as "Americans"—people who also apparently get to decide how long the stamp of "alien" should define certain immigrants and sometimes even their non-immigrant descendants.

Yet even if "Decide an Immigrant's Fate" might aptly subtitle too many current fantasies, plans, and acts, not the least being the Patriot Act, such affinities still doesn't tell us much about the relation of the cultural program with that title to the attitudes of the people who participate in it. As I learned from attending the program and from talking to some of the people involved in staging it, both the intentions and effects of the program involved a lot besides, and sometimes instead of, any justification of migrant subordination. This chapter works to people the production and consumption of history at Ellis Island through the changing cast of rangers, actors, and audience participants that I encountered at "Decide an Immigrant's Fate." I argue more fully here for what I have been suggesting throughout this book: that what is needed is not the ability to name or control interpretation, but the possibility of tweaking its ingredients.

AN HOMAGE TO RANGERS

In most books the author's acknowledgments generally lie outside the body of the text: before it, after it, or in the notes. But since a major focus of this book is on what I found missing at Ellis Island, it is crucial to repeat what readers who started with the acknowledgments section have already read: I owe a lot to Ellis Island park rangers. I do not refer here merely to those, like the one who called himself "Deep Throat," who offered me insider tips, or the amazing library staff members with their gift for "How about this?" that went beyond conventional models of research help. A lot of tips I got just by attending rangers' guided tours. Just about every tour I went on taught me something new. "Interpretation" is the name of the department responsible for educational programs, and it also is the term for activities like leading tours through which education happens. As Freeman Tilden defined it in his classic guide *Interpreting Our Heritage: Principles and Practices for Visitor Services in Parks, Museums, and Historic Places,* published in 1957 and still sometimes referred to as the "bible" of the field, interpretation is "an educational activity which aims to reveal meanings and relationships through the use of original objects, by firsthand experience, and by illustrative media, rather than simply to communicate factual information."[2] Daniel T. Brown, the chief ranger of interpretation at the Statue of Liberty and Ellis Island, told me that the primary goal of programming is to have people leave wanting to know more.[3] Or, as the ranger orientation material explains, paraphrasing Tilden, interpretation is "not instruction so much as what we may call provocation."[4] The attempted provocation worked on me, and I'm not implying any constant oppositional stance here: I left thinking, "find out more" more often than "wait a minute."

I also came away from my visits to Ellis Island with a great appreciation for the education work that rangers do, often with modest pay and with relatively few opportunities for professional development. Interpreters who are not in administrative supervision generally work on the lower half of the government's GS pay scale, with limited, and shrinking, chances to advance. One ranger said that the government had suspended the category "master interpreter," which paid in the GS 11 range, so that now rangers in "interpretation" can no longer pass the level of GS 9. Another ranger, a GS 7 who had spent "years" at GS 5, told me of a "5–7–9" program intended to bump employees up after a certain number of years; the federal budget, however, lacked the money to implement it.[5] Indeed, continuing budget cuts affected more than salaries. In my discussions with Brown and Vincent DiPietro, the education specialist, both mentioned various educational niceties that the Park Service budget didn't allow for, including extensive initial training or access to off-site workshops that could enhance interpreters' skills and help them take more advantage of what Brown called the "Interpretive Revolution" regarding approaches to social issues and interpretive processes themselves.[6] Other employees mentioned wanting more training and time for research. One mentioned a former component of interpreter training that shrunken budgets may have contributed to axing: future interpreters used to complete a research paper that added new material to the on-site library (notably, here, it is from one such paper that I first learned about the confiscated obscene photograph that I discuss in chapter 1).[7] While this ranger attributed dropping the requirement to the diminishing interest of supervisors in historical accuracy, budget-induced corner cutting also seems likely to have been a cause for the change.

Interpreters also faced restrictions in the content of their presentations. Like all national parks, Brown explained, the Statue of Liberty National Monument has an interpretive prospectus determined by Congress that dictates the primary themes that interpreters should cover. The use of a prospectus itself doesn't necessarily bode badly: the list of themes and objectives given in the documents for the statue and for Ellis Island, which generally concern their histories, structure, and functions, as well as the goal to present U.S. immigration "as a historic and contemporary phenomenon," makes sense for these monuments. Nonetheless, certain omissions recall those I've noted elsewhere, like the desire of some migrants for nonpermanent residence among other forms of "peopling" beyond immigration, and the failure to mention the statue's relation to slavery, which also has little place in the material I received that goes to people bringing students on fieldtrips. The 1995 *Teaching Guide for Grades 3–6*, which concerns the statue only, has activities that discuss slavery in relation to the inequalities that persisted despite alleged valuation of equal liberties, but these are not given in relation to the statue. "Pre-Visit Activities for School Groups, Grades 4–8," designed for both monuments, begins with the statement, "Your class has made the choice to come to the New World," and then continues in that vein throughout.[8] Since rangers have a fair amount of leeway in terms of expanding on the basic themes and information, however, what is missing on paper is not necessarily missing from presentations. Another hint at the limitations in content presentation comes from one objective listed for rangers working the statue: "To reduce the visitor impact on the resource by providing information and education on the adverse impact of gum, litter and graffiti."[9] Interpreters have less lofty responsibilities than inspiring inquiry, both during educational programs and in a variety of tasks like staffing the information desk and working the various exhibit areas.

One more restriction relates to a directive I heard about often, from people giving it and given it, to avoid being political: interpreters should try to indicate various issues regarding immigration without appearing to get on a soapbox.

Then, of course, there are the formidable challenges of addressing Ellis Island, which, as Brown said, many visitors saw as a "magical" place, and of the basic task of presenting a lot of material in a relatively small amount of time to people of diverse background, age, knowledge, attention, and interest. General tours last forty-five minutes. That's not much time, especially for guides who use techniques like engaging audience participation to keep the participants thinking and involved—or when, as happened on occasion, tours included an incessant questioner with idiosyncratic interests, like lighting fixtures, that made it hard to follow prepared plans.

These challenges explain the frequent use by rangers of analogies between past and present, some better than others. Some rangers pushed the boundaries of required neutrality by invoking identification or sympathy: one ended tours by suggesting that even though the past may seem different, the story of Ellis Island immigrants "is really a story about ourselves"; another asked us to think of her own immigrant ancestors when we consider advocating policies to curtail immigration now. Others worked by cuing, and confirming, common perceptions that one might instead want to shake up—What do we call LPC (liable to become a public charge) today? Right, welfare!—or by drawing connections between things that need more differentiation. One such common tidbit related that immigrants often feared Ellis Island officials because the uniformed people they saw in the old country were sometimes murderous police; the implication was that police brutality resided only in the past and far away. Another item, as I discussed in chapter 5, was the likening of slavery to indentured servitude.

My point is not to dismiss the strategy of analogy. I heard an excellent analogy regarding slavery on the "Other Half" tour at Colonial Williamsburg which exposed the injustices masked by the common apologist assertion that certain enslavers considered some of their enslaved part of the family. The interpreter asked us whether we thought females should decide what happens to their offspring, and then who considered their pets part of the family. The interpreter chose a volunteer who had answered yes to both questions, and then asked her whether she would sell her dog's puppies if she could get a lot of money for them. After she said yes, he pointed out that slaveholders' right to sell the children of people they enslaved needed to be held up against any protestations of family feeling and that the concept "part of the family" did not preclude differential treatment or presume expectations of like opportunity.[10] (The latter is a point I try to make to my students when they use "like family" to characterize the college's low-paid custodians and food service workers, whose annual pay may not match half of the annual price of tuition.)

Ellis Island interpreters offered good analogies and explanatory aids that added vivid, memorable imagery to explanation. One ranger, who was recommended to me by another as the best tour guide around, compared steerage to the subway at rush hour. When I took his tour a year later, he described it as the subway at rush hour with rotting fruit salad and coleslaw. Other rangers got people thinking about why the six-second medical inspection might mistakenly cause health officials to suspect excludable conditions. Maybe you were limping because the only decent-looking shoes you could get weren't the right size; maybe you got out of the ferry "dazed and confused"; maybe your luggage holding all of your possessions was too heavy, but you wouldn't give it up. Another cause for analogy: How much back then was $25, which people needed to show in order to be admitted? Today for $25 you can't even take your two kids to a movie; back then it was equal to six months of income.

Rangers also often worked to add information or commentary that altered the standard rap on some explanatory must haves. A great example here concerns trachoma. I noted earlier, in comparing material products to products of interpretation, that frequently repeated narratives can be as canned in presentation as the figures in the snow globe. A general fit into this category are narratives about trachoma, which explain that it was a contagious disease causing blindness, that medical inspectors checked all Ellis Island migrants for trachoma by using a buttonhook or fingers to lift up and check under their eyelids, and that a diagnosis of trachoma meant mandatory exclusion. Today at Ellis Island one can encounter the trachoma narrative on tours, on wall plaques, and in some contextual introductions to "Decide an Immigrant's Fate." It appears in the Ellis Island souvenir guide, and serves as a plot point in the play "Embracing Freedom," just as it does in numerous histories and historical novels for adults and children. It is one of those narratives that attentive or informed visitors may likely recognize encountering more than once, the kind that credentializes itself and its bearers through repetition. The more one encounters the narrative, the more it looks like information that one already knew: the historical novel, then, must be based on good research; the tour guide must have known what she was talking about; the guide book must be hitting the key points; I must be getting a handle on the basics. The more the details match up each time, the more they may appear to tell the whole story.

The frequent appearance of the trachoma narrative makes sense. By many accounts, the trachoma exam was memorable—standing out in the ordeal, and sometimes standing for it. "Ellis Island: doctors peered in my eyes, officials scrutinized my passport, and the gates were thrown open," wrote Claude McKay, a Jamaica-born writer associated with the Harlem Renaissance, about beginning in 1921 his second long sojourn in the United States. (That McKay had intimate relations with men as well as women is worth noting here too as another counterexample to the usual story.)[11] Given how much there is to tell about Ellis Island, the brevity of accounts makes sense, too. But, of course, with any capsule summary there is more to the topic, so changes and additions have a double benefit. Besides suggesting what the more to the topic is, they work as a reminder to keep an eye out for reification, for what gets frozen in or frozen out. For example, until I heard a ranger mention that trachoma still exists—in "Third World countries," he said, "without good water supplies"—I realized that, because I hadn't heard of trachoma before I started studying Ellis Island, I had inferred, from the (logical) use of the past tense to describe the trachoma testing there, that trachoma itself was a disease of the past. I learned that instead it is a disease of the impoverished. Another tour guide, the one of the rotting coleslaw, jiggled the link between trachoma and LPC risk, or LPC risk and human potential. Ascribing the trachoma exclusion to "people of small minds and small imagination," he cited Helen Keller and Franklin Roosevelt as a caution against presuming that disabilities meant more cost than contribution. His comments made me realize how often narratives about trachoma stopped short of noting what was wrong with the policy, although some certainly called it into question.[12] At least as typical, however, is the plot of "Embracing Freedom," in which officials almost mistake an innocent scratch on the eye, acquired in a minor mishap, for the disease; by implication, the flaws lie in the application of the policy rather than the policy itself.

For me, at least, the steps away from the standard line sent me looking for more. Regarding the trachoma of the past, I learned, especially from the work of Amy Fairchild and Nayan Shah, that public health and immigration personnel used racial and national stereotypes both in characterizing trachoma as a "loathsome and dangerous contagious disease" requiring deportation and in diagnosing individual cases of trachoma, about which doctors disagreed concerning the symptoms.[13] The buttonhook exam, then, did not produce a foolproof tool of diagnosis nor were standards as universally applied as the typical short narrative about trachoma suggests. I found regarding trachoma today a phenomenon I've mentioned earlier: the celebration of private funding and largesse as reasonable solutions to problems that might be better served under a different economic system altogether. Key to the current situation is the drug company Pfizer, which markets azithromycin (more well known as Zithromax), an oral antibiotic shown effective in treating trachoma. In 1998, Pfizer introduced a much-publicized drug donation program to treat trachoma in five countries. What the publicity might obscure is that the drug's preventative cost for those who must purchase it, Pfizer's use and promotion of patent laws to deter the production of generic equivalents, and the very fact that medicine is a for-profit business have limited the scope of prevention and treatment that might otherwise be possible, even though Pfizer's donations have increased dramatically from the first years of the program.[14]

In the last few paragraphs I have been emphasizing my own responses— I realized, I found, I studied—for two reasons. First, I want to keep visible the resources involved in assembling my imaginary tour. A few rangers, as a humorous gesture, gave me a junior ranger badge, the kind usually bestowed on visiting children. If it shines at all brightly, it does so because of resources I had that, in many ways, extend beyond those of the rangers. With trachoma and the Ellis Island narratives about it, these resources include the personal connections, of professional origin, that led me to helpful contacts at Pfizer and at Doctors without Borders (MSF), the credentials that helped get me interviews (although no one at Ellis Island asked to see evidence of them, and people were quite helpful before I described them), and, of course, the time and funding to visit Ellis Island numerous times, to read supplementary material, and to follow up on leads; rangers, as far as I know, don't get sabbaticals. Second, I want to underscore that I am not ascribing my own reactions to other visitors. They typify responses to programming primarily in their particularity, and illustrate how the specifics of what people bring to educational events affect what they take from them. One thing I brought, increasingly and more than most other participants, was prior experience with coverage of the material on the topic.

It was certainly possible, however, just within one visit to Ellis Island, to encounter the same material enough times to recognize repetition and difference among on-site iterations. In "Decide an Immigrant's Fate," visitors' prior knowledge was one variable affecting how the program went. I discuss this one and others in the sections following.

COMING TO POWER

When I first began attending "Decide an Immigrant's Fate" in 2000, it had been running for three years, according to Vincent DiPietro, the education specialist at Ellis Island. He explained that the program began partly as a strategy to maximize the use of the room where it is staged, which had actually functioned as a Board of Special Inquiry hearing room during Ellis Island's years as an immigration station. Unlike most of the other small rooms in the main building, which represent Ellis Island's history through photographs, texts, and objects in display cases, the hearing room had been restored with period furnishings to re-create its look during the early twentieth century. When it turned out that the relative isolation of the room facilitated vandalism, it was closed out of concern for the artifacts. But the museum curator eventually agreed that the room could be opened when staffed. Thus "Decide an Immigrant's Fate" was developed with two primary functions in mind: to enable access to the room and to inform visitors about what used to happen in it. DiPietro also suggested two other services that the program performed: it explained a part of Ellis Island's proceedings that were less likely than others to be part of family lore, since most migrants through Ellis Island never dealt with the BSI; and it gave visitors a chance to feel empowered about immigration. Most people, he said, have an opinion about immigration but are powerless to do anything about it and may feel helpless. Here, they get to decide, at least in fantasy.[15]

Whether or not "Decide an Immigrant's Fate" ever makes people feel empowered about contemporary immigration, one key variable in the program is the ranger's call on how, and how much, audiences should be empowered to perform the fictional task at hand. The program, which, rangers explain, is based on an actual incident, involves the case of a would-be immigrant commanded to appear before the BSI because he didn't have $25, the sum required in 1910 to demonstrate that one wasn't likely to become a public charge. When Ellis Island officials asked the immigrant's brother to come vouch for him, according to the story, the brother, unable to miss work, sent a letter that wound up creating more trouble. Not only would he house his brother, the letter said, but also he had already found him a job: his own employer had agreed to hire the brother, too, and had even paid for his passage. Oops. Where the brother must have seen evidence of the employer's good faith, the BSI saw a debt for the boat ticket that the immigrant would have to pay off, and consequently a violation of the Contract Labor Law of 1885, which prohibited people with a job in the United States already secured from entering the country on the grounds that prior contracts often created indentured servitude. As rangers explained, however, the prohibition was designed to keep jobs from going to new immigrants instead of natives or long-term residents at least as much as to protect migrants from exploitation.

The twenty-minute program generally proceeds as follows: a park ranger gives some historical background and solicits three volunteers to serve as the board. The ranger then summons an actor, from the crew that puts on "Embracing Freedom," who is introduced as Boris, Olga, or Mario (or Yankl in 2000) depending on the actor's sex and on whether the actor looks more plausibly Russian or Italian. Although I never heard a ranger mention it in this context, these nationalities are particularly appropriate for a 1910 case begun as an LPC hearing. A year earlier, Commissioner Williams had upped the required display to $25, as a legal means, he candidly stated, of weeding out the undesirable immigrants it was most likely to nab: southern and eastern Europeans, particularly Italians and Jews. Another such means appeared in 1912 when IQ tests began to be administered "to test the hereditary shortcomings of immigrants." As Nancy Ordover explains in *American Eugenics*, over 80 percent of Jewish, Polish, Italian, Hungarian, and Russian immigrants were labeled " 'feeble-minded defectives,' " thus making them eligible for exclusion. Migrants through Ellis Island were the first group in the United States subjected to IQ tests. This test, like others, encoded presumptions about economic status and the differential interest in evicting based on it; migrants with the money to avoid the island avoided the test, too.[16]

Once the players for "Decide an Immigrant's Fate" are all in place, a volunteer swears in the immigrant by reading an oath (on the order of "Do you promise that the testimony you are about to give concerning your admission to the United States is the truth, the whole truth, and nothing but the truth?"), and the three proceed to question the immigrant, more or less from a list of questions provided to them. Questioning usually reveals that the immigrant is a tailor (if male) or seamstress (if female) whose money was "swindled on the boat" by men with dice (if male) or stolen (if female). After a bit of questioning, the ranger introduces the brother's letter (or a sister's letter if the immigrant is female), which the ranger or a board member reads. More questions follow. Then, sometimes after being directed to confer with each other, the volunteers either vote or announce a consensus; rangers sometimes poll the audience before or after. The ranger then says something like "Welcome to America" or "You are excluded," sometimes after a little flourish by a panelist, like "Go forth and be a productive citizen." The ranger stamps a slip of paper in an official-looking way, hands it to the actor, and sends him or her off. If the immigrant is admitted, which usually happens, the audience often claps and cheers as the actor leaves — whether for the decision or for the performance, it is not always clear. Most rangers then reveal and explain the "real" decision, that the immigrant was excluded in the original case, and then answer some further questions as people drift away.

Variations in the program from the presentation side depend on the teaching strategies and the politics of the rangers who offer it, all of whom have volunteered to participate. It is not a mandatory rotation. One ranger who refused to participate disdained it for one of the same reasons that DiPietro liked it: the fact that a small percentage of migrants faced the BSI. Why, then, give the hearings all this attention? This ranger also had issues with what he perceived as the misplaced priorities of some other rangers more interested in entertaining than informing.

Those who teach may recognize in this comment the signs of a common conflict among teachers, one that may signal or mask other issues; sometimes, for instance, faculty who are younger, female, queer, of color, and/or simply popular are those against whom the charge of "entertainer" is leveled. While I did not get enough clues confidently to assert a particular subtext in this case, I did notice among participating rangers various levels of attention to issues like gender in running the program. Most rangers drew audience attention to gender when women volunteers joined the panel, generally asking the audience if we could identify what made our panel different from the historical ones. That usually brought the chorus, "women!" indicating one area of common knowledge about restrictions of the past. Some rangers went further, visibly aiming for gender diversity in picking among volunteers. One ranger in particular kept an eye on gender dynamics as the program went along; once when she noticed a male volunteer doing all of the questioning, she gently reminded the other panelists that they could ask questions, too.

Another issue that may recall freighted debates in other contexts concerned the processes for decision making. The historical BSI hearings, most rangers explained, involved hierarchy and voting: the two "junior" administrators on the board voted, with the "senior" member voting only to break a tie. In the fictional hearing, only some rangers designated one panelist the senior, and only some—not exactly the same "some"—centered the decision making on voting; others, as I said above, first solicited a consensus. Rangers also varied in whether they simply told panelists to read the prepared list of questions or encouraged them to come up with additional or alternative questions, and in whether they tried to get the rest of the audience involved in decision making.

One of the most determining decisions that rangers make concerns what to do with their introductory material. Before the "immigrant" enters, rangers have about five minutes to introduce enough information about Ellis Island so that even people who make the program their first stop can follow what is happening. Everyone explains the preliminary medical and legal inspections and the $25 rule. But what about the Contract Labor Law on which the original case hinged? Some withhold that information until the end, keeping for themselves the starring role in the moment of truth. For those rangers, however, things go awry if visitors already know the law and ask about it, which sometimes they do; rangers then expose their own deliberate withholding, and the law winds up with even more attention than it might otherwise have had. Other rangers explain the Contract Labor Law at the beginning, thus giving participants all the information they need to figure out the likely verdict. In one interesting variation I saw in 2000, some rangers got together with the main actor and, after clearing the plan through a supervisor in the interpretation department, they introduced the narrative detail that the immigrant was also a musician, along with introductory comments about a loophole in the law permitting people in certain professions, such as musicians, nurses, and clergy, to contract for their labor in advance. The pieces didn't quite fit here, however, since the contract in question concerns tailoring work rather than performance, but the idea, according to one ranger I interviewed, was to come up with a way for the visitors, who almost always admitted the immigrant, to be able to do so according to law.[17]

Here, of course, politics again enters in this desire to help people follow laws, even in the fantasy world. I was very interested, and a bit disheartened, to find this presumption of a responsibility to be law-abiding among numerous participants, including visitors. If it is the law, you have to follow it, even if the law is unjust, which many people thought it was. As one visitor put it, "You were screwed either way": if you had a job waiting for you, you were likely to become a contract laborer; if you had no clear prospects for employment, you were likely to become a public charge.[18] Visitors also saw easily, sometimes with various cues from rangers, that requiring assets contradicted the professed open arms of Liberty—"'give me your tired, your poor,' but not your dirt poor," as one ranger put it—and that the process for determining LPC and contract labor violations seemed designed for, or at least very conducive to, tripping up migrants, especially considering language barriers. How would you know that having no employment was preferable?

Nonetheless, people often thought that the law should be followed anyway. I spoke to one visitor, a white woman in her sixties, who served on a panel that rejected "Mario." She told me that while she liked the program, which she found educationally successful, and agreed with her panel's decision, having learned on-site about the Contract Labor Law in the movie *Island of Hope—Island of Tears*, she had really wanted to admit him. She added that she had even cried during the movie over the plight of the immigrants, but she still felt that she had to obey the law.[19] During another program, led by a ranger who didn't reveal the law in advance, the panelists called the ranger over and said, "We all like the guy and want to let him in but we think he broke the Contract Labor Law." An interesting departure from the usual ensued when the actor interrupted, in character as Boris, to say that coming here should be his decision. A panelist then took the role of explaining the law, saying to him, "If I own a business and pay your ticket, then you have to work for me," to which the immigrant responded that he didn't have to take the job if he didn't want to because "There's no slavery in America." He didn't prevail.[20]

What to make of the program deciding about Boris? From one angle, it all makes easy sense. Visitors act out the role of administrators charged to uphold migration laws, so they follow the laws that they know about. Yet nothing in the scene really goes without saying, beginning with a number of presumptions, concerning, for example, why migrants need to stop at geopolitical borders, and what is meant by borders as barriers and the crossing of borders. (As Caren Kaplan points out, "The notion of a world without boundaries . . . appeals to conservative, liberal, and progressive alike," for different reasons; "the multinational corporation and the libertarian anarchist might choose to phrase their ideal worlds in just such terms."[21]) Another presumption concerns whether staying put constitutes the core from which migrations constitute a "supplement," as James Clifford puts it in asking do "roots always precede routes?"[22] Or, conversely, whether, as Katharyne Mitchell emphasizes, conceptualizing travel or mobility as core elides key barriers, structured by gender, race, and economic status among other factors, that for numerous people impede or prohibit mobility "on the ground."[23] (But, too, a question I derive from a casual familiarity with the talk show and self-help genres: What does it mean that so many people now think they're "on a journey"?) Finally, there is the presumption of how individual biographies, real or fictional, bear on and illuminate history.[24] Such historical framing had some issues taken for granted that are worthy of note.

Worthy of attention, too, is what wasn't taken for granted in framing both the history and the fiction. The rangers had different ways of setting the scene, sometimes even providing a rationale for constituting a board with newcomers: we were a room of trainees, thus explaining our need for instruction; or the regular board is at lunch, thus explaining our sudden call to duty. They also gave a range of explanations about the current fictional task and the historical role at its base. One ranger would begin by intoning, "Inspectors, you are here to protect America," while another, deliberately signaling high drama, would say "Thank you for coming to help [voice deepens and gets louder] Decide an Immigrant's Fate." Sometimes rangers directed visitors to abandon their own values or personality: "Anyone have compassion? Throw it out. This isn't 2000; everything is black or white." The ranger who said that then added a seemingly contradictory point that the hearing was nonetheless a gift, "The first time these people were treated evenhandedly." Another ranger offered a similar mixed message: "Remember, it's not a judicial hearing because you have no legal rights. [But] how about that? You are not a citizen but you still get to have a hearing and if you don't like the answer you can appeal all the way to Washington." (Few people rejected at Ellis Island exercised this difficult-to-execute option.) Importantly, these comments don't quite seem as politically neutral as rangers were supposed to be.

The relation of visitors to the fictional set-up varied, too, sometimes independently of ranger directions. The woman I mentioned above who reluctantly rejected Mario took her job extraordinarily seriously and really got into it; she told me that "it felt kind of real, even though you knew in the back of your mind that it wasn't." In contrast, the woman who explained the Contract Labor Law to Boris seemed more interested in getting the right answer, snapping her finger in a "Yes!" gesture when the ranger explained the "real" verdict. People sometimes connected present to past, or fiction to nonfiction in other ways, too. One man in the audience on an occasion when the ranger polled the whole group joked that he had voted "no" because "then there'd be room for me."[25] Another man, geared even more toward entertainment, followed up Olga's negative response to "Have you been married?" by asking "Do you have dinner plans?" (The ranger humorously interjected "She needs to be a citizen first.")[26]

Occasionally participants had conflicting agendas. During one program in 2002, no actor was available for the immigrant's role and so the ranger solicited a volunteer from the audience, suggesting that the person might use one of his or her own immigrant ancestors for inspiration. A white male teenager volunteered. After answering "What is your nationality?" by saying, "Jewish, no, wait, Russia" (yet another interesting trace of the common articulation of Jewish as an ethnic identity and mark of the foreign) he played his character almost totally as a miscreant, or as his migrant ancestor might have said, a nogoodnick. He was a butcher because "I like killing animals," he was indeed a polygamist, with seven wives, and yes, he'd been in jail for robbery. (One interesting exception: He first answered "anarchist" to the question "are you an anarchist or a communist?" But it turned out, when he was asked if he knew what the word meant, that he had guessed, from the phrasing of the question, that "anarchist" was the opposite of "communist." Apparently, communism is beyond the bad that he wanted to assume in fiction.) His obnoxious goofing was somewhat thwarted, however, when one of the panel members, a white woman about fifty, tried to soften him with amateur psychology. Could it be, she asked, that he "really stole the money because he missed his family, but was too embarrassed just to say so." Besides not sounding particularly correct historically, this interpretation also required her invention of narrative detail, since it had not been established that his family had already relocated to the United States. To my surprise, he went for it. He assented to her theory, but to no avail. The two other people on the panel, white boys a bit younger than the "immigrant," refused to let him in no matter how many excuses she made for him.

Their insistence at booting him out points to another factor sometimes involved in the program: the age of participants. Children frequently volunteered, thus presenting challenges to running the program (which at least one ranger avoided by saying that panelists had to be eighteen or over). The tasks were sometimes a bit beyond younger children: those with the most need for the prepared questions might have great trouble reading them. Children also occasionally behaved disrespectfully, without the skill of the man who joked at sexual interest in (or harassment of) Olga to give the impression that his dubious comments were meant tongue in cheek. During one program, a Boy Scout on the board snickered at Olga's accent, generating other titters. The ranger interrupted the proceedings to chastise the group, albeit in historical form: "We are deciding something very serious here, whether someone comes into this country or gets sent back. If you can't handle it, please leave."

But more often, the comments of one ranger suggest, children affected the program by being harsher judges. I had asked him in August 2002 if he had seen changes in the program after the events of 9/11. Did visitors more frequently send the immigrant away? No, he said, citing youth as a big-ger factor than anything in current events. Children were much more rigid about punishing law-breaking than were the adults, who were often willing just to say "what the hell." The case of the polygamist butcher then typi-fied certain developmental habits, although another encounter I had sug-gests how contextually specified those are, too. I attended the program with the disrespectful Boy Scout in the company of some high school students from Upward Bound, a program funded by the Department of Education to help low-income high school students get to and succeed in college. For the students enrolled in the Upward Bound program run at the University of Southern Maine, this New York trip to see sights and colleges was a culmi-nation of the summer program.[27] Two of the students told me that they liked "Decide an Immigrant's Fate," and found it educational. But they consid-ered it insufficiently harsh, yet for different or additional reasons than the rigid morality that the ranger attributed to young people in general: being immigrants themselves, they thought that the program made the process of admission look far easier than it is. Meanwhile, DiPietro suggested another reason for the adult leniency I'd seen.[28] He told me that in the winter, when the actors aren't on site and the program runs with an audio instead of live people, the exclusion rate is higher. He speculated that looking in the face of even a fictional immigrant made it harder to say no.

THE FICTIONAL IS THE POLITICAL

Any list of common factors falls short in terms of explaining "Decide an Immigrant's Fate." Individual programs often seemed to depend as much as anything on idiosyncratic or personal circumstances. Despite everything I said, for instance, about seeing evidence of a pattern about wanting to uphold laws when the panelists who said they liked Boris threw him out anyway, his ouster seemed partly to be punishment for something uncon-nected to fictional narrative: the actor was late. Near the start of the pro-gram the ranger had to page so-and-so "from the acting company" in earshot of the whole group, and the tenor of the subsequent hearing had a certain combative, if lightheartedly combative, quality. When "Boris" said he was a musician, one of the judges interjected, "Maybe we should ask him to hum a few bars." In another program, which evicted "Olga," a white female judge repeated disdainfully, during the hearing and later to the man she was with, that Olga would probably become a prostitute.[29] Her intensity about the topic suggested that something was going on beyond a distanced analysis of the case, and maybe also beyond the garden-variety derision of sex work and sex workers that many people feel free to express as if there is a logic or morality to that position and it goes without saying. In *Interpreting Our Heritage* Tilden talked about having once called National Park Service interpreters "middlemen of happiness."[30] Not here.

These examples show the difficulties of discerning visitor interpretation. People engage "Decide an Immigrant's Fate" on various registers of reality and representation, sometimes simultaneously. The program can be about the tardy actor and the Contract Labor Law all at the same time; from one person to another it may concern those alternately, differently, or not at all. Similarly, what people bring to the program is neither attitudes about immigration only nor attitudes only about immigration. Ideas about immigration are mediated, created, and articulated by and through conceptualizations and practices concerning gender, money, race, sex, and more. Meanwhile, a lot besides immigration is at issue. The spectacle of a woman spitting anti-prostitute tirades to her companion after booting out a fictional immigrant well illustrates this point. Furthermore, none of these matters factor into the program only in the realm of attitudes. Most simply, money affects who may wind up attending "Decide an Immigrant's Fate" in the first place. As I stated earlier, the ferry ticket costs almost the equivalent of two hours' pay for many Aramark workers at Ellis Island, and that's before payroll deductions; it requires resources including funds, time, and mobility to position oneself at the dock.[31]

A wide range of factors bring people to "Decide an Immigrant's Fate." What people bring to the program is diverse, too: ideas, beliefs, and politics; bodies, their own and maybe others; histories understood to be personal and/or shared, with groups constituted by (concepts of) kinship, ethnicity, nation, and more; temporal particularities like the dynamics of the day. One can hardly, then, guarantee the effects of exhibits and programming or the meanings people take from them. One of my favorite examples of failed direction in meaning involves a conversation I heard on the ferry in 2001 among a family that, from appearance and sound, seemed to be constituted by a man, a woman, and their two children, all of South Asian descent;

the contrast between the parents' inflections and those of the children, a girl about ten and a boy several years younger, suggested that the children had been raised in the United States, with the parents possibly adult migrants. To the parents' dismay, the children seemed totally uninterested in the Statue of Liberty despite a lot of prompting. The father finally went into his daughter's pink backpack, yanked out the camera, and told her to take a picture. The boy eventually gave in to his mother's attempts to get his attention: "What's the Statue of Liberty? Just a lady holding some fire?"[32] Why would something like that be remarkable? Figuring out what would make anyone take notice depends on a lot besides taking notice oneself.

What exhibits, programming, and their presenters do provide, however, are components of interpretation. To be sure, these components are already products of interpretation themselves. This is one reason that, as Gable and Handler point out regarding Colonial Williamsburg, the roles of interpreter and visitor cannot really be mapped onto distinct categories of producer and consumer. Interpreters are themselves consumers of the "museum messages," as well as of "prepackaged ensembles of artifacts or texts" that they encounter in research and trainings.[33] I do not intend here to imply sinister manipulation on the part of trainers or exhibition planners. Anyone who uses secondary sources gets prepackaged material. Anyone who recommends, assigns, assembles, or writes about material is involved in packaging; the very act of attending or drawing attention to something as noteworthy pulls it into that realm. Visitors, likewise, function as producers of meanings. They "make something of" what they engage.

But to emphasize that component material rarely exists somehow before, beneath, or unmarked by interpretation, or that it gets transformed and supplemented by people who encounter it, is not to dismiss the factors that enable or encourage particular directions in interpretation by advancing particular (interpreted) materials and interpretations about them. Memory, both individual and collective, is as Michael Frisch suggests a "deeply cultural artifact" that can be guided and manipulated in various ways.[34] What if "Decide an Immigrant's Fate" concerned the case of Frank Woodhull, who came before the BSI when he had to admit to having a body that conformed to his given name, Mary Johnson? A lot more people would walk away from Ellis Island with a sense that migrants had relations to sex and gender that perhaps shouldn't be taken for granted.

I understand why "Decide an Immigrant's Fate" revolves around contract labor and the cash-in-hand requirement instead. Those restrictions affected a lot more people. Plus, a focus on the contract labor law has several excellent features. It offers a chance to explain in some depth the complex and contradictory features of a policy that are hard to pick up on immediately. It focuses concern on the relation of migration policy to demands for and ideas about labor, which continue to impact U.S. policy. It also has the great merit of showing how border laws can function rather malevolently. Then again, Woodhull's case offers some of the same features, although I still see the rationale and can envision making the same call myself.

I also understand a lot of programming decisions that made me cranky before I liked them. For example, one ranger explained in her introduction to the program that trachoma was a form of conjunctivitis. I mentioned to her afterward that trachoma was actually a form of chlamydia, explaining, on further questioning, that chlamydia is a sexually transmitted disease (although trachoma is generally spread when people with the disease wipe their eyes with their hands, which then come into contact with others). The ranger replied, "Oh, I would never tell people that." One of my first, silent, responses was to put that incident into the category of banned sexual matters. But when I thought more about it, I realized that while I wouldn't mislabel trachoma as a form of conjunctivitis, I wouldn't raise the topic of chlamydia either. With twenty minutes available for "Decide an Immigrant's Fate" or even the forty-five minutes available for a tour, the chlamydia connection, which did not really constitute a sexual secret anyway, hardly seemed like a good use of time, especially because, apparently, chlamydia itself would need to be explained. (This might actually be a reason for including it—the ranger's lack of familiarity with chlamydia points to a need for more public information about sexual health).

What does bother me are some of the exclusions and directions of interpretation that certain consistencies and repetitions across Ellis Island exhibits and programming seem to encourage, abetted by dominant trends off-site regarding the immigration station and its nearby statue. I have described some of those in previous chapters: silences about sexuality and about sex and gender complexities; the presumptive association of kinship and family with procreation only; the linkings between the island and the statue that work to evacuate the latter's connection to slavery; the gestures about the monuments' universal significance that sometimes function to mask the direction of major heritage resources to honor immigrants now generally considered white; and the disconnects regarding both contemporary incarceration and the exploitation of labor that occur in making a tourist site, complete with snacks and souvenirs, of a migrant detention center. For me, the issue regarding the case chosen for "Decide an Immigrant's Fate," then, is not that the program concerns contract labor rather than Frank Woodhull, but that Frank Woodhull's story resides primarily in a small caption within the souvenir guide, only available for purchase and not so easily run across.

The title "Decide an Immigrant's Fate" matters for related reasons. The program itself may not promote the imperious callousness and unjust assumption of privilege that I read into the title, and my reading may not be the dominant one, although I've heard many horrified gasps when I've recited it. Yet why put into repeated circulation a title that echoes some of the worst policies and impulses occurring today beyond the museum's boundaries?

CONCLUSION: LOOK HERE

In a way, this project turned me into a tour guide, at least for its duration. I began with an idea of writing a book about how people engaged Ellis Island souvenirs and wound up wanting to offer my own tour of the site and of material, ideas, and events linked to it. Look over here; let me show you this. Stay with me, please, while I relay information, suggest connections, and share my interpretations. Look at Liberty Weekend in relation to *Bowers v. Hardwick*. Look at "Frank Woodhull" as Frank Woodhull, not necessarily as *really* Mary Johnson. Look at the souvenir guide made in Korea next to the snow globe made in China next to the image of immigrant vendors that is regulated by the city to evoke poor peddlers of yore while abetting the well capitalized today.

I chose my project for several reasons, some of which are linked to the inevitable transformations involved in formulating any project. As I explained in the introduction, I came to see various features of my original plan as impossible, uninteresting, or limited by methodological habits that pushed me in two directions that weren't quite right: using context to explain ob-

FIGURE 24. Ellis Island snow globe key chain. Purchased at the gift
shop in 2003. (Photograph by Robert Diamante)

jects or objects to explain context. I also became intrigued by what I did not
find on offer in tours, displays, merchandise, and programs. I wanted to get
in there myself, adding material to the mix of what people might bring to
Ellis Island—the site, the history, the concept.

I don't expect my tour to function as a definitive read or last word, for
many reasons. The least is that the site keeps changing in terms of exhibitions, programming, staff, and products. Since I began my research, for
instance, my immigrants in a snow globe gave way to a smaller but multi-
tasking snow-globe key chain (figure 24)—multi, that is, if one finds, as I
do, a vital function in watery, glittery shake-and-show. It is still $2.99 and
"made in China" but the new one pictures the building on one side and a
waving U.S. flag on the other. No huddled masses, no other flags; the departure of the latter is differently unappealing than is their diminutive presence
in the "Destination America" motif. A new book by Barry Moreno, librarian
at Ellis Island, includes a picture of Charles Trenet, who, as the caption explains, was detained at Ellis Island for twenty-six days in 1948 on charges
of homosexuality. While his case does not bear on immigration process-

ing, since Ellis Island had long ceased that function by then and Trenet was traveling for theater engagements rather than trying to relocate, it surfaces the issue of sexual policing in ways welcome and, I hope, promising of more surfacing to come.[35] A page in the "Teacher's Corner" of the Park Service's Web site for the Statue of Liberty, discussing Liberty's broken chains, states that "the Statue of Liberty creation has a direct connection with America's abolition movement and the Civil War." That I found this information most easily through a link in an article in *Black History Magazine*, which also emphasizes the lack of such information in the Park Service's primary description of the statue's origins, points to changes that remain to be advocated.[36]

The material I considered is far from static; so, too, remains its context, both on-site and off. In 2003, the Supreme Court overthrew *Bowers v. Hardwick*, investigators worried about the statue and Ellis being terrorist targets, retailers hoped that capturing Saddam Hussein might put Christmas shoppers in a good mood for spending, and the National Ice Cream Council followed Jell-O in using Ellis Island to vouch for its all-American status.[37] "By 1921," according to an article based on council materials, "ice cream had become so identified with American culture that the commissioner of Ellis Island decided to include it in the first meal served to arriving immigrants": here again, through business promotion offered as news, is the implication of Ellis Island food as a welcoming pleasure extended to all rather than a detention ration dispensed as cheaply as possible.[38] Sex, money, products, nation: some things change, some things don't. Conservatives step up efforts to keep marriage heterosexual — not to mention just to keep marriage, an institution that fewer and fewer seem to question. Silences around Liberty's 1986 centennial are echoed, if silences can be said to echo, in the canonization of Reagan after his death, as mainstream press coverage minimized any mention of the terrible and sometimes deadly effects of his refusal to address AIDS, his economic and social policies, and his support for right-wing governments in Central America. Prosecutors still grab old laws to perpetrate new outrages, like when a 1872 law designed to keep brothel workers from boarding ships was used in 2002 against Greenpeace.[39] Meanwhile, the perceived need to "Decide an Immigrant's Fate" goes on and on. Virtually every week that I worked on this book, a new example (or six) appeared even in my minimally informative local paper, and not just about who stays or goes. In late 2003, for instance, Massachusetts terminated most nonemergency health care for a number of immigrants and refugees; and a governor's veto in November killed a bill to restore health insurance to disabled and elderly legal immigrants.[40]

In any case, regardless of changes and same-olds in various contextual out-theres, interpretations are neither solo shows nor catalysts that can be designed to push in singular directions. As I have been arguing in this chapter, people make meanings from what they encounter. As I have been suggesting throughout the book, meaning making does not proceed in a linear way: ideas, materials, practices, and representations come together in more knotty ways.

To me, these features of interpretation constitute a model more than a burden. I don't want this book to function as a truth deposit, were such a feat even possible. I want instead, trite as this may sound, to participate in collective projects of advancing understanding, social justice, and many, many pleasures. These three projects, I believe, do not come separately. By looking at scenes around Ellis Island and the Statue of Liberty where sex, money, products, and ideas of the nation come together, I aim to participate in projects of making them come together better.

NOTES

1 The quotes here are based on my conversation with Marion in Miami on December 2000. In general, for the purposes of maintaining the privacy of the people to whom I spoke, I omit or alter identifying details unless I am quoting someone such as the National Park Service supervisor who spoke to me more formally in an official capacity. Although Marion spoke of Eleanor Roosevelt as "ambassador" to the United Nations, she was technically a "delegate." Moreover, I could not find external corroboration of Marion's assertion that Roosevelt directly intervened in the particular matter of bringing Polish deportees back from Siberia. Whether Roosevelt's intervention remained largely unknown, undocumented, or unpublicized, or whether Marion mistakenly attributed her sister's release to Roosevelt, I don't know. Roosevelt was widely recognized as an advocate for human rights and the oppressed, including Jews. She led the U.N. creation of the "Universal Declaration of Human Rights," approved in 1948, the year in which she also won a medal from the *American Hebrew* for promoting better relations between Christians and Jews. See "Mrs. Roosevelt Honored; Gets Award for Aiding Amity of Christians and Jews," *New York Times*, 3 March 1949, p. 30. Thanks to Alex Wenger for her research help on this matter.

2 Chris Burbach, "All Aboard! Train Station Gallery Opens," *Omaha World-Herald*, 2 July 2000, sec. B, p. 1, http://www.lexis-nexis.com/. I discuss this habit of reference further in the introduction.

3 While some insist that the dimensions of the physical relationship between the two women remain a matter of speculation, their letters, even after many were discarded and those remaining often heavily edited, are suggestive of correspondence between lovers, as indicated by the much quoted letter dated 7 March 1933, written by Roosevelt, which begins "Hick darling," and goes on to say "I want to put my arms around you, I ache to hold you close. Your ring is a great comfort, I look at it & think she does love me, or I wouldn't be wearing it!" The letter, which can easily be found on the Internet, is reprinted in *Empty without You: The Intimate Letters of Eleanor Roosevelt and Lorena Hickok*, ed. Rodger Streitmatter (New York: Free Press, 1998), 19. Roosevelt also had lesbians among her close friends, who, Streitmatter notes, "served as

the conduit through which Eleanor moved into the community of politically astute women who were effecting social reform" (2–3). Blanche Wiesen Cook details these social relations and political activities in *Eleanor Roosevelt*, vol. 1 (New York: Viking, 1992). See chapter 12, "Eleanor Roosevelt and the New Women of the 1920's: Esther Lape and Elizabeth Read, First Feminist Friends," 288–301, especially 292–98, and chapter 13, "Convalescence, Marital Unity, and Separate Spheres: Polio, Val-Kill, and Warm Springs," 302–37, especially 319–27 and 331–37. As this material suggests, the political work that shaped Marion's perception of Roosevelt was informed, at the very least, by the openness of her affiliations.

INTRODUCTION

1 According to the Statue of Liberty—Ellis Island Foundation, Inc., *Annual Report* (New York: SOLEIF) for the fiscal year ending 31 March 2003, between 1,400,000 and 1,500,000 people visited in each of the fiscal years ending in 2001, 2002, and 2003 (p. 4).

2 On the particulars of Asian chic in 1997, see, for example, Dan Deluca, "Asian Chic," *Philadelphia Inquirer*, 30 November 1997, sec. H, pp. 1–2. In terms of arenas in which the racial and ethnic contents of "white" is being articulated, I am thinking, for example, of struggles over Affirmative Action, "whiteness studies," and various ethnic-pride initiatives among groups in which lighter-skinned people deemed to belong to that group are now generally labeled white, such as Irish, Polish, and German. See Charles Gallagher, "White Reconstruction in the University," *Socialist Review* 24, nos. 1 and 2 (1995): 165–87 for an interesting study of how white college students understand their race and ethnicity in relation to what they (mis)understand to be a climate that favors people of color.

3 It also exposed how little I knew about certain markers of status and pedigree, since while Sallie could indeed join the DAR, it was not her Mayflower descent that rendered her eligible but, as the name suggests, her descent from someone who had fought in the war called the American Revolution.

4 The cards, produced by Madison and Co. (New York, 1990) give the following statistics for the number of immigrants arriving between 1899 and 1931: Japan, 265,092; France, 533,644; Mexico, 700,134; Africa, 142,559. Assuming that these numbers come from the most generous accounting, they still add up to far less than 20 percent of Ellis Island immigrants. Note also that the inclusion of all of Africa in a group otherwise constituted by country is one of many telling and common inconsistencies in geopolitical categorizing.

5 *Remembering Ellis Island: Every Man's Monument*, hosted by Telly Savalas. (Cinescope Enterprises: A Panorama International Production, 1995).

6 Mark Landsman, with Yaron Avni, Reut Elkouby, Bushra Jawabri, Amer K. Ranon, Hazem El Sanoun, Yossi Zilberman, *Peace of Mind* (New York Global Action Project, 1999).

7 "Proposition 187 Was Struck Down Today," press release by the California Latino Civil Rights Network, 14 November 1997, reproduced on the A-Infos News Service=. Whether or not the state of California should challenge this decision was a source of subsequent political conflict.

8 See, for instance, Josie Huang, "Prison Sentence Spells Deportation," *Portland Press Herald*, 28 May 2002, which concerns the case of a man, born in a refugee camp on the Thai border to Cambodian parents, who faced deportation to Cambodia for his conviction in a drunk driving accident that killed his sister.

9 On the politics and poetics of language concerning migration and travel, see Eithne Luibhéid, *Entry Denied: Controlling Sexuality at the Border* (Minneapolis: University of Minnesota Press, 2002); Caren Kaplan, *Questions of Travel: Postmodern Discourses of Displacement* (Durham: Duke University Press, 1996); and James Clifford, *Routes: Travel and Translation in the Late Twentieth Century* (Cambridge, Mass.: Harvard University Press, 1997).

10 For a survey of the exhibits, along with interviews with people from MetaForm Inc., the design firm that created them, see Robert A. Parker, "The Ellis Island Immigration Museum," *Communication Arts* (January/February 1991): 82–93. A survey of the exhibits, along with historical background and a documents section, is also given in *Ellis Island and the Peopling of America: The Official Guide*, written by Virginia Yans-McLaughlin and Marjorie Lightman (with The Statue of Liberty–Ellis Island Foundation, as the cover credit reads) (New York: New Press, 1997).

11 I discuss later the complicated scenario by which Iacocca, actually tagged to run a government commission on restoring the monuments, also wound up running the foundation, which ultimately ran the show.

12 The acronym DOMA indicates the Defense of Marriage Act, passed by Congress in 1996, to fend off attempts to legalize "same-sex marriage" by specifying legal marriage as occurring only between (people legally identified as) one man and one woman.

13 Barbara Kirshenblatt-Gimblett, *Destination Culture: Tourism, Museums, and Heritage* (Berkeley: University of California Press, 1998), 184–86.

14 Ella Shohat, "Lynne Yamamoto, Reflections on Hair and Memory Loss," in *Fresh Talk/Daring Gazes: Conversations on Asian American Art*, ed. Elaine H. Kim, Margo Machida, and Sharon Mizota (Berkeley: University of California Press, 2003), 168.

15 The case hinged on the matter of landfill. In 1998, the Supreme Court ruled in *New Jersey v. New York* (523 US 767) that, based on an 1834 compact that gave New Jersey the submerged part of Ellis Island, the state owned the more than twenty-four acres above water that had been created by adding the landfill. By 2002, the more casual vending at the dock in New Jersey, suggesting endeavors of entrepreneurial migrant vendors working with a small outlay of capital, had given way to vendors with the more standard I ♥ NY and Statue of Liberty gear and the overall look of a franchise. I discuss vending at the New York dock more thoroughly in chapter 6.

16 *HRC Quarterly* (fall 1998): 12, 9. In this issue, in subsequent publications, and in

other texts such as membership-solicitation mailings, HRC repeatedly used some variation on the phrase "lesbian and gay equality," as opposed, for instance, to using "lesbian, gay, bisexual, and transgender equality," or articulating its mission in terms of a broader social-justice model. Bisexual and transgender concerns have more lately become part of HRC's named focus. By May 2004, its home page at http://www .hrc.org/ had "Working for Lesbian, Gay, Bisexual and Transgender Equal Rights" as the slogan under its name. Thanks to David Becker for drawing to my attention these HRC marketing issues.

17 Barbara Smith, "The Fight Is for Social, Political, and Economic Justice," *Gay Community News* 23, no. 4 (1998): 41. The issue has extensive coverage of the Millennium March controversy. See, also in that issue, Geeta Patel, "Stories for the Millennium: Disrupting Time" (52–53, 56–57); and Melanie Kaye Kantrowitz, "Whose Millennium?" (58–59).

18 The NRA Web site is http://www.nrastore.com/nra.

19 *Appendices to the referral to the United States House of Representatives pursuant to Title 28, United States Code, section 595(c) submitted by the Office of the Independent Counsel, September 9, 1998: communication from the Office of the Independent Counsel, Kenneth W. Starr, transmitting appendices to the referral to the United States House of Representatives pursuant to Title 28, United States Code, section 595(c) submitted by the Office of the Independent Counsel, September 9, 1998*, 116–26. The official title of the Starr report is *Referral to the United States House of Representatives pursuant to Title 28, United States Code, [section] 595(c) / submitted by the Office of the Independent Counsel* (Washington, D.C.: U.S. House of Representatives, 1998).

20 Ibid., 115.

21 For example, in Monica Lewinsky's deposition of 26 August 1998, reprinted in the Starr report appendices, she stated that Bill "brought [her] to orgasm" four times (1329). Interestingly, lines are blacked out after her affirmation of a Clinton-induced orgasm on 7 February of that year (1309), despite details throughout about whether Bill touched Monica's breasts and "genitals" over or under her clothes (both), if he sometimes used his mouth on her breasts or genitals (yes, no), and how often he was the one who unzipped his pants (sometimes). My point here is not to suggest that something would necessarily be wrong in a sexual relationship directed toward the orgasms of only one person involved, which might well be a mutual choice, but to note that in this case removing the mention of Monica's orgasms misrepresents their relationship and contributes to common readings of Monica as a victim or fool.

22 Tyson's particular role in the design has been variously described. According to the QVC press release, Tyson used drawing to express her overwhelming feelings there and at other sites in Africa. She then asked a friend (never named) to make jewelry from her designs for her own personal use; subsequently she decided to create a line after receiving so many compliments. "Cicely Tyson — Master of Many Trades — Interprets Her Passion for Elegance with 'Jewels of Unity' on QVC," reproduced by Yemi Toure, "We Don't Make This Stuff Up," *Hype: Monitoring the Black Image in*

the Media, 21 March 1999, http://www.pan.afrikan.net/hype/wwwboard/messages/590; htm.

23 Robben Museum, "New Year's Eve on Robben Island," 14 December 2000, http://www.robben-island.org.za/welcome.htm.

24 An excellent text is Alexandra Chasin, *Selling Out: The Gay and Lesbian Movement Goes to Market* (New York: St. Martin's Press, 2000), which, relevant to the issues explored here, points out that advertising aimed at gays and lesbians "has often promised full inclusion in the national community of Americans," an identity itself, as she discusses, frequently linked to consumption (101). Another excellent text is Lauren Berlant and Lisa Duggan, eds., *Our Monica Ourselves: The Clinton Affair and the National Interest* (New York: New York University Press, 2001). In this volume, in their essay "The Symbolics of Presidentialism: Sex and Democratic Identification" (34–52), which addresses revelations offered by organizing sex acts and gifts by dates, Dana D. Nelson and Tyler Curtain nicely point out a certain discernable queer content. For instance, Monica's Gap dress got stained on "a day that included the bestowal of a copy of Walt Whitman's *Leaves of Grass* by William Jefferson Clinton on Monica Lewinsky and a rim job by Monica Lewinsky on William Jefferson Clinton" (41).

25 For two articles clearly written from the press release, see Kimberly Roberts, "Cicely Tyson to Showcase Her Jewelry Line: The Famed Actress Will Present Her African-Inspired Jewels of Unity," *Philadelphia Tribune*, 3 March 1999, sec. B, p. 5; "Tyson Creates Jewelry Line," *Sacramento Observer*, 12 May 1999, sec. E, p. 5.

26 Conversation with Leslie Hill, fall 2001.

27 Irit Rogoff, *Terra Infirma: Geography's Visual Culture* (London and New York: Routledge, 2000), 8.

28 Matt Carroll, "Boston Architectural Firm Helps Restore Ellis Island," *Boston Globe*, 21 July 1990, p. 37.

29 Overheard, 19 September 2000.

30 On the increasing importance of sexual matters in terms of shaping conceptions of citizenship, see Lauren Berlant, *The Queen of America Goes to Washington City: Essays on Sex and Citizenship* (Durham: Duke University Press, 1997).

31 On the role of high cost in confirming pricelessness, see Igor Kopytoff, "The Cultural Biography of Things," in *The Social Life of Things: Commodities in Cultural Perspective*, ed. Arjun Appadurai (Cambridge: Cambridge University Press, 1986), 82.

32 Christine, Fidi, Jenieve, Ro, and Toni, "Talking Class: Working Class SM Dykes Lay Down the Line, Part Two," *Brat Attack*, no. 3 (1993): 39. As Pat Califia notes, products clearly designated for sexual use, such as the crotchless panties available in sex shops, generally cost much more and are made to wear out much faster than products not so clearly designated for that purpose alone, such as lingerie bought at a department store. Thus, people are made to pay (in the dual sense of price and punishment) for certain sexual accoutrements and the uses and values they imply (Pat Califia, "San Francisco: Revisiting the City of Desire," in *Queers in Space: Communi-*

ties, Public Places, Sites of Resistance, ed. Gordon Brent Ingram, Anne-Marie Bouthill-ette, and Yolanda Retter [Seattle: Bay Press, 1997], 183). The notion that production and pricing relate to respect for the perceived consumer comes up also, as I will discuss later, with regard to the Ellis Island gift shop.

33 Miranda Joseph, *Against the Romance of Community* (Minneapolis: University of Minnesota Press, 2002), 57. For another consideration of these issues, articulated regarding accounts of developments of queer identities in relation to capitalism, see Ann Pellegrini, "Consuming Lifestyle: Commodity Capitalism and Transforma-tions in Gay Identity," in *Queer Globalizations: Citizenship and the Afterlife of Colonial-ism*, ed. Arnaldo Cruz-Malavé and Martin F. Manalansan IV (New York: New York University Press, 2002), 134–45.

34 F. Ross Holland, *Idealists, Scoundrels, and the Lady: An Insider's View of the Statue of Liberty–Ellis Island Project* (Urbana: University of Illinois Press, 1993), 86.

35 Peter Morton Coan, ed. *Ellis Island Interviews* (New York: Checkmark Books, 1997), 109, 161.

36 B. Colin Hamblin, *Ellis Island: The Official Souvenir Guide* (Santa Barbara, Calif.: Companion Press, 1994).

37 On this function of the souvenir as "a trace of authentic experience" that needs to be supplemented by narrative, which I would argue to be a bit more occasional, see Susan Stewart, *On Longing: Narratives of the Miniature, the Gigantic, the Souvenir, the Collection* (Durham: Duke University Press, 1993), 135–36.

38 See, for instance, the classic essay by Joan Scott, "The Evidence of Experience," in *The Lesbian and Gay Studies Reader*, edited by Henry Abelove, Michèle Aina Barale, and David M. Halperin (New York: Routledge, 1993).

39 Thanks to Eric Smoodin for his insistent and persistent grumbling, as we sat to-gether once during a conference session, about whether one can call any videos "progressive" if their physical manufacture depends on the exploitation of labor.

40 I further discuss this poster, an offset lithograph printed in 1981, in chapter 5.

41 Arjun Appadurai, "Introduction: Commodities and the Politics of Value," in Ap-padurai, ed., *The Social Life of Things*, 13. Appadurai' s use of "exchangeability" is based on his argument that a commodity is "any thing intended for exchange" (9), and on his useful suggestion that besides exchanging objects for money, the usual definition of understanding commodities, gift giving and barter sometimes func-tion as forms of commodity exchange (9–13).

42 Stewart, *On Longing*, 21.

43 Interview, 19 September 2000.

44 Statue of Liberty–Ellis Island Foundation, Inc., *Annual Report: 1986–1987*, 9.

45 Mary Voelz Chandler, "Story of Refugees from Mexican Revolution Unfolds on DIA Wall," *Denver Rocky Mountain News*, 2 February 2000, sec. D, p. ; Kelley Bouchard, "A Thousand Miles: The People of Suburban Clarkston, Ga.,—Aka 'Ellis Island South'—Reveal Why Hundreds of Somali Immigrants Living There Are Looking

North, Toward Lewiston, Maine," *Maine Sunday Telegram*, 30 June 2002, sec. A. pp. 1, 10–11.

46 Daniel B. Wood, "Why 12 People Are Settling in L.A. Each Hour," *Christian Science Monitor*, 17 March 2000, p. 2.

47 Sherman Evans, co-creator with Angel Quintero, quoted in Jack Hitt, "Confederate Chic," *Gentleman's Quarterly*, November 1997 (reprinted on the Web site for Nu-South, http://www.nusouth.com/#).

48 As indicated by Benedict Anderson's famous definition of the nation as an "imagined community," nations themselves are constituted partly in the imagining of what constitutes them (Benedict Anderson, *Imagined Communities: Reflections on the Origin and Spread of Nationalism* [London: Verso, 1983]). Criteria that seem most habitually associated with belonging to a nation, such as residence within certain geopolitical boundaries or conformity to legal definitions of citizenship, vary themselves and do not always function as named or clear delimiters. For an excellent account of one case study regarding the politics of changing articulations of national belonging, see Inderpal Grewal, "Traveling Barbie: Indian Transnationality and New Consumer Subjects," *positions* 7 (1999): 799–826.

49 "Honoring with Pride: An Evening on Ellis Island," http://www.amfar.org/pages/pride.html#honor.

50 Denny Lee, "A Night Out with Eric McCormack; Diva for a Day," *New York Times*, 25 June 2000, sec. 9, p. 3.

51 As I discuss later, while most early fund-raising featured the statue, less than a third of the $277 million that Iacocca announced in July 1986, during Liberty Weekend when the newly restored statue was unveiled, went to restore the statue. See Holland, *Idealists, Scoundrels, and the Lady*, 98.

52 "About the Foundation," on the Web site for SOLEIF, http://www.ellisisland.org. This page is copyright 2000, although parts of the site are more recent.

53 Interview with Ron Lieberman, director of concessions, New York City Department of Parks and Recreation, 18 September 2000.

54 For a good account of the differences and relations between gender attribution, gender identity, gender expression, gender assignment, and of the fiction that there are only two sexes, see Kate Bornstein, *Gender Outlaw: On Men, Women, and the Rest of Us* (New York: Routledge, 1994), chapter 4, "Naming all the Parts," 22–40.

55 *Island of Hope—Island of Tears: The Story of Ellis Island and the American Immigration Experience* (New York: Guggenheim Productions, Inc., n.d.). The video is narrated by Gene Hackman, and depended for production on funding from American Express. A book also exists by that name: David M. Brownstone, Irene M. Franck, Douglass L. Brownstone, *Island of Hope, Island of Tears* (New York: Penguin, 1986 [1979]).

56 Erica Rand, *Barbie's Queer Accessories* (Durham: Duke University Press, 1995), 17.

57 September 2000.

58 Interview, 13 September 2000.

59 One great example of changing meanings as well as modes of interpretation regarding the same objects can be found in Juliet Ash's two essays on the tie, one analyzing the tie's social history and another using her own relation to her deceased husband's ties to consider memory and loss (Juliet Ash, "The Tie: Presence and Absence" and "Memory and Objects," in *The Gendered Object*, ed. Pat Kirkham [Manchester: Manchester University Press, 1995]).

CHAPTER 1: BREEDERS ON A GOLF BALL

1 Jane Perry Clark, *Deportation of Aliens from the United States to Europe* (New York: Columbia University Press, 1931), 41. Thanks to Dereka Rushbrook, Jasbir Puar, and especially Louisa Schein for their help, through many drafts and revisions, with the material in this chapter.

2 Ibid., 53.

3 See Mary Spongberg, *Feminizing Venereal Disease: The Body of the Prostitute in Nineteenth-Century Medical Discourse* (New York: New York University Press, 1997), on the development of the ideas that prostitution and the venereal diseases associated with it were largely morally or physically congenital, with people of certain "races," religions, national origins, and ethnicities more prone to it than others.

4 Paul Farmer, *AIDS and Accusation: Haiti and the Geography of Blame* (Berkeley: University of California Press, 1992), 224–25.

5 Eve Kosofsky Sedgwick, "Privilege of Unknowing," *Genders* 1 (1988): 102–3.

6 Farmer, *AIDS and Accusation*, 142–47.

7 Kirshenblatt-Gimblett, *Destination Culture*; Mike Wallace, "Boat People: Immigrant History at the Statue of Liberty and Ellis Island," in *Mickey Mouse History and Other Essays on American Memory* (Philadelphia: Temple University Press, 1996).

8 Interview by the author, 9 September 2000.

9 Interview by the author, 5 September 2000.

10 Statue of Liberty–Ellis Island Foundation, "About the Foundation."

11 Michael Warner, "Introduction," in *Fear of a Queer Planet*, ed. Michael Warner (Minneapolis: University of Minnesota Press, 1993); Alan Sinfeld, "Diaspora and Hybridity: Queer Identities and the Ethnicity Model," in *Diaspora and Visual Culture: Representing Africans and Jews*, ed. Nicholas Mirzoeff (London: Routledge, 2000), 95–114.

12 Ioannis Mookas, "Faultlines: Homophobic Innovation in *Gay Rights, Special Rights*," *Afterimage* 22 (1995): 14–18.

13 Berlant, *The Queen of America Goes to Washington City*, 1.

14 Messages read on 9 and 13 September 2000. The sign-in book, true to the popular meaning of the term "millennium," was gone by spring 2001.

15 Kerry O'Brien, who has worked in a variety of historic museum spaces, suggested that the missing smells might have stood out, for some people, all the more because of the odd combination of an overwhelming historic building and the exhibition ma-

terial filling it, which was out of context as much as in context: artifacts isolated in display cases, "the whole irony of a historic building museum" (e-mail message to author, 13 September 2000).

16 The image also shows up frequently in other contexts that concern nation and migration. In 2001, it appeared on the back of a T-shirt for the Museum of Jewish Heritage, which is located near the Battery Park pier where boats take off for the Statue of Liberty and Ellis Island. It also serves, with some blue colorization and the phrase "Freedom: a History of US," on a postcard advertising a 2003 exhibit of that name, subtitled "Photographs and Documents that Define American Freedom, 1776–1968." The exhibit took place at the Housatonic Museum of Art in Bridgeport, Connecticut, from 13 March through 18 April 2003. The lack of punctuation for "US" is part of the original title, playing off the similarity between the collective pronoun and the abbreviation for the United States, and exemplifying, in the process, the issue at hand for Ellis Island, about whether this image can stand for all of "US."

17 Kath Weston, *Long Slow Burn: Sexuality and Social Science* (New York: Routledge, 1998), 58–63.

18 Coan, *Ellis Island Interviews.*

19 "Commissioner Williams Explains the Charges Against McSweeney," *Boston Journal*, 20 August 1903; Harry Sullivan, "A Look at William Williams' First Administration as the Commissioner of Ellis Island," 1983, unpublished paper on file at the Statue of Liberty/Ellis Island Library, Ellis Island, New York; William C. Williams, letter to President Theodore Roosevelt, 16 February 1903, 3–4, Williams C. Williams Papers, New York Public Library.

20 Kiss and Tell (Persimmon Blackbridge, Lizard Jones, and Susan Stewart), *Her Tongue on My Theory* (Vancouver: Press Gang Publishers, 1994), 3.

21 Louisa Schein, "Diaspora Politics, Homeland Erotics, and the Materializing of Memory," *positions* 7 (1999): 724.

22 Cindy Patton and Benigno Sánchez-Eppler, "Introduction," in *Queer Diasporas* (Durham: Duke University Press, 2000), 2–3. Note that "intricate realignments" does not imply a linear or one-directional movement, although as Martin Manalansan notes, immigrant narratives often posit a "line of progression" from an old to a new identity, simplifying changes that may better be described, he suggests, "not in terms of self-contained modes of identity but as permeable boundaries of two co-existing yet oftentimes incommensurable cultural ideologies of gender and sexuality." Martin F. Manalansan IV, *Global Divas: Filipino Gay Men in the Diaspora* (Durham: Duke University Press, 2003), 21.

23 George Chauncey, *Gay New York: Gender, Urban Culture, and the Making of the Gay Male World, 1840–1940* (New York: Basic Books, 1994).

24 "Refused an Entry to the Promised Land: One of the Tragic Phases of Ellis Island — Turned Back from Liberty's Gateway," *New York Times*, 12 August 1906, sec. 3, p. 1. According to Fiorello La Guardia, who worked as a translator at Ellis Island from

1907 to 1910, the women were not always on the receiving end of unpleasant surprises with sexual or marital content. On rare occasions, he said, a woman that a man had sent for showed up with a baby born long after his sperm had left her continent. Fiorello La Guardia, *The Making of an Insurgent: An Autobiography, 1882–1919* (New York: Capricorn Books, 1961 [1948]), 68.

25 Abraham Cahan, *"Yekl" and "The Imported Bridegroom" and Other Stories of the New York Ghetto* (New York: Dover Publications, 1970 [1898]).

26 Ibid., 34.

27 Rebecca Herzig, "Removing Roots: "North American Hiroshima Maidens," *Technology and Culture* 40 (October 1999): 723–745; Rebecca Herzig, "The Woman beneath the Hair: Treating Hypertrichosis, 1870–1930," *NWSA Journal* 12 (fall 2000): 50–66. On mainstream publications' promotion of hair removal, see Christine Hope, "Caucasian Female Body Hair and American Culture," *Journal of American Culture* 5 (spring 1982): 93–99.

28 "Four Rules for Women," *Jewish Daily Forward*, 25 July 1915, excerpted in Irving Howe and Kenneth Libo, *How We Lived: A Documentary History of Immigrant Jews in America 1880–1930* (New York: Richard Marek Publishers, 1979), 147, as cited in Kathy Peiss, *Cheap Amusements: Working Women and Leisure in Turn-of-the-Century New York* (Philadelphia: Temple University Press, 1986), 72.

29 Luibhéid, *Entry Denied*, 37.

30 Lisa Lowe, *Immigrant Acts: Asian American Cultural Politics* (Durham, N.C.: Duke University Press, 1996), 4–5.

31 Luibhéid, *Entry Denied*, 36–37.

32 Bill Ong Hing, *Making and Remaking Asian America through Immigration Policy, 1850–1990* (Stanford: Stanford University Press, 1993), 23.

33 Nayan Shah, *Contagious Divides: Epidemics and Race in San Francisco's Chinatown* (Berkeley: University of California Press, 2001), 13.

34 "More Protection for Immigrants," newspaper clipping hand-dated "Nov 26 1903," William C. Williams Papers, New York Public Library. Unfortunately, while the William C. Williams papers offer an extensive collection of relevant clippings, many have been clipped in a way that excludes printed information about the name, date, or page numbers of the sources. Sometimes, as in this case, a written notation offers some of the information.

35 Memorandum, 12 June 1902, William C. Williams Papers, New York Public Library.

36 Letter to Secretary of the Treasury, "Hon. L. W. Shaw," 1 May 1902, William C. Williams Papers, New York Public Library.

37 The article states, "We referred briefly on Thursday in the Lewiston Journal," and has a handwritten date of 1904. The clipping includes only a portion of the article, subtitled "two issues for Maine." William C. Williams Papers, New York Public Library.

38 Undated memorandum, William C. Williams Papers, New York Public Library.

39 "A Nasty Cross-Examination," clipping hand-marked "Chic. Tribune Jy. 1902," pre-

sumably referring to a July article from the *Chicago Tribune*, William C. Williams Papers, New York Public Library.

40 "Commissioner Williams, Ungallant Old Bachelor that He Is, Is the Culprit," *New York World*, 5 September 1909 ["World, Sept. 5, 1909" is typed onto the clipping], William C. Williams Papers, New York Public Library.

41 "More Protection for Immigrants," William C. Williams Papers, New York Public Library.

42 James R. Sheffield, letter to "Hon. William Williams," 25 January 1905, William C. Williams Papers, New York Public Library.

43 Anne McClintock, *Imperial Leather: Race, Gender, and Sexuality in the Colonial Context* (New York: Routledge, 1995); Elizabeth Stephens, "Looking-Class Heroes: Dykes on Bikes Cruising Calendar Girls," in *The Passionate Camera: Photography and Bodies of Desire*, ed. Deborah Bright (London: Routledge, 1998), 278.

44 Aiwha Ong, "The Gender and Labor Politics of Postmodernity," in *The Politics of Culture in the Shadow of Capital*, eds. Lisa Lowe and David Lloyd (Durham: Duke University Press, 1997), 62–66.

45 Rosemary Hennessy, "Queer Visibility in Commodity Culture," in *Social Postmodernism: Beyond Identity Politics*, eds. L. Nicholson and S. Seidman (Cambridge: Cambridge University Press, 1995), 175–77.

46 Reginald Wright Kauffman, *The House of Bondage* (Upper Saddle River, N.J.: Gregg Press, 1968 [1910], 2, 10).

47 Timothy J. Gilfoyle, *City of Eros: New York City, Prostitution, and the Commercialization of Sex, 1790–1920* (New York: Norton, 1992), 292. Dennis Altman, in *Global Sex* (Chicago: University of Chicago Press, 2001), 12, also notes an international network of Jewish immigrant prostitutes at the end of the nineteenth century.

48 Gilfoyle, *City of Eros*, 288. See also Joanne J. Meyerowitz, *Women Adrift: Independent Wage Earners in Chicago, 1880–1930* (Chicago: University of Chicago Press, 1988), xviii–xix, 104–107; and Peiss, *Cheap Amusements*, 51–55.

49 Kate Simon, *Bronx Primitive: Portraits in a Childhood* (New York: Viking Press, 1982), 123–26.

50 Shah, *Contagious Divides*, 13; Chauncey, *Gay New York*; and Christopher Mele, *Selling the Lower East Side: Culture, Real Estate, and Resistance in New York City* (Minneapolis: University of Minnesota Press, 2000).

51 La Guardia, *The Making of an Insurgent*, 69.

52 Shah, *Contagious Divides*, 242–43.

53 Jennifer Ting, "Bachelor Society: Deviant Heterosexuality and Asian American Historiography," in *Privileging Positions: The Sites of Asian American Studies*, eds. G. Okihiro, M. Alquizola, D. F. Rony, and K. S. Wong (Pullman: Washington State University Press, 1995), 278.

54 Cathy J. Cohen, "Punk, Bulldaggers, and Welfare Queens: The Radical Potential of Queer Politics?" *GLQ* 3 (1997): 453, 442. See also Linda Singer, *Erotic Welfare: Sexual*

Theory and Politics in the Age of Epidemic (New York: Routledge, 1993). Singer suggests that an interesting by-product of the "campaign for safe sex" is "the discursive framework for remarketing the nuclear family as a prophylactic social device" (68), a point that bears consideration, too, in light of the push for gay marriage and the attendant promotion of a same-sex version of a nuclear family.

55 Immigration and Naturalization Service, "Frequently Asked Questions for Form I-693, Medical Examination of Aliens Seeking Adjustment of Status," http://www.ins .usdoj.gov/graphics/i-693faq.htm.

CHAPTER 2: GETTING DRESSED UP

1 "Underneath Your Clothes," lyrics by Shakira, 2001; music by Shakira and Lester Mendez. Thanks to Jed Bell and Jason Goldman for their close reading of this chapter and for their invaluable suggestions.

2 The bra might seem to be some of the laundry in the album's title, *Laundry Service*, but images of clothes don't float throughout the liner notes, and the choice of this particular item seems noteworthy in any case.

3 Essex Hemphill, "The Occupied Territories," *Ceremonies* (New York: Penguin, 1992), 72–73.

4 Hamblin, *Ellis Island*, 22.

5 Thanks to Marnina Gonick for pointing out the U.S. chauvinism in the lack of attention to Canada as a site of importance for Woodhull in newspaper accounts — and in my thinking on that point.

6 "Detain Woman Garbed as Man," *New York Herald*, 5 October 1908, p. 5. The article in the *New York Times*, "Woman in Male Garb Gains Her Freedom," 6 October 1908, n.p., states that Woodhull's intended destination was England, but there is no comment about why.

7 Joyce Murdoch and Deb Price, *Courting Justice: Gay Men and Lesbians v. the Supreme Court* (New York: Basic Books, 2001), 89–92. See Luibhéid, *Entry Denied*, 1–29, for the history of exclusion laws explicitly or implicitly concerning homosexuality, especially pp. 20–21 on the 1952 law that affected Fluti.

8 Amy Fairchild, *Science at the Borders: Immigrant Medical Inspection and the Shaping of the Modern Industrial Labor Force* (Baltimore: Johns Hopkins University Press, 2003), 276, 124–25.

9 "Lived 15 Years as a Man: Woman Wore Disguise until Halted at Ellis Island," *New York Daily Tribune*, 5 October 1908, p. 14; "Trousered Woman Allowed to Land," *New York Post*, 6 October 1908, p. 16; "Woman Voyager Posing as a Man Gains Her Liberty," *New York World*, 6 October 1908, p. 2; "Detain Woman Garbed as Man," *New York Herald*, 5 October 1908, p. 5; "Woman Travels as Man," *New York Press*, 5 October 1908, p. 5; "A Boy Guessed Her Sex," *New York Press*, 6 October 1908, p. 1; "Woman in Male Garb Gains Her Freedom, 6 October 1908, n.p.; "Woman Dons Man's Clothes to Make Living," *Daily People*, 6 October 1908, p. 2.

10 Although I am stating that Woodhull's gender trouble is a different matter than the class trouble he might have gotten into, I do not mean to suggest that they function fully independently, or have connections limited to issues regarding the likelihood of getting caught. See Leslie Feinberg, *Transgender Warriors: Making History from Joan of Ark to RuPaul* (Boston: Beacon Press, 1996), for an extended historical analysis of relations between gender and class oppressions.

11 Fairchild, *Science at the Borders*, 90.

12 Victor Heiser, *An American Doctor's Odyssey, Adventures in 45 Countries* (New York: Norton, 1936), 16; quoted in Alan M. Kraut, *Silent Travelers: Germs, Genes, and the "Immigrant Menace"* (New York: Basic Books, 1994), 63.

13 Fairchild, *Science at the Borders*, 166–67, 158; Shah, *Contagious Divides*, 184–95 (also, chapter 7, "Making Medical Borders at Ellis Island," 179–203, is extremely helpful). On the image of Jews as tubercular, see also Kraut, *Silent Travelers*," chapter 6, *Gezunthayt iz besse vi Krankhayt*: Fighting the Stigma of the "Jewish Disease," 136–65.

14 Fairchild, *Science at the Borders*, 150–59.

15 George J. Sánchez, *Becoming Mexican American: Ethnicity, Culture, and Identity in Chicano Los Angeles, 1900–1945* (Oxford: Oxford University Press, 1993), 55–57. The Bracero Program, which from 1942 to 1964 brought migrants from Mexico for temporary labor in the United States, also required forced stripping at the border. See also Eric Schlosser, *Reefer Madness: Sex, Drugs, and Cheap Labor in the American Black Market* (Boston: Houghton Mifflin, 2003), 100.

16 Fairchild, *Science at the Borders*, 65.

17 By mentioning the complexity of psychic effects, I mean here both to depart from assumptions of homogeneity and, more bravely, to gesture toward a direction of interpretation, which might in some cases be fruitful, that is suggested by the overlap in vocabulary between this scene and some standard sex scenarios, albeit ones often attractive to people without direct correspondences in personal history. As Ann Cvetkovich points out in *An Archive of Feelings: Trauma, Sexuality, and Lesbian Public Cultures* (Durham: Duke University Press, 2003), 4, it is often taboo to discuss how some sexual pleasures may have "roots in pain and difficulty," including the experience of incidents such as sexual abuse (see especially chapters 2 and 3, "Trauma and Touch: Butch-Femme Sexualities" and "Sexual Trauma/Queer Memory: Incest, Lesbianism, and Therapeutic Culture," 49–117). I think also here of a friend's comment that her experience of being a victim of police brutality, which she saw as precisely that, nonetheless enhanced the erotic charge for her of fantasies like the one in "The Surprise Party" from Pat Califia's *Macho Sluts: Erotic Fiction* (Boston: Alyson Publications, 1988), 211–42, which involves forced sex with police officers.

18 Luibhéid, *Entry Denied*, 11–12.

19 Edward Corsi, *In the Shadow of Liberty: The Chronicle of Ellis Island* (New York: Macmillan, 1935).

20　Ibid., 81–82, 71.

21　"To Deport Saxon 'Murray Hall': Otillie Castnaugle, Who Came Here as a Girl, Will Be Sent Back in Men's Clothes." Like many clippings in the Williams papers, this one was cut out right around the edges of the story itself, with no printed marker of the name of the paper or the date. It is possible that the date is 1902 because the clipping appears among others from 1902 in a group of materials dating from Williams's first period as commissioner, 1902 to 1905. The reference to "Murray Hall," who died in 1901, suggests a date from this period also. A handwritten notation, "Ju 23," also appears on the clipping, but in looking at New York newspapers from June and July, 1902–1905, I could not find reference to Castnaugle. Thanks to Julia Getzel and Penelope Malakates who retraced my footsteps on this research project and undertook other microfilm tasks for this chapter.

22　Jonathan Ned Katz documents press coverage concerning the death of Murray Hall in *Gay American History: Lesbians and Gay Men in the U.S.A.* (New York: Thomas Y. Crowell, 1976), 232–38. The chapter in which the Murray Hall material appears, "Passing Women: 1782–1920," 209–279, testifies to the scope of the phenomenon. See also my discussion below.

23　Marian West, "Women Who Have Passed as Men: A Curious Phase of the Problem of Sex—Historical Instances of Women Who Have Fought Their Way Through the World in Masculine Disguise," *Munsey's Magazine* 25 (1901): 273–81, 273.

24　Ibid., 274.

25　Corsi, *In the Shadow of Liberty*, 81–82.

26　Clark, *Deportation of Aliens from the United States to Europe*, 162–74. According to Clark, the moral turpitude provision was actually introduced by "humanitarian friends of the politically oppressed in other countries" and was intended to forestall "exclusion for commission of mere political crimes" (162).

27　Thanks to Deborah Bright pointing out that the absence of concern about Woodhull's intrusion into a male workforce was notable.

28　The full headline reads, "Murray Hall Fooled Many Shrewd Men, How for Years She Masqueraded in Male Attire, Had Married Two Women, Was a Prominent Tammany Politician and Always Voted—Senator Martin Astounded," 19 January 1901, quoted in Katz, *Gay American History*, 232.

29　Lisa Duggan, "The Trials of Alice Mitchell: Sensationalism, Sexology, and the Lesbian Subject in Turn-of-the-Century America," in *Queer Studies: An Interdisciplinary Reader*, ed. Robert J. Corber and Stephen Valocci (Oxford: Blackwell, 2003), 73. As Duggan emphasizes, press accounts need to be studied for elements of self-representation as well as distortion; despite lurid sensationalism, they were often "nonetheless based on the stories women told about their own relationships" (78). Assessing self-representation in terms of matters like fact and authenticity is complicated, too, in ways historically specific and gendered. As Jesse Alemán suggests, "The act of cross-dressing . . . may in fact trouble the notion of authenticity altogether in autobiography, authorship, and even identity (Aleman, "Authenticity,

Autobiography, and Identity: *The Woman in Battle* as a Civil War Narrative," in *The Woman in Battle: The Civil War Narrative of Loreta Janeta Velasquez, Cuban Woman and Confederate Soldier*, by Loreta Janeta Velasquez [Madison: University of Wisconsin Press, 2003], xix). Velasquez was another person identified as a female-to-male cross-dresser who had a lot of notoriety in advance of Woodhull.

30   Katz, *Gay American History*, 207–279; the San Francisco Lesbian and Gay History Project's "'She Even Chewed Tobacco': A Pictorial Narrative of Passing Women in America," in *Hidden from History: Reclaiming the Gay and Lesbian Past*, ed. Martin Bauml Duberman, Martha Vicinus, and George Chauncey Jr. (New York: New American Library, 1989), 183–94 (a video documents the slide show on which the article was based: Elizabeth Stevens and Estelle Freedman, *"She Even Chewed Tobacco,"* 1983). See also Esther Newton, "The Mythic Mannish Lesbian: Radclyffe Hall and the New Woman," in *Margaret Mead Made Me Gay: Personal Essays, Public Ideas* (Durham: Duke University Press, 2000), 176–77 (note that this essay originally appeared in *Signs* 9 [1984]); and Lillian Faderman, *Odd Girls and Twilight Lovers: A History of Lesbian Life in Twentieth-Century America* (New York: Columbia University Press, 1991), 42–48. Faderman, who notes that it was Katz who first popularized the term "passing women" (316, n. 8), calls such individuals "female transvestites," a term that egregiously downplays the many factors that go into trans presentation besides the clothing.

31   Bram Stoker, *Famous Imposters* (New York: Sturgis and Walton, 1910), 227.

32   Nevada Barr, *Bittersweet* (San Francisco: Spinsters/Aunt Lute, 1984). Also relevant to the material in my next two chapters, which argue that the Statue of Liberty fundamentally concerns race and sex—but skip this if you don't want me to spoil the mystery—*Liberty Falling* hinges on white supremacists who consider Liberty the symbol of a country where the government wants "to let the Jews make it mandatory our kids are taught to love their little mud brothers"; they try to destroy the statue partly by detonating explosives packed in Liberty's breasts. Nevada Barr, *Liberty Falling* (New York: Avon Books, 1999), 337.

33   Stoker, *Famous Imposters*, 230–31.

34   Corsi, *In the Shadow of Liberty*, 81–82.

35   Feinberg, *Transgender Warriors*, 83–85. See her chapter "Not Just Passing" for a more complete articulation of these points. Feinberg suggests that without access to hormones and surgery (or maybe even with access), someone with a female sex attribution is likely to have been transgendered to some degree in order to pass: "While a woman could throw on men's clothing and pass as a man for safety on dark roadways, could she pass as a man at an inn where men slept together in the same beds? Could she maintain her identity in daylight? Pass the scrutiny of co-workers? Would she really feel safer or more free?" (84–85). Further, I was amused by what Feinberg imagined telling a feminine friend who presumed that she would have chosen to pass in earlier times: maybe "in the dead of winter, if she was bundled up against the cold, with a hood or hat covering her head, some man in a deli *might* call her

'sir'" (84–85). Trade the deli for a pharmacy and that describes precisely my one adult experience of being taken for male.

36 Conversation with Jed Bell, 28 May 2004.

37 Panel for the course "Women, Gender, Visual Culture," Bates College, March 2003; Leslie Feinberg, *Stone Butch Blues* (Ithaca: Firebrand Press, 1993).

38 Patton and Sánchez-Eppler, *Queer Diasporas*, 3.

39 On named categories in relation to identity, feeling, and policing, see Riki Wilchins, "Changing the Subject," in *GenderQueer: Voices from Beyond the Sexual Binary*, ed. Joan Nestle, Clare Howell, and Riki Wilchins (Los Angeles: Alyson Books, 2002), 48–52.

40 Jennifer Miller explains in the video *Juggling Gender* another way that perceptions of others transform perceptions of self. Although Miller identifies primarily as a woman with a beard and mustache, being treated as male sometimes causes her to see herself as male in certain circumstances (Tami Gold, *Juggling Gender: Politics, Sex and Identity* [New York: Tamerik Productions, 1997]).

41 Joan Scott, "The Evidence of Experience," in *The Lesbian and Gay Studies Reader*, ed. Henry Abelove, Michèle Aina Barale, and David M. Halperin (New York: Routledge, 1993), 409, 412.

42 Nicholas Rose, "Identity, Genealogy, History," in *Questions of Cultural Identity*, ed. Stuart Hall and Paul du Gay (London: Sage, 1996), 132, 137.

43 In Del LaGrace Volcano and Judith Halberstam, *The Drag King Book* (London: Serpent's Tail, 1999), 36, 39, Judith "Jack" Halberstam offers a good account of contemporary variation within a category in discussing various relations to understandings of authenticity, performance, and masculinity, both onstage and offstage, among drag kings. Another great resource on gender variation within and among identities is Joan Nestle, *The Persistent Desire: A Femme-Butch Reader* (Boston: Alyson Publications, 1992).

44 On the development of consumer culture in the late nineteenth and early twentieth centuries, see Richard M. Ohmann, *Selling Culture: Magazines, Markets, and Class at the Turn of the Century* (London: Verso, 1996).

45 Max Probst describes his experience with such misperception in "Diversity of the Transgender Community," which also offers another example of how different systems of interpretation affect each other. Raised as female, Probst started getting facial hair at age fifteen. Although he was immediately taken to the doctor, it wasn't until many years later, when he decided to stop getting rid of the hair, that a hormonal cause was diagnosed: "When I went to the OB/GYN for my yearly, proudly sporting my beard, I was diagnosed with Polycystic Ovarian Syndrome otherwise known as PCOS. When my lab results came back with high levels of testosterone, it was confirmed. Seven years had passed since my first visit concerning this matter. And in those seven years, the issue was never brought up." Now, he writes, he is subject to a different misunderstanding, ironically issuing from the more enlightened: "Today, people assume I am on testosterone and that my experience is the

same as other Female to Males or that I just started transitioning when in fact, my journey has been quite different." Like the category "passing women," "female to male" now has a dominant narrative that stories may be distorted to fit (Max Probst, "Diversity of the Transgender Community," paper presented at "Transecting the Academy," Brown University, 2003, and published in "Trans Matters in Education: Insights from Students," edited by Erica Rand, with essays by Danielle Nika Askini, Jordon Bosse, Lyndon Cudlitz, Max Probst, and Mea Tavares, *Radical Teacher* 67 [summer 2003]: 14). For another take on having a female sex attribution or identity with facial hair, see Wendy Chapkis, *Beauty Secrets: Women and the Politics of Appearance* (Boston: South End Press, 1986). Chapkis points out the work, including emotional work, involved in any woman's path to femininity: "Despite the fact that each woman knows her own belabored transformation from female to feminine is artificial, she harbors the secret conviction that it should be effortless. A 'real woman' would be naturally feminine while she is only in disguise" (5). Her comment serves as a reminder that while gender-crossing or perceived gender irregularity often gets the attention these days in terms of complexity, presenting as one sex or another may be quite complicated in any case.

46 American Park Network, "Statue of Liberty National Monument, Photography," http://www.americanparknetwork.com/parkinfo/sl/photo/ (APM Media, 2001).

47 Alan Sekula, "The Body and the Archive," *October* 39 (1986): 3–64, 18.

48 Ibid., 56.

49 American Park Network, "Statue of Liberty National Monument, Photography."

50 For a discussion of the visual and archival evidence regarding immigrants' contributions to official photographs in another context, see Brain Osborne, "Constructing the State, Managing the Corporation, Transforming the Individual: Photography, Immigration and the Canadian National Railways, 1925–30," in *Picturing Place: Photography and the Geographical Imagination*, ed. Joan Schwartz and James Ryan (New York: I. B. Tauris, 2003), 186–90.

51 Kiss and Tell, *Her Tongue on My Theory*, 49.

52 Thanks to Penelope Malakates and Julia Getzel for researching this topic.

53 Bram Stoker, *Famous Imposters*, 283–345. The book's frontispiece offers a visual suggestion of evidence in its illustration of "Queen Elizabeth as a Young Woman" with an apparently flat chest under her dress.

54 I say "illustrate or symbolize" because some accounts identify the women as nurses. See, for instance, Wilton S. Tifft, *Ellis Island* (Chicago: Contemporary Books, 1999 [1990]). Others, like Fairchild (*Science at the Border*, 66), fail to specify their jobs at all. In Barry Moreno, *Ellis Island: Images of America* (Charleston, S.C.: Arcadia Press, 2003), a caption states: "In 1914, Dr. Rose A. Bebb was appointed the first woman physician at Ellis Island. This made gynecological examinations for signs of pregnancy or disease more endurable for the patient" (43). Note that the caption doesn't state whether Dr. Bebb is in the picture, but it does mention gynecological exams, which the image doesn't seem to be portraying.

55 La Guardia, *The Making of an Insurgent*, 65–66. Interestingly, a typescript with an earlier draft of the paragraph has La Guardia imagining the girl to be from virtually a different period, but only possibly new to solo encounters with men: "Imagine this girl who had always been protected, according to the custom of her province (medieval?) and who was perhaps never in the company of a man alone" (manuscript in the La Guardia and Wagner Archives, Fiorello H. La Guardia Community College, City University of New York). Thanks to Liz Clark for bringing this manuscript to my attention.

56 A. G. Smith, *Statue of Liberty and Ellis Island Coloring Book* (New York: Dover Publications, 1985), 29.

CHAPTER 3: TRAFFIC IN MY FANTASY BUTCH

1 Daniel Marom points out that size has always mattered regarding the Statue of Liberty: during the initial U.S. fund-raising for her pedestal in the 1870s and 1880s, her greater stature than the Colossus of Rhodes was used to solicit contributions (Marom, "Who Is the "Mother of Exiles"? An Inquiry into Jewish Aspects of Emma Lazarus's 'The New Colossus,'" *Prooftexts* 20 [autumn 2000]: 233). Regarding this chapter as a whole, I thank Lionel Cantú and Eithne Luibhéid for their enthusiasm, ideas, and support, and Luibhéid notably for her extensive and invaluable commentary on many drafts.

2 Thanks to James Clifford for introducing this point about the statue changing size and to the other participants in the discussion after I presented this material at a colloquium sponsored by the Center for Cultural Studies at the University of California at Santa Cruz, April 2002. On the topic of size, in summer 2003 Penelope Malakates reported to me conversations with several friends visiting New York who expressed a fear of seeing the statue lest it be disappointingly small.

3 Toby Keith, "Courtesy of the Red, White, and Blue (The Angry American)," lyrics © Tokeka Tunes (BMI), on the CD *Unleashed* (Nashville: Dreamworks, 2002).

4 Although I haven't been able to date the image precisely, it appears on one Web page that gives the date of its last update as 16 October 2001 (Current Events Humor Archive, http//kd4dcy.net/rthumor). Searching under "Statue of Liberty" plus "Osama" yields numerous sites with the image.

5 Jasbir K. Puar and Amit S. Rai, "Monster, Terrorist, Fag: The War on Terrorism and the Production of Docile Patriots," *Social Text* 72 (fall 2002): 126. See this essay, too, for a description of other representations in this genre.

6 Lawrence Grossberg, *We Gotta Get Out of This Place: Popular Conservatism and Postmodern Culture* (New York: Routledge, 1992), 63.

7 Paula Span, "Liberty Trash," *Washington Post*, 27 June 1986, sec. D, p. 1; Holland, *Idealists, Scoundrels, and the Lady*, 68, 86.

8 For another consideration of the limits of linear expository narrative, see Manalan-

san's *Global Divas*, 89–92. Manalansan argues that the "unruliness" of his "criss-crossing narratives that never seem to finish stems in part from the rhythms of everyday life."

9   Besides sources otherwise mentioned in this chapter, resources on the statue and her apprehension include Christian Blanchet and Bertrand Dart, *Statue of Liberty: The First Hundred Years*, trans. Bernard A. Weisberger (New York: American Heritage Publishing Co., 1985); Nancy Jo Fox, *Liberties with Liberty: The Fascinating History of America's Proudest Symbol* (New York: E. P. Dutton, 1985); *Liberty: The French American Statue in Art and History*, New York Public Library and the Comité officiel franco-américain pour la célébration du centenaire de la Statue de la Liberté (New York: Perennial Library, 1986); Barry Moreno, *The Statue of Liberty Encyclopedia* (New York: Simon & Schuster, 2000).

10 Henry A. Giroux, *The Mouse That Roared: Disney and The End of Innocence* (Lanham, M.D.: Rowman and Littlefield, 1999), 8.

11 Susana Peña, "Visibility and Silence: Mariel and Cuban American Gay Male Experience and Representation," in *Queer Migrations: Sexuality, U.S. Citizenship, and Border Crossings*, ed. Lionel Cantú and Eithne Luibhéid (Minneapolis: University of Minnesota Press, 2005).

12 This program aired on 14 March 2001.

13 Al Robb, "Lady Liberty" in *Dear Miss Liberty: Letters to the Statue of Liberty*, ed. Lynne Bundeson (Salt Lake City: Peregrine Smith Books, 1986), 71.

14 Evelyn Wilde Mayerson, *The Cat Who Escaped from Steerage* (New York: Charles Scribner's Sons, 1990), 46.

15 Kathy High, *Icky and Kathy Find Liberty* is part of the Icky and Kathy trilogy. *Betty and Pansy's Severe Queer Review of New York* (San Francisco: Bedpan Productions, 1994), vi.

16 In Coan's *Ellis Island Interviews*, Estelle Miller recalls seeing the statue from the ship at the age of thirteen in 1909: "Nobody knew what it was. One man said, 'Don't you know? That's Columbus.' . . . So we thought it was Columbus. For years I thought that" (221). Theodore Spako, who was sixteen when he arrived at Ellis Island in 1911, recalled questioning a cabin mate who made the same identification, "Listen, this don't look like Christopher Columbus. That's a lady there" (277–78).

17 Kathleen Chevalier, quoted by Neil G. Kotler in "The Statue of Liberty as Idea, Symbol, and Historical Presence," in *The Statue of Liberty Revisited*, ed. Wilton S. Dillon and Neil G. Kotler (Washington, D.C.: Smithsonian Institution Press, 1994), 13.

18 Marvin Trachtenberg, *The Statue of Liberty*, rev. ed. (New York: Penguin Books, 1986), 104. The painting is *Truth* by C.-V.-E. Lefebvre, 1859.

19 Linda Zerelli, "Democracy and National Fantasy: Reflections on the Statue of Liberty," in *Cultural Studies and Political Theory*, ed. Jodi Dean (Ithaca: Cornell University Press, 2000), 180.

20 Michael Kinsley, "Liberty Deflowered," *New Republic*, 19 December 1983; Garnet

Chapin, in "Taking Care of Miss Liberty," *20/20*, aired 12 December 1985; Richard Cohen, "Franchising the Statue of Liberty," *Washington Post*, 28 September 1985, A25. All are cited in Holland, *Idealists, Scoundrels, and the Lady*, 84, 181, 85.

21 Roberta Brandes Gratz and Eric Fettman, "The Selling of Miss Liberty," *Nation* 241, no. 15 (9 November 1985): 465–76.

22 Trachtenberg, *Statue of Liberty*, 195–96.

23 Barbara A. Babcock and John J. Macaloon, "Everybody's Gal: Women, Boundaries, and Monuments," in *The Statue of Liberty Revisited*, ed. Wilton S. Dillon and Neil G. Kotler (Washington, D.C.: Smithsonian Institution Press, 1994), 90.

24 Ibid., 94.

25 Ibid., 92. Rattan Davenport, "Statuary Rape," *Social Anarchism* 13 (1987): 32–33. Babcock and Macaloon obscure by omission that their source, calling anarchists to trash "icons of the state religion," implies a stance toward rape metaphors of which I doubt they would approve.

26 Martha Grove and Deborah Whitefield, "N.Y. Singing Red, White, and Bucks to Miss Liberty," *Los Angeles Times*, 29 June 1986, sec. 1, p. 1.

27 Span, "Liberty Trash," sec. D, p. 1; Maureen Dowd, "The Statue as Souvenir," *New York Times*, sec. 6, part 2, p. 8.

28 Hall, *Idealists, Scoundrels, and the Lady*, 126–27, illustration facing page 36. Iacocca was the parade's grand marshal.

29 As Kamala Kempadoo emphasizes, the concepts of who has even the possibility of agency in sex work are highly marked by racism, as stereotypes of the "Third World/non-western woman" often position her as absolutely victimized. At the same time, as Kempadoo states, racism is at work in other complex ways, from exoticizing racial and ethnic otherness to, simultaneously, putting exoticized others still secondary to white women within the global sex industry (Kempadoo, "Introduction: Globalizing Sex Workers' Rights," in *Global Sex Workers: Rights, Resistance, and Redefinition*, ed. Kamala Kempadoo and Jo Doezema (New York: Routledge, 1998), 1–27. On agency and other issues regarding women today who migrate for labor, see Barbara Ehrenreich and Arle Russell Hochschild, eds., *Global Woman: Nannies, Maids, and Sex Workers in the New Economy* (New York: Holt, 2002).

30 Clark, *Deportation of Aliens*, 53, 63–69. For an account of how ideas about agency and innocence affect current laws, policies, and attitudes about sexual labor, see Wendy Chapkis, "Soft Glove, Punishing Fist: The Trafficking Victims' Protection Act," in *Controlling Sex: The Politics of Intimacy and Identity*, ed. Elizabeth Bernstein and Laurie Schafner (New York: Routledge, 2004).

31 Lauren Berlant, *The Anatomy of National Fantasy: Hawthorne, Utopia, and Everyday Life* (Chicago: University of Chicago Press, 1991), 27–28.

32 *New York Times*, 3 July 1986, sec. A, p. 31.

33 M. Jacqui Alexander, "Erotic Autonomy as a Politics of Decolonization: An Anatomy of Feminist and State Practice in the Bahamas Tourist Economy," in *Feminist Gene-*

alogies, Colonial Legacies, Democratic Futures, ed. M. Jacqui Alexander and Chandra Talpade Mohanty (New York: Routledge, 1997), 64–65. See also the anthology *Gender Ironies of Nationalism: Sexing the Nation*, ed. Tamar Mayer (London: Routledge, 2000). As Mayer states in her introduction, "Gender Ironies of Nationalism: Setting the Stage," " 'Purity,' 'modesty' and 'chastity' are common themes in national narrative of gender, nation, and sexuality" (10).

34 Immigration Marriage Fraud Amendments of 1986, Pub. L. No. 99–639, 100 Stat. 3537 (codified as amended at 8 U.S.C. §§ 1154, 1184, 1186a [1994]). On the inaccuracy of the data cited by the INS, see James A. Jones, "The Immigration Marriage Fraud Amendments: Sham Marriages or Sham Legislation?" *Florida State University Law Review* 24 (1997): 679–701.

35 United States Senate Committee of the Judiciary, Subcommittee on Immigration and Refugee Policy, "Immigration Marriage Fraud," Hearing Before the Subcommittee on Immigration and Refugee Policy of the Committee of the Judiciary, 99th Cong, 1st Sess., July 26, 1985 (Washington, D.C.: Government Publications Office, 1986).

36 On how IMFA provisions for ensuring the authenticity of marriages have made immigrant women vulnerable to abuse and the (insufficient) attempts to remedy the law, see Jones, "The Immigration Marriage Fraud Amendments," and Michelle J. Anderson, "A License to Abuse: The Impact of Conditional Status on Female Immigrants," *Yale Law Journal* 102 (April 1993): 1401–30.

37 *Bowers v. Hardwick*, 478 U.S. 186 (1986). The Georgia antisodomy law in question criminalized all acts involving "the sex organs of one person and the mouth or anus of another," (Ga. Code Ann. 16-6-2[a] [1984]). Indeed, as Justice Blackmun wrote in his dissent, the state's code, which, until 1968, defined sodomy as "the carnal knowledge and connection against the order of nature, by man with man, or in the same unnatural manner with woman" (Ga. Crim. Code 26–5901 [1933]), may actually have been revised in 1968 to include heterosexual acts, such as "heterosexual cunnilingus," that had been ruled exempt in previous cases (Blackmun, dissent, footnote 1). However, the decision of *Bowers v. Hardwick* ignored the scope of the actual statute. Its primary finding was that "the Constitution does not confer a fundamental right upon homosexuals to engage in sodomy."

38 Janet Halley, "The Construction of Heterosexuality," in *Fear of a Queer Planet: Queer Politics and Social Theory*, ed. Michael Warner (Minneapolis: University of Minnesota Press, 1993), 91–92.

39 Burger, Chief Justice, concurring, *Bowers v. Hardwick*, 478 U.S. 186 (1986).

40 Sara Rimmer, "Nation Rekindles Statue of Liberty as Beacon of Hope; Across U.S., a Ceremony for History, *New York Times*, 4 July 1986, sec. A, p. 1; Bob Drogan, "Chief Justice Leads Massive Swearing In of New Citizens," *Los Angeles Times*, 4 July 1986, sec. 1, p. 1. Rimmer states that 100 countries participated; Drogan says that it was 109.

41 Peter Freiberg, "Supreme Court Decision Sparks Protests: 'New Militancy' Seen in Angry Demonstrations," *Advocate*, 5 August 1986, p. 12.

42 William H. Blair, "City's Homosexuals Protest High Court Sodomy Ruling," *New York Times*, 3 July 1986, sec. B, p. 5; Alan Finder, "Police Halt Rights Marchers at Wall St.," *New York Times*, 5 July 1986, sec. A, p. 32.

43 Deborah B. Gould, *Sex, Death, and the Politics of Anger: Emotions and Reason in* ACT UP's *Fight Against* AIDS, (Ph.D. diss., University of Chicago, 2000). As both Gould's text and the *Advocate* article point out, demonstrations against the verdict, which occurred before the advent of ACT UP stepped up the pace of demonstrations and civil disobedience on queer rights issues, stood out also by size and visible anger.

44 John Rechy, "A High Court Decision and a Sense of Betrayal," *Los Angeles Times*, 6 July 1986, sec. 5, p. 1.

45 Michael Hanlon, "4 million Liberty-Lovers Take Over Streets of New York," *Toronto Star*, 5 July 1986, sec. A, p. 3; Maural Dolan and Siobhan Flynn, "Coast Guard Kept Scrambling; N.Y. Waters Roiled but Streets Peaceful," *Los Angeles Times*, 5 July 1986, sec. 1, p. 8.

46 Elizabeth Mehren, "Joyous Creature Roams N.Y.," *Los Angeles Times*, 5 July 1986, sec. 1, p. 1; Cass Peterson, "Celebrating Liberty Weekend in Manhattan Not for Claustrophobics," *Washington Post*, 5 July 1986, sec. A, p. 15; Jay Sharbut, "Battery Park Hosts Show of Its Own," *Los Angeles Times*, 7 July 1986, sec. 6, p. 1.

47 David Deitcher, "Law and Desire," in *The Question of Equality: Lesbian and Gay Politics in America Since Stonewall*, ed. David Deitcher (New York: Scribner, 1995), 150. Deitcher also includes a report that police went out of their way to avoid arresting even protestors who tried to get arrested, suggesting how narratives about "keeping the peace" need to take account of the intended beneficiaries—here, it seems, not the protestors but the corporate and government sponsors of the festivities.

48 "Crime in the Bedroom" and "Day of Sail, Night of Fire," *New York Times*, 2 July 1986, sec. A. p. 30; "The Right to Remedy, Affirmed," *New York Times*, 3 July 1986, sec. A. p. 30.

49 Bundesen, *Dear Miss Liberty*, 18, 52, 31, 33.

50 "Girl Wins Freedom Essay; Family May Lose Benefits," *San Diego Union-Tribune*, 22 May 1986, sec. A, p. 17; Peter Rowe, "Happy Ending," *San Diego Union-Tribune*, 27 May 1986, sec. E, p. 2; Holland, *Idealists, Scoundrels, and the Lady*, 222–23; Michael Hanlon, "U.S. Puts on the Ritz for Liberty," *Toronto Star*, 4 July 1986, sec. A., p. 15.

51 Peter Wyden, *The Unknown Iacocca* (New York: William Morrow, 1987), 17.

52 Mike Wallace, *Mickey Mouse History and Other Essays on American Memory* (Philadelphia: Temple University Press, 1996), 57–58. For one critique of the myth of bootstrap individualism, including the use of it to obscure racism, see Karen Brodkin Sacks, "How Did Jews Become White Folks?" in *Race*, ed. Steven Gregory and Roger Sanjek (New Brunswick: Rutgers University Press, 1994), 78–102. Brodkin Sacks discusses the specific benefits Jews received, including access to the advan-

tages offered by the GI bill that were not extended to African American veterans. See also Michael Omi and Howard Winant, *Racial Formation in the United States: From the 1960s to the 1990s*, 2nd ed. (New York: Routledge, 1994), 20–22, on how the bootstrap myth is part of an "ethnicity paradigm" inaccurately applied to the groups differentially treated by race—and with no interest in, for instance, in "ethnicity *among* blacks" (22).

53 Aristide R. Zollberg, "Reforming the Back Door: The Immigration Reform and Control Act of 1986 in Historical Perspective," in *Immigration Reconsidered: History, Sociology, and Politics*, ed. Virginia Yans-McLaughlin (Oxford: Oxford University Press), 334. Section 201(h) of the act states that in most cases "an alien [who] was granted lawful temporary resident status" is ineligible for any federal assistance programs for five years.

54 Hue Cao, "A New Life," *Los Angeles Times*, 29 June 1986, magazine section, p. 15.

55 Besides Wallace, see, for instance, Lynn Johnson, "Ellis Island: Historical Preservation from the Supply Side," *Radical History Review* 28–30 (1984): 164–67. I consider this issue further in chapter 5.

56 On the promotion by those in economic power of the idea that it is not the benevolent lender or donor but the recipient of loan and largesse who may be of dubious nature and on suspect moral ground, see Lorrayne Carroll and Joseph Medley, "'Whooping It Up for Rational Prosperity': Narratives of the East Asian Financial Crisis," in *World Bank Literature*, ed. Amitava Kumar (Minneapolis: University of Minnesota Press, 2003), 150–52. The essay discusses the revival of the nineteenth-century term "moral hazard" in IMF/World Bank literature to justify structural adjustment measures. Moral hazard is the notion that extending benefits could lead to bad behavior and attitudes; if you have fire insurance, why not burn down the barn?

57 Amber L. Hollibaugh, *My Dangerous Desires: A Queer Girl Dreaming Her Way Home*. (Durham: Duke University Press, 2000), 4–5. The omissions she identifies related to her own history touch on many topics discussed in this chapter and the next: "My life as a queer woman, a too-poor girl, a mixed-race hooker, a left-wing activist, was never meant to be remembered or told, never meant to endure or to count." For a good fictional account of economic struggle under Reaganism, see Laura Moriarty, *The Center of Everything* (New York: Hyperion, 2003).

58 Dorothy Allison, *Skin: Thinking about Sex, Class, and Literature* (Ithaca, N.Y.: Firebrand Books, 1994), 17.

59 Eduardo Galeano notes that Iacocca ventured another rationale, at a press conference in Buenos Aires in late 1993, for the model of giving a little but not too much to the economically struggling. Galeano recounts that Iacocca, musing about whether advancing education is a good strategy for reducing unemployment, wondered, since education turned unemployed Germans into "frustrated professionals who then turned to socialism and rebellion," whether "it wouldn't be better for the unem-

ployed to smarten up and go straight to McDonald's to find a job" (Galeano, *Upside Down: A Primer for the Looking Glass World*, trans. Mark Fried [New York: Henry Holt, 2000], 169).

60 *Bring It On* (Beacon, 2000). There is also a good implicit subplot here about disproportionate public school funding and the increasing reliance by schools on inequitably available local private resources, but it is hampered by relegating discussions of race to code phrases like "inner city" and scenes where race issues are meant to seem so obvious that they go without saying. They actually do need some saying.

61 R. L. Jones, *Great American Stuff: A Celebration of People, Places and Products that Make Us Happy to Live in America* (Nashville: Cumberland House, 1997), 3.

62 Announcement for the "Liberty Love Boat" event, reproduced in Annie Sprinkle, *Hardcore from the Heart: The Pleasures, Profits and Politics of Sex in Performance. Annie Sprinkle: Solo*, edited and with commentaries by Gabrielle Cody (London: Continuum, 2001), 40.

63 Ibid., 41.

64 Signs displayed on the boat ride to Liberty Island, visible in a photograph by Dona Ann McAdams, reproduced in Sprinkle, *Hardcore from the Heart*, 42.

CHAPTER 4: GREEN WOMAN, RACE MATTERS

1 Lee Iacocca, with William Novak, *Iacocca: An Autobiography* (Toronto: Bantam Books, 1984), 152–53.

2 I employ here the concept of homosociality as developed by Eve Kosofsky Sedgwick in *Between Men: English Literature and Male Homosocial Desire* (New York: Columbia University Press, 1985).

3 Moreno, *The Statue of Liberty Encyclopedia*, "Enabling Legislation," 83–84.

4 John Higham, *Send These to Me: Immigrants in Urban America*, rev. ed. (Baltimore: Johns Hopkins University Press, 1984), 75–79.

5 Lowery Stokes Sims, "Interview with William Pope.L," in *William Pope.L: The Friendliest Black Artist in America*, ed. Mark H. C. Bessire (Cambridge, Mass.: MIT Press, 2002), 63. Thanks to the artist for his insights on this chapter and elsewhere.

6 On Lazarus's involvement with and writings about refugees, see Dan Vogel, *Emma Lazarus* (Boston: Twayne, 1980), 139–41; Eve Merriam, *Emma Lazarus: Woman with a Torch* (New York: Citadel Press, 1956), 60–62; Carol Kessner, "Matrilineal Dissent: The Rhetoric of Zeal in Emma Lazarus, Maria Syrkin, and Cynthia Ozick," in *Women of the Word: Jewish Women and Jewish Writing* (Detroit: Wayne State University Press, 1994), 198–205; Ranen Omer-Sherman, "Emma Lazarus, Jewish American Poetics, and the Challenge of Modernity," *Legacy* 19, no. 2 (2002): 170–91; and Max Cavitch, "Emma Lazarus and the Golem of Liberty," forthcoming in *American Literary History*, 2005.

7 Edward A. Steiner, *On the Trail of the Immigrant* (New York, 1906), 60, quoted in Higham, *Send These to Me*, 75.

8   Higham, *Send These to Me*, 76–79.

9   "A Twentieth Anniversary Message from Lee Iacocca," in SOLEIF, *Liberty Highlights: The Official 20th Anniversary Newsletter* 1, no. 1 (summer 2002): 1.

10 Gratz and Fettman, "The Selling of Miss Liberty," 465–70; Holland, *Idealists, Scoundrels, and the Lady*, 12–13.

11 Gratz and Fettman, "The Selling of Miss Liberty," 469; Cass Peterson, "Commission Has Offered Little Advice; Statue of Liberty's Public Panel Overshadowed by Private Group," *Washington Post*, 14 February 1986, sec. A, p. 12.

12 Lee Iacocca, *Liberty for All*, ed. Barbara Grazzini (Wilmington, Del.: Miller Publishing, 2002), 13, 19, 20.

13 Gratz and Fettman, "The Selling of Miss Liberty," 472–74; Holland, *Idealists, Scoundrels, and the Lady*, 61–65.

14 Lee Iacocca, with Sonny Kleinfield, *Talking Straight* (New York: Bantam Books, 1988), 3. Iacocca also points here to the actual source of his appointment, recounting that when his "Chrysler people down in Washington" told him about the invitation, they thought it wouldn't be prestigious enough, being a Department of the Interior commission rather than a presidential one (5). His point was that the lowliness of the commission shows that the administration did not understand the importance of the restorations.

15 Peterson, "Commission Has Offered Little Advice"; Gratz and Fettman, "The Selling of Miss Liberty," 469.

16 Holland, *Idealists, Scoundrels, and the Lady*, xvii–xviii.

17 Cass Peterson, "Iacocca Assails Hodel's Action as Almost 'Un-American,'" *Washington Post*, 14 February 1986, sec. A, p. 1; "O'Neill Leads Clamor for Iacocca's Reinstatement to Statue Commission," *San Diego Union-Tribune*, 15 February 1986, sec. A, p. 2.

18 *The New Republic* points out that both the donation and the $4 million in publicity costs could be deducted, leading to a tax break higher than the amount of money the government received as a gift. "Liberty Deflowered," *The New Republic*, 19 December 1983, 6.

19 The ad's small print indicates a cap of $3,000,000 to the donation, with $500,000 donated outright and the rest to come from a one-cent donation per credit card purchase from 1 December 2003 to 31 January 2004.

20 Martin Gottlieb, "Marketing of Statue Alters Nature of Fund-Raising," *New York Times*, 15 June 1986, sec. 1, p. 29.

21 Ibid.

22 "The Right to Remedy, Affirmed," *New York Times*, 3 July 1986, sec. A, p. 30.

23 On the importance to fighting racism of attending to racial differences, as opposed to trying to will color blindness into existence, see Patricia J. Williams, *Seeing a Color-Blind Future: The Paradox of Race* (New York: Noonday Press, 1997), especially chapter 1, "The Emperor's New Clothes," 3–16. See also the book whose title I echo in the title of this chapter, Ruth Frankenberg's *White Women, Race Matters: The So-*

cial Construction of Whiteness (Minneapolis: University of Minnesota Press, 1993), in which she discusses the problems that attend white people accounting for experience in ways that miss its "'racialness,'" ways that it is racially structured (9 and throughout).

24 Saum Song Bo, "A Chinese View of the Statue of Liberty," *American Missionary* 39. no. 10 (October 1885), quoted by Juan Perea, "The Statue of Liberty: Notes from Behind the Gilded Door," in *Immigrants Out! The New Nativism and the Anti-Immigrant Impulse in the United States*, ed. Juan Perea (New York: New York University Press, 1997), 52–53.

25 David Proctor, *Enacting Political Culture: Rhetorical Transformations of Liberty Weekend* (New York: Praeger, 1991), chapter 3, "The Struggle for Identity: Black America's Liberty Rhetoric," 35–56. Proctor's evaluation of this commentary is not as adept as his drawing attention to it is important. It is also worth noting, regarding the omissions I discussed in the previous chapter, that Procter mentions *Bowers v. Hardwick* only in a footnote about the protest.

26 Wolper is quoted by James M. Banner Jr. in "The Wrong Symbol," letter to the editor, *New York Times*, 15 June 1986; "The Torch Shines for Blacks," *US News and World Report*, 16 June 1986, p. 65.

27 On the transformation of racial perceptions regarding particular groups, see Sacks, "How Did Jews Become White Folks"; Noel Ignatiev, *How the Irish Became White* (New York: Routledge, 1995); Liz Curtis, *Nothing but the Same Old Story: The Roots of Anti-Irish Racism* (Belfast: Sasta, 1996); and David R. Roediger, *The Wages of Whiteness: Race and the Making of the American Working Class* (London: Verso, 1991). See also David Theo Goldberg, *Racial Subjects: Writing on Race in America* (New York: Routledge 1997), especially chapter 3, "Taking Stock: Counting by Race," which analyzes the history of racial categories in the U.S. census, including the curious matter of why "Jewish" was never formed as a category, despite its racialization, but "Hindoo" was. The census, Goldberg also writes, offers "overwhelming evidence of a racialized social structure" such that "the continuing insistence on implementing an idea of color-blindness either denies historical reality or serves to cut off any claims to contemporary entitlements" (55).

28 Jim Haskins, *The Statue of Liberty: America's Proud Lady* (Minneapolis: Lerner Publications, 1986), 12.

29 Jim Haskins, "Jim Haskins, from my Viewpoint," http://web.clas.ufl.edu/users/jhaskins/. The essay itself is undated but the site includes a resume with data given up to 1994; however, the e-mail gained wide circulation about five years later, suggesting a later date.

30 This widely circulating e-mail is reproduced at http://urbanlegends.about.com/library/weekly/aa020900a.htm.

31 Calvin R. Robinson, Redman Battle, and Edward W. Robinson, *Journey of the Songhai People*, a publication of the Pan African Federation Organization (Philadelphia:

Farmer Press; Pan African Federation Organization, 1987), 160–63. Occasionally sole authorship is attributed to either Edward Robinson or PAFO.

32 "Was the Statue of Liberty First Conceived as a Black Woman?" *Black History Magazine,* http://www.blackhistorymagazine.net/statueofliberty.html.

33 The text in the book states: "According to Dr. Jim Haskins, a member of the National Education Advisory Committee of the Liberty—Ellis Island Committee, professor of English at the University of Florida, and prolific Black author, points documentarily to what stimulated the original idea for that 151 foot statue in the harbor" (160).

34 Mark Hyman, "Introduction," in *Journey of the Songhai People,* by Robinson, Battle, and Robinson, xv.

35 Barbara Mikkelson, "Urban Legends Reference Pages: History (Statue of Liberty)," http://www.snopes.com/history/american/liberty.htm. When I first encountered the e-mail it was marked "last updated 14 February 2000". This date was later changed to 13 October 2003, although the content seems virtually the same. For Mikkelson's citation on other matters, see, for instance, Hugo Martin, "Web Keeps Legends of the Road on a Roll," *Portland Press Herald,* 18 October 2002, sec. E, p. 4.

36 See, for instance, "Theory Shakes Up Lady Liberty," *Lewiston Sun-Journal,* 8 February 2000, sec. A, p. 1.

37 "Watching Dr. Jeffries Self-Destruct," *New York Times,* 25 August 1991, sec. D, p. 14, cited in Mikkelson, "Urban Legends Reference Pages."

38 Manning Marable, "Beyond Racial Identity Politics: Toward a Liberation Theory for Multicultural Democracy," in *Privileging Positions: The Sites of Asian American Studies,* ed. Gary Y. Okihiro, Marilyn Alquizola, Dorothy Fujita Rony, and K. Scott Wong (Pullman: Washington State University Press, 1995), 322–23.

39 Ibid., 31–33.

40 Robinson, Battle, and Robinson, *Journey of the Songhai People,* 161–62.

41 William E. Geist, "The Iacocca Touch," *New York Times,* 18 May 1986, sec. 6, part 2, p. 32.

42 Clarke Taylor, "CNN Says It Will Cover Liberty Despite ABC Pact," *Los Angeles Times,* 5 June 1986, sec. 6, p. 1; "ABC, CNN Work Out Pact for Liberty Coverage," *Los Angeles Times,* 14 June 1986; Gus Stevens, "Buying, Selling of Miss Liberty Is Not a Pretty Sight," *San Diego Union-Tribune,* 12 July 1986, sec. E, p. 9.

43 "Theory Shakes Up Lady Liberty," *Lewiston Sun-Journal,* 8 February 2000, sec. A, p. 1. The ABC news story, by Geraldine Sealy, appeared on the same date at http://more.abcnews.go.com/sections/us/dailynews/statue000208.html.

44 Williams, *Seeing a Color-Blind Future,* 8.

45 Toni Morrison, *Playing in the Dark: Whiteness and the Literary Imagination* (New York: Vintage, 1992), 65, quoted in *Representations of Slavery: Race and Ideology in Southern Plantation Museums* by Jennifer L. Eichstedt and Stephen Small (Washington, D.C.: Smithsonian Institution Press, 2002), 268.

46 For several reasons on which I cannot elaborate, I have chosen to respect this au-

thor's wish not to be associated with the topic. That Moses Lazarus, Emma's father, was in the business of sugar refining is noted generally without any elaboration in the biographies of her. See, for instance, Merriam, *Emma Lazarus*, 10. A study of Lazarus's other poetry suggests some complicated imagined relationship of Jews to people of other diasporas, partly forged in trying to write against the ideological conditions producing the Russian pogroms, the refugees of which occupied much of her activism.

47   Anne McClintock, *Imperial Leather: Race, Gender and Sexuality in the Colonial Context* (New York: Routledge, 1995), 152–54; see also, in the same book, "Soft-Soaping Empire: Commodity Racism and Imperial Advertising," 207–31.

48   See Walter Johnson, *Soul by Soul: Life inside the Antebellum Slave Market* (Cambridge, Mass.: Harvard University Press, 1999), for an excellent elaboration of slaveholding in terms of the sales relationship. As Johnson emphasizes, the fact that slavery made people for purchase must not be elided, although many slaveholders tried to do it, some seeing the slave traders as "a caste apart" and responsible for the slave trade's evils (24–25). On the relationship of enslaved people to commodity access and ownership, see Elizabeth Chin, *Purchasing Power: Black Kids and American Consumer Culture* (Minneapolis: University of Minnesota Press, 2001), 34–42.

49   Regina Austin, "'A Nation of Thieves': Consumption, Commerce, and the Black Public Sphere," *Public Culture* 7 (fall 1994): 225–48. See also Melvin Oliver and Thomas M. Shapiro, *Black Wealth/White Wealth: A New Perspective on Racial Inequality* (New York: Routledge, 1997), for another excellent analysis of disparate relations to money in historical and political content. As Oliver and Shapiro note, for instance, unlike various immigrant groups, who used self-employment to deal with the financial barriers imposed by prejudice against them, "with predispositions like those of immigrants to the idea of self-employment, blacks faced an environment where they were by law restricted from participation in business on the open market, especially from the postbellum period to the middle of the twentieth century. Explicit state and local policies restricted the rights and freedoms of blacks as economic agents" (46).

50   Holland, *Idealists, Scoundrels, and the Lady*, 80.

51   SOLEIF formally named its total as $305.4 million in March 1987 and $450 million ("and counting") on its Web site in 2001. See Holland, *Idealists, Scoundrels, and the Lady*, 98; The Statue of Liberty–Ellis Island Foundation "About the Foundation," http://www.ellisisland.org/Eiinfo/about.asp. Figures vary about what money went where. *Ellis Island and Statue of Liberty Magazine*, which is less a periodical with changing articles than it is a booklet published with changing advertisements, states in its tenth edition that of more than $295 million raised, $86 million went to the statue.

1   Combined Federal Campaign National List, www.opm.gov/cfc/natlist/Introduction
.htm; Statue of Liberty–Ellis Island Foundation, Inc., Independent Auditor's Report, 31 March 2002. Thanks to Julia Getzel for help in researching this point.

2   "Ellis Island Makes History Accessible to Everyone at www.ellisisland.org," 2003,
Oracle Corporation Web site, http://www.oracle.com/customers/9i/ellis.html. Oracle Corporation produced and manages the ship-manifest database software.

3   Steven Greenhouse, "Actors in Ellis Island Show Vote, 7 to 1, to Join Union," *New
York Times*, 15 August 2002.

4   Mike McIntire, "U.S. Is Investigating Use of Donors' Gifts to Statue of Liberty,"
New York Times, 5 April 2004, sec. 1, p. 22. As a correction published on 6 April
(accessed at www.nytimes.com) indicated, the free weekly paper *amNew York* first
broke the story in February. A controversy arose later in February when it came out
that Alex Storozynski had written a letter to Bill O'Reilly after seeing the story discussed on the *O'Reilly Factor* on 19 February without crediting his 2 February story.
See Lloyd Grove's column, "The Lowdown," from 24 February 2004, from the *Daily
News Front Page*, accessed at http://www.nydailynews.com/front/story/167675p-
146553c.html. (Lloyd also indicates that Storozynski was a former member of the
Daily News editorial board.) The *Times* correction, meanwhile, gives no author for
the story it didn't credit. Various statements and explanations were issued by SOLEIF
for its defense. Several can be found at both ellisisland.org and statueofliberty.org.
These do not deny so much as defend the practices attributed to SOLEIF.

5   It is worth noting here that ellisisland.org, which might appear from its name to
be the official, primary site, comes up first in most Internet searches, followed by
ellisisland.com. The Park Service site is nps.gov/elis/. Opportunities created by the
federal government's use of "gov" as its suffix is clear also regarding the White
House. For example, www.whitehouse.com is a porn site and www.whitehouse.org
is a parody site at which one can buy, for instance, a poster with the Homeland
Security Advisory System, where code yellow is marked, "Paranoia: Sustain. Re-
Elect. Repeat." Thanks to Mary Boyle for the tip on www.whitehouse.com and
www.whitehouse.org.

6   Receipt for evening performance, Colonial Williamsburg, 2003.

7   Lynn Johnson, interview with Moffitt, 24 March 1983, quoted in her "Ellis Island,"
160.

8   Mike Wallace, "Visiting the Past: History Museums in the United States," *Radical
History Review* 25 (fall 1981): 63, in Johnson, "Ellis Island," 162, 164. Wallace's essay
also appears in his *Mickey Mouse History*, 4–32.

9   Johnson, "Ellis Island," 165. For an excellent account of how radical political traditions informed migrants' subsequent lives in the United States, see Annelise Orleck's *Common Sense and a Little Fire: Women and Working-Class Politics in the United
States, 1900–1965* (Chapel Hill: University of North Carolina Press, 1995), 16–23. As

a biography of four immigrant Jewish women labor activists, the book is extremely useful for Orleck's analysis of class diversity and conflict among immigrants, before and after migration, and within labor movements, and for her discussion of her subjects' complicated personal and political lives, including the decades-long relationship between Pauline Newman, a force in the Women's Trade Union League (WTUL) and the International Ladies' Garment Workers' Union (ILGWU), and her activist ally and lover Frieda Miller. Since Newman came through Ellis Island when she was around nine years old, where according to Orleck her family was separated from their belongings (25), her sexual identity, presumably, did not bear on her actual passage through Ellis Island. However, her biography indicates the greater varieties of sexual history among Ellis Island immigrant narratives than is usually suggested in accounts.

10   Ibid., 165.

11   Roy Rosenzweig and David Thelen, *The Presence of the Past: Popular Uses of History in American Life* (New York: Columbia University Press, 1998), 116 (see also pp. 10, 149–53).

12   Ibid., 155.

13   "Ellis Island Makes History Accessible to Everyone at www.ellisisland.org." Oracle Corporation Website.

14   Interview, 28 September 2000.

15   Holland, *Idealists, Scoundrels, and the Lady*, 244.

16   The Statue of Liberty–Ellis Island Foundation, Inc., "Financial Statements," 2002, p. 5. SOLEIF received $1,096,119 for that year and $1,154,434 for the fiscal year ending 31 March 2001. Although the "Financial Statements" document I received is dated 31 March 2002, it includes an auditor's report, prepared by "Goldstein Golub Kessler LLP," that is dated 22 May 2002, so the document I received clearly dates to that time or later.

17   Interview, 10 September 2000.

18   Peter Wyden, in *The Unknown Iacocca*, 15, states that polls showed Iacocca's name recognition at 92.7 percent (where 70 percent is considered high), and with a high rating of 78 percent viewing him favorably.

19   Vietnam Veterans Memorial Fund, "The Wall That Heals," www.vvmf.org; program for the exhibit held in Kennedy Park, Lewiston, Maine, 1–3 June 2001; " 'The Wall That Heals,' " *Lewiston Sun Journal*, 30 May 2001, sec. B, p. 1. The exhibit also includes historical information along with documents and mementos specific to the location. As with the memorial in Washington, D.C., visitors to the replica often leave mementos and messages.

20   Urban Legends Reference Pages, "Politics: Target Practice" ("last updated: 23 March 2003") http://www.snopes.com/politics/military/target.asp.

21   Universal Fellowship of Metropolitan Community Churches, "The Wedding," http:// www.ufmcc.com/wedding1.htm and http:/secure.ufmcc.com/wedregpay.htm.

22   Consider also the mishmash in the signs on I-95 that welcome visitors to New York.

The state's imperialist slogan, "The Empire State," coexists with the Statue of Liberty, generally seen to honor another sort of government, and the consumer/tourist staple "I ♥ NY."

23 Mailings from the Southern Poverty Law Center, "National Campaign for Tolerance." The letters in the mailing are dated 16 May 2001 (small certificate), 15 May 2002 (large certificate), and 15 May 2003 (received by a friend). The first two letters are identical in text with different format; the third, which comes with yet a different-looking certificate, has been slightly revised.

24 Previously SOLEIF issued certificates to people who contributed to the Statue of Liberty restoration. My grandfather received one, dated 1983, that began by stating the importance of freedom in "the hearts of men everywhere" and that the Commission presented the certificate "on behalf of all those people who decades past forsook their homes . . ." and "in recognition of [the donor's] selfless sacrifice." It also gave reproduced signatures from Iacocca and Gerald Ford, listed as SOLEIF's honorary chairman.

25 Eileen Myles, *Cool for You* (New York: Soft Skull Press, 2000), 12.

26 Southern Poverty Law Center, "Wall of Tolerance," http://www.splcenter.org/cgi-bin/goframe.pl?dirname=/centerinfo&pagename=walloftolerance.html.

27 Jennifer Jacobson, "Historians Ask Smithsonian to Rethink Donor's Role in Exhibit on 'American Achievers,'" *Chronicle of Higher Education*, 11 June 2001, www.chronicle.com; "Smithsonian cash 'withdrawn,'" BBC News, 5 February 2002, http://news.bbc.co.uk/2/hi/entertainment/1801974.stm.

28 The revised pamphlet I picked up in 2002 spells out the forty-character limit that is implicit in the order form of the earlier version of the brochure.

29 Overheard 21 September 2000.

30 I introduce this point about sex, art, and money in the introduction.

31 Actually, however, they could not have discovered the grandmother for a few more years because her name did not appear in the databank until the next segment of the wall was erected several years later.

32 See for instance, Ann E. Berman, "Family Tree," in *Martha Stewart Living*, April 1999, pp. 221–31, and her book *Favorite Comfort Food: A Satisfying Collection of Home Cooking Classics* (New York: Clarkson N. Potter, 1999).

33 *Martha Stewart's Christmas Dream*, first aired 6 December 2000.

34 Deirdre Carmody, "Squatters Put Life into Ellis Island," *New York Times*, 25 July 1970, p. 25; Murray Schumach, "Squatters to Leave Ellis Island on Saturday but 'Will Be Back,'" *New York Times*, 26 July 1970, p. 56; Deirdre Carmody, "Ellis Island Squatters Get Permit to Develop Center, *New York Times*, 19 August 1970, pp. 1, 78; Deirdre Carmody, "Black Group Plans Ellis I. Monument to Immigrants," *New York Times*, 21 August 1970, p. 53. Note that except for one article, none appear on the front or first pages. The precise history of the ambitious plan is unclear, but the subsequent publicity about Matthew includes (among various claims to be a political mover and shaker in communication with the likes of Richard Nixon and the Jewish

Defense League) a conviction for Medicaid fraud that likely helped to terminate the Ellis Island plans. ("U.S. Group Appeals to Kosygin to Allow Visit to Jewish Area," *New York Times*, 4 August 1971, p. 5; Lee Dembert, "Ellis Island," *New York Times* 26 May 1974, p. 27).

35 Hortense J. Spillers, "Mama's Baby, Papa's Maybe: An American Grammar Book," *Diacritics* 17 (1987): 73–75.

36 The blanket use of "immigrant" shows up on www.ellisisland.org. A link called "The Immigrant Experience" leads to a brief immigration time line, one of the few links to any historical material, and "Family Histories," which is comprised of "six stories of Americans from different backgrounds researching immigrant ancestry." One of these stories concerns a woman locating information about enslaved ancestors. While the account itself is respectful and might offer valuable hints to people researching their own related histories, putting it under the umbrella "immigrant ancestry" is disrespectful and makes the material largely unattainable via Internet search inquiries.

37 The activist and writer Barbara Smith is one of several African Americans who, after hearing my description of my project, mentioned remembering the material on slavery as noticeably and inexcusably meager (conversation with Barbara Smith, State College, Pennsylvania, fall 2001).

38 Wallace, *Mickey Mouse History*, 69.

39 *Audio Tour of Ellis Island with Tom Brokaw.* The copyright information on the packaging is given as "©2000 by Ellis Island and Acoustiguide Corp.," but according to Vincent DiPietro the tape is of earlier genesis (interview, 19 September 2000). In the tape, Brokaw welcomes the listener "on behalf of the National Park Service"; Aramark handles the rentals and produced the flier with the languages given without the proper accent marks.

40 Richard Handler and Eric Gable, *The New History in an Old Museum: Creating the Past at Colonial Williamsburg* (Durham: Duke University Press, 1997), 121, 18, 84–89.

41 "Overview of Themes and Objectives" from the "Basic Information for Program Planning" sent to me by Vincent DiPietro, in response to my request, during my interview with him on 28 September 2000, for more information about the primary themes. The themes, he and Brown explained, came from the "interpretive prospectus," which, like the directive given to each national park, is authorized by Congress.

42 September 2000 and 9 July 2001. Both statements occurred during presentations of "Decide an Immigrant's Fate," which I discuss further in chapter 8.

43 "Visitor Relations," in the unpaginated document "Statue of Liberty National Monument Division of Interpretation Orientation Packet #2." In the interest of preserving the anonymity of the person who passed it on to me, I indicate here that I received it from someone who had received it during a training session between 2000 and 2002. This is not, however, to suggest that I could not have received it through official channels had I asked.

44 Tour, 21 October 2000.

45 Angel Island Association, "Immigration Station," http://www.angelisland.org/immigro2.html (page copyright 1998–2003).

CHAPTER 6: IMMIGRANT PEDDLERS

1 *Sky* (Delta Airlines), October 2000, p. 169.

2 Interview, 21 October 2000. Sherman also indicated that he and the other teacher leading the fieldtrip, Kim Gilles, purchased educational materials on Angel Island, including a video and book, for use in their classes. In describing the class status of his students, Sherman suggested that the median price of a home was $250,000, which fell in the bottom half for the Bay Area. An article in the next issue of *San Francisco* magazine, "What a Difference a Year Makes," November 2000, p. 84, indicates that he was right on target: in July 2000, the median price of a house in Hayward was $269,500, up almost $60,000 from the year before, while the median price in San Francisco was $470,000.

3 The Alcatraz proclamation is available on the Internet as part of the Fourth World Documentation Project, sponsored by the Center for World Indigenous Studies, Olympia, Washington, www.cwis.org.

4 Joseph Lelyveld, "Outboard Balks Ellis I. Coup," *New York Times*, 17 March 1970, p. A45.

5 I glean this information about the Ellis Island proclamation from the article cited above by Lelyveld. The episode gets little if any attention in Ellis Island chronologies. The National Park Service does, however, offer a link to the Alcatraz proclamation on its Web site for Alcatraz, http://www.nps.gov/alcatraz. A click on this link leads first to a page stating that "you are now leaving Parknet" and that the National Park Service "does not control and cannot guarantee the relevance, timeliness, or accuracy" of the material.

6 See also Eichstedt and Small, *Representations of Slavery*, for the presence of "negritude memorabilia," marketing racist stereotypes, at the gift shops of many plantation museums (68–69), and even the occasional conversion of some former slave quarters into gift shops (98).

7 Susan Taylor Martin, "Use of 'Palestine' Provokes Attack on Sam's Club; Retailer Embroiled in Global Debate," *St. Petersburg Times*, 19 December 2000, sec. A, p. 2. This article was widely circulated on the Internet (and frequently plagiarized). After an initial circulating e-mail stated that the globe was marked "Palestine" instead of Israel, it turned out that "Palestine" was listed next to Israel, floating in the Mediterranean. Martin's article states that Sam's Club, without plans to pull the globes, was nonetheless "still trying to determine why its Chinese supplier put 'Palestine' on the globes in the first place," a comment that supports the widespread perception at the time that every position on "Palestine" as a map location constitutes a deliberate political position.

8   David Hench, "State on Alert for Possible Terrorists, *Portland Press Herald*, 13 September 2003, sec. A, pp. 1, 8; Associated Press, "Gunman Kills Himself after Taking Hostages at Tenn. College," *Portland Press Herald*, 18 September 2003, sec. A, p. 8; David Hench, "Border Agents Nab 10 People in Local Sweep," *Portland Press Herald*," 28 January 2004, sec. B, pp. 1, 5; David Hench, "Sweep Sparks Fear among Latinos," *Portland Press Herald*, 30 January 2004, sec. B, pp. 1, 4; Bill Nemitz, "Search for Illegal Aliens Alienates City," *Portland Press Herald*, 30 January 2004, sec. B, p. 1. I visited the Maine Highland Games in August 2003 and a carnival in Berkeley Springs, West Virginia, the previous month. Nothing seemed to regulate the weapons one could carry but, at the games, people under eighteen couldn't buy swords and, at the carnival, people under eighteen couldn't win knives with blades more than three inches long.

9   "Vermont Court Allows 'IRISH' on License Plate," *Maine Sunday Telegram*, 9 February 2003, sec. B, p. 6.

10 Manning Marable, for instance, uses "common sense" to challenge an "assimilationist" and "color-blind" approach to understanding race in the United States, saying that it "defies common sense and denies the crucial difference race still makes in daily life. The vast majority of African Americans are absolutely convinced that race is the fundamental division in U.S. society" (Manning Marable "The Problematics of Ethnic Studies," in *Dispatches from the Ebony Tower: Intellectuals Confront the African American Experience*, ed. Manning Marable [New York: Columbia University Press, 2000], 2480.

11 Ian F. Haney-López, *White by Law* (New York: New York University Press, 1996), 1–4. The other rationale besides common knowledge was scientific evidence; eventually, however, as Haney-López documents, common knowledge won out. His appendix A, 203–8, summarizes the basis for the decisions in 1878 through 1944.

12 *United States v. Bhagat Singh Thind*, 261 U.S. 204 (1923), excerpted in Haney-López, *White by Law*, 222–23. López discusses the case on pp. 87–91. The case that had just then been decided, *Takao Ozawa v. United States*, 260 U.S. 178 (1922), denied citizenship for a Japanese man who, among other arguments, said his skin color was white; the decision against him cited common knowledge that white people were "Caucasian" (see Haney-López, *White by Law*, 81–85).

13 Ibid., 87–88.

14 Ibid., 26.

15 Dean MacCannell, *The Tourist: A New Theory of the Leisure Class*, rev. ed. (Berkeley: University of California Press, 1999), 101–2, 137–38. Robert Kahn, ed., *City Secrets: New York City* (n.p.: Little Bookroom, 2002).

16 The wedding favor choices were introduced on 20 August 2003, and the winner was revealed one week later.

17 I use the phrase "beyond the pale" both for its general sense of being outside the limits of accepted norms and proprieties and for the geopolitical referents that contribute to that general meaning. "The pale" historically was used to demarcate the

exclusion or ghettoization of undesirable residents in various areas, such as Catholics in Ireland and Jews in Russia.

18 "Michael and Hushi," *Full Frontal Fashion* designer profiles, *New York Magazine and Metro TV on the Web, NewYorkMetro.com,* http://www.newyorkmetro.com/metrotv/ fff/designers/bios/michael&hushi.htm.

19 Christopher Mele, *Selling the Lower East Side: Culture, Real Estate, and Resistance in New York City* (Minneapolis: University of Minnesota Press, 2000), 25–26. On pp. x–xii, Mele discusses how the different names given to the Lower East Side and segments of it function as evidence of the "struggle over space."

20 As MacCannell (in *The Tourist,* 92–93) explains, he applies to tourism the terminology of front and back regions developed by Erving Goffman.

21 Interview with Hushidar Mortezaie, 22 September 2000.

22 In a 2003 interview in *Salam Worldwide,* Mortezaie, who describes there that part of his goal is to challenge the stereotypes of "terrorist" and "oppressed women" that have been dominant since the Hostage Crisis [capitalization in the original], indicated that his increasing fame had not yet brought significant financial reward ("Fashion Revolution: Iranian Designers Are Taking America by Storm," *Salam Worldwide,* 1 July 2003, http://www.salamworldwide.com/fashion10th.html).

23 The ferry ride and interviews took place on 2 September 2000.

24 Annette Dragon, e-mail correspondence, 3 September 2000.

25 Announcement made on the Circle Line ferry as it approached Battery Park from Ellis Island, 28 June 2001.

26 Regarding the iconic in vending, see, for an amusing contrast, the song "Detachable Penis," in which a man with a detachable penis (which "comes in handy," he says because "I can leave it at home when I think it's gonna get me into trouble, or I can rent it out if I don't need it") loses it at a party and finds it for sale next to a broken toaster on Second Avenue, "where all those people sell used books and junk on the street." King Missile, "Detachable Penis," lyrics by John S. Hall, *Happy Hour* (Atlantic, 1992).

27 Abraham Cahan, *The Rise of David Levinsky,* with an introduction by Jules Chametzky (New York: Penguin Books, 1993). The ascent and eventual failure of his pushcart career is described on pp. 104–39. On the visibility and numbers of Jewish peddlers and pushcart vendors on the Lower East Side, see Nancy Foner, *From Ellis Island to JFK: New York's Two Great Waves of Immigration* (New Haven: Yale University Press, 2000), 83.

28 Hasia R. Diner, *Lower East Side Memories: A Jewish Place in America* (Princeton: Princeton University Press, 2000), 8, 5.

29 Reproduced in Marilyn Halter, *Shopping for Identity: The Marketing of Ethnicity* (New York: Schocken Books, 2000), 150. A *Boston Globe* article from 16 December 1990, soon after Ellis Island opened, offers an indication of how much spending activity the search for ethnic roots can generate; the author begins at Ellis Island and then visits shops, restaurants, and cultural venues, among other places, on the Lower

East Side and elsewhere. See Larry Tye, "In NYC, Ethnic Traditions and Memories," *Boston Globe*, 16 December 1990, sec. B, p. 1.

30 John Corry, "Liberty Weekend/The Harbor; We Formed a New Nationality," *New York Times*, 4 July 1986, sec. B, p. 4.

31 Foner, *From Ellis Island to JFK*, 34–35.

32 Mele, *Selling the Lower East Side*, 24.

33 Dangerous Bedfellows, ed., *Policing Public Sex* (Boston: South End Press, 1996); see especially Jay Boltcher, "The ~~Fuck Suck~~ Buck Stops Here," 25–44, and David Serlin "The Twilight (Zone) of Commercial Sex," 45–52. Mele, *Selling the Lower East Side*, 10.

34 Robert Lederman, "West African Street Vendor Dies in Hail of Police Bullets as Vendors Prepare City Hall Demonstration," 5 February 1999 and addendum on 6 February 1999, openair-market net, http://www.openair.org/alerts/artist/nywaf.html. See also the "Anti-Giuliani Kiosk" at *Mid Atlantic InfoShop, Your Guide to Anarchy on the Web*, http://www.infoshop.org/nyork/vendor_killed.html.

35 Interview with Ronald Lieberman, director of concessions, New York City Department of Parks and Recreations, 18 September 2000. All subsequent references to our conversation refer to this interview. Lieberman estimated that his office dealt with more than 550 businesses, including the Mets and Yankees, to whom the city leased the ball parks—in deals that gave the city "50 percent naming rights" to new minor league teams.

36 City of New York Parks and Recreation, "Request for Proposals for the Operation of Two Mobile Souvenir Carts at Historic Battery Park, Manhattan," Solicitation M5-SV 3/99, March 11, 1999, 2.

37 Foner, *From Ellis Island to JFK*, 83.

38 Interview, Battery Park, 7 September 2000.

39 Joseph Berger, "For City's Repairmen, Shop May Be the Sidewalk," *New York Times*, 10 September 2003, sec. B, p.4. The article's description of repair people who set up shop on the street as a "twist on the immigrant peddlers who have long been a feature of the city's commercial hubs" is a typical example of "immigrant peddlers" referenced as common knowledge.

40 City of New York Parks and Recreation, "Application for Artist Vendor Permits for New York City Parks and Recreation," October 2000 (n.p.).

41 The Summit took place from 5–8 September in 2000; I spoke to the vendor on 11 September.

42 City of New York Parks and Recreation, "Request for Proposals for the Operation of Two Mobile souvenir Carts at Historic Battery Park, Manhattan," 1999, 4–6. The city kept only the check of the "successful proposer," to be "retained as liquidated damages in the event that this proposer fails to enter into an agreement with Parks."

43 Lieberman told me that the Battery Park licenses brought in $3,271,000, and concession licenses for the city as a whole brought in over $48 million. The food carts brought in $413,550.

44 City of New York Parks and Recreation, "Request for Proposals for the Operation of Two Mobile Souvenir Carts at Historic Battery Park," 2–3.

45 Ibid., 2.

46 Interviews, 5 September 2000, 28 September 2000, and 10 August 2002, along with some casual conversations in July 2001.

47 I spoke to both of these men on 7 September 2000.

48 This group of conversations took place on 11 September 2000.

49 Interview, 9 September 2000. I engaged her in conversation about an incident that had occurred earlier in the day when a man showed up with a Statue of Liberty costume and tried to get in on her business. I had overheard her annoyance, as she muttered loudly, "He needs a sex change." I'm not sure exactly what she meant, but he did, I thought, have more of that stock Statue of Liberty butch look going on.

50 Interview, 5 September 2000.

51 Regina Austin, "An Honest Living: Street Vendors, Municipal Regulation and the Black Public Sphere," *Yale Law Review* 103 (1994): 2119–131, 2121. See also Daniel M. Bluestone, "'The Push Cart Evil': Peddlers, Merchants, and New York City's Streets, 1890–1940," *Journal of Urban History 68* (1991): 69–92. As Austin also emphasizes, vending fills important social, political, and economic functions: "Street vending fills a small part of the void created by the economic marginalization of black Americans as workers, owners, and consumers. Illegal, informal street vending employs people. It supplies blacks with goods they need and want. It contributes to the maintenance of black culture" (2123).

52 Michael Tomasky, "Rudy's Rules of Order," *New York Magazine*, 22 June 22 1998, NewYorkMetro.com, http://www.newyorkmetro.com/nymetro/news/politics/new york/features/2798/.

53 Amnesty International, "Police Shootings," in "Police Brutality and Excessive Force in the New York City Police Department," 1996, http://www.amnestyusa.org/rights forall/police/nypd/nypd-07.html#Racial. The report details "evidence suggesting that a disproportionate number of people shot in apparently non-threatening or questionable circumstances in New York City are racial minorities. At least 32 of the 35 suspects shot by police in the cases examined by Amnesty International were minorities (16 were Latino, 15 were black, 1 was Asian, 1 was white and in two cases the race of the deceased was unknown). They included two black plain clothes police officers who were shot by white officers who mistook them for suspects."

54 Human Rights Watch, "Shielded from Justice: Police Brutality and Accountability in the United States," June 1998, http://www.hrw.org/reports98/police/uspo99.htm.

55 Amy Waldman, "Bias Case Gains Against the City," *New York Times*, 5 February 2001, sec. A., p.1. According to Jeremiah Timothy Driscoll, formerly in the excursion boat business, racism figured in various dealings there, too. For instance, he states, the Westchester County Park Commission refused to allow "open boats" to land at Rye, "which would, on a Saturday or Sunday, scatter as many as 10,000 brown bodies

on the all white sands of Westchester County" (Driscoll, *Crime Circles Manhattan* (New York: n.p., 1980), 122–23. While Driscoll's intense hostility to many officials and entrepreneurs is evidenced in his title's allusion to the Circle Line, which runs cruises around Manhattan and the ferry to the Statue of Liberty and Ellis Island, his assessment here should not thereby be dismissed.

56 Overheard, 22 September 2003.

57 October 2000. I asked about this later that day at the Angel Island gift shop where the docent at work there (the volunteers who staffed the gift shop also were involved at many levels on Angel Island) told me that the design had been approved by the appropriate national parks people.

58 NYPD ads, seen on the subway, September 2000. Romano's brother later quit the force for a department outside the city with better pay.

CHAPTER 7: PRODUCT PACKAGING

1 Deborah Bright, unpublished statement on *Glacial Erratic Series*.

2 United American Indians of New England, "Background Information," http://home .earthlink.net/~uainendom/.

3 Plimoth Plantation, "Rambles in Pilgrimland: Tourism in Plymouth, Massachu-setts, 1845–1945," 2000, http://www.plimoth.org. By 2004, the Web site no longer described the event. A link on the events page, announcing the Day of Mourning leads to UAINE's site.

4 Joseph Lelyveld, "Outboard Balks Ellis I. Coup," *New York Times*, 17 March 1970, p. 45.

5 United American Indians of New England, "Statement" 19 October 1998, http:// home.earthlink.net/~uainendom/. A press release by the ACLU of Massachusetts outlined the settlement: "The Agreement provides that UAINE will be allowed to hold the Day of Mourning in Plymouth each year without having to secure a formal permit from the town so long as they notify the town of their intentions in advance. The town, in turn, will provide UAINE with appropriate facilities for the event, will list the day of Mourning in the calendar of town events and will make UAINE litera-ture available to visitors to Plymouth. The agreement also provides that $100,000 will be donated to the Metacom Education Fund, which will be used, among other things, for publications and educational programs about the history and treatment of native peoples in Massachusetts. (Metacom, also known as King Philip, was the son of Massasoit who led the Wampanoags in a war against the English in the 17th century). An additional $15,000 will be held in escrow for the erection of two his-torical plaques: one will be placed in the town square explaining that this was the location where Metacom's severed head was mounted on a pile after he was killed, and a second on Cole's Hill commemorating the Day of Mourning. A $20,000 dona-tion will also be made to the ACLU of Massachusetts" (ACLU of Massachusetts, "ACLU of Massachusetts Prevails in Court: Agreement Reached between Town of Plym-

outh and the United American Indians of New England," press release, 19 October 1998, http://users.aol.com/mcluf/home.htm). The text of the plaque on Cole's Hill, appropriately embedded into a rock, and its dedication line, also show the extent of UAINE's victory: "Since 1970, Native Americans have gathered at noon on Cole's Hill in Plymouth to commemorate a National Day of Mourning on the US Thanksgiving holiday. Many Native Americans do not celebrate the arrival of the Pilgrims and other European settlers. To them, Thanksgiving Day is a reminder of the genocide of millions of their people, the theft of their lands, and the relentless assault on their culture. Participants in a National Day of Mourning honor Native ancestors and the struggles of Native peoples to survive today. It is a day of remembrance and spiritual connection as well as a protest of the racism and oppression which Native Americans continue to experience. Erected by the Town of Plymouth on behalf of the United American Indians of New England."

6   Bright, comment to me, July 2003, and statement on *Glacial Erratic Series* (forthcoming).

7   Bright, statement on *Glacial Erratic Series* (forthcoming).

8   Interview, 29 September 2000.

9   T-shirt seen in summer 1999. Its text capitalizes "the" but not "of," suggesting "The World" as the title of the place.

10 Overheard on 29 September 2000.

11 Martin Bernal, *Black Athena: The Afroasiatic Roots of Classical Civilization; Vol. 1: The Fabrication of Ancient Greece, 1785–1985* (New Brunswick: Rutgers University Press, 1987), 241. On the habits of picturing Egypt and Greece, see, for instance, Horst de la Croix and Richard G. Tansey, *Gardner's Art through the Ages*, 8th ed. (San Diego: Harcourt Brace Jovanovich, 1986); and Hugh Honour and John Fleming, *The Visual Arts: A History*, 3rd ed. (Englewood Cliffs, N.J.: Prentice Hall, 1992). In contrast, H. W. Janson's *History of Art*, 5th ed. (New York: Abrams, 1995), 46–47, has a map called "The Ancient World" placed at the beginning of the section on that topic, which includes Europe and Egypt visible in an area marked North Africa. However, the inside cover of the volume has separate maps of "Egypt and Ancient Near East" and "the Greek World."

12 *The Source for Everything Jewish*, Chanukah 2002, Hamakor Judaica, Inc. Thanks to Marjorie Feld for sending this catalog my way.

13 *Portland Press Herald*, 2 June 2003, sec. A, p. 4.

14 Steven C. Dubin, *Displays of Power: Memory and Amnesia in the American Museum* (New York: New York University Press, 1999), 232–33. An Associated Press article on the eventual permanent home of the restored plane, in a new annex of the Smithsonian's Air and Space Museum, indicates how the museum decided to try to avoid conflict and conform to the wishes expressed by members of the Military and the U.S. Congress by omitting material on the damage caused by the bombing ("Enola Gay, restored, to Be Museum Centerpiece," *Portland Press Herald*, 19 August 2003, sec. A, p. 3).

15 "Cuban Can-do Dinner," *Glamour*, July 2000, p. 73.

16 Sarah Banet-Weiser, "Elián González and 'The Purpose of America': Nation, Family, and the Child-Citizen," *American Quarterly* 55, no. 2 (June 2003): 154.

17 "eBay Yanks Alleged Elián Stuff," *Lewiston Sun Journal*, 3 May 2000, sec. C, p. 18; "Elián Gonzalez Stuff Flooding Internet," *Lewiston Sun Journal*, 5 May 2000, sec. B, p. 4; "Pam Smart Memorabilia Snapped Up," *Lewiston Sun Journal*, 19 May 2000, sec. B, p. 6.

18 Leonard Pitts Jr., "Auctioning a Relic from a Tragedy Would Be Offensive," *Miami Herald*, 5 May 2001, sec. E, pp. 1, 6.

19 Thanks to Ken Wissoker for making this point.

20 Marilyn Halter, *Shopping for Identity: The Marketing of Ethnicity* (New York: Schocken Books, 2000), 49.

21 Multicultural Marketing Resources, Inc., http://www.multiculturalmarketing resources.com (*Source Book* information at http://www.multicultural.com/products /sourcebook.html).

22 Halter, *Shopping for Identity*, 21. For an excellent account of various stakes in multicultural marketing, see Katharyne Mitchell, "In Whose Interest? Transnational Capital and the Production of Multiculturalism in Canada," in *Global/Local: Cultural Production and the Transnational Imaginary*, ed. Rob Wilson and Wimal Dissanayake (Durham: Duke University Press, 1996), 218–51.

23 Doreen Massey, "The Spatial Construction of Youth Cultures," in *Cool Places: Geographies of Youth Cultures*, ed. Tracey Skelton and Gill Valentine (London: Routledge, 1998), 123, 121.

24 Telephone interview, 24 September 2000.

25 For the range of activist strategies on labor and manufacture, see Andrew Ross, ed., *No Sweat: Fashion, Free Trade, and the Rights of Garment Workers* (New York: Verso, 1997).

26 Jennifer Wilson, in the "Family Travel" section of *Better Homes and Gardens*, May 2003, p. 182, states that according to Karen Axelrod, "co-author, with her husband Bruce Brumberg," of *Watch It Made in the U.S.A.: A Visitor's Guide to the Companies that Make Your Favorite Products* (New York: Avalon, 1997), patriotism is a major reason that "families take factory tours."

27 "Feng Shui Remodeled Gift Shop Leads to Great Results," 124–25; Tony De Masi, "Father's Day: Spending Should Be Up," 104; and "Economic Trends Worth Watching," 71, all in *Souvenirs, Gifts and Novelties* 40, no. 2 (March 2001).

28 For instance, the magazine provides a general service through which one can request information from its advertisers by filling out a postcard with information about the business one works for.

29 Thanks to Mathea Dietz Daunheimer for emphasizing this point about variations among factories in China.

30 "Into the Blue," *Martha Stewart Living*, July/August 2000, p. 180.

31 Joanna Kadi, *Thinking Class: Sketches from a Cultural Worker* (Boston: South End Press, 1996), 44–45.

32 *The Source for Everything Jewish*, pp. 54, 2.

33 Erica Jong, *Inventing Memory: A Novel of Mothers and Daughters* (New York: Harper-Paperbacks, 1997), 276.

34 "Alien Food Lube," paper presented at the conference Objects and/in Visual Culture, Pennsylvania State University, March 2004.

35 In his essay on the designing of the exhibit, Robert Parker quotes Jack Masey, the project manager for the exhibit's designer MetaForm, as indeed saying "our goal was to bring the immigrant experience to life" (Parker, "The Ellis Island Immigration Museum," 82). But I refer here more generally to this commonly expressed goal.

36 From a mailing advertising Berman, *Favorite Comfort Food*.

37 Colonial Williamsburg Foundation, *Colonial Williamsburg Tavern Cookbook*, edited by Charles Pierce, recipes by John R. Gonzales (New York: Clarkson Potter Publishers, 2001), 12.

38 Menu of the King's Arms Tavern, online at the Colonial Williamsburg Web site, www.history.org. When I ate there, in July 2003, the waiter explained that the relishes of the evening were derived from a 1690s cookbook and the bread was a popular eighteenth-century treat.

39 Radhika Viyas Mongia, "Race, Nationality, Mobility: A History of the Passport," *Public Culture* 11 (1999): 527, 528.

40 One ranger who understood the meals to be ill imagined in terms of culinary pleasure or broadly extended government generosity saw another bit of evidence regarding their nature in the sign at the back of the photograph. He told me it said "Silence While Eating." I did not find other evidence of either the sign text or that policy, however.

41 Tom Bernardin, *The Ellis Island Immigrant Cookbook* (New York: Tom Bernardin, Inc., 1991).

42 For meat production in the United States, see Eric Schlosser, *Fast Food Nation: The Dark Side of the All-American Meal* (Boston: Houghton Mifflin, 2001); and the novel by Ruth L. Ozeki, *My Year of Meats* (New York: Penguin, 1999). I do not mean to imply here any charges about the specific meat used by Aramark at Ellis Island but rather to indicate now-standard features of meat production in general. Given the specialty status and cost of meat now produced without antibiotics or hormones and with "free range" breeding, one can assume from the cost of food at the Ellis Island snack shop a more ordinary production of the meat served there.

43 In the signifying system of a certain kind of tourism, the alcohol itself may be seen to reference international cosmopolitanism, at least if a related situation at Disney World suggests a meaningful pattern. At Disney World, the Magic Kingdom is alcohol-free; costumed waiters addressing customers as "Milady" at Cinderella's castle cannot provide the ale suggested by the aura. But at Epcot Center's World

Showcase, where each pavilion represents the culture, food, and, centrally, the shopping of a different country, restaurants do offer alcohol. Similarly, in New York Harbor, alcohol is forbidden at Liberty Island but it is sold at Ellis Island.

44 In 2004 the feature "Q & A on the News" in the *Portland Press Herald* (25 January, sec. A, p. 1) related an interchange on National Public Radio in which a reporter recounted being told that an act of Congress had changed the name. As numerous news sources indicated around the date of the name change, 11 March 2003, the changes were the work of Representative Bob Ney, Republican from Ohio, of the Committee on House Administration, in response to a request circulated by Representative Walter Jones of North Carolina. See their press release, issued by the Committee on House Administration, 11 March 2003, "House Office Buildings to Serve 'Freedom Fries': Reps. Ney and Jones Remove 'French' Fries from House Restaurant Menus," http://www.house.gov/ney/freedomfriespr.htm.

45 Java City is a coffee company with an extensive wholesale business, including the "Java City Espresso Cart Systems" that are part of its "Licensed-Branded Programs," visible at the Java City Web site, http://www.javacity.com/wholesale/.

46 Bernardin, *Ellis Island Immigrant Cookbook*, Ellis Island bills of fare, 25; borscht, 40, 95; Good Friday supper, 59; cabbage, for example, 41, 66, 87, 94, 96, 104.

47 Overheard, 1 August 2000.

48 The credit line on the placemat states, "ARA Leisure Services, Inc. PM 200. Plasticrome. Photos Courtesy of Library of Congress." The two signal dates used in the text under the photograph make little sense. The year 1897 is when the first Ellis Island immigration building, opened in 1892, burned down; the new building, with this particular "front door to freedom," opened in 1900. The terminal date of 1938 is an unusual choice; most pick 1924, when restriction laws began greatly to curb migration, or 1954, when the station closed down.

49 David Treadwell, "American Album, Jersey Claims Ellis Tourists Get Taken for a Ride; Some Say a Free Pedestrian Bridge Should Take the Place of a Mandatory Ferry Trip," *Los Angeles Times*, 5 November 1990, sec. A, p. 5; James T. Humberd, "Bureaucratic Block," *Los Angeles Times*, 25 November 1990, sec. L, p. 18; Albert Parisi, "Celebrating Gateway to Nation, Debating Link to Jersey City," *New York Times*, 23 December 1990, sec. 12 NJ, p. 2.

50 Quoted in Parisi, "Ellis Island Journal."

51 Margaret Stratton, "Sentencing the Sentence: America's Abandoned Prisons," in *Detained in Purgatory*, in the series *Contact Sheet*, no. 110 (Syracuse, N.Y.: Light Work, 2000), 44.

52 Ibid.

53 Ibid.

54 Rachel L. Swarns, "Haitians are Held in U.S. Despite Grant of Asylum," *New York Times*, 25 July 2003, www.nytimes.com. In explaining government arguments for the detention of Haitians, Swarms writes of Attorney General John Ashcroft: "He said the State Department had learned that Haiti had become a staging point for

Pakistanis and Palestinians hoping to enter the United States illegally, a charge that has been disputed by advocates for immigrants." Note here also the presumptions that people should be suspect by virtue of being Pakistanis or Palestinians.

55 La Guardia, *The Making of an Insurgent*, 65–66.

56 ACLU, *Insatiable Appetite: The Government's Demand for New and Unnecessary Powers after September 11: An ACLU Report* (Washington, D.C.: American Civil Liberties Union), 4.

57 Arthur C. Helton, ". . . And No Way to Treat Refugees," *New York Times*, 14 March 1986, sec. A, p. 35.

58 Peace Child International, *Stand Up for Your Rights* (Chicago: World Book, Inc.), 1998. The mainstream publisher may explain the cheerful blurb also on the front cover that the book is "A Peace Child International Project celebrating 50 years of Human Rights," when the book itself actually attends in great detail to human rights not yet achieved.

59 David Wasson, "Cafeteria Contract a Failure in Ohio Prison," *Tampa Tribune*, 22 July 2001, 1.

60 Thomas C. Tobin, "Prison Food Costs Less, But at a Price," *St. Petersburg Times*, 17 July 2002, sec. A., p. 1.

61 Ibid.

62 Ibid.

63 Heather Sala, "George Washington U. Dining Employees Stop Work in Protest," *GW Hatchet* (n.d.); Parker Lee Nash, "Inquiry Reopened in HPU Dispute," *Greensboro (N.C.) News and Record*, 31 May 2001, sec. B, p. 6; "Class Action Race Discrimination Lawsuit Filed against Aramark Corporation; 2000-Employee Corporation Is Nation's Largest Outsourcing Provider," PR Newswire, 15 August 2001. The last source provided the revenue figure, which has been quoted widely elsewhere.

64 "Discrimination Suit no Shock to State Aramark Workers," *Ethnic Newswatch*, 8 September 2001, www.aft.org/privatization/psrp/TrackRec_FoodSer.pdf. Detroit had already been the site of labor activism by Aramark workers, as Charles E. Simmons, a professor at Eastern Michigan University, discussed in "Put Life and Love before Profit and War," 1 May 2001, posted to the Black Radical Congress Listserv, 8 May 2001.

65 Wasson, "Cafeteria Contract a Failure in Ohio Prison," *Tampa Tribune*, 22 July 2001; Robert Ruth, "Food-Service Contract at Prison Given to State Workers Union," *Columbus Dispatch*, 30 September 2000, sec. B, p. 6; "State employee takeover of controversial Aramark contract to yield $1 million savings to prison budget," news release, 29 September 2000, posted on the Web site of the Ohio Civil Service Employees Association, http://www.ocsea.org/celebrate_aramark_defeat.html (OSCEA is part of AFSCME, the American Federation of State, County and Municipal Employees).

66 Emma Goldman, *Living My Life* (New York: Knopf, 1934), 56, quoted in Alix Kates Shulman, "Dances with Feminists," *Women's Review of Books* 9 no. 3 (December

1991), posted at "The Emma Goldman Papers," Berkeley Digital Library SunSITE, http://sunsite.berkeley.edu/Goldman/Features/dances_shulman.html, 2002. I was directed to the site by Pam Williams, "Heathengirl Investigates," http://www.bit-net.com/~grenadin/goldman.html, last updated 7 May 2002. Shulman explains how a short-handed version of material she presented at a talk wound up in 1973 on T-shirts in the form, "If I can't dance, I don't want to be in your revolution," which then became widely circulated, sometimes in variant form. Shulman quotes Goldman's own account of her response: "I was tired of having the Cause constantly thrown into my face. I did not believe that a Cause which stood for a beautiful ideal, for anarchism, for release and freedom from conventions and prejudice, should demand the denial of life and joy. I insisted that our Cause could not expect me to become a nun and that the movement should not be turned into a cloister. If it meant that, I did not want it. I want freedom, the right to self-expression, everybody's right to beautiful, radiant things. Anarchism meant that to me, and I would live it in spite of the whole world—prisons, persecution, everything. Yes, even in spite of the condemnation of my own comrades I would live my beautiful ideal."

67 Joanne Maddern reports on an interview with Alan Kraut, author of *Silent Travelers: Germs, Genes, and the "Immigrant Menace,"* in which he speculates that the provision of tourist amenities was a guiding feature of Ellis Island's renovation that also got rid of some of the "magic" of the place that might have remained were part of the accessible site left as "a ruin," as it was when he visited in the 1970s: "'American visitors . . . like the conveniences of clean bathrooms and souvenirs and being able to buy a Coca-Cola when they want to.'" The tourist features, then, also work to banish "ghosts," although as Maddern documents, and aptly evaluates, testimonies to ghosts remain a prominent feature of narratives about visiting. Joanne Maddern, "The Aestheticization of the Spectropolitical Migrant Landscape," paper presented at the conference "Geography in the University of Wales," May 2003.

CHAPTER 8: "DECIDE AN IMMIGRANT'S FATE"

1 In the interest of preserving the anonymity of rangers staffing the program, I do not indicate the specific dates of individual programs unless there is a particular reason to indicate a date or the reference primarily concerns visitors.

2 Freeman Tilden, *Interpreting Our Heritage: Principles and Practices for Visitor Services in Parks, Museums, and Historic Places* (Chapel Hill: University of North Carolina Press, 1957), 8. While Tilden's book is particularly focused on the National Park Service, it has wider reach. Several interpreters I met at Colonial Williamsburg in July 2003 directed me to it as the key text.

3 Interview with Vincent DiPietro, education specialist in the Department of Interpretation, and Daniel T. Brown, chief ranger of Interpretation, 28 September 2000.

4 "Six Principles of Interpretation," in Statue of Liberty National Monument, Division of Interpretation, "Orientation Packet #2," n.d. (obtained around 2000), n.p.

A caption at the bottom of the page states "from Freeman Tilden's *Interpreting Our Heritage.*" Although the orientation packet doesn't specify, the text to which it refers appears on p. 9 of Tilden's text, which actually states that the purpose "is not instruction, but provocation," thus suggesting the Park Service manual to be hedging a bit at turning away from instruction.

5 From interviews on 28 September 2000 and 6 July 2001.

6 Interview with Brown and DiPietro, 28 September 2000.

7 This research paper requirement was also mentioned to Michael H. Frisch and Dwight Pitcaithley by the guide who led the tour they took in late 1984, before the restoration had gotten underway. See their essay "Audience Expectations as Resource and Challenge: Ellis Island as a Case Study," in *Past Meets Present: Essays about Historical Interpretation and Public Audiences,* ed. Jo Blatti (Washington, D.C.: Smithsonian Institution, 1987), 164.

8 *Teaching Guide for Grades 3–6* has the seal of the National Park Service on the cover but the copyright is by SOLEIF, 1995; I received the undated "Pre-Visit Activity Guide" in a packet for educators that I got at Ellis Island in 2000, along with the *Teaching Guide.*

9 "Overview of Themes and Objectives," Statue of Liberty. Excerpt from instructional material provided to me by the National Park Service in 2000.

10 "The Other Half Tour," Colonial Williamsburg, 16 July 2003.

11 Claude McKay, *A Long Way from Home* (New York: Arno Press and the *New York Times,* 1969 [1937]), 95. On the sex of McKay's sexual partners, see Wayne F. Cooper, *Claude McKay: Rebel Sojourner in the Harlem Renaissance, a Biography* (Baton Rouge: Louisiana State University Press, 1987), 30.

12 In the 1983 novel *Ellis Island,* by Fred Mustard Stewart (New York: William Morris and Co.), an immigrant from Ireland discovered to have trachoma at Ellis Island manages to get into the United States after some bribing and maneuvering on her behalf (and another ocean voyage). Her ultimately happy life may be testimony against the impetus to expel, although having family, not the government, to take care of her also manages to sidestep some of the issues.

13 Amy L. Fairchild, *Science at the Borders,* 37–39; Nayan Shah, *Contagious Divides,* 187–89.

14 On the scope of publicity, see the undated booklet "International Trachoma Initiative: Launching a Great Philanthropy Effort," produced by Pfizer, which itemizes the media coverage. In 2003, Pfizer announced its intention to donate enough azithromycin to treat 90 percent of people with trachoma, donating 135 million doses in the next five years, up from 8 million between 1998 and 2003. See "Pfizer to Provide 135 Million with Trachoma Treatment," *U.N. Wire,* United Nations Foundation, www.unwire.org/UNWire/20031113/449_10356.asp. As a 2001 Oxfam Company briefing paper, called *Pfizer: Formula for Fairness: Patient Rights before Patent Rights* (Pfizer briefing paper no. 2) pointed out, however, Pfizer's work to defend and, indeed, increase the patent rights of pharmaceutical companies has simulta-

neously worked against access to needed medicines, including azithromycin, which has many other crucial uses from which developing countries could benefit. Thanks to Rachel Cohen of Doctors without Borders (MSF) for her help on this topic.

15 Interview, 19 September 2000.

16 Nancy Ordover, *American Eugenics: Race, Queer Anatomy, and the Science of Nationalism* (Minneapolis: University of Minnesota Press, 2003), 11–12.

17 I heard different narratives about the source and development of this idea. In 2000, rangers described coming up with the plan, doing a little research, and then running it by their superiors. In 2001, one of the actors told me it was all his idea, which seemed to me at least a bit of exaggeration.

18 September 2000.

19 Interview, 9 July 2001.

20 September 2000.

21 Caren Kaplan, "'A World without Boundaries': The Body Shop's Trans/national Geographies," in *With Other Eyes: Looking at Race and Gender in Visual Culture*, ed. Lisa Bloom (Minneapolis: University of Minnesota Press, 1999), 139.

22 Clifford, *Routes*, 3, 44.

23 Mitchell, "In Whose Interest?" 219–20. Thanks also to Lydia Savage for her insistent emphasis on this point.

24 In addition to sources cited previously, see Jean Comaroff and John Comaroff, *Ethnography and the Historical Imagination* (Bolder: Westview Press, 1992), 25–27, for a discussion of how "the 'life-story' [as] an instrument of bourgeois history in the making" is far from politically, ideologically, or epistemologically neutral in origin and deployment.

25 July 2001.

26 June 2001.

27 The Web site Upward Bound at USM explains that the program assists "qualified, low income students . . . to prepare to become the first in their families to graduate from college. . . . The summer, residential program serves 70+ juniors and seniors with academic coursework, part-time employment, college and career exploration, and cultural, recreational, and community service experiences for six weeks on the Gorham campus of the University of Southern Maine. Career exploration, tutoring, academic advising, college visits, cultural experiences, and college admissions and financial aid planning assistance are provided to 100+ sophomores, juniors, and seniors during the school year" (http://www.usm.maine.edu/upwardbound/home .html). Thanks to Johannah Burdin, director of the USM program, for enabling me to spend the day with the group.

28 Interview, 18 July 2001.

29 July 2001.

30 Tilden, *Interpreting Our Heritage*, 12.

31 Relations between money and heritage engagement can be quite complex. In 2002, near Herkimer in upstate New York along the Erie Canal, I was on a school bus char-

tered for a short trip to a historic house. When someone asked the driver, who was describing the area's history, about how she knew so much (a rather presumptuous and condescending question, I thought), she replied that because the economy was so bad in the area and employment opportunities had dried up, "heritage is all we have."

32 July 2001.

33 Handler and Gable, *The New History in an Old Museum*, 13, 80. At Colonial Williamsburg, they emphasized, these "prepackaged ensembles" were often described as "just the facts" (80). As a result, as they discuss, when and what interpreters thought they were "interpreting" varied.

34 Michael Frisch, *A Shared Authority: Essays on the Craft and Meaning of Oral and Public History* (Albany: State University of New York Press, 1990), xxiii. Two extremely helpful anthologies concerning theories and practices involved in representing the past, especially as they involve places, artifacts, and diverse participants in the process, are Jo Blatti, ed., *Past Meets Present: Essays about Historic Interpretation and Public Audiences* (Washington, D.C.: Smithsonian Institution Press, 1987); and David Boswell and Jessica Evans, eds., *Representing the Nation: Histories, Heritage, and Museums* (New York: Routledge, 1999).

35 Moreno, *Ellis Island*, 110.

36 "Broken Chains," *Teacher's Corner*, http://www.nps.gov/stli/teachercorner/page14 .html; "Was the Statue of Liberty First Conceived as a Black Woman?" *Black History Magazine*, http://www.blackhistorymagazine.net/statueofliberty.html.

37 Associated Press, "Report: 'Icons' Lack Federal Protection," *Portland Press Herald*, 6 September 2003, sec. A, p. 3; Associated Press, "Retailers Hope Capture Spurs Spending," *Portland Press Herald*, 15 December 2003, sec. A, p. 16.

38 "Frozen Facts," *Centre Daily Times* (State College, Pennsylvania), 9 August 2003, sec. C, p. 1. A text at the bottom of the article says, "Source: National Ice Cream Council."

39 Associated Press, "1872 Law Used to Target Greenpeace," *Portland Press Herald*, 21 January 2004.

40 Associated Press, "Romney Insurance Veto Criticized by Advocates," *Portland Press Herald*, 29 November 2003, sec. B, p. 8.

BIBLIOGRAPHY

ACLU. *Insatiable Appetite: The Government's Demand for New and Unnecessary Powers after September 11. An ACLU Report*. Washington, D.C.: American Civil Liberties Union, 2002.

Alemán, Jesse. "Authenticity, Autobiography, and Identity: *The Woman in Battle* as a Civil War Narrative." In *The Woman in Battle: The Civil War Narrative of Loreta Janeta Velasquez, Cuban Woman and Confederate Soldier*. Madison: University of Wisconsin Press, 2003.

Alexander, M. Jacqui. "Erotic Autonomy as a Politics of Decolonization: An Anatomy of Feminist and State Practice in the Bahamas Tourist Economy." In *Feminist Genealogies, Colonial Legacies, Democratic Futures*, edited by M. Jaqui Alexander and Chandra Talpade Mohanty. New York: Routledge, 1997.

Alexander, M. Jacqui, and Chandra Talpade Mohanty, eds. *Feminist Genealogies, Colonial Legacies, Democratic Futures*. New York: Routledge, 1997.

Allison, Dorothy. *Skin: Thinking about Sex, Class, and Literature*. Ithaca, N.Y.: Firebrand Books, 1994.

Altman, Dennis. *Global Sex*. Chicago: University of Chicago Press, 2001.

Anderson, Benedict. *Imagined Communities: Reflections on the Origin and Spread of Nationalism*. London: Verso, 1983.

Anderson, Michelle J. "A License to Abuse: The Impact of Conditional Status on Female Immigrants." *Yale Law Review* 102 (April 1993): 1401–30.

Appadurai, Arjun. "Introduction: Commodities and the Politics of Value." In *The Social Life of Things: Commodities in Cultural Perspective*, edited by Arjun Appadurai. Cambridge: Cambridge University Press, 1986.

———, ed. *The Social Life of Things: Commodities in Cultural Perspective*. Cambridge: Cambridge University Press, 1986.

Ash, Juliet. "The Tie: Presence and Absence" and "Memory and Objects." In *The Gendered Object*, edited by Pat Kirkham. Manchester: Manchester University Press, 1995.

Austin, Regina. "An Honest Living: Street Vendors, Municipal Regulation and the Black Public Sphere." *Yale Law Review* 103 (1994): 2119–31.

————. "A Nation of Thieves: Consumption, Commerce, and the Black Public Sphere." *Public Culture* 7 (fall 1994): 225–48.

Babcock, Barbara A., and John J. Macaloon. "Everybody's Gal: Women, Boundaries, and Monuments." In *The Statue of Liberty Revisited*, edited by Wilton S. Dillon and Neil G. Kotler. Washington, D.C.: Smithsonian Institution Press, 1994.

Banet-Weiser, Sarah. "Elián González and 'The Purpose of America': Nation, Family, and the Child-Citizen." *American Quarterly* 55, no. 2 (June 2003): 149–78.

Barr, Nevada. *Bittersweet*. San Francisco: Spinsters/Aunt Lute, 1984.

————. *Liberty Falling*. New York: Avon Books, 1999.

Berlant, Lauren. *The Anatomy of National Fantasy: Hawthorne, Utopia, and Everyday Life*. Chicago: University of Chicago Press, 1994.

————.*The Queen of America Goes to Washington City: Essays on Sex and Citizenship*. Durham: Duke University Press, 1997.

Berlant, Lauren, and Lisa Duggan, eds. *Our Monica Ourselves: The Clinton Affair and the National Interest*. New York: New York University Press, 2002.

Berman, Ann E. *Favorite Comfort Food: A Satisfying Collection of Home Cooking Classics*. New York: Clarkson N. Potter, 1999.

Bernal, Martin. *Black Athena: The Afroasiatic Roots of Classical Civilization*. 2 vols. New Brunswick: Rutgers University Press, 1999.

Bernardin, Tom. *The Ellis Island Immigrant Cookbook*. New York: Tom Bernardin, 1999.

Bessire, Mark H. C., ed. *William Pope.L: The Friendliest Black Artist In America©*. Cambridge, Mass.: MIT Press, 2002.

Betty and Pansy's Severe Queer Review of New York. San Francisco: Bedpan Productions, 1994.

Blanchet, Christian, and Bertrand Dart. *Statue of Liberty: The First Hundred Years*. Translated by Bernard A. Weisberger. New York: American Heritage Publishing, 1985.

Blatti, Jo, ed. *Past Meets Present: Essays about Historic Interpretation and Public Audiences*. Washington, D.C.: Smithsonian Institution Press, 1987.

Bluestone, Daniel M. " 'The Push Cart Evil': Peddlers, Merchants, and New York City's Streets, 1890–1940." *Journal of Urban History* 68 (1991): 69–92.

Boltcher, Jay. "Sex Club Owners: The ~~Fuck Suck~~ Buck Stops Here." In *Policing Public Sex: Queer Politics and the Future of AIDS Activism*, edited by Dangerous Bedfellows. Boston: South End Press, 1996.

Bornstein, Kate. *Gender Outlaw: On Men, Women, and the Rest of Us*. New York: Routledge, 1994.

Boswell, David, and Jessica Evans, eds. *Representing the Nation: Histories, Heritage, and Museums*. New York: Routledge, 1999.

Brownstone, David M., Irene M. Franck, and Douglass L. Brownstone. *Island of Hope, Island of Tears*. New York: Penguin Books, 1986 [1979].

Bundeson, Lynne, ed. *Dear Miss Liberty: Letters to the Statue of Liberty*. Salt Lake City: Peregrine Smith Books, 1986.

Cahan, Abraham. *The Rise of David Levinsky*. New York: Penguin Books, 1993.

———. *"Yekl" and "The Imported Bridegroom" and Other Stories of the New York Ghetto*. New York: Dover Publications, 1970 [1898].

Califia, Pat. "San Francisco: Revisiting the City of Desire." In *Queers in Space: Communities, Public Places, Sites of Resistance*, edited by Gordon Brent Ingram, Anne-Marie Bouthillette, and Yolanda Retter. Seattle: Bay Press, 1997.

———. "The Surprise Party." In *Macho Sluts: Erotic Fiction*. Boston: Alyson Publications, 1988.

Cantú, Lionel, and Eithne Luibhéid, eds. *Queer Migrations: Sexuality, U.S. Citizenship, and Border Crossings*. Minneapolis: University of Minnesota Press, 2005.

Carroll, Lorrayne, and Joseph Medley. " 'Whooping It Up for Rational Prosperity': Narratives of the East Asian Financial Crisis." In *World Bank Literature*, edited by Amitava Kumar. Minneapolis: University of Minnesota Press, 2003.

Cavitch, Max. "Emma Lazarus and the Golem of Liberty." In *American Literary History*. Forthcoming.

Chapkis, Wendy. "Soft Glove, Punishing Fist: The Trafficking Victims' Protection Act." In *Controlling Sex: The Politics of Intimacy and Identity*, edited by Elizabeth Bernstein and Laurie Schafner. New York: Routledge, 2004.

———. *Beauty Secrets: Women and the Politics of Appearance*. Boston: South End Press, 1986.

Chasin, Alexandra. *Selling Out: The Gay and Lesbian Movement Goes to Market*. New York: St. Martin's Press, 2000.

Chauncey, George. *Gay New York: Gender, Urban Culture, and the Making of the Gay Male World, 1840–1940*. New York: Basic Books, 1994.

Chin, Elizabeth. *Purchasing Power: Black Kids and American Consumer Culture*. Minneapolis: University of Minnesota Press, 2001.

Christine, Fidi, Jenieve, Ro, and Toni. "Talking Class: Working Class sm Dykes Lay Down the Line, Part Two," *Brat Attack*, no. 3 (fall 1993): 30–36.

Clark, Jane Perry. *Deportation of Aliens from the United States to Europe*. New York: Columbia University Press, 1931.

Clifford, James. *Routes: Travel and Translation in the Late Twentieth Century*. Cambridge, Mass.: Harvard University Press, 1997.

Coan, Peter Morton. *Ellis Island Interviews: In Their Own Words*. New York: Checkmark Books, 1997.

Cody, Gabrielle, ed. *Hardcore from the Heart: The Pleasures, Profits and Politics of Sex in Performance. Annie Sprinkle: Solo*. London: Continuum, 2001.

Cohen, Cathy J. "Punk, Bulldaggers, and Welfare Queens: The Radical Potential of Queer Politics?" *GLQ* 3 (1997): 437–65.

Comaroff, Jean, and John Comaroff. *Ethnography and the Historical Imagination*. Boulder: Westview Press, 1992.

Cooper, Wayne F. *Claude McKay: Rebel Sojourner in the Harlem Renaissance, a Biography*. Baton Rouge: Louisiana State University Press, 1987.

Corsi, Edward. *In the Shadow of Liberty: The Chronicle of Ellis Island*. New York: Macmillan, 1935.

Cruz-Malavé, Arnaldo, and Martin F. Manalansan IV, eds. *Queer Globalizations: Citizenship and the Afterlife of Colonialism*. New York: New York University Press, 2002.

Curtis, Liz. *Nothing but the Same Old Story: The Roots of Anti-Irish Racism*. Belfast: Sasta, 1996.

Cvetkovich, Ann. *An Archive of Feelings: Trauma, Sexuality, and Lesbian Public Cultures*. Durham: Duke University Press, 2003.

Dangerous Bedfellows, ed. *Policing Public Sex: Queer Politics and the Future of AIDS Activism*. Boston: South End Press, 1996.

Davenport, Rattan. "Statuary Rape." *Social Anarchism* 13 (1987): 32–33.

Deitcher, David, ed. "Law and Desire." In *The Question of Equality: Lesbian and Gay Politics in America since Stonewall*. New York: Scribner, 1995.

Dillon, Wilton S., and Neil G. Kotler, eds. *The Statue of Liberty Revisited*. Washington, D.C.: and London: Smithsonian Institution Press, 1994.

Diner, Hasia R. *Lower East Side Memories: A Jewish Place in America*. Princeton: Princeton University Press, 2000.

Driscoll, Jeremiah Timothy. *Crime Circles Manhattan*. New York: n.p., 1980.

Dubin, Steven C. *Displays of Power: Memory and Amnesia in the American Museum*. New York: New York University Press, 1999.

Duggan, Lisa. "The Trials of Alice Mitchell: Sensationalism, Sexology, and the Lesbian Subject in Turn-of-the-Century America." In *Queer Studies: An Interdisciplinary Reader*, edited by Robert J. Corber and Stephen Valocci. Oxford: Blackwell, 2003.

Ehrenreich, Barbara, and Arle Russell Hochschild, eds. *Global Woman: Nannies, Maids, and Sex Workers in the New Economy*. New York: Harry Holt, 2002.

Eichstedt, Jennifer L., and Stephen Small. *Representations of Slavery: Race and Ideology in Southern Plantation Museums*. Washington, D.C.: Smithsonian Institution Press, 2002.

Faderman, Lillian. *Odd Girls and Twilight Lovers: A History of Lesbian Life in Twentieth-Century America*. New York: Columbia University Press, 1991.

Fairchild, Amy. *Science at the Borders: Immigrant Medical Inspection and the Shaping of the Modern Labor Force*, Baltimore: Johns Hopkins Press, 2003.

Farmer, Paul. *AIDS and Accusation: Haiti and the Geography of Blame*. Berkeley: University of California Press, 1992.

Feinberg, Leslie. *Stone Butch Blues*. Ithaca, N.Y.: Firebrand Press, 1993.

———. *Transgender Warriors: Making History from Joan of Ark to RuPaul*. Boston: Beacon Press, 1996.

Foner, Nancy. *From Ellis Island to JFK: New York's Two Great Waves of Immigration*. New Haven: Yale University Press, 2000.

Fox, Nancy Jo. *Liberties with Liberty: The Fascinating History of America's Proudest Symbol*. New York: E. P. Dutton, 1985.

Frankenberg, Ruth. *White Women, Race Matters: The Social Construction of Whiteness.* Minneapolis: University of Minnesota Press, 1993.

Frisch, Michael. *A Shared Authority: Essays on the Craft and Meaning of Oral and Public History.* Albany: State University of New York Press, 1990.

Frisch, Michael, and Dwight Pitcaithley. "Audience Expectations as Resource and Challenge: Ellis Island as a Case Study." In *Past Meets Present: Essays about Historical Interpretation and Public Audiences,* edited by Jo Blatti. Washington, D.C.: Smithsonian Institution Press, 1987.

Galeano, Eduardo. *Upside Down: A Primer for the Looking Glass World,* translated by Mark Fried. New York: Henry Holt and Company, 2000.

Gallagher, Charles. "White Reconstruction in the University." *Socialist Review* 24, nos. 1 and 2 (1995): 165–87.

Gilfoyle, Timothy J. *City of Eros: New York City, Prostitution, and the Commercialization of Sex, 1790–1920.* New York: Norton, 1992.

Giroux, Henry A. *The Mouse That Roared: Disney and the End of Innocence.* Lanham, Md: Rowman and Littlefield, 1999.

Gold, Tami. *Juggling Gender: Politics, Sex and Identity.* Tamerik Productions, 1997.

Goldberg, David Theo. *Racial Subjects: Writing on Race in America.* New York: Routledge, 1997.

Goldman, Emma. *Living My Life.* New York: Knopf, 1934.

Gould, Deborah B. "Sex, Death, and the Politics of Anger: Emotions and Reason in ACT UP's Fight Against AIDS." Ph.D. diss., University of Chicago, 2000.

Gratz, Roberta Brandes, and Eric Fettman. "The Selling of Miss Liberty." *Nation* 241, no. 15 (9 November 1985): 465–76.

———. "The Battle for Ellis Island." *Nation* 241, no. 18 (30 November 1985): 579–89.

Grewal, Inderpal. "Traveling Barbie: Indian Transnationality and New Consumer Subjects." *positions* 7 (1999): 799–826.

Grossberg, Lawrence. *We Gotta Get Out of This Place: Popular Conservatism and Postmodern Culture.* New York: Routledge, 1992.

Hall, Stuart, and Paul du Gay, eds. *Questions of Cultural Identity.* London: Sage, 1996.

Halley, Janet. "The Construction of Heterosexuality." In *Fear of a Queer Planet: Queer Politics and Social Theory,* edited by Michael Warner. Minneapolis: University of Minnesota Press, 1993.

Halter, Marilyn. *Shopping for Identity: The Marketing of Ethnicity.* New York: Schocken Books, 2000.

Hamblin, B. Colin. *Ellis Island: The Official Souvenir Guidebook.* Santa Barbara: Companion Press, 1994 [1991].

Handler, Richard, and Eric Gable. *The New History in an Old Museum: Creating the Past at Colonial Williamsburg.* Durham: Duke University Press, 1997.

Haney-López, Ian F. *White by Law: The Legal Construction of Race.* New York: New York University Press, 1996.

Haskins, Jim. *The Statue of Liberty: America's Proud Lady.* Minneapolis: Lerner Publications, 1986.

Heiser, Victor. *An American Doctor's Odyssey, Adventures in Forty-five Countries.* New York: Norton, 1936.

Hemphill, Essex. *Ceremonies: Prose and Poetry.* New York: Penguin Books, 1992.

Hennessy, Rosemary. "Queer Visibility in Commodity Culture." In *Social Postmodernism: Beyond Identity Politics,* eds. Linda Nicholson and Steven Seidman. Cambridge: Cambridge University Press, 1995.

Herzig, Rebecca. "Removing Roots: North American Hiroshima Maidens." *Technology and Culture* 40 (October 1999): 723–45.

———. "The Woman Beneath the Hair: Treating Hypertrichosis, 1870–1930." *NWSA Journal* 12 (fall 2000): 50–66.

Higham, John. *Send These to Me: Immigrants in Urban America.* Rev. ed. Baltimore: Johns Hopkins University Press, 1984.

Hing, Bill Ong. *Making and Remaking Asian America through Immigration Policy, 1850–1990.* Stanford: Stanford University Press, 1993.

Holland, F. Ross. *Idealists, Scoundrels, and the Lady: An Insider's View of the Statue of Liberty–Ellis Island Project.* Urbana: University of Illinois Press, 1993.

Hollibaugh, Amber L. *My Dangerous Desires: A Queer Girl Dreaming Her Way Home.* Durham: Duke University Press, 2000.

Hope, Christine. "Caucasian Female Body Hair and American Culture." *Journal of American Culture* 5 (spring 1982): 93–99.

Howe, Irving, and Kenneth Libo. *How We Lived: A Documentary History of Immigrant Jews in America 1880–1930.* New York: Richard Marek Publishers, 1979.

Iacocca, Lee. *Liberty for All.* Edited by Barbara Grazzini. Wilmington, Del.: Miller Publishing, 2002.

———, and Sonny Kleinfield. *Talking Straight.* New York: Bantam Books, 1988.

———, and William Novak. *Iacocca: an Autobiography.* Toronto: Bantam Books, 1984.

Ignatiev, Noel. *How the Irish Became White.* New York: Routledge, 1995.

Ingram, Gordon Brent, Anne-Marie Bouthillette, and Yolanda Retter, eds. *Queers in Space: Communities, Public Places, Sites of Resistance.* Seattle: Bay Press, 1997.

Johnson, Lynn. "Ellis Island: Historical Preservation from the Supply Side." *Radical History Review* 28–30 (1984): 157–68.

Johnson, Walter. 1999. *Soul by Soul: Life Inside the Antebellum Slave Market.* Cambridge, Mass.: Harvard University Press.

Jones, James A. "The Immigration Marriage Fraud Amendments: Sham Marriages or Sham Legislation?" *Florida State University Law Review* 24 (1997): 679–701.

Jones, R. L. *Great American Stuff: A Celebration of People, Places and Products that Make Us Happy to Live in America.* Nashville: Cumberland House, 1997.

Jong, Erica. *Inventing Memory: A Novel of Mothers and Daughters.* New York: Harper-Paperbacks, 1997.

Joseph, Miranda. *Against the Romance of Community*. Minneapolis: University of Minnesota Press, 2002.

Kadi, Joanna. *Thinking Class: Sketches from a Cultural Worker*. Boston: South End Press, 1996.

Kahn, Robert, ed. *City Secrets: New York City*. N.p.: Little Bookroom, 2002.

Kantrowitz, Melanie Kaye. "Whose Millennium?" *Gay Community News* 23, no. 4 (1998): 58–59.

Kaplan, Caren. " 'A World Without Boundaries': The Body Shop's Trans/national Geographies." In *With Other Eyes: Looking at Race and Gender in Visual Culture*, edited by Lisa Bloom. Minneapolis: University of Minnesota Press, 1999.

———. *Questions of Travel: Postmodern Discourses of Displacement*. Durham: Duke University Press, 1996.

Katz, Jonathan Ned. *Gay American History: Lesbians and Gay Men in the U.S.A.* New York: Thomas Y. Crowell, 1976.

Kauffman, Reginald Wright. *The House of Bondage*. Upper Saddle River, N.J.: Gregg Press, 1968 [1910].

Kempadoo, Kamala. "Introduction: Globalizing Sex Workers' Rights." In *Global Sex Workers: Rights, Resistance, and Redefinition*, edited by Kamala Kempadoo and Jo Doezema. New York: Routledge, 1998.

Kessner, Carol. "Matrilineal Dissent: The Rhetoric of Zeal in Emma Lazarus, Maria Syrkin, and Cynthia Ozick." In *Women of the Word: Jewish Women and Jewish Writing*. Detroit: Wayne State University Press, 1994.

Kirshenblatt-Gimblett, Barbara. *Destination Culture: Tourism, Museums, and Heritage*. Berkeley: University of California Press, 1998.

Kiss and Tell. *Her Tongue on My Theory: Images, Essays and Fantasies*. Vancouver, B.C.: Press Gang Publishers, 1994.

Kopytoff, Igor. "The Cultural Biography of Things." In *The Social Life of Things: Commodities in Cultural Perspective*, edited by Arjun Appadurai. Cambridge: Cambridge University Press, 1986.

Kotler, Neil G. "The Statue of Liberty as Idea, Symbol, and Historical Presence." In *The Statue of Liberty Revisited*, edited by Neil G. Kotler and Wilton S. Dillon. Washington, D.C.: Smithsonian Institution Press, 1994.

Kotler, Neil G., and Wilton S. Dillon, eds. *The Statue of Liberty Revisited*. Washington, D.C.: Smithsonian Institution Press, 1994.

Kraut, Alan M. *Silent Travelers: Germs, Genes, and the "Immigrant Menace."* New York: Basic Books, 1994.

Kumar, Amitava, ed. *World Bank Literature*. Minneapolis: University of Minnesota Press, 2003.

La Guardia, Fiorello H. *The Making of an Insurgent: An Autobiography, 1882–1919*. New York: Capricorn Books, 1961 [1948].

Landsman, Mark, with Yaron Avni, Reut Elkouby, Bushra Jawabri, Amer K. Ranon, Hazem El Sanoun, Yossi Zilberman. *Peace of Mind* (Global Action Project), 1999.

Lowe, Lisa. *Immigrant Acts: Asian American Cultural Politics*. Durham: Duke University Press, 1996.

Lowe, Lisa, and David Lloyd. *The Politics of Culture in the Shadow of Capital*. Durham: Duke University Press, 1997.

Luibhéid, Eithne. *Entry Denied: Controlling Sexuality at the Border*. Minneapolis: University of Minnesota Press, 2002.

MacCannell, Dean. *The Tourist: A New Theory of the Leisure Class*. Rev. ed. Berkeley: University of California Press, 1999.

Maddern, Joanne. "The Aestheticization of the Spectropolitical Migrant Landscape." Paper presented at the conference "Geography in the University of Wales," May 2003.

Manalansan IV, Martin. *Global Divas: Filipino Gay Men in the Diaspora*. Durham: Duke University Press, 2003.

Marable, Manning. "Beyond Racial Identity Politics: Toward a Liberation Theory for Multicultural Democracy." In *Privileging Positions: The Sites of Asian American Studies*, edited by Gary Y. Okihiro, Marilyn Alquizola, Dorothy Fujita Rony, and K. Scott Wong. Pullman: Washington State University Press, 1995.

———, ed. *Dispatches from the Ebony Tower: Intellectuals Confront the African American Experience*. New York: Columbia University Press, 2000.

Marom, Daniel. "Who Is the 'Mother of Exiles'? An Inquiry into Jewish Aspects of Emma Lazarus's 'The New Colossus.'" *Prooftexts* 20 (autumn 2000): 231–61.

Massey, Doreen. "The Spatial Construction of Youth Cultures." In *Cool Places: Geographies of Youth Cultures*, edited by Tracey Skelton and Gill Valentine. London: Routledge, 1998.

Mayer, Tamar, ed. *Gender Ironies of Nationalism: Sexing the Nation*. London: Routledge, 2000.

Mayerson, Evelyn Wilde. *The Cat Who Escaped from Steerage*. New York: Charles Scribner's Sons, 1990.

McClintock, Anne. *Imperial Leather: Race, Gender and Sexuality in the Colonial Context*. New York: Routledge, 1995.

McKay, Claude. *A Long Way from Home*. New York: Arno Press and the *New York Times*, 1969 [1937].

Mele, Christopher. *Selling the Lower East Side: Culture, Real Estate, and Resistance in New York City*. Minneapolis: University of Minnesota Press, 2000.

Merriam, Eve. *Emma Lazarus: Woman with a Torch*. New York: Citadel Press, 1956.

Meyerowitz, Joanne J. *Women Adrift: Independent Wage Earners in Chicago, 1880–1930*. Chicago: University of Chicago Press, 1998.

Mirzoeff, Nicholas, ed. *Diaspora and Visual Culture: Representing Africans and Jews*. London: Routledge, 2000.

Mitchell, Katharyne. "In Whose Interest? Transnational Capital and the Production of Multiculturalism in Canada." In *Global/Local: Cultural Production and the Transna-*

tional Imaginary, edited by Rob Wilson and Wimal Dissanayake. Durham: Duke University Press, 1996.

Mongia, Radhika Viyas. "Race, Nationality, Mobility: A History of the Passport." *Public Culture* 11 (1999): 527–56.

Mookas, Ioannis. "Faultlines: Homophobic Innovation in *Gay Rights, Special Rights*." *Afterimage* 22 (1995): 14–18.

Moreno, Barry. *Ellis Island: Images of America*. Charleston, S.C.: Arcadia Press, 2003.

———. *The Statue of Liberty Encyclopedia*. New York: Simon and Schuster, 2000.

Moriarty, Laura. *The Center of Everything*. New York: Hyperion, 2003.

Morrison, Toni. *Playing in the Dark: Whiteness and the Literary Imagination*. New York: Vintage, 1992.

Murdoch, Joyce, and Deb Price. *Courting Justice: Gay Men and Lesbians v. the Supreme Court*. New York: Basic Books, 2001.

Myles, Eileen. *Cool for You*. New York: Soft Skull Press, 2000.

Nestle, Joan. *The Persistent Desire: A Femme-Butch Reader*. Boston: Alyson, 1992.

Nestle, Joan, Clare Howell, and Riki Wilchins, eds. *GenderQueer: Voices from Beyond the Sexual Binary*. Los Angeles: Alyson Books, 2002.

Newton, Esther. *Margaret Mead Made Me Gay: Personal Essays, Public Ideas*. Durham: Duke University Press, 2000.

———. "The Mythic Mannish Lesbian: Radclyffe Hall and the New Woman" (1984). In *Margaret Mead Made Me Gay: Personal Essays, Public Ideas*. Durham: Duke University Press, 2000.

New York Public Library and the Comité officiel franco-américain pour la célèbration du centenaire de la Statue de la Liberté. *Liberty: The French American Statue in Art and History*. New York: Perennial Library, 1986.

Nicholson, Linda, and Steven Seidman, eds. *Social Postmodernism: Beyond Identity Politics*. Cambridge: Cambridge University Press, 1995.

Ohmann, Richard M. *Selling Culture: Magazines, Markets, and Class at the Turn of the Century*. London: Verso, 1996.

Oliver, Melvin, and Thomas M. Shapiro. *Black Wealth/White Wealth: A New Perspective on Racial Inequality*. New York: Routledge, 1997.

Omer-Sherman, Ranen. "Emma Lazarus, Jewish American Poetics, and the Challenge of Modernity." *Legacy* 19, no. 2 (2002): 170–91.

Omi, Michael, and Howard Winant. *Racial Formation in the United States: From the 1960s to the 1990s*. 2nd ed. New York: Routledge, 1994.

Ong, Aihwa. "The Gender and Labor Politics of Postmodernity." In *The Politics of Culture in the Shadow of Capital*, edited by Lisa Lowe and David Lloyd. Durham: Duke University Press, 1997.

Ordover, Nancy. *American Eugenics: Race, Queer Anatomy, and the Science of Nationalism*. Minneapolis: University of Minnesota Press, 2003.

Orleck, Annelise. *Common Sense and a Little Fire: Women and Working-Class Politics in the United States, 1900–1965*. Chapel Hill: University of North Carolina Press, 1995.

Osborne, Brian. "Constructing the State, Managing the Corporation, Transforming the Individual: Photography, Immigration and the Canadian National Railways, 1925–30." In *Picturing Place: Photography and the Geographical Imagination*, ed. Joan Schwartz and James Ryan. New York: I. B. Tauris, 2003.

Ozeki, Ruth L. *My Year of Meats*. New York: Penguin Books, 1999.

Parker, Robert A. "The Ellis Island Immigration Museum." *Communication Arts* (January/February 1991): 82–93.

Patel, Geeta. "Stories for the Millennium: Disrupting Time." *Gay Community News* 23, no. 4 (1998): 52–53, 56–57.

Patton, Cindy, and Benigno Sánchez-Eppler. *Queer Diasporas*. Durham: Duke University Press, 2000.

Peace Child International. *Stand Up for Your Rights*. Chicago: World Book, 1998.

Peiss, Kathy. *Cheap Amusements: Working Women and Leisure in Turn-of-the-Century New York*. Philadelphia: Temple University Press, 1986.

Pellegrini, Ann. "Consuming Lifestyle: Commodity Capitalism and Transformations in Gay Identity." In *Queer Globalizations: Citizenship and the Afterlife of Colonialism*, edited by Arnaldo Cruz-Malavé and Martin F. Manalansan IV. New York: New York University Press, 2002.

Peña, Susana. "Visibility and Silence: Mariel and Cuban American Gay Male Experience and Representation." In *Queer Migrations: Sexuality, U.S. Citizenship, and Border Crossings*, edited by Lionel Cantú and Eithne Luibhéid. Minneapolis: University of Minnesota Press, 2004.

Perea, Juan. "The Statue of Liberty: Notes from Behind the Gilded Door." In *Immigrants Out! The New Nativism and the Anti-Immigrant Impulse in the United States*, edited by Juan Perea. New York: New York University Press, 1997.

Pierce, Charles, ed. *Colonial Williamsburg Tavern Cookbook*. New York: Clarkson Potter Publishers, 2001.

Probst, Max. "Diversity of the Transgender Community." In "Trans Matters in Education: Insights from Students," edited by Erica Rand. *Radical Teacher* 67 (summer 2003): 9–14.

Procter, David. *Enacting Political Culture: Rhetorical Transformations of Liberty Weekend*. New York: Praeger, 1991.

Puar, Jasbir K., and Amit S. Rai. "Monster, Terrorist, Fag: The War on Terrorism and the Production of Docile Patriots." *Social Text* 72 (fall 2002): 117–48.

Rand, Erica. *Barbie's Queer Accessories*. Durham: Duke University Press, 1995.

———, ed. "Trans Matters in Education: Insights from Students," with essays by Danielle Nika Askini, Jordon Bosse, Lyndon Cudlitz, Max Probst, and Mea Tavares. *Radical Teacher* 67 (summer 2003): 9–14.

Robinson, Calvin R., Redman Battle, and Edward W. Robinson. *Journey of the Songhai People*. Philadelphia: Farmer Press; Pan African Federation Organization, 1987.

Roediger, David R. *The Wages of Whiteness: Race and the Making of the American Working Class*. London: Verso, 1991.

Rogoff, Irit. *Terra Infirma: Geography's Visual Culture*. London: Routledge, 2000.

Rose, Nicholas. "Identity, Genealogy, History." In *Questions of Cultural Identity*, edited by Stuart Hall and Paul du Gay. London: Sage, 1996.

Rosenzweig, Roy, and David Thelen. *The Presence of the Past: Popular Uses of History in American Life*. New York: Columbia University Press, 1998.

Ross, Andrew. ed. *No Sweat: Fashion, Free Trade, and the Rights of Garment Workers*. New York: Verso, 1997.

Sacks, Karen Brodkin. "How Did Jews Become White Folks?" In *Race*, edited by Steven Gregory and Roger Sanjek. New Brunswick: Rutgers University Press, 1994.

Sánchez, George J. *Becoming Mexican American: Ethnicity, Culture, and Identity in Chicano Los Angeles, 1900–1945*. Oxford: Oxford University Press, 1993.

The San Francisco Lesbian and Gay History Project. "'She Even Chewed Tobacco': A Pictorial Narrative of Passing Women in America." In *Hidden from History: Reclaiming the Gay and Lesbian Past*, edited by Martin Bauml Duberman, Martha Vicinus, and George Chauncey Jr. New York: New American Library, 1989.

Schein, Louisa. "Diaspora Politics, Homeland Erotics, and the Materializing of Memory." *positions* 7 (1999): 697–729.

Schlosser, Eric. *Fast Food Nation: The Dark Side of the All-American Meal*. Boston: Houghton Mifflin, 2001.

———. *Reefer Madness: Sex, Drugs, and Cheap Labor in the American Black Market*. Boston: Houghton Mifflin, 2003.

Scott, Joan. "The Evidence of Experience." In *The Lesbian and Gay Studies Reader*, edited by Henry Abelove, Michèle Aina Barale, and David M. Halperin. New York: Routledge, 1993.

Sedgwick, Eve Kosofsky. *Between Men: English Literature and Male Homosocial Desire*. New York: Columbia University Press, 1985.

———. "Privilege of Unknowing." *Genders* 1 (1988): 102–23.

Sekula, Alan. "The Body and the Archive." *October* 39 (1986): 3–64.

Serlin, David. "The Twilight (Zone) of Commercial Sex." In *Policing Public Sex: Queer Politics and the Future of AIDS Activism*, edited by Dangerous Bedfellows. Boston: South End Press, 1996.

Shah, Nayan. *Contagious Divides: Epidemics and Race in San Francisco's Chinatown*. Berkeley: University of California Press, 2001.

Shohat, Ella. "Lynne Yamamoto, Reflections on Hair and Memory Loss." In *Fresh Talk/Daring Gazes: Conversations on Asian American Art*, edited by Elaine H. Kim, Margo Machida, and Sharon Mizota. Berkeley: University of California Press, 2003.

Shulman, Alix Kates. "Dances with Feminists." *Women's Review of Books* 9, no. 3 (December 1991): n.p.

Simon, Kate. *Bronx Primitive: Portraits in a Childhood*. New York: Viking Press, 1982.

Sims, Lowery Stokes. "Interview with William Pope.L." In *William Pope.L: The Friendliest Black Artist In America©*, edited by Mark H. C. Bessire. Cambridge, Mass.: MIT Press.

Sinfeld, Alan. "Diaspora and Hybridity: Queer Identities and the Ethnicity Model." In *Diaspora and Visual Culture: Representing Africans and Jews*, edited by Nicholas Mirzoeff. London: Routledge, 2000.

Singer, Linda. *Erotic Welfare: Sexual Theory and Politics in the Age of Epidemic*. New York: Routledge, 1993.

Skelton, Tracey, and Gill Valentine, eds. *Cool Places: Geographies of Youth Cultures*. London: Routledge, 1998.

Smith, Barbara. "The Fight is for Social, Political, and Economic Justice." *Gay Community News* 23, no. 4. (1998): 41.

Spongberg, Mary. *Feminizing Venereal Disease: The Body of the Prostitute in Nineteenth-Century Medical Discourse*. New York: New York University Press, 1997.

Sprinkle, Annie. "Liberty Love Boat." In *Hardcore from the Heart: The Pleasures, Profits and Politics of Sex in Performance. Annie Sprinkle: Solo*, edited by Gabrielle Cody. London: Continuum, 2001.

Stephens, Elizabeth. "Looking-Class Heroes: Dykes on Bikes Cruising Calendar Girls." In *The Passionate Camera: Photography and Bodies of Desire*, edited by Deborah Bright. London: Routledge, 1998.

Stevens, Elizabeth, and Estelle Freedman, "She Even Chewed Tobacco," video, 1983.

Stewart, Fred Mustard. *Ellis Island*. New York: William Morris, 1983.

Stewart, Susan. *On Longing: Narratives of the Miniature, the Gigantic, the Souvenir, the Collection*. Durham: Duke University Press, 1993.

Stoker, Bram. *Famous Imposters*. New York: Sturgis and Walton, 1910.

Stratton, Margaret. *Detained in Purgatory. Contact Sheet*, no. 110. Syracuse, N.Y.: Light Work, 2000.

Sullivan, Harry. "A Look at William Williams' First Administration as the Commissioner of Ellis Island." Unpublished paper, 1983. Statue of Liberty–Ellis Island library, Ellis Island, New York.

Tifft, Wilton S. *Ellis Island*. Chicago: Contemporary Books, 1999 [1990].

Tilden, Freeman. *Interpreting Our Heritage: Principles and Practices for Visitor Services in Parks, Museums, and Historic Places*. Chapel Hill: University of North Carolina Press, 1957.

Ting, Jennifer. "Bachelor Society: Deviant Heterosexuality and Asian American Historiography." In *Privileging Positions: The Sites of Asian American Studies*, edited by G. Okihiro, M. Alquizola, D. F. Rony, K. S. Wong. Pullman: Washington State University Press, 1995.

Trachtenberg, Marvin. *The Statue of Liberty*. Rev. ed. New York: Penguin Books, 1986.

Vogel, Dan. *Emma Lazarus*. Boston: Twayne Publishers, 1980.

Volcano, Del LaGrace, and Judith Halberstam. *The Drag King Book*. London: Serpent's Tail, 1999.

Wallace, Mike. *Mickey Mouse History and Other Essays on American Memory*. Philadelphia: Temple University Press, 1996.

Warner, Michael, ed. *Fear of a Queer Planet: Queer Politics and Social Theory*. Minneapolis: University of Minnesota Press, 1993.

West, Marian. "Women Who Have Passed as Men: A Curious Phase of the Problem of Sex—Historical Instances of Women Who Have Fought Their Way Through the World in Masculine Disguise." *Munsey's Magazine* 25 (1901): 273–81.

Weston, Kath. *Long Slow Burn: Sexuality and Social Science*. New York: Routledge, 1998.

Wilchins, Riki. "Changing the Subject." In *GenderQueer: Voices from Beyond the Sexual Binary*, edited by Joan Nestle, Clare Howell, and Riki Wilchins. Los Angeles: Alyson Books, 2002.

Williams, Patricia J. *Seeing a Color-Blind Future: The Paradox of Race*. New York: Noonday Press, 1997.

Wilson, Rob, and Wimal Dissanayake, eds. *Global/Local: Cultural Production and the Transnational Imaginary*. Durham: Duke University Press, 1998.

Wyden, Peter. *The Unknown Iacocca*. New York: William Morrow and Company, Inc., 1987.

Yans-McLaughlin, Virginia, and Marjorie Lightman. *Ellis Island and the Peopling of America: The Official Guide*. New York: New Press, 1997.

Zerelli, Linda. "Democracy and National Fantasy: Reflections on the Statue of Liberty." In *Cultural Studies and Political Theory*, edited by Jodi Dean. Ithaca: Cornell University Press, 2000.

Zollberg, Aristide R. "Reforming the Back Door: The Immigration Reform and Control Act of 1986 in Historical Perspective." In *Immigration Reconsidered: History, Sociology, and Politics*, edited by Virginia Yans-McLaughlin. Oxford: Oxford University Press, 1990.

INDEX

79; detention of, 68, 77; in Ellis Island materials, 69, 258–59; entrance of, to the United States, 79, 81–82; gender presentation of, 49, 68, 72–73, 77–80, 97–98; medical inspection of, 73, 80–81; naming and, 82–83; photograph of, 68–70, 72, 73, 92, 96–97; work and residence history of, 72–73

Workers, 36, 37–38, 153–56, 241–48. *See also* Labor

"Yekl: A Tale of the New York Ghetto" (Cahan), 55

Zerelli, Linda, 114
Zitko, Peg, 155
Zollberg, Aristide R., 285 n.53
Zybysko, 96

Erica Rand is a professor of art and visual
culture and the chair of the women's and gender
studies program at Bates College.

Library of Congress Cataloging-in-Publication Data

Rand, Erica

The Ellis Island snow globe / Erica Rand.

p. cm.   Includes bibliographical references and index.

ISBN 0-8223-3578-6 (cloth : alk. paper)

ISBN 0-8223-3591-3 (pbk. : alk. paper)

1. Ellis Island Immigration Station (N.Y. and N.J.)

2. United States—Emigration and immigration—Historiography.

3. Ethnicity—United States—Historiography.

4. Nationalism—United States—Historiography.

5. Sex role—United States—Historiography.

6. Consumption (Economics)—Social aspects—United States.

7. Souvenirs (Keepsakes)—United States.

I. Title.

JV6484.R36 2005   304.8'73—dc22

2004030134